Corporate Cash Management Handbook

Richard Bort, CCM

Richard Bort & Associates

WARREN, GORHAM & LAMONT
Boston • New York

Preface

WITHIN THE LARGER GAME of business corporate cash management is a game, the object of which is to optimize the amount of funds available to the enterprise. This is achieved by accelerating collections, controlling disbursements, and managing the balances by borrowing to cover shortfalls and investing excess funds. The cash manager uses information to accomplish this objective and, therefore, is more of an information and systems manager than a cash manager.

The game has rules—banking rules, accounting rules, rules of ethics, conventions, and accepted customs and practices. Therein lie some of the challenges to corporate cash managers—the better one understands these rules, the more able he is to play the game profitably.

This book describes the objectives and many of the rules of corporate cash management, thus enabling the players to play the game more effectively. There are usually several players involved: corporate financial managers, bankers, accountants, students, educators, and even a few financial reporters who want to understand the intricacies of the game as professional observers.

The book starts with an overview of the environment of cash management, including the role of funds management in the firm, a discussion of the structure and regulatory features of the U.S. banking system, and a description of the payment mechanisms in the United States. Before launching into the nuts and bolts of cash management techniques and technologies, the book addresses the matter of managing accounts receivable, the asset from which funds flow in most companies.

The next four chapters tackle the tools, techniques, and technologies involved in the modern corporate cash management system. They address both the prosaic paper-based mechanisms (checks), as well as the electronic funds transfer and computer-based information delivery systems that have gained a prominent position in the current state of the art. This part includes a chapter on treasury workstations and a chapter on managing banking relationships that covers bank compensation and techniques for buying banking services.

Having established the fundamental mechanisms for channeling flows of funds through the firm, the book addresses the all important area of liquidity management—making sure the firm has the "right" amount of funds available, not too much and not too little. Following a discussion of some of the practical principles of managing liquidity and working capital, a chapter on short-term funds flow forecasting sets the stage for those two counterbalancing tools: borrowing to cover shortfalls and investing excess funds. A chapter is devoted to each of these topics.

Some of the myth and mystery surrounding international financial operations are dispelled in two chapters, one focusing on some practical approaches to treasury management in a company's foreign operations, and the other delving into foreign exchange, letters of credit, and international trade transactions.

This book catalogs the many cash management services, techniques, and technologies available to cash managers. It includes some helpful operating suggestions drawn from the actual corporate and banking experience of the author and some successes of other cash managers. The reader is advised to look for "Cash Management Suggestions" that are scattered throughout the book.

This book will be supplemented annually and will include material on the related fields of treasury management and working capital management. We will keep tabs on emerging technologies such as electronic data interchange and the use of computers in enhancing and controlling the flow of funds through the firm, and between firms.

Acknowledgments

Eugene Simonoff, executive vice-president and publisher of Warren, Gorham & Lamont, Inc. (WG&L) first suggested that I write *Corporate Cash Management Handbook*. His perception that a handbook on corporate cash management was needed—that none had been written until now—was ingenious. The continual encouragement of WG&L's Philip Gabel early in the project was critical for one who had never written more than a few magazine articles and an MBA thesis. He urged me to base the book on my own experience without substantial research and interviews; after all, my 9 years as a banker and 14 more as a corporate treasury manager at three large and very different companies, not to mention several years currently as a consultant, seemed to be excellent preparation for the task. Little did I know that the project would take more than two years and would directly involve more than 20 people, although only a small portion of the book was actually contributed by others.

One thing led to another and the book is now a reality, but not without the advice, assistance, and forebearance of many people. My wife, Judi, who acted as my sounding board and often had her patience stretched to the limit, keyboarded almost the entire manuscript. The cheerleading (and scolding) of our son, Randy (the investment banker), from his office in Beverly Hills and later by long distance from his Tokyo office, was always encouraging. The editors, first Steven Sayre and later JoAnne Haffeman, allowed me the freedom to cover the subject matter as I saw fit and taught me to rely on the good sense of others who suggested changes.

Treasury workstations, those children of the personal computer, so filled with marketing potential but a sales disappointment for most banks and vendors, have been the particular interest of Robert J. Leahy. Leahy is an erstwhile hacker, former "Sysop" of the world's only known cash management electronic bulletin board (an idea that was ahead of its time in 1984) and editor of the leading cash management publication, *The Leahy Newsletter*. Bob contributed Chapter 9, "Treasury Workstations."

Paul "Pete" Peterik, who mastered the art of borrowing from banks during his tenure as assistant treasurer of Wickes Companies, Inc., contributed Chapter 13, "Short-Term Borrowing." His acute understanding of the mechanics and psychology of managing lenders is unusual to say the least, and he was kind enough to share some of his knowledge with us.

Money manager and author Alan G. Seidner graciously allowed us to borrow material from his WG&L book, *Corporate Investments Manual,* to form the basis for Chapter 14, "Short-Term Investing."

Otherwise, all of the chapters are homegrown.

Considerable inspiration for the organization and shape of the book must be attributed to the National Corporate Cash Management Association's (NCCMA) *Essentials of Cash Management: A Study Guide.* That work was developed and published by the NCCMA in 1985 to define the body of knowledge of cash management and to assist candidates for the Certified Cash Manager credential to prepare for the requisite examination.

To minimize the risks of being off base in some of the factual content, several people were kind enough to review and comment on parts of the material. While the author retains full responsibility for any inaccuracies and omissions, their contributions to this book are gratefully acknowledged.

Richard C. Ercole, Charles G. Whitney, Bill McSwain, and Rejana Stallings of Security Pacific National Bank; Andrew B. Laub and D. E. Berresford of Southwest Gas Company; John J. Cipriano and Samuel T. Fox of Bank of California, N.A.; Basil P. Mavrovitis of Cyro Industries; Julie Roberts of TranSettlements, Inc.; Martin Decere, CCM, former corporate treasurer and a colleague on the NCCMA's Certification Council; Joel Newkirk, former banker who reviewed an early draft of several chapters; and at least one banker who has requested anonymity because of ''bank policy.''

This book would not have been possible without them.

RICHARD BORT

Sherman Oaks, California
February 1989

Summary of Contents

SUMMARY OF CONTENTS

PART VI—INTERNATIONAL OPERATIONS

Table of Contents

3   The U.S. Banking and Payments System

PART II *Funds Mobilization*

4 *Management of Accounts Receivable*

5 Depository Systems: Channeling and Accelerating Receipt of Funds

PART III Disbursement Systems

6 Paper-Based Disbursements

7 *Electronic Payment Systems*

TABLE OF CONTENTS

PART IV Funds Management Systems

8 Designing and Managing the Funds Management System

9 *Treasury Workstations*
Robert J. Leahy

10 *Managing the Banking Relationship*

TABLE OF CONTENTS

PART V *Liquidity*

11 *Managing Liquidity*

12 *Short-Term Funds Flow Forecasting*

13 Short-Term Borrowing
Paul Peterik

14 *Investing Excess Funds*

PART VI *International Operations*

15 *Managing Funds in Foreign Subsidiaries*

16 *Executing International Trade Transactions*

TABLE OF CONTENTS

PART I

Overview of Cash Management

CHAPTER 1

The Role of Funds Management in the Firm

INTRODUCTION

To practice cash management effectively requires a fundamental understanding of how funds flow through the banking system, as well as a knowledge of banking products and services used to operate a configuration of bank accounts suitable to the company's requirements. The effective cash manager must also understand the electronic tools available for moving funds and for managing the information related to the funds flows and balances. The professional cash manager must also master techniques for balancing the firm's liquidity position, involving both borrowing and investing. Finally, those who practice cash management in companies that do business outside the United States must have a firm grasp of payment systems and banking practices in each of the relevant countries.

Even though cash management functions comprise only a portion of the typical treasury manager's time, the combination of tasks and judgments add up to an exciting and critically important role in the success of every company. Whether the company has ample funds with which to work or even if it is chronically short of available funds, the practice of good cash management is integral to the success of the firm.

"Cash Management" is defined as the systematic gathering of information about a firm's collections, disbursements, and balances, and the use of that information to manage effectively the funds available to the firm. Cash management principles are not specific to a particular form of organization, or to any particular group of industries. This has been amply demonstrated by the fact that cash managers have been known to advance their careers by changing jobs without any real concern about changing industries. The techniques, devices, and structures useful in managing the funds of a firm in one industry are usually equally useful in a firm in any other industry.

Cash management is a subset of treasury management, which incorporates the tasks of providing funds and funding to the firm and influencing the elements of working capital for the purpose of increasing the firm's liquidity. Treasury management involves the broader areas of managing the sources of funds, both internal and external, and providing protection to the firm's physical and human assets. Internal sources of funds with which the treasury manager is concerned generally include asset management and efforts to reduce the amount invested in working capital. Protection of physical assets involves risk insurance; protection of human assets involves pensions and health and welfare programs, all of which are also treasury functions.

The practice of cash management can be by default and rudimentary; or it can be very conservatively and inefficiently practiced by the company controller, for example, who ordered the suspension of check issuance when the general ledger cash account reached a zero balance. It can also be practiced aggressively to the point where every available dollar is fully used either to cover the payment of checks or invested in income-producing securities.

The professional cash manager strives to achieve a balance among aggressive mobilization of funds, prudent investing of these funds, and paying appropriate compensation to the banks that provide the cash management services, including information and control services; depository accounts; checking accounts; funds concentration systems; lockboxes; account reconcilement; and investment services. In fact, the practice of cash management uses and encompasses all of the noncredit services of the bank as well as those of some nonbank service providers.

BACKGROUND

The origin of modern cash management in the United States dates back to The Great Depression when banks sometimes sought control over the cash flows of borrowers. By insisting that the borrower have its customers direct their remittances to a post office box, the bank would control the post office box and apply all of the collections to the outstanding loan, meanwhile advancing fresh funds to keep the company afloat.

The post office box, or lockbox, device was legitimatized as a cash management tool in 1947, when the Radio Corporation of America (RCA) asked several major banks to establish a lockbox system for its corporate collections. Instead of the banks capturing the remittance funds to protect their loans, however, they merely deposited the funds to RCA's deposit accounts and notified the company of the total amount received and the details of the individual remittances.

The motivation for shifting remittance processing to the banks in 1947 was undoubtedly different from the motivation today. In 1947, a bank's labor costs were lower than at a manufacturing company. Therefore, savings could be realized by shifting the processing work to a bank. Unlike today, interest rates were not a factor. Interest rates were low at that time and remained low for many years, providing little incentive for corporate treasurers to invest short-term liquidity funds. The conventional wisdom was to maintain liquidity by hoarding sufficient funds in the corporate checking account to cover any eventuality. Sometimes if funds exceeded a certain level, the treasurer would then invest in treasury bills (T-bills) or a bank fixed time deposit.

In the early 1960s, however, interest rates began to climb steadily, and banks began to manage their liabilities and assets aggressively. A major contribution to bank liability management was the invention of the negotiable time certificate of deposit (CD) and the development of a secondary market for the trading of these deposit instruments. When The First National City

Bank of New York (now known as Citibank) invented this instrument in 1961, the bank merely provided the element of legal negotiability to fixed time deposits by issuing a certificate payable to the bearer to reflect ownership of the fixed time deposit. When several other major banks decided to follow suit, and they all decided to buy and sell the certificates issued by each other, a secondary market was born. It was not long before treasurers realized that they could invest their cash hoards in safe bank deposits that would earn somewhat more than the nominal yield of T-bills, yet have access to the funds before maturity if they were needed.

As interest rates continued to rise in the 1970s, bankers aggressively solicited large corporate deposits, forcing the other banks to offer market interest rates to their existing customers just to defend the deposits they already had. But the die had been cast, because deposits that had been available for free would now cost the bank an interest rate.

Figure 1-1 shows the progression of several key interest rates from the 1930s through the 1980s, including the peaks in the prime rate, which was a key bank lending rate for many years.

As interest rates rose, the corporate cash asset grew in value because of its ability to generate income, and the management of that asset therefore became increasingly critical and sophisticated. In 1967, National Data Corporation (NDC), a small company in Atlanta, Ga., devised a new cash management application for its computer service bureau business, and a number of banks began to remarket this service. NDC had assembled a telephone network that blanketed the country, which enabled companies with multiple remote depositing units to report the amount of the day's deposit for each unit and thereby automatically initiate the transfer of funds from the depository accounts to a central funds concentration account. The telephone network collected the data, a computer stored and organized the data, and depository transfer checks moved the funds accurately, timely, inexpensively, and reliably to the concentration bank. The depository transfer check continues as a mainstay of cash management, even as it has evolved from paper into electronic form.

Computer usage surged in the 1960s in both companies and banks. In the 1960s, banks converted their demand deposit accounts (DDAs) from ledger cards posted by electro-mechanical accounting machines to mainframe computers. In 1964, the Federal Reserve (the Fed) mandated that all checks be encoded with a magnetic ink character recognition (MICR) line to identify electronically the drawee bank and the amount of the check, thus enabling the Fed and others involved in the check clearing process to read, sort, and direct checks through the system.

FIG. 1-1

Selected Key Interest Rates, 1934–1987

Year	Average	Bank Prime Rate	Average 1-Year T-Bills	Average Yield 20-Year Government Bond
1987	8.20	7.75–9.25	6.33	+8.59
1986	8.33	7.50–9.00	6.08	7.85
1985	9.93	9.50–10.50	7.81	10.97
1984	12.04	10.75–13.00	9.92	12.48
1983	10.79	10.50–11.00	8.80	11.34
1982	14.84	11.50–17.00	11.07	12.92
1981	18.87	15.95–20.50	13.16	13.72
1980	15.27	11.00–21.50	10.89	11.39
1979	12.67	11.50–15.75	9.75	9.33
1978	9.06	7.75–11.75	7.74	8.48
1977	6.83	6.25–7.75	5.71	7.67
1976	6.34	6.25–7.25	5.52	7.86
1975	7.86	7.50–10.00	6.28	8.19
1974	10.81	8.75–12.00	7.70	8.05
1973	8.03	6.25–10.00	7.01	7.12
1972	5.25	4.75–6.00	4.77	6.01
1971	5.72	5.25–6.00	4.67	6.12
1970	7.91	6.75–8.00	6.48	6.86
1969	7.95	7.00–8.50	6.79	
1968	6.31	6.00–6.75	5.46	
1959– 1967	4.78	4.00–6.00	3.80	
1948– 1958	2.98	2.00–4.50	*1.86	
1934– 1947	1.50	1.50	N/A	

* 9–12 month issues
+ 30 year bond

Sources: Banking and Monetary Statistics, 1941–1970; Annual Statistical Digests, 1980–1987, *Board of Governors of the Federal Reserve System (Courtesy San Francisco Fed).*

In 1976, another revolutionary development occured when Chemical Bank of New York introduced its ChemLink system, which furnished account transaction and balance data to its customers electronically. This system provided customers with a daily report from the bank as to the prior day's debits, credits, balances, and float. These reports were made available via interactive terminal, telex, or teletype for a modest fee. The data that ChemLink brought to the treasurer's office electronically was previously available to the company from many banks, but it was manually generated and reported and, therefore, prone to error. It was also usually delivered free of charge. Each morning an army of clerks would comb the bank's internal records from the preceding day and reconstruct the activity in the customer's account to reconcile the starting and ending balances. Once the data-gathering was completed, a clerk would telephone the company's treasury department and verbally report the data. Corporate treasury managers had come to rely on the timely receipt and accuracy of this data in order to manage the disbursement and collection float aggressively. After all, interest rates had climbed to 6 percent for short-term investments, making the cash asset potentially one of the most productive assets of the firm, whether the company was a borrower or an investor.

Other banks followed Chemical Bank's lead either by buying licenses from Chemical or other vendors or by developing their own systems.

Managing float was the cash manager's principal role in the 1970s. It became a zero-sum game between trading partners. The seller sought ways to reduce the mail float and clearing time on checks received from customers, and customers sought ways to extend the mail and clearing float. As lockbox studies proliferated and companies implemented new lockbox sites, they also opened checking accounts at banks located in remote places that promised the checks would take longer to clear if they were drawn on those banks.

With the passage of the Monetary Control Act of 1980, the Fed was given a mandate to reduce float in the banking system. Throughout the 1980s, the Fed's "War on Float" was successful in wringing billions of dollars of float from the system by speeding up the transportation of paper (checks) from bank to bank, and by introducing multiple daily presentment of checks to banks. As a result, the role of the cash manager shifted in the 1980s from float management to information management and cost containment and, more importantly, funds management system design. This entailed learning about computers and software systems, integration of treasury management software with corporate mainframes, and the use of telecommunications and computers for the exchange of routine business data, both within the company as well as with providers of financial services and other trading partners. The modern cash manager is fully conversant with techniques for borrowing and investing, as well as desktop computers and systems management. Often, the tasks of forecasting and tracking cash flows and tinkering with float mechanisms has been relegated to a supervisory or even semiclerical level in the company.

BASIC FUNCTIONS OF CASH MANAGEMENT

Cash management has four basic functions: deposits, funds concentration, disbursements, and information and control. The establishment of an effective

FIG. 1-2

Funds Flow Schematic Diagram

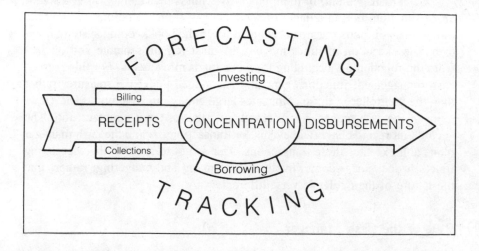

cash management system must incorporate all of these functions, as well as interface with the accounting system's general ledger. Supporting these four basic functions are systems for forecasting and tracking the flows of funds. Figure 1-2 is a schematic diagram of the flow of funds through the company.

The depository function is concerned with moving receipts, whether retail store receipts or the proceeds from the collection of accounts receivable, into a bank account of the collecting firm. The objective of the depository function is to deposit the receipts into the bank account as quickly as possible and to obtain the information sufficient to account for the source of the funds.

The funds concentration function, which often is unnecessary in small companies with simple bank account configurations, is concerned with moving the funds from the depository account to a central bank account of the company where the funds can be used to cover disbursements, repay debt, or be invested.

The disbursement function is the one in which the obligations of the firm are discharged by payment either through a check or draft, or an electronic funds transfer (EFT).

The information and control function ties together the depository, funds concentration, and disbursement functions by reflecting all significant funds movements and balances. This enables the cash manager to plan the funds flows and balances and thereby anticipate borrowing requirements and investing opportunities. The use of effective funds forecasting and monitoring, or tracking, the actual flows provides the cash manager with the essential element of control over the system.

Cash management, or more precisely "funds management," is a stand-alone function, not an adjunct of accounting system operations. Of course, movements of funds must be accounted for in the bookkeeping system; however, the execution of funds movements must remain separate and distinct from the function of accounting for those funds movements. For this reason, cash management functions generally are lodged under the treasurer rather than the controller in those companies large enough to have both. The viewpoint of the cash manager is different from that of the accountant, too. The accountant records historical events, or transactions, while the cash manager plans and executes these transactions. That is not to say that the accounting function does not become involved in planning and budgeting; rather, that the nature of their roles is very different.

Role of the Cash Manager

In addition to managing the four functions previously mentioned, the cash manager's role is to design and implement improvements in the existing funds management system; become involved in broader aspects of the treasury function, including investing, borrowing, and forecasting; day-to-day management of banking relationships; accessing and managing intermediate-term and long-term sources of funding; improving working capital management in the firm by liasing with accounts payable, accounts receivable, procurement, inventory management, marketing, legal, insurance, and audit; and any other functions that may affect or be affected by the movement of the company's funds.

Figure 1-3 depicts the core functions of the treasury department, which typically consists of the treasurer, assistant treasurer, and cash manager, with cash management in the center, surrounded by additional functions typically performed by the assistant treasurer. In the outer ring are the functions that are often performed by the treasurer. It should be noted, however, that the clear lines in this graphic depiction are usually not lines at all in actual practice. Instead, the three professionals in the treasury function most often function as a team with the assistant treasurer in the middle crossing over into the respective domain of the cash manager and the treasurer.

The function, strategy, and execution of these management tasks are the important considerations, not which of these professionals performs the particular tasks. Accordingly, the use of the terms "cash manager" or "financial manager" here is intended in its broadest sense without any implication as to which of the professionals or staff members actually performs the work.

FIG. 1-3
The Treasury Function

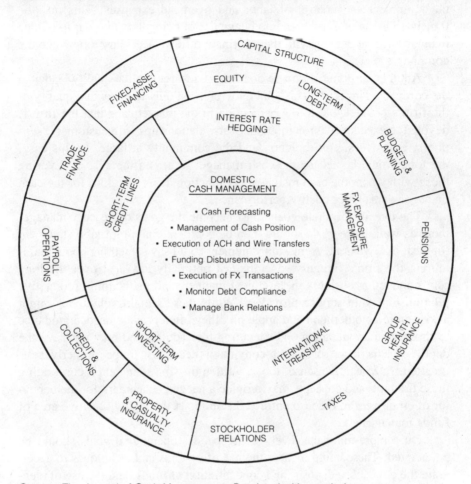

Source: The Journal of Cash Management. *Reprinted with permission.*

STRATEGIC PLANNING FOR CASH MANAGEMENT

Cash management strategies do not have to be written, but they should at the very least be articulated and understood by all of the participants. Moreover, the cash management strategy must complement and support the overall strategic mission of the enterprise. For example, a straightforward corporate goal of being the low-cost producer in an industry may set the tone throughout the company, encouraging investment in technologically advanced capital equipment and control of labor and overhead expenses. This may be translated in the treasury area into heavy use of computers in order to reduce manual effort in dealing with the information flows necessary to manage the company's funds.

Another corporate strategic goal may be to remain the quality leader in the company's industry. This goal may refer not only to the actual quality of the firm's product, but to the perception in the marketplace that the firm is devoted to excellence throughout all of its relationships with customers, suppliers, employees, stockholders, and the community at large. In this case, the tone would be set for the cash manager to err on the side of favoring those with whom the cash management function deals, in return for the cash manager demanding quality performance.

The overall corporate goals must become the goals of treasury management as well; these goals should then be combined into a mission statement for cash management. A mission statement could say something about maintaining the firm's liquidity, operating at optimally low cost over the long run, conducting business in an ethical manner, and maintaining productive relationships with service providers. While these seeming platitudes might also mention motherhood and apple pie, they often provide needed guidance to those who are planning and executing transactions and may not have the depth of experience or moral conviction necessary to be properly self-directed. In a negative sense, too, a written mission statement incorporating these thoughts and concepts may provide a needed benchmark for the behavior of employees in order to enforce discipline in the highly sensitive area of funds management.

On a more mundane level, some specific operational goals should be enunciated. These could include the use of systems and techniques to accelerate the collection, deposit, and concentration of funds, and the use of electronic information management systems wherever feasible to manage the entire process. To the uninitiated, this may sound like the prelude to a major budget request, which just might be the case. Considering the volume of funds flowing through the firm, prudence dictates the funding of appropriate systems and controls with which to achieve the goals desired by the company. While treasury departments are typically understaffed, management would be remiss to deny the resources necessary to develop and operate at least a baseline cash management system.

EMPLOYMENT OF A CASH MANAGEMENT SYSTEM

The primary goals of a cash management system are to provide pathways for the unimpeded inflow of funds to a central concentration point; to provide controls over the outflow of funds; and to have sufficient information available to manage the funds balances.

As a company grows, its administrative infrastructure often fails to keep pace with its sales and production capabilities. It is regretable but not unusual to have an antiquated system for receiving customer remittances and mobilizing the funds to where they can be used for disbursements, debt repayment, or investment. In those instances where some modern banking services may be used, credit for upgrading the company's cash management system usually goes to the persuasive banker who sold the product to the company.

Were it not for bankers presenting such products as lockboxes, funds concentration systems, and controlled disbursing, many financial managers would not be aware of them. For this reason, many companies find useful the process of networking with other financial managers by attending meetings and programs held by regional cash management associations and the National Corporate Cash Management Association (NCCMA), a nationwide association of treasury professionals.

Funds collected from customers should easily find channels from the point of deposit to the concentration point, and the system should not require an overt act by company personnel to move the funds to the concentration point. By the same token, the company should not depend on the banking system to initiate the transfer from the depository accounts to the concentration account, since the banking system can benefit by its omission to act timely.

Unlike receipts, which should flow in automatically, disbursements should flow out in an orderly but controlled manner requiring overt action by management.

The funds remaining in the concentration account are the temporary result of cumulative receipts minus cumulative disbursements, plus long-term capital funds not presently employed. The cash manager must have an information management system to predict future receipts, disbursements, and balances. In addition, the cash manager must have a funding source available when a shortfall of funds is imminent, and a method and medium for investing when there is a temporary surplus.

These objectives—easy inflow, controlled outflow, and a workable balancing mechanism—comprise the basic strategy of cash management. A corollary goal is to achieve these functions at an optimally low cost. This requires the effective deployment of personnel in concert with the appropriate computer hardware and software. It also requires a clear set of written policies, guidelines, and procedures; a rational configuration of operating bank accounts to provide the channels for the funds; and proper management of the firm's banking relations to provide adequate sources of credit. Also necessary are reasonably reliable forecasts of funds flows and sufficient information about actual funds flows, together with tools to organize and analyze the information to prepare the forecasts and monitor the actual results. When large amounts of information are needed, such as in large and complex banking configurations, computers may be necessary tools.

Another corollary goal is to have the funds management system generate information for bookkeeping on two fronts: to record all funds movements in the firm, and to provide sufficient remittance data to enable the cash application process within the accounts receivable management function. The cash management system must be capable of capturing and delivering the necessary data, in the required detail on a timely basis.

Each of the cash management subsystems—collections, funds concentration, disbursements, and information and control—must be designed to function efficiently, effectively, and at minimal cost. With sound design, proper operation, and occasional maintenance, the cash management system can generate meaningful profit through reduced costs and effective use of the liquidity resources available to the firm.

Elements of a Cash Management System

An effective cash management system is based on the prevailing payment system. Payment systems vary from country to country; in the United States the predominant system for effecting payments is paper based (check). The check is actually a written instruction by a payor addressed to the payor's bank unconditionally ordering the bank to make a payment to the payee. Besides being a payment order, a check becomes a bookkeeping mechanism in the payment system when the depository bank, acting as agent for the payee, credits the account of the payee. The check continues its role as a bookkeeping mechanism when it is transported through the banking system to the payor's bank and is charged to the payor's account. While this paper-based payment system operates well for the most part, it has pockets of inefficiency, tends to be expensive to operate, and often is slow.

An electronic payment system has been developing in the United States over the past 20 years or so that eliminates the delays, and reduces the pockets of inefficiency and costs that exist in the paper-based payment system.

However, financial managers' misplaced devotion to disbursement float, coupled with the banks' desire to continue using the traditional method of paper-based payments, have severely hampered the growth of electronic payment systems in the United States. Many countries are much further advanced in their acceptance and use of electronic business-to-business payments than the United States.

Banks have developed innovations that enable customers to take advantage of both of these payment systems to channel, predict, track, and account for their flow of funds. The challenge facing each cash manager is to understand a company's unique characteristics, how those characteristics affect the company's receipt and disbursement patterns, and to select and implement the appropriate banking and information tools to use the payment system to the company's advantage.

BANKING RELATIONSHIPS

Of the 15,000 commercial banks in the United States, only a relatively small number—a few hundred at most—are in a position to offer the full range of sophisticated cash management products and services that are often required by large companies. The vast majority of commercial banks primarily serve consumers and small businesses, and they occasionally provide routine banking services to large companies.

To provide the cash management services required by large companies requires the commitment of human, technical, and financial resources that usually exceed the capability of small banks. In fact, a very large number of the smaller banks in this country even contract out their basic "demand deposit accounting," which is their checking account activity and balances. It is usually the larger banks that provide this service, for a fee, to their smaller competitors.

The task of the cash manager is to define the cash management services that are required and then to select a bank or banks that can deliver those services most effectively. In this connection, the cash management strategy begins to influence the bank selection process by raising the question of whether to buy cash management services from the same bank that provides credit services, or to unbundle the requirements for other advantages.

It should be noted that banks tend to react to customer demand but unfortunately, most companies fail to let their banks know what they want. Most companies respond to the banker's pitch of a product rather than taking a proactive approach and letting the banker know what value-added services the company would like. It would be to a financial manager's credit to let the banker know when there is a service that could benefit the company. The bank will probably not react favorably for just this one request; however, someone else may also be making the same request, or the bank may be able to cherry-pick existing products to fashion the one suggested.

LIQUIDITY MANAGEMENT

Managing the firm's liquidity is the number one responsibility of the cash manager. This is because the cash manager, who is responsible for constantly monitoring and adjusting the firm's collection and disbursement systems to maximize the amount of funds available to the firm, must be aware of the company's funds position at all times. Thus, when the cash manager realizes there is either an excess or a shortage of funds, appropriate action must be taken. The resulting action is either to invest the excess or borrow to cover the shortfall (or to pray that the worst case disbursements scenario will not come to pass). Daily liquidity management is that simple.

Liquidity management on a more strategic plane involves forecasting the funds flows and, based on these forecasts, developing lines of credit for shortfalls and investing policy and guidelines for handling excess funds. Without some long-range planning in these areas, liquidity is not managed—rather, liquidity problems will consume a lot of management's time. Moreover, the lack of such planning will lead to fiscal embarrassment at best, and reduced profits at worst. Embarrassment occurs when the bank balance is not sufficient to cover checks; profits are affected both as a result of this embarrassment and by the inefficient investing of temporarily excess funds. Even firms with more funds available than required can improve investment results through forecasting funds flows and developing a set of investing guidelines. At the very least, they can avoid loss from investing unwisely.

Extending the liquidity management function to the long term takes into account the broader realm of treasury management, and the concepts of working capital management and long-term funding. What took the cash manager in the 1970s all morning to accomplish now takes a few minutes thanks to desktop computers and the direct exchange of electronic data between the bank and the corporation. With more time available and the demise of the "float game," the cash manager of the late 1980s has begun to seek broader challenges in financial management. Thus, where the practice of cash management once involved managing float, it is now directed toward managing all elements of working capital.

The late 1980s has also seen the birth of new techniques and tools that enable attentive managers to reduce nearly permanent investments in accounts receivable and inventory, and to control disbursement patterns more closely. These tools and techniques involve the use of computers, tele-communications systems, and standardized formats for exchanging routine business transactions in machine readable form, such that pairs of trading partners can communicate not just computer-to-computer, but application-to-application. When the buyer's purchase order system communicates directly with the seller's order entry system, and when the seller's billing system communicates with the buyer's accounts payable system, which in turn communicates with the seller's accounts receivable/cash application system, a "win-win" situation is created. Both partners gain greater control over their respective systems through enhanced software, the costs of oper-ating the system are reduced, including reduced errors and research, and inventories and receivables are reduced owing to faster order lead times and quicker cash application, respectively. Further, cash flow forecasting accu-racy is improved for both partners.

No one is better positioned than the treasury manager (formerly cash manager) to lead the parade toward "electronification" of the working capi-tal systems and subsequently, their management. The treasury manager is uniquely situated to enjoy a global view of the company's working capital operations, and to exert some influence to wring funds from these accounts. A dollar permanently released from investment in working capital is a dollar of new long-term capital that is obtained virtually free of charge, with no underwriting costs or debt service or dividend requirements.

CASH MANAGEMENT DEPARTMENT

The Department as a Profit Center

The concept of the cash management department operating as a profit center has been controversial throughout the industry. Most experienced cash man-agers respond that it could be dangerous to the health of the firm to make the cash management department a profit center because it would misplace incentives. Instead, they argue that the cash management department is properly considered a cost center on which certain expense constraints and certain revenue-producing goals may be placed.

The main argument against making the cash management department a profit center is that the funds available for investment and interest rates, the principal elements necessary to make a measurable profit, are beyond the control of the cash manager. Thus, it would be unwise for a company to require the cash manager to meet specific profit goals. Rather, the preferred course of action is to negotiate a set of revenue objectives for the cash manager that are dependent upon the amount of funds available for investment and that are related to prevailing interest rates, rather than to a specific dollar objective. The danger of a specific dollar objective is that the overzealous cash manager will stretch the rules to achieve the goal and assume greater risk than desired. More than one cash manager has caused great loss to the firm by overextending the company's exposure to risk in order to meet an overly optimistic profit goal. The cash manager may believe that he will lose his job either way: by failing to meet the goal because of market conditions or by losing money in trying by taking on risk.

Staffing

Because cash management department staffing varies widely from company to company, there truly is no typical staffing structure. This is because staffing patterns tend to follow the functions that are lodged there, and no two companies charge cash management with precisely the same functions. There is one common thread, however: cash management departments are typically understaffed in relation to their functions. Perhaps this is because cash management is viewed as a cost center and management wants to avoid being lavish or because management simply expects more productivity from such highly paid personnel. The real reason is not clear.

The functions listed in the core of Figure 1-3 are typical and basic to the cash management function in most companies. But additional functions are overlaid on these in all but the very largest of companies. In those companies, pure cash management is virtually a full-time concern. However, in companies smaller than the top tier, cash management generally is not a full-time occupation for the professional staff. After the core cash management tasks are completed each day, the professional staff in the cash management department performs other tasks, including accounts receivable or accounts payable (one or the other, but seldom both), capital budgeting, long-range planning, risk insurance management, employee benefits, and capital markets and capital formation. A number of other functions, including designing and implementing improvements to the cash management system, also fall to the department.

The basic functionality often requires that a professional cash manager work alone for most companies with up to approximately $100 million in revenues, with the addition of one clerical support person for companies with revenues of up to about $200 million, and the addition of a secretary for those with up to approximately $300 million. Above that revenue level, the nature and complexity of the company tends to dictate the staffing requirements. Often, a clerical support staffer will obtain the bank balance report and manipulate the relevant data into a coherent report format, which the cash manager then uses to make decisions concerning borrowing, investing, and funding. Meanwhile, the cash manager executes funds transfers and foreign exchange transactions. Following the setting of the daily cash position with the requisite borrowing or indicated investing action, the cash manager often contacts divisional financial managers for updates on expected remittances and funding requirements. Then the cash manager updates the daily forecast for the next day and the remainder of the week. When all of this is completed, often within an hour or two after arriving at the office, the cash manager then moves on to other tasks and projects.

The cash manager usually reports up the treasury line to the treasurer through the assistant treasurer (if there is one). It would be very unusual for the cash manager to report up the controllership line as long as there is a treasurer because of the auditing requirement for the separation of these duties. The cash manager executes transactions, which normally requires that the booking of those transactions into the company's accounting records be made by someone not reporting up the same line. This is not a problem in large companies, where the treasurer and controller each form separate reporting lines. In smaller companies, however, usually those with revenues of $100 million or less, there often is only one financial officer, usually designated as the controller, who is responsible for executing and recording all financial transactions. In these situations, separating these duties is difficult.

Networking

Most cash managers are curious as to how cash is managed in other companies. Most cash management systems are homegrown, developed over the years by a succession of financial managers with varying levels of knowledge and sophistication in cash management. The company's banks, too, have had some input to the process and very often the result is a system that barely holds together thanks only to the ingenuity and long experience of the incumbent treasury manager.

The financial professional who has responsibility for cash management is constantly seeking new techniques and tools that will solve bottlenecks and that will make the firm's cash management system function better.

To meet this need, financial managers have found membership in regional cash management associations and the National Corporate Cash

Management Association (NCCMA), ''the association of treasury professionals'' useful, as well as attending the regular meetings, conferences, and seminars that these organizations present thoughout the year. The NCCMA was founded in 1980. Its activities include publishing a journal containing articles on state-of-the-art cash and treasury management techniques and issues, operating a professional certification program, influencing banking legislation and regulation with the corporate viewpoint, developing and maintaining standards, and holding a major annual conference and seminars throughout the year in various cities.

Contact the NCCMA for information regarding membership, certification programs, conferences, seminars, and for contacts with regional cash management associations.

NCCMA
52 Church Hill Road
Newtown, Conn. 06470
(203) 426-3007

There are also several independent monthly magazines and newsletters available with useful information for the financial manager who wishes to stay in touch with the profession. The following are the names and addresses of some of these publications.

Newsletters:

Cash Management Digest (monthly)
Warren, Gorham & Lamont, Inc.
210 South Street
Boston, Mass. 02111
(617) 423-2020

Corporate EFT Report (monthly)
c/o Phillips Publishing, Inc.
7811 Montrose Road
Potomac, Md. 20854
(301) 340-2100

The Leahy Newsletter (monthly)
P. O. Box 467
Tustin, Cal. 92680
(714) 832-7811

Practical Cash Management (monthly)
c/o Bankers Research, Inc.
P. O. Box 431
Westport, Conn. 06881
(203) 227-1237

The Treasury Manager (monthly)
c/o IBC (Holdings) U.S. Inc.
P. O. Box 6640
Holliston, Mass. 01746
(508) 429-5930

Treasury Pro (monthly)
c/o Treasury Communications, Inc.
277 Fairfield Road, Suite 331
Fairfield, N.J. 07006
(201) 575-5740

Magazines:

Corporate Cashflow (monthly)
c/o Communications Channels, Inc.
6255 Barfield Road
Atlanta, Ga. 30328
(404) 256-9800

U.S. Banking Structure and Regulation

OVERVIEW

Domestic Banking

The commercial banking system in the United States has a dual nature. This nature arises from the fact that commercial banking is regulated by both federal and state agencies. In addition, there are two types of banking institutions: commercial banks and thrifts.

Thrift institutions, which include some 9,000 savings banks, savings and loan associations, and credit unions, deal primarily with the interest-bearing deposit accounts of individuals. These institutions also make loans to finance homes, automobiles, and other consumer purchases, provide financing for real estate projects, and often participate in other forms of secured financing. However, thrifts seldom become involved in the traditional commercial banking business of making unsecured loans to businesses for working capital purposes.

Commercial banks provide the everyday banking resources and the cash management services that are required to operate a business. As of the end of 1986, there were approximately 15,000 commercial banks in the United States. Of the 25 largest banks in the world (ranked by deposits),[1] only one was based in the United States. Japan, on the other hand, had 16 banks among the top 25, including the seven largest banks in the world. The largest U.S. bank was ranked no. 17 in deposits and no. 9 in total assets. In 1966, American banks had dominated the list, with 7 out of the 10 largest banks in the world, and 10 of the top 25. Some analysts argue that the decline in the dominance of U.S. banks is the result of restrictive laws governing geographic expansion, regulations requiring excessive capital-to-assets ratios compared to other countries, and prohibitions against ownership

---

[1] "The Top 500 Banks in the World—U.S. and Overseas Banks Ranked by Deposits on December 31, 1986," *Am. Banker* (July 30, 1987), pp. 48–52, and "The Top 500 Banks in the World—U.S. and Overseas Banks Ranked by Assets on December 31, 1986," *Am. Banker* (July 31, 1987), pp. 28–32.

of banks by industrial enterprises (and vice versa). The rise of the Japanese banks has been attributed to the great strength of the yen against the dollar and other world currencies and considerably less restrictive capital requirements than in the United States. (A strong foreign currency tends to inflate the size of the foreign banks' deposits and assets when stated in terms of the dollar.)

Commercial banks can be either federally or state chartered. The differences between a national bank and a state-chartered bank are much more important to the banker than they are to the customer. The source of the charter determines which regulatory agency, federal or state, has primary responsibility for monitoring the bank's soundness and operations.

There are three agencies responsible for regulating the banking system: (1) the Office of the Comptroller of the Currency (OCC); (2) the Board of Governors of the Federal Reserve System; and (3) the Federal Deposit Insurance Corporation (FDIC). The regulatory agencies for state-chartered banks are each state's banking department or commissioner of banking. All national banks and any state bank insured by the FDIC come under the regulatory jurisdiction of that agency as well. State-chartered banks may apply for membership in the Federal Reserve System (the Fed), in which case their deposits must be insured by the FDIC.

Commercial banks tend to have broad powers to accept deposits, make loans, and act in a fiduciary capacity with all classes of customers, including consumers, legal business entities, other banks, government units, and nonprofit organizations. Commercial banks have historically attracted demand deposits and short-term time deposits, which traditionally have funded the banks' short-term business loans.

International Banking

The United States is the dominant center of banking activity for world financial markets, although some insist that the London financial markets are more important. However, most of the world's currencies are quoted in terms of the U.S. dollar; the prices of oil, gold, and other major commodities are quoted in terms of U.S. dollars; and English is generally thought of as the universal language of international business. U.S. banks are among the most powerful forces in financing the world's international trade, even if they are no longer the largest in the industry. This dominance is attributed to both the size of the U.S. economy compared to the rest of the world, and U.S. political and economic stability. These factors make the United States the Reserve Bank to the world, by default.

As previously noted, U.S. banks have been surpassed in size by other countries' banking institutions, especially Japan's, in part because of the legal restrictions that have, until the late 1980s, confined domestic deposit-taking functions to the state in which the bank is headquartered. This restriction has characterized U.S. banking since the McFadden Act of 1927. As a result, money center banks have developed in a few major cities that are regional hubs of commerce and industry. While few of these have reached the world class level of New York City banks, some of the money center banks conduct considerable business nationwide and worldwide.

New York City is effectively the center of financial activity for the United States in world markets. While the volume of financial transactions executed in New York far surpasses that of any other U.S. city, a considerable volume of financial transactions is conducted by banks in other U.S. money centers such as Los Angeles and Chicago.

There are several major factors contributing to the dominance of New York. One factor is that the Federal Reserve Bank of New York acts as agent for the Federal Reserve Board in conducting open market transactions in U.S. government securities and foreign exchange. Another factor is that the trading floors of the two largest stock exchanges in the country are in New York. In addition, because New York is in the eastern time zone only five or six hours behind London and the rest of Europe, cities further west are at a time disadvantage. Thus, in the foreign exchange area, the New York market becomes a continuation of the London market. When the New York markets close, the global markets pause until Tokyo opens two hours later; when it is 5 P.M. in New York, it is 7 A.M. the next day in Tokyo. Although California foreign exchange trading could fill in this gap, California traders tend to operate concurrently with New York.

Nationwide Interstate Banking

Congress introduced a new level of competitiveness in banking with the Depository Institutions Deregulation and Monetary Control Act of 1980. Since then, encouraged by changing state laws that allow reciprocal interstate banking, major money center banks have been preparing for the inception of nationwide interstate banking. Thus, by 1991, a major legal impediment to the growth of American banks in the world economy may be removed when several major states permit the entry of out-of-state banks to begin taking deposits.

Interstate banking was carried out in certain situations for many years prior to the passage of the McFadden Act. Under the McFadden Act, several banks were permitted to operate in states beyond their home states; they have done so without much fanfare or creativity. Figure 2-1 lists those banks and holding companies that have "grandfather" status either by virtue of their franchises predating the McFadden Act or for some other reason.

In the early 1980s, as thrift institutions began experiencing financial troubles resulting from an interest rate crunch and, in some cases, poor management, federal regulators prevented several collapses by inducing sound out-of-state thrifts to take over the failing institutions. To do so, the regulators occasionally were forced to permit the merger (rather than acquisition) of the two units, allowing the resuting entity to operate branches that accept deposits in more than one state.

FIG. 2-1
Interstate Banks and Bank Holding Companies

Bank and Home Base	Out-of-State Branch
Bank of California	California, Oregon, Washington
Bank of Montreal, Canada	New York, Illinois, California
Barclays Bank, England	New York, California
Canadian Imperial Bank of Commerce	New York, California
Sumitomo Bank Ltd., Japan	California, Hawaii
Otto Bremer Foundation St. Paul, Minn.	Minnesota, North Dakota, Wisconsin, California
First Interstate Bancorp. Los Angeles, Calif.	California, Arizona, Colorado, Idaho, Montana, Nevada, New Mexico, Oregon, Utah, Washington, Wyoming
First Bank System Minneapolis, Minn.	Minnesota, Montana, North Dakota, South Dakota, Wisconsin
Norwest Corp., Minneapolis, Minn.	Minnesota, Iowa, Nebraska, Montana, North Dakota, Wisconsin
First Security Corp. Salt Lake City, Utah	Utah, Idaho, Wyoming
First American Bancshares Corp. Washington, D.C.	District of Columbia, Maryland, Virginia, Tennessee, New York
General Bancshares Corp. St. Louis, Mo.	Missouri, Illinois, Tennessee
NCNB Corp., Charlotte, N.C.	North Carolina, Florida
Northern Trust Co., Chicago, Ill.	Illinois, Florida

The advent of nationwide interstate banking for commercial banks may result in a number of significent structural and operating changes. Although these changes may at first be unsettling to cash managers, they should view the advent of nationwide interstate banking as beneficial to their cause. Some of these benefits include consolidation of interstate operations into fewer banks, consolidated lockbox collections, easier coordination among different banks in a multibank relationship, better capitalized banks, and greater capabilities within a given bank.

To the corporate treasury manager, one possible short-term effect of nationwide interstate banking is improvement in the funds collection/concentration process. Companies that collect from customers in many states must either have their customers mail their remittances to a central or regional concentration point or suffer the cost and administrative headaches of dealing with many different banks. This may involve at least one bank in each state where the company wants to maintain a depository point.

With nationwide interstate banking, several of the larger and more aggresive banks can be expected to accept those deposits in virtually all business centers in the country, concentrating those funds internally and automatically whenever the customer's cash management system directs. This will truly be a value-added service by those banks that can adapt the existing systems and technology to achieve it. Aside from inhibiting state laws, the greatest challenge that banks will have to face will be to install common and compatible operating systems throughout the merged institution.

The advent of nationwide interstate banking may also cause an upheaval in federal antitrust policy if money center banks find it to their advantage to merge. Mergers among banks in the same region may result in very powerful regional banks that can compete with nationwide banks. Mergers among banks in different regions will result in additional super-regional or nationwide banks. In the late 1980s, potential mergers were being lined up through acquisitions of banks across state lines by bank holding companies.

Large corporations will probably benefit from these mergers as the resulting national and super-regional banks offer more complete product lines to their corporate customers. Social Darwinism also has strong business applications here: only the more fit bank management teams will survive; there will be upheavals in bank personnel, customer relations, and pricing. The strong will probably become stronger, and the weak will fail or (more likely) be absorbed by stronger institutions.

The number of banks will likely slip from 15,000 to a more manageable level, perhaps by as much as one-third. Most of the survivors will be small, local independent banks or medium-sized banks with strong niches in particular market specialties such as international trade financing, real estate development, or private (personal), merchant, or investment banking.

These evolutionary changes in the banking system, which started to take place in the mid-1980s, will most likely be far-reaching over several years. The banking system will probably not settle down until the late 1990s. In the meantime, the burden of providing a safety net to the entire system falls on the federal regulatory apparatus, particularly the Fed. It is important for psychological, political, and economic reasons that the U.S. banking system remain strong and viable in order to provide the necessary financial services not only to the businesses of the United States, but to the world in general. Foreign investors are quick to realize that the United States is a major supplier, consumer, and financier in the world markets and that any economic woes in the United States are quickly exported to its trading partners.

FEDERAL RESERVE SYSTEM

Structure

The Fed manages the U.S. monetary policy, regulates member banks' operations, provides banking services as a wholesaler, and acts as the fiscal agent for the U.S. Treasury. The Fed is an independent agency within the federal government. The members of Fed's Board of Governors (the Board) are appointed by the President with the advice and consent of the Senate. The Board reports to Congress and maintains active contact with other federal agencies that develop and execute fiscal policy or that otherwise affect the financial health of the United States.

The Fed consists of three components: the Board, the Federal Open Market Committee (FOMC), and 12 Federal Reserve Banks and their branches (see Figure 2-2).

Board of Governors. Each of the seven members is appointed to a 14-year term by the President and confirmed by the Senate. The Board's primary responsibilities involve formulation of credit and monetary policy and supervision of the Reserve Banks, bank holding companies, and member banks.

Federal Open Market Committee. The FOMC consists of the seven members of the Board and five Reserve Bank presidents who serve on a rotating basis, except for the president of the New York Federal Reserve

FIG. 2-2

Organization of the Federal Reserve System

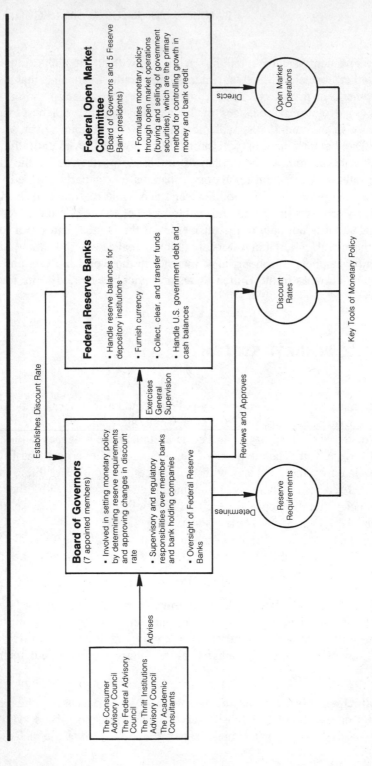

Board of Governors
(7 appointed members)

- Involved in setting monetary policy by determining reserve requirements and approving changes in discount rate

- Supervisory and regulatory responsibilities over member banks and bank holding companies

- Oversight of Federal Reserve Banks

The Consumer Advisory Council
The Federal Advisory Council
The Thrift Institutions Advisory Council
The Academic Consultants

Advises

Federal Reserve Banks

- Handle reserve balances for depository institutions

- Furnish currency

- Collect, clear, and transfer funds

- Handle U.S. government debt and cash balances

Exercises General Supervision

Establishes Discount Rate

Federal Open Market Committee
(Board of Governors and 5 Feserve Bank presidents)

- Formulates monetary policy through open market operations (buying and selling of government securities), which are the primary method for controlling growth in money and bank credit

Determines

Reviews and Approves

Directs

Reserve Requirements

Discount Rates

Open Market Operations

Key Tools of Monetary Policy

Source: Federal Reserve Board

Bank, who is a permanent member. The FOMC meets frequently to assess the condition of the U.S. economy and its international trade balance, and to determine the course of the Fed's open market policy for controlling money and credit. To implement monetary policy, the FOMC directs the purchase or sale of U.S. Treasury securities in the open market, which alters the level of reserves in the banking system and thereby influences the supply of money and credit in the financial markets. These activities are executed through the Federal Reserve Bank of New York.

Federal Reserve District Banks. There are 12 Federal Reserve districts, with one Reserve Bank serving each district. The 12 Reserve Banks have 25 branches and 11 additional regional check processing centers (RCPCs) (see Figure 2-3).

Figure 2-4 shows the boundaries of the districts and the locations of each Reserve Bank, branch, and RCPC.

Reserve Banks. The Reserve Banks are unusual legal entities in that their stockholders, who are the member banks in their respective districts, do not have the customary powers and privileges of corporate stockholders. Each Reserve Bank has a board of nine directors: three directors represent the member banks, three directors are independent members who are not involved in lending (often selected from the business and academic communities served by the bank), and three directors are appointed by the Board of Governors, which also designates the Reserve Bank's chairman and deputy chairman. The Board of Directors of each Reserve Bank appoints (with the approval of the Board of Governors), the president, who is chief executive officer, and the first vice-president; the president and first vice-president serve five year terms.

The result of this complex arrangement is that the member banks in a district own the capital stock of the Reserve Bank that regulates them. The Reserve Bank's Board of Directors is composed of equal representation from the member banks and from the Board. Each Reserve Bank's Board of Directors appoints the management of the bank, but it does so only with the approval of the Board.

The Fed's monetary and credit policies and supervisory powers are carried out through the Reserve Banks. In addition, the Reserve Banks perform services such as maintaining reserve and clearing accounts, accepting deposits, executing payment orders, providing coin and currency, and operating the payment systems for paper-based and electronic payments. In addition, the Reserve Banks carry out the Fed's responsibilities as fiscal agent and depository for the United States, as well as Treasury, foreign cen-

FIG. 2-3

Federal Reserve Banks, Branches, and Regional Check Processing Centers

Federal Reserve District No.	Reserve Bank Headquarters City	Branches	RCPCs
1	Boston	—	Lewiston Windsor Locks
2	New York	Buffalo	Cranford Jericho Utica
3	Philadelphia	—	—
4	Cleveland	Cincinnati Pittsburgh	Columbus
5	Richmond	Baltimore Charlotte	Columbia Charleston
6	Atlanta	Birmingham Jacksonville Miami Nashville New Orleans	—
7	Chicago	Detroit	Des Moines Indianapolis Milwaukee
8	St. Louis	Little Rock Louisville Memphis	—
9	Minneapolis	Helena	—
10	Kansas City	Denver Oklahoma City Omaha	—
11	Dallas	El Paso Houston San Antonio	—
12	San Francisco	Los Angeles Portland Salt Lake City Seattle	—

FIG. 2-4

Boundaries of Federal Reserve Districts and Their Branch Territories

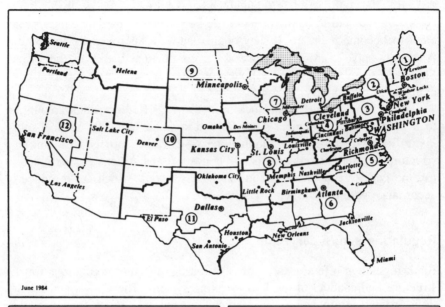

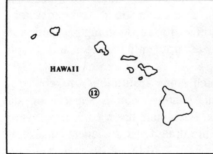 

June 1984

LEGEND

— Boundaries of Federal Reserve Districts

— Boundaries of Federal Reserve Branch Territories

★ Board of Governors of the Federal Reserve System

◉ Federal Reserve Bank Cities

• Federal Reserve Branch Cities

▪ Federal Reserve Bank Facility

▲ Regional Check Processing Office

Source: Federal Reserve Board

tral banks, and international organizations such as the International Monetary Fund.

Member Banks. Of the approximately 15,000 commercial banks in the United States, only about 5,700 are members of the Fed. Federally chartered banks are required to be members of the Fed; banks with state charters may elect to become members if they qualify and are approved by the Board. Although only about 38 percent of the commercial banks in the United States are member banks, they hold more than 70 percent of the total bank deposits in the country.

Each member must hold stock in its district's Reserve Bank amounting to 3 percent of the member's capital and surplus. In 1980, all depository institutions—members and nonmembers—became subject to a uniform structure of reserve requirements. All depository institutions are permitted to use the Fed's credit facilities and purchase services, which are provided in accordance with established fee schedules.

Regulation and Supervision

Bank regulation refers to the promulgation of rules and regulations for the structure and conduct of the U.S. banking system. These laws and regulations provide a framework within which financial institutions are expected to operate in order to promote and maintain a safe and sound banking system. Bank supervision, on the other hand, refers to the on-going inspection of individual institutions to ensure that they are prudently managed and comply with applicable laws and regulations.

The dual banking system, in which some institutions are chartered under federal laws and others hold state charters, entails supervision and regulation by federal and state agencies. Each state has a bank supervisory agency. As previously discussed, there are three federal agencies that regulate banks: the Fed, the OCC, and the FDIC. Although there is potential overlap among the three federal agencies, they have established a system that enables them to address their primary interests. This system also serves to reduce the potential problems that arise from multiple examinations and sources of supervision. Each agency's respective "turf" is as follows:

1. *Fed*—The Fed generally regulates and supervises all banks that are members of the Fed. This includes federally chartered banks and those state-chartered banks that elect to be Fed members. The Fed also supervises all bank holding companies.

2. *OCC*—The OCC grants charters to national banks and has direct responsibility for their regulation, supervision, and examination, as contrasted with the Board which has only general regulatory and supervisory responsibility over national banks, confining itself to reviewing financial statements and OCC examination reports.

3. *FDIC*—Since all national banks and state-chartered Fed member banks are regulated and supervised by the OCC and the Fed, the FDIC directly supervises only insured commercial banks that are not Fed members, as well as insured state-chartered savings banks.

In addition to these three federal agencies, there are two other federal agencies that supervise and regulate nonbank financial institutions: the Federal Home Loan Bank Board (FHLBB) and the National Credit Union Administration Board (NCUAB). The FHLBB covers the Federal Home Loan Banks and the Federal Savings and Loan Insurance Corporation (FSLIC), which in turn, regulates savings and loan associations and savings banks that are federally chartered, and savings and loan holding companies. It shares supervisory responsibility with the states over state-chartered savings and loan associations. The NCUAB charters, supervises, and insures all federal credit unions and those state-chartered credit unions that elect and qualify for NCUAB insurance.

Federal Reserve Regulations. The Fed administers some 29 regulations that embody both the banking laws adopted by Congress and the administrative regulations adopted by the Board. These regulations cover a wide variety of financial activities, including the Fed's functions as the central bank, the Fed's relationships with financial institutions, the activities of commercial banks and their holding companies, and consumer credit transactions. Figure 2-5 lists the Federal Reserve Regulations.[2]

Of principal interest to corporate financial managers are Regulations G, T, U, and X, which are frequently mentioned in the negative covenants sections of bank loan agreements. These four regulations restrict credit extensions by lenders to finance securities transactions.

Regulation G applies to lenders, other than broker-dealers and banks, who make loans of $200,000 or more (or more than $500,000 in total at any one time outstanding), which are secured, directly or indirectly, by margin stock. Such a lender might be a corporation that finances the purchase by

---

[2] Copies of the Federal Reserve Regulations may be obtained free of charge from Publications Services, Mail Stop 138, Board of Governors of the Federal Reserve System, Washington, D.C. 20551.

FIG. 2-5

Federal Reserve Regulations

A —Loans to Depository Institutions

B —Equal Credit Opportunity

C —Home Mortgage Disclosure

D —Reserve Requirements

E —Electronic Fund Transfers

F —Securities of Member Banks

G —Margin Credit Extended by Parties Other Than Banks, Brokers, and Dealers

H —Membership Requirements for State-Chartered Banks

I —Member Stock in Federal Reserve Banks

J —Check Collection and Funds Transfer

K —International Banking Operations

L —Interlocking Bank Relationships

M —Consumer Leasing

N —Relationships With Foreign Banks

O —Loans to Executive Officers of Member Banks

P —Member Bank Protection Standards

Q —Interest on Deposits

R —Interlocking Relationships Between Securities Dealers and Member Banks

S —Reimbursement for Providing Financial Records

T —Margin Credit Extended by Brokers and Dealers

U —Margin Credit Extended by Banks

V —Guarantee of Loans for National Defense Work

W —Extensions of Consumer Credit (revoked in 1952)

X —Borrowers who Obtain Margin Credit

Y —Bank Holding Companies

Z —Truth in Lending

AA —Consumer Complaint Procedures

BB —Community Reinvestment

CC —Funds Availability

one of its executives of a sizeable amount of margin stock—stock that is publicly traded and subject to the Fed's margin rules. That corporation would be required to register with the Fed promptly after extending the financing. However, lenders that extend credit to purchase margin stock through an eligible employee stock option plan are exempt from this registration requirement.

Regulation T, which applies to securities brokers and dealers, and Regulation U, which applies to banks, govern the extension of credit for the purpose of purchasing or carrying margin stock.

Regulation X is designed to fill in any gaps that may exist among Regulations G, T, and U, and it applies in particular to persons who obtain credit outside of the United States for the purpose of purchasing or carrying U.S. securities, not just margin securities.

Regulation Z implements the Federal Truth-in-Lending and Fair Credit Billing acts and seeks "to promote the informed use of consumer credit by requiring disclosures about its terms and cost."

Regulation V "facilitate(s) the financing of contracts or other operations deemed necessary to national defense production." These loans, commonly referred to as "V-loans," are made by banks and other private financing institutions to defense contractors, and are guaranteed by agencies or departments of the federal government.

New Regulation CC implements the Expedited Funds Availability Act of 1987. This regulation limits the period that a depository institution may place a "hold" on a customer's deposit of checks while the checks clear, and governs the timely return of dishonored items.

Supervisory Examination. Depository institutions are generally examined on an annual basis; institutions that are identified as having significant problems are examined more frequently. The examination typically involves the following five areas of inquiry:

1. An appraisal of the soundness of assets. Since loans receivable usually constitute the largest category of assets, examiners delve into the creditworthiness of major borrowers and the adequacy of loan documentation. Examiners also appraise the value of securities and other investments owned by the institution.

2. An evaluation of internal operations, policies, and management capability. Weaknesses in these areas can be a signal of potential problems in future asset quality.

3. An analysis of capital, earnings, liquidity, and interest rate sensitivity. These factors all bear on an institution's potential

ability to withstand sudden changes in the economic environment that may cause rapid changes in interest rates and deterioration in loan quality.

4. A review of compliance with banking laws and regulations.

5. A determination of the institution's solvency, taking into account all of the information obtained in the course of the examination.

Most examinations produce some type of criticism on some aspect of the institution's condition or operations. However, the results of the examination are discussed privately with management since public disclosure might cause depositors to withdraw their funds. However, where the number of violations or the severity of criticism places the solvency or liquidity of an institution in jeopardy, that institution is scheduled for more intense supervision by the supervising agency. If liquidity is the institution's principal problem, the Fed's discount window is available for borrowings. When the problems of an institution reach a critical level, the supervisory agencies cooperate to facilitate the acquisition of the institution by a more sound institution, or to arrange for the liquidation of the problem institution by the appropriate insurance agency.

The Fed as Central Bank

The three main purposes of the Federal Reserve Act of 1913 are:

- To provide an elastic currency base that can grow with economic activity in the United States;
- To provide credit facilities for member banks to re-discount commercial credits and loans; and
- To supervise the banking system.

The Act has since been expanded to include the following broader national financial and economic objectives:

- To maintain stability and growth of the U.S. economy;
- To maintain a high level of employment;
- To maintain stability of the U.S. dollar in world markets;
- To maintain reasonable trade balances with foreign countries;

- To manage the supply of money and credit to encourage growth in the economy with reasonable price stability;

- To manage inflationary and deflationary pressures as they arise; and

- To be the lender of last resort to prevent liquidity crises and financial panics.

Monetary Policy

The principal tool used by the Fed to attain these goals is called "monetary policy," which is reflected in the Fed's daily activities in influencing the amount of money and credit in the U.S. economy. Monetary policy controls the expansion and contraction of the money supply through open market operations involving the buying and selling of U.S. government securities. Monetary policy should not be confused with "fiscal policy," which is the management of the federal government's activities in taxation, spending, and debt management. Although each activity ultimately has an effect on the other, fiscal policy is managed through the budget process by the executive branch of the federal government, while monetary policy is managed solely by the Fed.

There are many forces that influence the U.S. economy. Some of these forces impede economic progress while other forces generate inflationary pressures. Some of the more important influences on the health and direction of the U.S. economy include the fiscal policy of the federal government; the productivity and wage and price policies of the private sector; the policies of foreign countries that affect the levels of supply and demand and the prices of commodities in world markets; and exogenous factors such as environmental aberrations that affect agricultural crops, or political turmoil that affects oil prices. As these forces are influencing the nation's economy, the Fed must ensure that the supply of money and credit are adequate to facilitate the transactional volume of the U.S. economy. The Fed's responsibility extends to both the short-term, involving cyclical inflation and deflation, and the longer-term considerations of a growing economy and the need for stability of prices.

The Fed constantly measures the growth of the economy, relative price stability, and pressures of inflation and deflation, and mediates these pressures and forces through monetary policy. Each of the 12 Reserve Banks maintains a watch on the economy; most of the banks publish monthly or quarterly journals that report their economic research and analysis. The results of this research are made available to the economics staff of the

Board and to the FOMC, which meets periodically in Washington. This economic research is used by the Board to determine monetary policy. The policy is then executed by the FOMC through the purchase and sale of U.S. government securities in the open market and by the advance of loans by the Reserve Banks to their depository institutions. The Board may also execute policy by adjusting reserve requirements. The FOMC also manages the Fed's investment portfolio.

Open Market Operations. Actual securities trading is conducted by the trading desk at the Federal Reserve Bank of New York. The traders at this desk are in constant contact with the primary dealers in government securities. There are approximately 44 primary dealers with which the Board conducts most of its business. Although any financial institution or investor may buy and sell government securities, the primary dealers stand ready to deal in any issue of the federal government. They also report their financial condition to the Board on a regular basis. This group of primary dealers becomes, in effect, the antennae for the Board as to interest rates and activities in the government securities market.

The markets for all debt securities, long- and short-term, public and private, are keyed to the government securities market. U.S. government securities are considered, by definition, to have the highest credit rating in the world. Consequently, interest rates on all other securities are based on U.S. government securities for similar maturities.

The FOMC can gently but firmly affect interest rates in the economy by buying or selling government securities for its own portfolio. The Fed's portfolio of U.S. government and agency securities was nearly $240 billion (as of the end of 1988); thus, it can easily deal in any maturity in any size it desires.

For example, suppose the FOMC intends to raise short-term interest rates. It would seek quotes on different short-term maturities of government securities by having Fed traders telephone the primary dealers to solicit bids to buy each security. After receiving all bids, the traders simultaneously "hit" the bids in the market among all of the primary dealers. This means that the Fed sells the securities that were bid for by the primary dealers at the best prices and within the dollar limits determined by the FOMC's trading office. This process occurs many times during the day; the cumulative effect of this process is to sell securities into the portfolios of the primary dealers. Dealers are forced to finance the portfolios with funds borrowed from banks (dealers are always heavy borrowers) or to sell other securities aggressively. Since some of the primary dealers are banks themselves, the effect on the bank dealers is to reduce their nonearning reserve funds on deposit with the

Fed to below the required reserve level. This occurs because the banks pay for the purchased securities out of their reserve accounts at the Fed.

As reserve funds are removed from the banking system, lenders either slow down their lending activities, increase their interest rates, sell some portfolio securities (thereby driving up interest rates as the supply of securities increases), or use a combination of these actions. The FOMC has achieved its goal of raising interest rates, which was perhaps part of the larger strategy to rein in inflationary tendencies that may have been spotted by the economists of the Board and the Reserve Banks around the country.

Although the Fed's trading activities are not conducted with a profit motive, the Fed earns billions of dollars of interest income annually on its portfolio of government securities. In addition, the Fed charges its members and other depository institutions for services such as check clearing, deposit and delivery of coin and currency, and securities clearance and custody services. The Fed pays an annual "dividend" (the technical reason used is payment of interest on the Federal Reserve notes, or currency, in circulation) to the U.S. Treasury. This dividend consists of the bulk of its net income and amounted to more than $18 billion each year in 1986 and 1987.

Reserve Requirements. Under the Monetary Control Act of 1980,[3] each depository institution is required to maintain reserves against its deposit base. The level of required reserves was initially set at 12 percent of demand deposits and 3 percent of most time and savings deposits. The level of required reserves is set by the Board and may be adjusted to accommodate the objectives of monetary policy. In actual practice, however, the level of required reserves at depository institutions is adjusted very infrequently. Any action that reduces a bank's reserves without reducing its reserve requirement will cause the bank to take immediate action to restore its reserve position. Bank-dealers restore their reserve positions to the required level by borrowing from the Reserve Bank's discount window or by borrowing excess reserves from other banks. This process creates ripples through the financial community as reserve-short banks absorb excess reserves from other banks.

Federal Reserve Discount Window. The second most important element of monetary policy (after maintaining the nation's economy on an even keel) is the lending operations through the discount window of each of the Reserve Banks.

---

[3] The Monetary Control Act is Title I of the Depository Institutions Deregulation and Monetary Control Act of 1980.

OPEN MARKET OPERATIONS IN ACTION

The Fed's open market operations were put to the test on October 19, 1987, the day the stock market crashed by a record 508 points on the Dow Jones Industrial Average. The Fed's actions that day clearly showed the influence that it has over the economy of the United States and the world.

The stock market had been taking record beatings for several days previously, and it had been down more than 3 percent the previous trading day, Friday, October 16. Over the weekend, world leaders pondered actions they might take on the following Monday because they feared a continuation in the severe losses of value and the consequent erosion of net worth of banks and dealers worldwide. Alan Greenspan, the chairman of the Board, met with key members of the Reagan Administration and after much discussion and some dissent, a plan was devised. The plan was simple: the Fed had to provide liquidity to the markets lest a liquidity crisis compound the sell-off. This plan borrowed a lesson from the Great Depression, when the Fed threw gasoline on the fire by tightening credit and liquidity at a time when the very survival of key financial institutions was at stake.

The Federal Reserve Bank of New York conducts its normal buying and selling operations each morning by calling the primary dealers on their direct lines almost simultaneously at 11:40 A.M., which is known as "Fed Time." If for any reason the Fed decides to conduct a higher than normal volume of transactions, the calls are made a few minutes early to allow the Fed's traders a little more time to complete their work.

With instantaneous worldwide telecommunications, everyone was poised for a disaster because the Tokyo, Singapore, and London markets had experienced their own disasters Sunday night. Speculation began to

The primary purpose of the credit extended at the discount window is to allow banks the short-term adjustment of their reserve positions. This need arises owing to seasonal or sudden changes in deposit levels, the need to fund unexpected increases in loans, or to bridge temporary gaps in obtaining funds from other sources. Discount window activity usually rises in periods of tight credit, and its most active users tend to be institutions that rely heavily on volatile checking account deposits or that have heavy short-term loan commitments.

This lending program is available to all depository institutions subject to the Fed's required reserves, whether they are Fed members or not. Even

build about what actions the Fed might take, if any. As the financial markets opened in New York at 9 A.M. Monday, the Fed's plan was ready for execution.

The New York stock exchange plummeted from the opening bell, and it quickly became clear that the losses that were suffered in Tokyo and Singapore had overtaken the United States as well. When the Fed's calls went out at 11:30 A.M., the head traders at the primary dealers were alerted to the Fed's plan.

As the head traders answered their direct lines to the Fed, they quickly responded by shouting aloud to the other traders in their trading rooms, "two day system." This is "traderese" denoting that the Fed was in the market trading for its own "system" account (rather than trading on behalf of a foreign government) with two-day repurchase agreements, buying Treasury securities from the dealers. In this way, the Fed was acting immediately and decisively to inject cash reserves into the banking system, at least on a temporary basis.

To confirm its resolve to provide liquidity rather than to restrict trading, the Fed came into the market every day for more than a week, buying more Treasury securities, sometimes placing the phone calls as early as 10 A.M. Aside from the direct effect these operations had on the measured liquidity in the market, the psychological impact of these actions was tremendous, giving confidence to all U.S. markets and to markets abroad that the Fed was going to support the markets during this period. Unlike the normally concealed intentions of the Fed, the FOMC's actions left no doubt as to the Fed's policy and intentions.

Source: Fortune, *(Nov. 23, 1987), p. 82.*

though the Fed stands ready to make loans to depository institutions, it discourages use of this facility except as a last resort. Discount window loans are designed to accomplish the following two objectives:

- To complement the Fed's open market operations by assisting depository institutions to restore their reserve positions; and
- To provide liquidity to the banking and financial system when it is under economic stress.

Advance and discount loans are made through the discount window. Depository institutions may borrow by taking loan advances secured by the pledge of adequate collateral such as the debt securities of federal, state, and local governments, certain types of mortgage loans, and certain forms of business and consumer loans owned by the depository institution. Advances are the predominant form of borrowing at the discount window. However, the discount of loans and other investments carrying the endorsement of the institution is also permitted and, in fact, was the traditional means of borrowing from the Fed until the passage of the 1980 Act. That act not only required all depository institutions holding transaction (checking) accounts and nonpersonal time deposits to maintain reserves with the Fed, but it also opened the Fed's discount window to nonmember institutions.

When making advances and discounts to depository institutions, a Reserve Bank charges interest at the discount rate, which is periodically adjusted by the Board and which is watched by market analysts. However, this is an administered rate, not a market rate, which tends to lag the market rather than be an economic bellwether.

Fed Funds. Fed Funds are short-term unsecured loans between banks. Fed Funds loans are usually made for a term of overnight, but may be extended. The prevailing market interest rate on Fed Funds loans is a key indicator of the supply and demand for money and credit in the economy. Fed Funds loans are made because at any given moment, some banks have reserves in excess of their required amount while other banks are short of their required reserves. Therefore, banks "buy and sell" (they actually "borrow and lend") these excess reserves among themselves at negotiated interest rates. This interbank market exists principally because the Fed tends to discourage depository institutions from using the discount window except under severe conditions. These conditions may exist in periods of tight credit when the supply of excess reserves is not adequate to satisfy the demand, or where the credit of a particular depository institution has deteriorated to the point where banks in the Fed Funds market will not lend to that institution.

Large regional and money center banks operate as buyers and sellers in the Fed Funds market as a service to their smaller correspondent banks across the country. The amount of Fed Funds offered or bid for by a small bank may not attract interest in the interbank market because the amount is too small and the bank may not be well known. Therefore, the big city correspondent stands ready to buy the small bank's excess funds or to sell funds to the small bank when it is short, regardless of the larger bank's own reserve position. Naturally, the larger bank quotes a spread to buy and sell small blocks of Fed Funds and makes a profit on these transactions while it is adjusting its own net funds position. The large banks often find that they can cover their own reserve shortage by buying funds from smaller banks at below-market interest rates.

CASH MANAGEMENT SUGGESTION:

A cash manager who seeks to improve the yield on short-term investments without appreciably increasing risk might consider making a Fed Funds loan to its bank in lieu of placing the funds in a certificate of deposit (CD). The CD requires the bank to maintain reserves, while the Fed Funds loan does not require reserves. Therefore, the bank can offer a slightly higher interest rate on the loan than it could on the CD. The opportunity to make a Fed Funds loan depends, of course, on the bank's appetite for borrowed funds.

Implications of Monetary Policy for Cash Managers

The manager of a firm's funds position must always be cognizant of the level and direction of interest rates in the economy. Treasury managers are usually concerned with either borrowing or investing funds and in many situations, both. Although the firm may be a net borrower in its primary business, it may have a portfolio of investments in its pension fund. Or a firm may be a net investor in its primary business while it participates in a capital project that is being funded by short-term borrowings.

Interest rates directly affect revenue, the cost of doing business, and the availability of credit. Even if the firm is not a borrower, high interest rates and reduced credit availability usually have an adverse effect on accounts receivable collections. When interest rates are high, customers almost automatically slow down their bill payments. Net investors slow down payments in order to increase their interest income, while net borrowers slow down their payments to conserve their borrowings and interest expense.

The treasury manager cannot escape the influence of interest rates on the treasury management function. Therefore, it is important to understand why interest rates change, how these changes affect the economy at large, and how they affect the manager's firm. This is not to imply that the manager should attempt to compete with professional economists in predicting interest rates. Indeed, even with their massive data and computer resources, economists are more often wrong than right. What is implied, though, is the need to anticipate changes in the general direction or level of interest rates and the need to prepare and protect the firm against the consequent loss of liquidity and deterioration of assets.

Professional economists monitor data from every facet of the economy. Their analyses of that data influence the perception of investors, traders, and speculators in the worldwide marketplace. Tentative conclusions are tested by actual changes in interest rates, prices, and employment, which in turn lead to adjustments of those perceptions and more testing based on the next set of empirical evidence. Moreover, perceptions have a time dimension that is often overlooked by inexperienced observers. For instance, to say "interest rates are rising" sometimes overlooks the time reference. Short-term rates may indeed be rising while long-term interest rates remain relatively stable. This scenario may reflect the market's perception that there are some short-term forces at work that are causing rates to rise but that these forces do not affect the longer view of the economy.

Market Perception

The markets for stocks, bonds, short-term money market instruments, and other forms of investment often behave in ways that baffle the casual observer. Yet, to the astute observer, the markets often behave very rationally. These latter observers believe that market movements reflect the collective knowledge and all information available in the market place, which includes historic data and anticipated trends. It is the weight of this collective knowledge, for example, that causes the Dow Jones Industrial Average (or any other index, for that matter) to rise by 20 points in a day and to fall by 20 points the next day. This collective knowledge among all of the players in a market is a very powerful force.

The chairman of the Fed's Board of Governors is probably the single most influential person with respect to economic and business conditions in the country. What the chairman says and does is extremely important to the direction and rate of change of interest rates and should therefore command the attention of cash managers. The chairman is also very influential among fellow governors. The chairman, along with the FOMC, which consists of the seven governors and five Reserve Bank presidents, use the most current and complete economic data available to control the operation of the largest portfolio of U.S. government securities in the world. They also have the capacity to affect bank reserves directly and immediately. In an economy as large and complex as the United States', where there are so many market participants, observers, critics, and measurement takers, the weight of the Fed is perhaps equal to the weight of all the other experts combined. As the effect of economic changes becomes magnified with the growth of the economy, the stakes grow as well, leaving little margin for error or experimentation.

Fiscal Agent for U.S. Treasury

The Reserve Banks and their branches function as the banker for the federal government. They maintain the Treasury Department's checking accounts, clear Treasury checks drawn against them, and act as the fiscal agent for the Treasury Department to issue, redeem, and transfer ownership of government securities. The Treasury maintains "Treasury Tax and Loan Accounts" at more than 15,000 depositories for the purpose of accepting tax receipts from individual and corporate taxpayers. The Treasury periodically draws funds down from these accounts and concentrates them in a Reserve Bank.

As the banker for the Treasury, the Reserve Banks pay checks drawn against them by the Treasury to pay the bills of the government. These include vendor payments, transfer payments such as social security, and salaries and retirement benefits of government employees. The Treasury initiates Automatic Clearing House (ACH) payments to vendors, employees, and recipients of social security and retirement benefits through the Federal Reserve Bank of New York.

The Reserve Banks act as fiscal agent for the Treasury in handling the operations involved in selling, servicing, and redeeming marketable Treasury securities (bills, notes, and bonds). They distribute information regarding new issues, accept tenders from the public, collect payment for the securities, credit the Treasury's account with the proceeds, and deliver the securities in book entry form to customers' accounts. The Fed also operates the communications network that transfers ownership of Treasury securities from sellers to buyers. In addition, the Fed issues, services, and redeems U.S. savings bonds and qualifies depository institutions and corporations as agents to issue and redeem savings bonds.

FINANCIAL MANAGEMENT SERVICE

The Financial Management Service (FMS) is an agency of the U.S. Treasury Department and is the federal government's central financial manager. Cash managers of companies that have nondefense contracts with the federal government might benefit by becoming familiar with the organization and functions of the FMS. The FMS, which is headquartered in Washington and has seven regional financial centers, is responsible for the collection, accounting, credit administration, and cash management of Federal monies, as well as making payments on behalf of many agencies of the federal government. This agency manages the government's receipts and disbursements and its central accounting and reporting system, and provides a broad range of financial management and consulting services to other government agencies on working capital management, accounting, systems development, disbursements, and claims.

The FMS manages cash flows averaging $7 billion a day. The FMS receives approximately $15 billion annually through a series of lockboxes at banks; approximately $647 billion annually through Treasury Tax and Loan accounts at about 15,000 financial institutions; about $118 billion annually through a network of approximately 450 banks that receive deposits from more than 100 federal agencies; and about $110 billion annually from collections made through the Fed.

The FMS sets policy for federal collection and disbursement systems, manages more than 100 accounts, including the Social Security Trust Fund and the Highway Trust Fund, and generates more than 700 million payments annually worth more than $700 billion. In addition, the FMS oversees the government's central accounting and reporting system.

The U.S. Banking and Payments System

BACKGROUND

The modern check has its roots in Dutch commerce dating back to the 1500s, when "cashiers" accepted deposits as a security measure against bandits and collected and cancelled debts for depositors. By the latter part of the seventeenth century in England, goldsmiths accepted deposits and issued receipts, which were written promises to pay either the depositor or someone designated by the depositor. As the banking industry developed, banks offered to collect on goldsmith notes for customers and to exchange these instruments with other banks to facilitate their collection on behalf of customers.

The checking system was established in the United States—now the heaviest user of checks in the world—in 1681 by a group of Boston businessmen. At this time, currency was in short supply, and the businessmen pledged their assets to a fund called "The Fund at Boston in New England," receiving credit with the fund and a checkbook to draw against the credit balance. The shortage of currency was soon relieved, however, by the issuance of additional paper currency, which was more acceptable than checks.

Paper currency remained the standard medium for settling debts until after the Revoluntionary War. Deposit banking and checks increased in popularity as cities began to form and grow, transportation improved, and a postal system with low and uniform rates was developed. By the Civil War, more debts were being settled with checks than with paper currency. However, with no central bank to make settlements, banks were forced to set up accounts with each other to clear settlements. As this system of bilateral accounts developed, distant banks began to charge each other for the checks presented to them for payment. These exchange charges were levied against out-of-town banks by the drawee bank, which took a discount and remitted less than par value. To avoid these "nonpar" charges, banks began to send checks over circuitous routes through correspondent banks—often linking correspondent to correspondent—until the checks were presented by local correspondent banks for which the nonpar charges were usually waived.

As this "nonsystem" for clearing checks became more costly and inconvenient, action was taken to replace it with a centralized system for clearing checks at par. In 1913, the Federal Reserve Act was adopted by Congress to establish a series of Federal Reserve banks and branches to clear and collect checks for the banks that were members. This new system, which covered the nation and cleared checks at par, simplified and expedited the routing of checks throughout the country.

THE FED AS OPERATOR OF THE U.S. PAYMENTS SYSTEM

One of the principal ways in which the Federal Reserve System (the Fed) maintains stability in our economic system is by providing a centralized system for clearing checks. In fact, the Fed processes more than 15 billion checks out of the more than 45 billion checks written annually. The 30 billion or so checks not handled by the Fed are cleared in various ways, including internal processing within the depository bank, sending direct to the drawee bank by the depository bank, sending to correspondent banks in distant cities, and exchanging checks among several local banks in a clearinghouse arrangement.

The continued existence of multiple check clearing systems, and the fundamental nature of their operations, is important to the treasury manager who wishes to design a cash management system with optimal float (the time between the deposit of a check and its payment) and cost characteristics. To encourage other banks to maintain deposit accounts, a money center bank may decide to upgrade its processing capability and flexibility of time schedules to attract check clearing business away from the Fed. In addition, since the Fed must charge for these services under provisions of the Monetary Control Act of 1980, the money center bank may use pricing inducements to encourage correspondent bank deposits. Competition among banks within a money center often leads to different pricing and levels of service. Moreover, the city where a particular bank is located has characteristics such as airline connections, weather, transportation costs, and operating efficiency of the local Federal Reserve bank that all have a bearing on the cost to a correspondent of routing checks through the Fed or through a correspondent bank.

EXAMPLE: A bank located in Phoenix accepts a deposit of a sizeable number of checks drawn on Chicago banks. The Phoenix bank may either deposit those checks with the closest Federal Reserve branch (Los Angeles, located some 400 miles away), send the checks to the Chicago Federal Reserve bank, or send the checks to a Chicago correspondent bank where the Phoenix bank maintains a depository account. All three options entail a check clearing charge per check or per cash letter (deposit). To send the checks to Los Angeles will require meeting an early deadline in Los Angeles of perhaps 8 P.M. in order to receive next-day availability of funds. Sending the checks by courier to the Chicago correspondent, however, will extend that deadline to perhaps as late as 5 A.M. the next morning, which would allow the Phoenix bank more time for check processing. The manner in which the Phoenix bank manages its check clearing options is important to the corporate cash manager, because a well-managed bank transit operation will result in later deposit deadlines and faster availability of funds.

While float management is no longer the principal concern of cash managers, as it was in the 1980s, float will continue to exist until paper-based payments are eliminated. As long as checks represent a substantial portion of a company's receipts and disbursements, the prudent designer of a cash management system will need to consider the time it takes for checks to clear.

CHECK CLEARING ARRANGEMENTS

When a customer deposits a check at a bank (depository bank), the bank credits the customer's account and then physically moves the check to the bank on which it is drawn (drawee bank). The route the check travels from the depository bank to the drawee bank depends on the physical proximity of the two banks as well as any special arrangements that may exist between them or with another mutual clearing bank. Check clearing patterns are largely a function of geography. The basic geographical distinctions are local (same city), regional (same Fed district[1]), and distant.

---

[1] See Chapter 2 for locations of the Federal Reserve district banks, branches, and RCPCs.

Clearing Float

"Clearing float" is the amount of funds credited to an account upon the deposit of a check for which payment has not yet been settled in the banking system. Clearing float arises when the customer deposits some checks and the depository bank reflects the deposit liability on its books. The bank makes an offsetting entry to its books by debiting its asset account "Items in Process of Collection." The checks deposited by the customer are then dispatched in three directions:

1. They remain in the depository bank to be processed as on-us checks;

2. They are sent to the local clearinghouse for exchange with local drawee banks; and

3. They are delivered directly to another bank (either the Fed or a correspondent bank) for deposit.

Upon arrival at their destinations, the "Items in Process of Collection" asset account is relieved by a credit, and the amount is then debited to the asset account "Cash and Due from Banks" to reflect the deposit of funds in a correspondent bank or a Federal Reserve bank.

As long as people, businesses, governments, and others use paper checks to settle accounts with each other, there will be clearing float. Clearing float exists because the depository bank credits the depositor's account but must await settlement from the drawee bank. With modern transportation, this delayed availability usually takes one to three days.

Local Checks

Checks drawn on local banks include those drawn on the depository bank itself ("on-us" checks). On-us checks never leave the depository bank once they are deposited but are processed by the Proof Department to validate the deposit and sent directly to the bank's Demand Deposit Accounting Department to be charged to the issuer's account.

Checks drawn on other local or regional banks may be exchanged bilaterally between the depository and drawee banks or they may be deposited with the Fed's Regional Check Processing Center (RCPC) serving the region. There are 11 RCPCs in addition to the 12 Federal Reserve banks and the 25 Federal Reserve branches, all of which process checks for customers that are financial institutions.[2] While the 37 Fed district banks and branches provide full services to their depositors, the 11 RCPCs provide only check clearing services. For purposes of this section, the terms "RCPC" and "Fed" are used interchangeably and are applied to all 48 Fed facilities that process checks.

Clearinghouse Checks

The bilateral exchange of checks between a depository bank and a drawee bank has been a traditional banking process for hundreds of years. When bank messengers in seventeenth century London discovered that their impromptu meetings in coffee houses could serve as a central exchange point, eliminating the need for multiple deliveries of checks to different locations, the idea of the clearinghouse was born.

In the modern clearinghouse, the member banks exchange checks with each other and calculate the net amounts due to and from each other. There may be several clearinghouse meetings during the day. Following the final meeting, the banks settle with each other either through their Fed accounts or through their correspondent accounts.

The clearinghouse settlement normally occurs with a credit or charge for the net amount due to or from the bank, which is passed to the bank's account at the Fed. Clearinghouse checks normally give rise to one day of clearing float, because the depository bank typically does not receive the offset to its "Items in Process of Collection" account (in the form of on-us checks received from other clearinghouse members plus the net debit or credit to its Fed account) until the end of the day. This occurs usually one day after crediting the depositor's account. A typical time line for processing clearinghouse checks is depicted in Figure 3-1.

As is evident in Figure 3-1, clearinghouse checks deposited by a customer over the counter during Day 1, even early in the day, have no chance to be swapped with the other clearinghouse drawee banks because banks usually do not process deposits until the evening. An exception is lockbox deposits, which are usually processed early enough in the day to meet the clearinghouse deadlines. Over-the-counter deposits of clearinghouse checks are almost invariably cleared by the next day, barring any errors or unusual events.

Another exception is checks drawn on depository institutions that are not members of the local clearinghouse. In many cities, institutions such as savings and loans, savings banks, credit unions, and foreign banks are usu-

---

[2] See Chapter 6 for a detailed description of how banks process checks.

FIG. 3-1

Clearing Float Created by Clearinghouse Checks

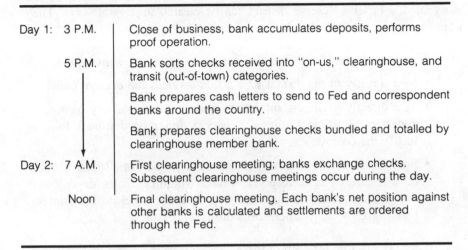

Day 1:	3 P.M.	Close of business, bank accumulates deposits, performs proof operation.
	5 P.M.	Bank sorts checks received into "on-us," clearinghouse, and transit (out-of-town) categories.
		Bank prepares cash letters to send to Fed and correspondent banks around the country.
		Bank prepares clearinghouse checks bundled and totalled by clearinghouse member bank.
Day 2:	7 A.M.	First clearinghouse meeting; banks exchange checks. Subsequent clearinghouse meetings occur during the day.
	Noon	Final clearinghouse meeting. Each bank's net position against other banks is calculated and settlements are ordered through the Fed.

ally not clearinghouse members. Checks drawn on these institutions usually clear through other channels, such as directly to the Fed through the Federal Home Loan Bank (FHLB) or through another commercial bank that is a clearinghouse member.

Regional Checks

Checks drawn on other banks within the same Fed district, that are not members of the local clearinghouse are often sent to the Fed for collection. To use the services of the Fed, the depository bank sends a cash letter (the form by which one bank makes a deposit to another bank) to the Fed for credit to its Fed account. The Fed credits the depository institution's account and assigns a deferred availability, or float, to the deposit based on the amount of time required to present the checks to the respective drawee banks.

If the depository bank sends its cash letter to a Fed processing center early in the day, perhaps containing checks deposited by customers through lockboxes during the night, the Fed may give same-day availability to at least a portion of the deposit. For deposits received later in the day, next-day availability may be granted. It is critical that deadlines be met in order to obtain available funds without suffering an extra day of float.

An alternative method for clearing regional checks is for the clearinghouse nonmember to use a member correspondent.

Distant Checks

Checks drawn on distant banks that are beyond the boundaries of the depository bank's Federal Reserve district can be cleared in several ways. They can be:

- Deposited with the RCPC that serves the *depository* institution;
- Sent directly to the distant RCPC that services the *drawee* bank;
- Sent directly to the distant drawee bank if the depository bank generates a sufficient volume of checks drawn on that bank to justify the cost; or
- Sent for deposit to a correspondent bank in the same locale as the drawee bank. The correspondent bank would credit the deposit to the sending bank's account and then clear the check to the drawee bank through the local clearinghouse.

There is a charge for each of these check-clearing alternatives. The Fed charges for each check deposited to it, as do correspondent banks. Even drawee banks may have charges for handling bundles of on-us checks presented to them. Moreover, presentment of checks to distant drawee or correspondent banks entails transportation charges, usually for courier services or freight on scheduled airlines. Most banks use the Fed's charges and availability schedules as a baseline against which to evaluate the charges and availability of the alternative clearing methods.

Very often, large banks that take in many thousands of checks daily from their customers find it advantageous to sort checks during the proof operation into categories by major city, and then to dispatch these checks to correspondent banks in each of those cities. The advantage of this routing system over depositing all items with the Fed may be lower costs, faster availability, or both.

After dispatching cash letters directly to correspondent banks in major cities, and after sending local checks to the clearinghouse, the depository bank often deposits all the remaining checks with the Fed. The Fed wins the dubious privilege, therefore, of having to clear all of the "other" checks, which are largely drawn on banks in smaller towns and cities, without winning a proportionate share of the big city volume. This increases the Fed's costs by saddling it with the more expensive clearing tasks. Nevertheless, the Fed stands ready to accept deposits from all depository institutions and to clear their checks. Each Fed district bank presents checks directly to banks in its own territory, and sends checks drawn on banks in other Fed districts to the RCPCs that serve them. At the end of each day, all of the Fed district banks settle with each other through the Fed's Interdistrict Settlement Fund (ISF). The ISF is also used for settlement of all other Fed interdistrict transactions such as wire transfers and securities settlements.

Transit Checks

Transit checks are checks that are sent by the depository bank to another bank for deposit. That bank may be a Federal Reserve bank or a correspondent bank, and its receipt of the check depends on schedules of trucks, trains, airlines, or private courier services. Generally, the depository bank can route each check to the next bank in the clearing chain before the close of business the next day. This gives rise to one-day float. Figure 3-2 is a time line showing the sequences and the approximate timing of each step in processing deposited transit checks. If the check is to be deposited at the drawee bank on the same day as received, then clearing float is limited to only one day. Such a situation exists where a depository bank sends the check directly to a drawee bank that is also a correspondent. In such a case, the correspondent credits the depository bank's account and charges the issuer's account virtually simultaneously. If the drawee bank is not a correspondent, a correspondent can send the check to the drawee the same day through the clearinghouse in the correspondent's city, in which case clearing float is limited to one day. If the correspondent (or the Fed district bank receiving the check from the depository bank) must further deliver the check to the drawee bank, then at least one additional clearing day may be consumed, making two days of clearing float.

As can be seen in Figure 3-2, most checks tend to clear and settle on the business day following the day of deposit. This is referred to as next-day settlement and gives rise to one-day availability of funds. Each bank along the time line has an incentive to obtain final settlement as quickly as possible, thus inducing it to process checks quickly and efficiently and to seek the fastest ways (at reasonable cost) to transport checks to their drawee banks.

Some checks take two days to reach their drawee banks. These checks generally are drawn on banks that are physically located a long distance from the Fed's nearest check processing center, adding an extra day or more to transit time. Referring to Case *A* in Figure 3-2, although the Fed normally ships cash letters out at 5 A.M. and they are received by the drawee banks within an hour or so, some banks are located in remote places so far from a commercial airport that transportation takes a full day.

FIG. 3-2

Clearing Float Created by Transit Checks

Case A—Check is sent by depository bank to Fed.

Case B—Check is sent by depository bank to drawee bank.

Case C—Check is sent by depository bank to correspondent bank, which in turn sends check to drawee bank through clearinghouse.

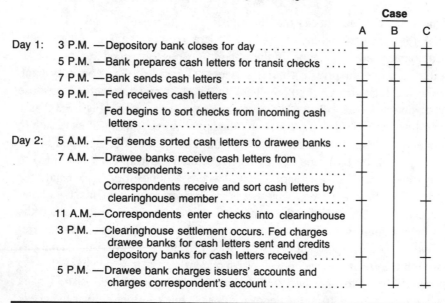

		Case		
		A	B	C
Day 1:	3 P.M. —Depository bank closes for day	+	+	+
	5 P.M. —Bank prepares cash letters for transit checks	+	+	+
	7 P.M. —Bank sends cash letters	+	+	+
	9 P.M. —Fed receives cash letters	+		
	Fed begins to sort checks from incoming cash letters	+		
Day 2:	5 A.M. —Fed sends sorted cash letters to drawee banks ..	+		
	7 A.M. —Drawee banks receive cash letters from correspondents	+		
	Correspondents receive and sort cash letters by clearinghouse member.....................	+		+
	11 A.M.—Correspondents enter checks into clearinghouse			
	3 P.M. —Clearinghouse settlement occurs. Fed charges drawee banks for cash letters sent and credits depository banks for cash letters received	+		+
	5 P.M. —Drawee bank charges issuers' accounts and charges correspondent's account	+	+	+

Noon Presentment

The Depository Institutions Deregulation and Monetary Control Act of 1980 mandated that the Fed reduce Fed float,[3] the amount of funds represented by credits the Fed has given to depository banks before the drawee banks have been charged. In an effort to comply with this mandate, the Fed initiated a second presentment (delivery) of checks during the day. The Fed's goal was to make the second presentment by noon—in fact, it typically occurs several hours earlier. The second presentment enables the Fed check processing centers to clear out the bulk of their check volume very early in the morning. But the items that miss the early cut-off need not be held over until the next day. They are presented to the drawee banks a few hours later.

---

[3] See Chapter 6 for a discussion of Fed float.

The second presentment is made only to those banks whose check volume exceeds $10 million per day. For smaller banks—and most of the 15,000 commercial banks in the United States are small banks—their volume of checks passing through the Fed does not warrant the expense of a second presentment by the Fed. The Fed continues to seek adjustments to its presentment schedules and to force banks to accept progressively later presentments of checks in order to reduce float in the banking system.

Availability Schedules

An availability schedule (see Figure 3-3) is the schedule of processing deadlines established by the individual bank in order to allocate float to checks deposited. The schedule, which most major cash management banks publish and make available on request to customers, notifies the customers of the precise time of day by which the bank's check processing center must receive the deposited item for it to be assigned no, one, two, or three days float. The schedule is usually organized by geographical location of the drawee bank and may refer to territories served by particular RCPCs rather than to specific cities.

With some 45 billion checks clearing annually, no depository institution can track each check through the clearing process to determine when final settlement is actually made. However, institutions do track cash letters to ensure their prompt disptach and arrival according to predetermined schedules, which are in turn based on predetermined routing patterns. Large banks tend to be aggressive in setting up their routing patterns, and those patterns are altered frequently to reflect changing availability schedules of correspondent banks and changes in airline routing and flight schedules.

Generally, a check deposited to the Fed that is drawn on a bank in the same Fed district receives same day or next day availability. Checks drawn on banks in other Fed districts located in areas far from the nearest RCPC receive two-day availability. This system of deferred availability is crucial to a company that is designing a system to collect remittances from customers. Availability is usually enhanced when a check remains within a single Fed district. Therefore, when selecting lockbox depository banks, careful consideration must be given to Fed district boundaries and not just to mailing schedules.[4]

---

[4] See Chapter 8 for a detailed description of wire transfers.

FIG. 3-3

Sample Availability Schedule (Partial)

Federal Reserve District	Transit Numbers	Deposit Deadline							
		0200	0500	1100	1500	1930	2030	2230	2330
		Availability							
6TH District									
Whitney Nat'l Bank	0650-0017	1	1	1	1	1	1	1	1
New Orleans RCPC	0651, 0652	1	1	2	2	2	2	1	1
New Orleans RCPC	0653, 0654, 0655	1	1	2	2	2	2	1	1
Miami	0660	1	1	2	2	2	2	1	1
Miami RCPC	0670	1	1	2	2	2	2	1	1
7TH District									
Chicago	0710	1	1	1	1	1	1	1	1
First National Bank	0710-0001	0	0	1	1	1	1	0	0
Continental Bank	0710-0003	0	0	1	1	1	1	0	0
Northern Trust	0710-0015	0	0	1	1	1	1	0	0
Harris Trust	0710-0028	0	0	1	1	1	1	0	0
Chicago RCPC	0711, 0712, 0719	1	1	2	2	2	2	1	1
Detroit	0720	1	1	1	1	1	1	1	1
Detroit RCPC	0724	1	1	2	2	2	2	1	1
Michigan Nat'l Bank, Lansing	0724-1174	1	1	1	1	1	1	1	1
Des Moines	0730	1	1	1	1	1	1	1	1
Des Moines RCPC	0739	1	1	2	2	2	2	1	1
Indianapolis	0740	1	1	1	1	1	1	1	1
Indianapolis RCPC	0749	1	1	2	2	2	2	1	1
Milwaukee	0750	1	1	1	1	1	1	1	1
Milwaukee RCPC	0759	1	1	2	2	2	2	1	1
8TH District									
St. Louis	0810	1	1	1	1	1	1	1	1
St. Louis Country	0812, 0815, 0865	1	1	2	2	2	2	1	1
St. Louis Country	0813, 0863	1	1	2	2	2	2	1	1
St. Louis RCPC	0819	1	1	2	2	2	2	1	1
Little Rock	0820	1	1	2	2	2	2	1	1
Little Rock RCPC	0821, 0829	1	1	2	2	2	2	1	1
Louisville	0830	1	1	1	1	1	1	1	1
Louisville RCPC	0839,	1	1	2	2	2	2	1	1
Memphis	0840	1	1	1	1	1	1	1	1
Memphis RCPC	0841, 0842, 0843	1	1	2	2	2	2	1	1
9TH District									
Norwest Bank	0910-0001	0	0	1	1	1	1	0	0
First Bank of Minn.	0910-0002	0	0	1	1	1	1	0	0
Minneapolis & St. Paul Clearinghouse	0910, 0960	1	1	1	1	1	1	1	1
Minneapolis Country	0911, 0912, 0913, 0914, 0915	2	2	2	2	2	2	2	2
Minneapolis RCPC	0918, 0919	1	1	2	2	2	2	1	1
Helena	0920	1	1	2	2	2	2	1	1
Helena Country	0921	2	2	3	3	3	3	2	2
LEDGER CREDIT 2030									

To the cash manager whose deposits are routinely made over-the-counter to the bank, an availability schedule is of little use since cut-off times apply to the receipt of deposits by the Proof Department at the bank's central processing facility. To the cash manager who delivers deposits directly to the bank's central processing facility or who uses the bank's lock-box service, however, the cut-off times are important both in absolute terms and when comparing the relative performance of banks.

One bank may offer later deposit cut-off times than its competitor. However, if the later deadlines result in a missed airline flight, resulting in actual longer clearing times for a significant amount of the company's deposits, then the later deadlines may actually be detrimental.

CASH MANAGEMENT SUGGESTION:

The cash manager who is interested in monitoring a bank's availability should consider asking the following questions of the bank:

1. Does the published availability schedule reflect actual availability obtained by the bank, or is it merely a schedule to establish how the bank charges for clearing float? Frequently, the bank will pad the availability schedule to make the deadlines appear earlier than they actually are in order to assure its ability to meet those deadlines. As a result, a bank may quote and charge for two day's float when it may actually obtain one-day availability some or most of the time.

2. Does the bank publish more than one availability schedule? Banks often publish one availability schedule for corporate/commercial depositors and another availability schedule for correspondent bank depositors. Bankers generally understand the check clearing process better, and correspondent banks tend to be more sensitive to differences in the availability schedules of banks. Accordingly, depository banks often publish an availability schedule for their correspondent banks that contains less padding of the deadlines. Correspondent banks may also be offered more favorable availability because they frequently encode the amount on checks deposited, enabling the depository bank to process the items more efficiently.

3. How frequently does the bank revise its published availability schedule? The actual availability schedule may change daily, but it is neither practical nor particularly useful for a bank to publish it that frequently. Some banks revise and publish availability schedules monthly, and others publish semiannually.

ELECTRONIC FUNDS TRANSFER PAYMENT MECHANISMS

The principal forms of electronic funds transfer are wire transfers and automated clearing house (ACH) transfers. Others include the Clearinghouse

Interbank Payments System (CHIPS) operated by the New York Clearing House Association, and the Society for Worldwide Interbank Financial Telecommunications (SWIFT), operated by an international consortium of banks for international payments and certain structured forms of nonpayment messages.

Any payment mechanism, whether paper-based or electronic, entails the transfer of value from the payor to the payee. Value is represented by credit balances on the bank's books reflecting customers' deposit balances. Value is transferred through bookkeeping entries that add value to the payee's account and subtract value from the payor's account. The electronic funds transfer mechanism is merely a means for communicating the instruction to add value to one account and subtract value from another account. Checks are inherently slow and the exact timing of the transfer of value uncertain; however, electronic funds transfer methods are fast and carry a greater degree of certainty as to the moment of final settlement.

Wire Transfers

"Wire transfer" usually refers to a same-day transfer of funds from an account at one bank to an account at another bank initiated over the Fedwire.[5]

Fedwire is the Federal Reserve Communications System, linking the 12 Federal Reserve district banks, their 25 branches, and certain eligible U.S. depository institutions. An eligible institution initiates a Fedwire transfer by sending instructions to the Federal Reserve bank or branch that serves the institution to charge the Fed account of the originating institution and to credit the Fed account of the receiving institution. The message also states the reason for the transfer, such as "to settle Fed funds loan" or "credit account #12345 I/N/O John Smith." If both the originating and receiving depository institutions are in the same Fed district, the Reserve Bank makes the appropriate entries to pass value from the originating institution's account to the receiving institution's account. The Reserve Bank then notifies the receiving institution of the transfer by sending a message over the Fedwire. If the two institutions are in different districts, the Reserve Bank in the originating district notifies the Reserve Bank in the receiving district, and they arrange to pass value between them, settling through the ISF.

The Fedwire network is a series of connections among the Federal Reserve banks, linking each bank with at least two other banks to provide

---

[5] See Chapter 7 for a detailed discussion of Fedwire transfers.

alternate communication lines in case of breakdowns. The Fed guarantees to pass value as of the date the Fedwire transfer is initiated, provided that the transfer meets all required criteria, including the initiation cut-off deadline.

The Fed endeavors to complete a given transaction within minutes after receiving it from the originating institution. Interdistrict transfers take longer because the message must be handled by two Reserve Banks. However, the total elapsed time normally is 30 minutes or less.

CASH MANAGEMENT SUGGESTION:

> When a bank knows it is being watched, it may perform better. When swift execution of a Fedwire transfer is required, the cash manager should note the time of day that the wire transfer instructions were given to the originating bank and request that the bank provide the Fedwire number (a sequential number that is used to trace Fedwires) and the time of dispatch (the time when the message was actually sent out on the Fedwire). The elapsed time from when the cash manager ordered the wire transfer to the time the wire actually went out is a function of internal processing by the originating institution and is totally within the control of that institution (assuming no intervening failure of the Fedwire system).

Daylight Overdrafts

Undue delays in the dispatch of Fedwire transfers usually occur for only two reasons: daylight overdrafts or internal inefficiency within the originating depository institution. A daylight overdraft occurs when a depositor orders a wire transfer to be made in anticipation of receipt of funds the same day. The result is an overdraft in the account for a period during the day. Daylight overdrafts must be taken into account by any company wishing to make a timely Fedwire transfer.

> **EXAMPLE:** The balance in Corporation A's account is $250,000. Corporation A is fully confident that its investment banker will send $800,000 into its account from the sale of investment securities. At 9 A.M. A's cash manager orders a wire transfer from its bank to the bank of Manufacturing Company B for $800,000 to pay for a machine. The wire transfer from the investment banker is not received until 11 A.M. If A's bank had acted to initiate the wire promptly at 9 A.M., a daylight overdraft would have occurred in A's bank account from that moment until the receipt of funds at 11 A.M. from the investment bank.

A daylight overdraft in a corporate bank account can lead to a corresponding daylight overdraft in the bank's account at the Fed. In the mid-1980s, with the rash of bank failures and total daylight overdrafts at the Fed averaging $110 to $120 billion a day, the Fed introduced a measure to limit the amount of daylight overdrafts at all depository institutions. The limit for each bank, which was initially imposed on a voluntary basis in March 1986, is called the "Sender's Net Debit Cap," referring to the limit or cap on the amount of the net debit balance (overdraft) a bank may have in its Fed account at any moment. The amount of a bank's net debit cap is based on a multiple of the bank's amount of capital funds, adjusted for its relative financial strength and the quality of its internal controls as determined through supervisory examinations. The Fed has insisted that banks not disclose the amount of their respective net debit caps because it is actually irrelevant to the community at large and could be misinterpreted. By adjusting the allowable net debit cap, the Fed can theoretically control its exposure to risk if any bank suddenly fails.

The other side of the daylight overdraft issue is that all banks are asked to control their wire transfer activities because of the excesses of a few. Such control may lead to a gridlock in the financial system if all of the major banks are frozen from making wire transfers until they receive incoming funds from each other.

The cash manager is concerned about the daylight overdraft issue because a company's outbound wire transfer traffic may be delayed when the originating bank bumps up against its net debit cap. The net debit cap may have even been reached by the bank's own operations rather than by the actions of its customers. The bank may have sold Fed funds or it may have purchased U.S. government securities, both of which settle through the bank's Fed account. If the bank was delayed in funding its Fed account, perhaps from a correspondent bank where funds have accumulated from direct-send cash letters, a daylight overdraft would occur.

CASH MANAGEMENT SUGGESTION:

By tracking the time of receipt and disbursement of wire transfers made through the company's account, the cash manager can determine the company's actual daylight overdraft position, if any. While this can be done only after the fact by obtaining documentation from the bank, the cash manager should discuss the situation with the bank with a view toward relieving the company from the burden of delays in its outbound wire transfer traffic.

From time to time, private wire transfer systems have been developed among groups of banks, such as the Bankwire system that folded in

1986. These systems tend to arise when the Fedwire system is slow to adopt technological change or its pricing policy leaves room for less expensive alternatives. Since a wire transfer system is actually only a communications medium for passing bookkeeping instructions, alternative wire transfer systems probably will continue to appear from time to time.

CASH MANAGEMENT SUGGESTION:

If an alternative wire transfer system is available, the cash manager need not specify which system the originating bank should use but may leave that choice up to the bank. However, the cash manager should specify the value date for settlement (e.g., same day, next day, or a specific future date). The risk of loss should not be affected by the particular medium selected by the bank, although the cost and risk of delay of the transaction could very well be affected.

ACH Transfers

Clearinghouse associations in many major cities have developed electronic methods of passing payments among members and other financial institutions in the region and of exchanging payments among the ACHs themselves. ACH transfers may be either credit transfers (sending funds out) or debit transfers (pulling funds in), and they may be initiated by either the payee or the payor. Figure 3-4 shows the names and locations of ACHs.

With ACH transfers, the parties are the "originator" and the "receiver" of the transaction, and the transaction is either a credit or a debit transfer.

EXAMPLE: When Corporation *C* makes a salary payment to its employee Jones, it is the originator, Jones is the receiver, and the transaction is a credit transfer ("for credit to Jones' account"). Likewise, *C*'s bank is the Originating Depository Financial Institution (ODFI) and Jones' bank is the Receiving Depository Financial Institution (RDFI). *C* is in the cable television business, and it has received permission from its customer, Smythe, to collect his monthly subscription fee by making a debit transfer directly from Smythe's bank account on the fifteenth day of each month. *C* is still the originator of this transaction, which is a debit transfer (the message would read, "debit to Smythe's account"), and Smythe is the receiver. *C*'s bank is still the ODFI and Smythe's bank is the RDFI.

FIG. 3-4
Names and Locations of ACHs

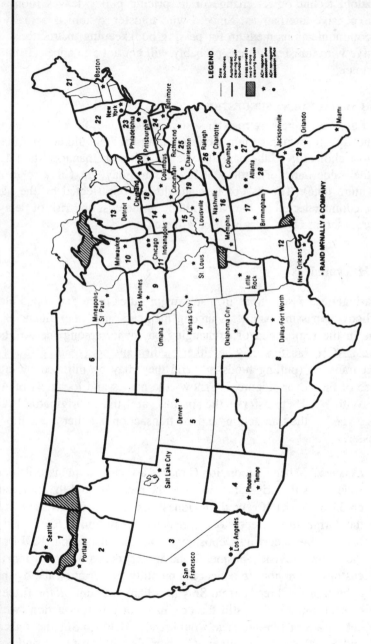

Source: *Reprinted with permission from the Rand McNally Banker's Directory.*

Map Reference Number	City	ACH Name	Acronym	Federal Reserve Bank District
28	Atlanta	Georgia ACH Association	GACHA	6 Atlanta
24	Baltimore	Mid-Atlantic ACH Association	MACHA	3 Philadelphia
17	Birmingham	Alabama ACH Association	ALACHA	6 Atlanta
21	Boston	New England ACH Association	NEACH	1 Boston
25	Charleston, W.V.	Virginias ACH Association	VACHA	5 Richmond
26	Charlotte	North Carolina ACH Association	NORCACHA	5 Richmond
11	Chicago	Midwest ACH Association	MACHA	7 Chicago
19	Cincinnati	Central Regional Automated Funds Transfer System	CRAFTS	4 Cleveland
18	Cleveland	Mid-America Automated Payments System	MAPS	4 Cleveland
27	Columbia, S.C.	South Carolina ACH Association	SOCACHA	5 Richmond
19	Columbus, Ohio	Central Regional Automated Funds Transfer System	CRAFTS	4 Cleveland
8	Dallas	Southwestern ACH Association	SWACHA	11 Dallas
5	Denver	Rocky Mountain ACH Association	RMACHA	10 Kansas City
9	Des Moines	Iowa ACH Association	IACHA	7 Chicago
13	Detroit	Michigan ACH Association	MACHA	7 Chicago
14	Indianapolis	Indiana Exchange, Inc.	INDEX	7 Chicago
29	Jacksonville	Florida Payment Systems, Inc.	FPSI	6 Atlanta
7	Kansas City	Mid-America Payment Exchange	MAPEX	10 Kansas City
7	Little Rock	Mid-America Payment Exchange	MAPEX	8 St. Louis
3	Los Angeles	Calwestern ACH Association	CACHA	12 San Francisco
15	Louisville	Kentuckiana ACH Association	KACHA	8 St. Louis
12	Memphis	Southern Financial Exchange	SFE	6 Atlanta
29	Miami	Florida Payment System, Inc.	FPSI	6 Atlanta
10	Milwaukee	Wisconsin ACH Association	WACHA	7 Chicago
6	Minneapolis	Upper Midwest ACH Association	UMACHA	9 Minneapolis
16	Nashville	Tennessee ACH Association	TACHA	6 Atlanta
12	New Orleans	Southern Financial Exchange	SFX	6 Atlanta
22	New York	New York ACH Association	NYACH	2 New York
7	Oklahoma City	Mid-America Payment Exchange	MAPEX	10 Kansas City
7	Omaha	Mid-America Payment Exchange	MAPEX	10 Kansas City
23	Philadelphia	Third District Funds Transfer Association	3DFTA	3 Philadelphia
4	Phoenix	Arizona Clearing House Association	ACHA	12 San Francisco
20	Pittsburgh	Tri-State ACH Association	TRISACH	4 Cleveland
2	Portland	Oregon ACH Association	OACHA	12 San Francisco
25	Richmond	Virginias ACH Association	VACHA	5 Richmond
3	Salt Lake City	Calwestern ACH Association	CACHA	12 San Francisco
3	San Francisco	Calwestern ACH Association	CACHA	12 San Francisco
1	Seattle	Northwest ACH Association	NWACHA	12 San Francisco
7	St. Louis	Mid-America Payment Exchange	MAPEX	8 St. Louis
4	Tempe	Arizona Clearing House Association	ACHA	12 San Francisco

3-19

The principal differences between wire and ACH transfers are as follows:

1. Wire transfers are oriented to a single transfer, while ACH transfers are oriented to handling multiple transfers in a batch mode.

2. Wire transfers are oriented to same-day settlement, while ACH transfers are oriented to future-date settlement, although same-day settlement for transactions within the same ACH is technically possible.

3. Wire transfers are expensive because of their customized, one-at-a-time nature, while ACH transfers are inexpensive because of their structured data format and high volume batch nature. Moreover, bank product managers have discovered that customers are willing to pay a premium for same-day settlement.

PRIVATE PAYMENT MECHANISMS[6]

The Fed operates the "Federal Reserve Communications System—80" (Fedwire) and has been retained as a contractor to operate all but a few of the ACHs as well. Therefore, the Fed dominates the payment system for most electronic funds transfers.

However, when specific electronic funds transfer requirements develop that can be handled outside the Fed, often a private solution develops. In recent U.S. history, both Bankwire and Cashwire existed for a time and then folded for one reason or another. However, CHIPS has survived as a domestic settlement mechanism, and SWIFT has grown as an international network for payments. Other settlement mechanisms have been developed for specific industries, such as Petro-clear for the petroleum industry, but these generally are not available to banks or to businesses not belonging to that industry.

CHIPS

CHIPS, operated by the New York Clearing House Association, handles large-dollar payments among approximately 140 banks with offices in New York. CHIPS is a computer-based system that enables its clearing banks to handle a high volume of daily payment transactions quickly, accurately, and efficiently. In addition, the New York Clearinghouse Association operates a

---

[6] See Chapter 7 for a detailed discussion of private EFT systems.

paper-based clearinghouse and the New York Automated Clearinghouse (NYACH). NYACH handles the same kinds of ACH transfers as other regional ACHs.

While the common perception is that CHIPS handles mostly international transactions, in fact all of its transactions are domestic, since they are payments from one CHIPS member bank to another CHIPS member bank. It is true, however, that a large proportion of these payments are in settlement of international transactions, such as remittances and foreign exchange transactions. For example, an Italian bank owing dollars to a large West Coast bank may send a telex to its New York correspondent, instructing it to charge the account of the Italian bank and pay the West Coast bank. In this example, the transaction is initiated abroad, but the actual dollar payment occurs between two domestic banks. The New York bank would have the choice of initiating a Fedwire transfer to the West Coast bank's headquarters in San Francisco, or of creating a CHIPS transfer. The CHIPS transfer is actually only a message between the two banks, followed by a net settlement of funds at the end of the day by each institution against the clearinghouse rather than against each other. CHIPS transfers are accumulated throughout the day, at the close of which each member's net position is calculated and settlement is effected through the Federal Reserve Bank of New York.

SWIFT

In 1973, a group of the largest banks in Europe, Canada, and the United States formed SWIFT, based in Brussels. By 1987, the membership of SWIFT grew to include more than 2,000 banks in approximately 54 countries around the world. SWIFT operates 24 hours a day, 365 days a year, as a carrier of message traffic among all of the banks in the SWIFT network. The messages are in standard formats structured by message type to facilitate understanding of the messages regardless of the sender's native language. The standard formats also provide a method for sending rapid, accurate, and secure messages inexpensively among the members. The types of messages that SWIFT handles include:

- Customer funds transfers
- Bank transfers
- Foreign exchange confirmations
- Loan and deposit advice and confirmations
- Collection advice and payment acknowledgements

- Letters of credit
- Account reconcilement statements
- Administrative messages
- Advice and confirmation of securities transactions

Like CHIPS, SWIFT is basically a message system rather than a funds transfer system such as Fedwire. SWIFT does not actually move funds concurrently with the message. Settlement of SWIFT transactions usually occurs through correspondent accounts of the sending and receiving banks or through mutual correspondents or central banks of the countries involved.

RISK IN THE PAYMENT SYSTEM

Payment system risk has been an increasing concern of the Fed, particularly since the mid-1980s when the volume of bank failures began to accelerate. Regardless of the reason for a bank failure, the costs can be extremely high, not only to the federal agency that has insured the deposits of the failed institution but to the entire payment system. The failure of a payor, whether a business organization or an individual, results in a dishonored payment transaction. When a depository institution fails, payment transactions can be dishonored by the thousands unless the regulatory and deposit insurance agencies can erect a safety net rapidly. The fear that the safety net may not be spread fast enough, and that the amount of insurance may be completely consumed, leaving no safety margin for the remaining players, has haunted the Fed.

Risk manifests itself in three different ways in the payment system: (1) systemic risk, resulting from inefficiencies and processing delays within the system; (2) credit risk, the risk of failure of either a corporate payor or a drawee bank, or the risk that a paying bank may become temporarily unable to move funds because of a daylight overdraft cap;[7] and (3) fraud risk, possibly resulting from lack of authentication and encryption in ACH transactions, or forged signatures or endorsements on checks. The fact that no losses due to the failure of a payor or an originating bank have yet been incurred in the ACH system does not prove that there is no risk.

The key element in payment system risk is the issue of finality of payment. When payment becomes final, neither side has recourse to the other and the transaction is complete. Unfortunately, the exact moment of finality

---

[7] For a detailed discussion, see "Daylight Overdrafts," this chapter.

in most types of transactions cannot be known in real time; rather, it is known only after it has occurred. But the task facing the payment system regulators is to move finality of payment into a more visible and recordable position in order to reduce or eliminate the uncertainty that attends almost every payment transaction.

Checks

Risk in paper-based payment systems exists between the time the account of the depositor of a check is credited and the time the item is charged to the account of the payor. This period is often for up to two days, and if the check is dishonored for any reason (e.g., insufficient or uncollected funds, payment stopped, signature or endorsement problem, account closed), it usually takes even longer for the item to be returned to the depository bank. In the meantime, if the depositor has withdrawn the funds and cannot be found, the depository bank is left holding the bag.

To minimize this problem, banks developed the concept of a "hold" on the deposited funds to prevent the depositor from withdrawing the deposited funds until such time as the item would normally be returned. Legislation in certain states in the late 1980s placed limits on the length of such holds because of the perception that banks were holding funds for unreasonably long periods. This issue was addressed by Congress in 1987 with the passage of the Expedited Funds Availability Act and the adoption by the Fed in 1988 of Regulation CC to implement the Act.

In a real sense, the mere existence of clearing float represents a risk in the payment system. Clearing float truly reflects double counting of funds in the banking system because the same funds are on deposit for a period of time in both the payee's account and in the payor's account. Any interference with the timely completion of the clearing transaction presents the risk of loss in the system.

Wire Transfers

The Fedwire presents little risk to the payment system because it is a true wire transfer system. That is, the message to create the bookkeeping entry and the actual entry are made simultaneously. If the entry cannot be made, then the message is truncated and the transaction is aborted. Risk does exist, however, in the form of daylight overdrafts; this is a matter of credit risk on the part of the overdrawn bank involved.

Automated Clearing Houses

The payment risk in an ACH environment arises in two possible ways:

1. The payor must authorize the transfer in advance, with the settlement date specified for some time in the future. If during the interim period the payor fails, the payee may receive payment while the payor is unable to complete the transaction. This problem could be resolved if the settlement were made simultaneously with verification that both sides of the transaction were being completed. However, the latter aspect of this control would destroy the bulk nature (and the low cost) of this form of payment. Therefore, ACH payment risk devolves into a credit risk borne by the system based on the solvency of the payor.

2. The completion of an ACH transaction depends on the solvency and liquidity of the paying bank. The failure of that bank to settle an ACH transaction could leave the ACH system in shambles while the parties decide who should bear the burden of the loss.

ATTEMPTS TO OVERRIDE THE SYSTEM

An attempt is often made to beat the system by adopting a device or technique to gain a momentary cash management advantage. The Fed or a bank would respond by changing the rules to discourage the aberrant behavior, only to find that the resourceful cash manager had discovered a new loophole in the system. Few of these devices or techniques have endured simply because most of them result in a zero sum; that is, to the extent that one player gains, another player loses. In the long run, the losers outnumber the winners, and they tend to end the game.

Those devices and techniques that have endured have done so usually because they are not zero sum; that is, one player wins but not at the expense of another player. Perhaps the best example of this is controlled disbursing, which was an outgrowth of the "outlawed" remote disbursing. Where remote disbursing is a zero-sum game and has been regulated out of existence by the Fed, controlled disbursing is a win-win opportunity for most of the players. Controlled disbursing has found a niche as a most useful technique for companies and a very important revenue-producing service for banks.

Remote disbursing. In remote disbursing, the payor draws checks on a bank located in a remote part of the United States, far from a Fed check processing center. The bank should also have few correspondent banks sending it cash letters, and it should have a relatively light volume of checks drawn against it in order not to attract correspondent cash letters or second presentments from the Fed. In 1980, the Fed effectively ended remote disbursing when it forbade banks to accept disbursing accounts from companies that had no other business reason than to create extended disbursement float.

Federal tax payments. Most commercial banks in the United States are official depositories of the U.S. Treasury. These banks accept tax deposits from companies for payment of employment and income taxes. Until the early 1980s, aggressive companies often made the tax deposit to a nearby convenient bank on the due date, using a check drawn on a distant bank. Banks used to encourage their clients to make tax deposits with them because the government used to leave the funds on deposit for several days or even a week. In fact, some banks even took these "Treasury Tax and Loan Account" (TT & L) balances into consideration in the customer's account analysis statement, even though the balances were in the government's account.

Another ploy was to send the tax payment to an Internal Revenue Service (IRS) office rather than to a bank. IRS offices took several days to deliver the check to a bank, but they acknowledged payment when it was received. A variation on this theme was to deliver the tax payment check directly to a Fed district bank or branch instead of to a commercial bank. Stories abounded about how it took up to two weeks for those checks to clear, the reasons for which have never been made apparent. The Fed and IRS ended this practice by requiring that the tax deposits be made to a commercial bank tax depository and that the check be drawn on a bank in the same Fed district.

With the Depository Institutions Deregulation and Monetary Control Act of 1980, the Treasury demanded that the U.S. government receive credit for these TT & L balances to offset services rendered by the banks to the Treasury; further, the Treasury began to draw down the balances from the TT & L accounts much more aggressively. It is not unusual for a major bank to hold federal tax deposit funds for an average of less than one day. Consequently, few banks allow credit on corporate account analyses for tax deposits any more.

Destroying the MICR line. Perhaps the most blatantly illegal practices, and therefore not widely practiced, were efforts to destroy the integrity of the magnetic ink character recognition (MICR) line. By "cooking" checks in a microwave oven, the ferrous material in the magnetic ink was scrambled to cause it to lose its magnetic property. Alternatively, by making a pinhole (too small to be readily visible) in one of the MICR numbers or symbols, the ability to read the MICR line by bank reader-sorters was destroyed. In either case, the tampered check would be rejected by the depository bank's equipment, causing a delay in processing the item until a substitute MICR line could be printed and pasted onto the defective item. These practices are clearly fraudulent and therefore illegal.

Remote check mailing. To extend mail float, some companies use their decentralized plants and offices to mail checks. Checks may be issued at a company's headquarters and shipped to a distant plant site for mailing to vendors in the vicinity of the headquarters. A refinement of this is to place check-printing equipment at the remote plant site and transmit the check data to the remote printer. This eliminates the time necessary for shipping the printed checks, although it also opens up potential control problems.

This practice is profitable to the issuer because most vendors that offer prompt payment discounts use the postmark date rather than the date of receipt of the check to determine eligibility for the discount. Obviously, if the check can be mailed timely but its delivery delayed in the postal system, the payor has gained at the corresponding expense of the payee.

Tampering with the postage meter. A variation of the remote check game that violates postal regulations is simply to set the date on the postage meter incorrectly. If payment is due on the tenth day of the month and vendors rely on the postmark to determine eligibility for the discount, the mail room can make some money for the company merely by setting the meter at the tenth, while mailing the checks several days later.

The forgotten signature. Usually an inadvertent error, the omission of an authorized signature from the check is often believed to buy time for a beleaguered payor who hopes that the payee will realize the error and return the check for a proper signature. Unfortunately, this ploy usually does not work because the informed payee will deposit the check even without the signature, and the check will usually clear through the banking system anyway. When the drawee bank receives the item, it will normally telephone an authorized signatory of the issuer for permission to pay it, and such permission is expected unless the check was erroneously or fraudulently issued.

The disregarded lockbox. The attentive disbursement manager can usually identify situations in which a vendor is switching the remittance address from the company to a lockbox processor.[8] The following are three tip-offs as to when this is the case:

1. The notice of the new remittance address carries an instruction to send all correspondence to an address different than the remittance address;

2. The remittance address is in a different locale from the accounting department of the payee; and

3. The new remittance address is to a particular post office or unique ZIP code known to be used by lockbox processors.

When starting up a lockbox remittance processing system, vendors realize that it often takes payors time to adjust the databases in their accounts payable systems. Disbursement managers sometimes take advantage of this fluid situation by dragging their feet while continuing to remit to the vendor's old street or post office box address. This forces the vendor to handle the check without the lockbox processor intervening, which usually buys an extra day or two.

----

[8] See Chapter 5 for a detailed discussion of lockboxes.

PART II

Funds Mobilization

CHAPTER 4

Management of Accounts Receivable

OBJECTIVES

Credit and collection policies are but two of the many elements determining the relative success of a business. Because of their importance, credit and collection policies should be in writing and periodically reviewed and revised. Too often, marketing management ignores credit and collection policies in the belief that product pricing is of sole importance. However, credit and collection policies are nearly as important a marketing tool as pricing, because the failure of these two procedures can wipe out even a large sales figure very quickly.

The profitability of a firm can be seriously affected by inadequate credit and collection policies. For example, the firm that operates on a gross profit margin of 33 percent and writes off $1 of accounts receivable has realized the loss of gross profit from $3 of sales. The $1 of receivables written off accounts for 33 cents of gross profit plus 67 cents of actual costs. It will take another $3 of sales with gross profit at 33 percent to recoup the loss. Another company that writes off $1 and operates at a 20 percent gross profit margin will require $5 of sales to recoup the loss. Through sound credit and collection policies, not only can the profitability of the firm be protected against calamity, but it can often be enhanced as well.

The cash manager is interested in accounts receivable management principally in order to be able to forecast cash receipts. Only through forecasting can a financial manager know that expected receipts have failed to materialize. In a well managed accounts receivable program, the combination of sound credit terms and some enforcement of discipline will pay off in terms of predictable collection patterns. To the extent that collection patterns can be made somewhat more predictable, the cash manager can better anticipate cash flows and manage with a lower overall level of funds.[1] To the treasury manager with broader interests than merely forecasting and planning funds flows, the challenge is to provide sufficient funding for the company's growth. Too often, a firm's growth in sales and profits is reflected mainly in an increasing investment in accounts receivable. Obviously, if the treasury manager can restrain the growth of this asset, the firm's funding and capital requirements will be reduced accordingly. Clearly, the treasury manager has a role to play in determining the optimum level of accounts receivable in order to maximize the flow of funds.

Accounts receivable often represents the largest asset group for the firm other than its fixed assets. The amount of capital invested in accounts receivable is large and bears a substantial part of the cost of doing business. The balance in each account continually turns over, with new and old accounts appearing and disappearing in an ongoing cycle. Although generally accepted accounting principles dictate that accounts receivable be reflected in the balance sheet as a current asset, from the viewpoint of capital employment the aggregate of accounts receivable is as fixed an asset as there is on the whole balance sheet.

The astute financial manager can influence the size of the investment in accounts receivable within the bounds of competition and profitability of the firm. As part of the overall planning and control function, the manager can and should make a conscious decision about the size of the investment in accounts receivable.

Determining the Optimum Level of Receivables

The principal determinants of the size of the firm's accounts receivable are the form in which credit is granted and the terms of sale that are customary (and the level of adherence to those terms, within a particular trade or industry).

Figure 4-1 shows an example of two companies that have identical sales of $100,000 per month but different credit terms that result in different collection patterns. Company *A* offers standard terms of sale of net 30 days and experiences a composite average collection time of 35 days sales outstand-

---

[1] See Chapter 12 for a detailed discussion of short-term funds flow forecasting.

FIG. 4-1

Terms of Sale and Resulting Days Sales Outstanding (DSO)

Billings:	$100,000 per month

Example A:

Industry Terms of Sale:	Net 30 days
Accounts Receivable:	$116,667
Average Collection Time:	35 days

Result—Receivables average 35 DSO

Example B:

Industry Terms of Sale:	2%/10 net 30
Compliance:	
60% of billings are collected in 12 days or less 2%	$24,000
25% of billings are collected in 37 days	30,833
15% of billings are collected in 60 days	30,000
Result—receivables average:	$84,833 = 25 DSO

ing (DSO), or $116,667 of accounts receivable. (Assuming a 30-day month, $116,667 receivables divided by $100,000 sales equals 1.167 months' sales outstanding, or 35 days).

Company B, on the other hand, offers a discount of 2 percent for payment within 10 days after invoice date, and some 60 percent of the billings are collected within that time period. Of course, Company B gives up 2 percent of its sales volume to these customers, or $480 ($24,000 × 0.002) of expense per month. An additional 25 percent of billings are collected without discount in a composite average of 37 days, and the remainder are slow payers who pay some 15 percent of billings in an average of 60 days.

Of these two companies, which is in a better financial position? To determine the answer requires one more piece of information: the "hurdle rate," or the composite cost of money to a company. One approach to setting the hurdle rate can be to use the firm's cost of equity capital or its cost of long-term debt capital, or a combination of these capital sources weighted for the respective proportions making up the firm's capital structure. Another approach is to take the variable portion of the asset only and apply a cost of short-term funds.

Under normal business conditions and assuming that the customer tends to pay its bills in a reasonably timely and consistent manner, the firm's level of accounts receivable is essentially a fixed asset. Seldom, however, does the amount of the accounts receivable asset remain fixed; a baseline amount could be postulated statistically, based on standard industry terms, to isolate the amount of receivables in excess of that amount. The excess amount invested in accounts receivable varies based on economic conditions and interest rates, product quality, and numerous other factors. This variable amount equals the excess over what would be the "normal" level of receivables if all customers paid on time. In looking at the overall financial structure of a firm, the fixed, or baseline, level of receivables should be financed with permanent or, at least, long-term capital. However, the variable portion is financed by short-term funding derived either internally or from external sources such as lenders and trade creditors. There is a clear and direct interest cost to carry these receivables. If the firm is a net borrower of short-term funds, then its borrowing interest rate would be appropriate; if it is a net investor, then the yield on the firm's short-term portfolio would be an appropriate opportunity cost for the hurdle rate. In this approach, the short-term interest rate is applied to the variable portion of the asset. That is the variance from the baseline amount of receivables that would exist under normal business conditions under standard terms of sale for the particular industry. To determine the variance from the baseline that the firm can tolerate, the financial manager treats all changes in terms of a short-term hurdle rate. A short-term hurdle rate of 10 percent is assumed here.

In the comparisons of Company A and Company B in Figure 4-1, the baseline level of accounts receivable would be $116,667, since both firms sell on the net terms of 30 days and that level of receivables would indicate a "normal" actual collection period. Company B enjoys a level of receivables that is $31,834 less than baseline and therefore has an annual saving in carrying costs of $3,183 ($31,834 at the hurdle rate of 10 percent). However, to achieve this, Company B allows prompt payment discounts of $5,760 ($480 per month × 12 months). Company B therefore has additional net costs of $2,577 to achieve its 25 DSO, compared to Company A's, which has 35 DSO. If Company B operates at a net operating profit margin of 10 percent of sales, then Company B must generate additional annual sales of $25,770 ($12,577 divided by 0.10) to compensate for this cost. That represents a sales increase on top of its present sales of $1.2 million or 2.1 percent.

As can be observed in this example, it is possible to influence to some extent the amount of the investment in accounts receivable. Such influence can take the form of alteration of selling terms, cash discounts, and varying degrees of discipline or leniency in enforcing or encouraging payments when due. Some such devices are positive in nature and usually make the customer want to pay early. If positive incentives to pay early fail to have an effect, this may be a warning that the customer may be in financial difficulty and should be monitored closely. Other devices are negative, such as overt penalties for late payment, or dunning letters, which are ultimately necessary but usually evoke a negative emotional response by the slow payer. Tactful personal contact is more expensive than dunning letters, but ultimately is probably more effective in making the collection and avoiding a negative emotional response.

Managing the Asset

Once the target level of receivables and the terms of sale have been determined, the financial manager focuses on implementation of the accounts receivable program. The program has two aspects: credit and collections.

"Credit" is the process of determining how and to whom deferred payment terms will be extended in the normal course of business to facilitate sales of the company's products and services. "Collections" deals with the process of following up with customers who have failed to make timely payment within the stated credit terms. The goals of collections are to minimize the variable portion of the accounts receivable asset and to maintain cash flow.

Sandwiched between credit and collections is the billing process and the cash management mechanism for receiving payments, such as lockboxes, depository bank accounts, electronic funds transfers, and cash application. The effective accounts receivable system integrates all of these elements to provide information to management about the timeliness of billing and collection from all customers in the aggregate, as well as from each customer individually. Usually this integration is accomplished through the use of computer applications software, which can range from simple in design and use to complex and expensive.

Cash Application. The "cash application" process frequently is a culprit in unnecessarily inflating the level of accounts receivable. Cash application is the process of matching customer remittances with open invoices and thereby extinguishing accounts receivable.

Cash application is achieved manually, electronically, or through some combination of manual and electronic processing. Manual processing, of course, involves the hand-posting of payments to customer account records. Of necessity, this method is limited to relatively small businesses that have few customers.

Electronic cash application takes many forms and requires that the open accounts receivable be maintained in a computer. A combination of manual and electronic cash application usually entails a clerk sitting at a computer terminal and manually reviewing the customer's remittance, such as a check stub or photocopy of the check (the original of the check having been deposited) and calling up the customer's account on the terminal screen. Upon finding the correct account and open invoice, the clerk makes electronic notation of payment in the customer's computer file.

Automated cash application is quite popular among companies with large volumes of remittances and some sophistication in their data processing capability. Automated cash application begins with the electronic capture of customer payment and remittance data, and then associating that data with the computer file of open accounts receivable in order for customer payments to be applied to open accounts or invoices automatically. The payment and remittance data may be captured by the company's lockbox bank or by the company, depending on the volume of checks, the bank's processing capabilities, and the costs.

There are two principal techniques used for automated cash application: "autocash" and "direct data capture." In both techniques, the lockbox bank processes wholesale remittances by electronically "reading" the magnetic ink character recognition (MICR) line of each check as it processes the payee's incoming remittances through high speed equipment. As it reads the MICR line, the reader records the drawee bank's transit routing number, the payor's account number, and the amount of the check. These data are arrayed in a data file that is either delivered to the payee for autocash cash application or used to record additional information about the remittance such as name of the remitter, invoice numbers, amounts paid, and discounts and adjustments taken. This information is captured by computer terminal operators making keystroke entries while physically reviewing the check stub, check, or an image of the check.

The computer file of remittance data is delivered to the company where the cash application process takes place. If the autocash method is used, the company must maintain a database to identify its customers through their bank transit routing and account numbers. Autocash processing first identifies the customer; then using mathematical algorithms, it attempts to find the one or more open invoices that in combination with each other equal the total amount of the payment. Autocash is particularly useful where remittances are applied to open accounts rather than to specific invoices, or where customers pay only a few invoices at a time and generally do not take discounts or make adjustments. Autocash tends to lose its efficiency when more than approximately five invoices are paid by a single remittance or where there are discounts and adjustments.

Direct data capture, in which the remittance data file contains not only customer identification but also the detail of specific invoices being paid and discounts and adjustments, is more straightforward from a data processing standpoint. The remittance data file is associated with the file of open invoices and remittances are matched electronically with open items.

In retail remittance processing, an optically scannable coupon (often termed a "return document") accompanies the remittance check. After balancing the payments with the coupons, the coupons are "read" electronically to create the remittance data file. The scan line on the coupon contains the customer's account number and payment amount.

Electronic application of remittance information to open items generally is accomplished accurately and more timely than by manual posting methods, thereby giving a clearer picture of open accounts receivable at any moment in time.

Credit and Collection Policies. There is a policy and a procedural aspect to both credit and collections. The policy aspect is essentially a statement by management of the major objectives and guidelines. The procedural aspect is a set of rules designed to implement the policy statement. The following are sample credit and collection policies.

Credit Policies: It is the policy of this firm

- To minimize bad debt write-offs;
- To accept reasonable credit risks in order to meet the competition;
- To extend credit aggressively to build sales.

Collection Policies: It is the policy of this firm

- To be courteous and professional in the routine collection of past due accounts;
- To be firm and fair in dealing with customers who become past due;
- To protect the firm's assets by being timely and aggressive in the pursuit of past due accounts;
- To do anything legal and possible to collect amounts due to the firm.

When given the policy statements concerning both credit and collections, the accounts receivable manager becomes duly charged with developing procedures and guidelines for granting credit and effecting collections. The absence of such policy statements creates a void for the accounts receivable manager and can result in credit and collection operations that are ineffective in protecting assets and counterproductive in achieving the target level of receivables.

Competitive pressures normally dictate the terms of sale and the amount of collection pressure that may be brought to bear on customers. Theoretically, the firm decides whether to extend credit. However, in reality, the effects of competition frequently dictate that decision. If competitors are willing to extend more liberal credit terms, or be more forebearing in collecting outstanding receivables, then the financial manager must either do the same or find another area of competition, such as price, product quality, or service. The financial manager who wants to meet the competitors' level of credit and collection standards may offer other sales incentives to customers.

ESTABLISHING A CREDIT POLICY

Four principal elements determine credit policy. They are:

1. Financial strength of the customer
2. Length of customer's own selling/collecting cycle
3. Length of acceptable credit terms
4. Industry norms

Credit risk increases with the length of time of exposure. This is evident not only with trade credit but with money-lending as well. It is not unusual at all, for example, for a large company to enjoy a top-notch credit rating on its short-term commercial paper but a more modest rating on its long-term bonds. This simply reflects the fact that credit risk is more susceptible to change over a longer period than over a shorter period. Similarly with trade credit, the longer the duration of exposure, the greater the risk.

Evaluating Credit Risk

The credit department is responsible for simultaneously approving sales and reducing credit risk. Its challenge is to determine whether to grant credit to marginal accounts, and, if so, how much. An uncollectible account directly affects the company's profits. Volumes have been written about techniques for evaluating credit risk, including quantitive credit scoring systems. Credit evaluation is primarily a process of predicting how timely a prospective customer will handle the future payment of its obligations. Successful credit evaluation has only one result: sales and timely collection from customers. Unsuccessful credit evaluation has two unhappy results:

- Rejection of a good credit risk, resulting in lost sales and profits; and

- Acceptance of a bad credit risk, resulting in at least significant monitoring and collection costs, and at worst, a bad debt write-off.

More likely, failure in the credit evaluation process may result in a "evergreen account" where a weak customer continuously buys and pays but always owes amounts past due. This situation could actually mask the ultimate realization of a loss, although it usually represents important sales revenue.

Five "Cs" of Credit Evaluation. Credit evaluation involves the analysis of some very intangible qualities that are best described as the "five Cs of credit." They are character, capacity, capital, collateral, and conditions.

Character. A determination of the underlying desire of the customer to pay.

Capacity. A prediction of the likelihood that the customer will have the funds to pay when the obligation becomes due.

Capital. A measure of the long-term resources available to the customer if its working capital is not sufficient. This is the incipient stage of planning a fallback position and anticipating the use of secondary sources of repayment if the primary source proves insufficient. The net worth and financial stability of the company may predict the company's capability to raise additional funds.

Collateral. Identification of assets that may be available in case the obligation is not paid in timely fashion.

Conditions. Evaluation of the environment external to the customer, such as the condition of the economy and substitute products, which may affect the buyer's ability to sustain cash flow.

Therefore, the process of credit evaluation depends on the development of a sufficient amount of reliable information about the potential customer. The usual sources of reliable information are other vendors and suppliers that have had credit experience with the prospective customer and are willing to share their credit history; credit reporting agencies that collect information from various sources; and the prospective customer's bank. The bank may grant considerable credit to the customer, and it usually has some insight into the financial behavior of the customer from its experience with the customer's depository and disbursing activities.

Two principal problems are associated with the actual use of the five Cs of credit:

1. The process of obtaining a sufficient amount of information on a timely basis to evaluate all of the categories of character, capacity, capital, collateral, and conditions for each customer is costly and lengthy. The cost and time involved need to be weighed against the size of the sale or credit line and the amount of profit likely to be derived. Because the credit decision often is so time-sensitive, an extensive analysis may not be feasible. But an adequate credit report should not be sacrificed because of the time it takes to obtain the basic data necessary to make an evaluation.

2. Once the required information is obtained, it is necessary to translate the data into a sound credit granting decision. Because there would be so much data to consider, this can usually be rationally accomplished only by financial statement analysis and a credit scoring model. It may be too expensive to develop a complete and valid credit scoring model.

Decision Tree Approach. A technique called a "decision tree" can be used more efficiently and inexpensively to gather sufficient information for making a credit decision. A decision tree takes a sequential approach to the decision-making process, seeking to determine at an early stage and without great expense whether the applicant should be accepted, rejected, or if more investigation is required. If more investigation is required, then the next branch of the decision tree is reached and the process of deciding acceptance, rejection, or more investigation is repeated. If the choice is still inconclusive, then the next branch must be approached, and so on until a decision to accept or reject is finally made. At each juncture a modest credit scoring model may be employed to determine quantitatively whether there is a clear basis for choice.

Following are two illustrations of the decisions of the decision tree approach.

Company *A* manufactures automated widgets and has annual sales of $100 million. It applied for a credit line of $50,000 to a manufacturer of framis sub-assemblies, a component of automated widgets. There are several other framis manufacturers in the region, all of which are viable competitors in quality, delivery, and price.

The credit application lists four current suppliers to Company *A*. The credit manager contacts each one by telephone and obtains the following credit history:

Supplier	High credit	Payments	Amount owed	Rating
1	$100,000	Prompt	$76,200	Satisfactory
2	48,000	Discount	46,000	Satisfactory
3	25,000	Prompt	10,000	Satisfactory
4	5,000	Slow 10 days	2,000	Satisfactory

In addition, the credit manager obtains a credit report from an agency showing that the principals of Company *A* have been in business for many years and are experienced; there is no history of bankruptcy or fires of suspicious origin, and the company's bank has had the account for two years with satisfactory experience. Further, for a line of credit of this size, the credit manager checks public records for liens on the assets of the proposed customer and finds none.

Based on this information, the credit manager accepts the application for a line of credit of $50,000 without further investigation. His reasoning is that character and capacity seem to be more than adequate for the amount involved (in relation to the volume of the buyer's business), and the other three Cs would be too expensive to check for a credit line of this size. Furthermore, a $50,000 credit line for a company the size of Company *A* is modest and it is very likely that a competitor would approve such an application. To follow up, the credit manager reports the new line to the credit reporting agency and requests "continuing service" for future credit report updates on Company *A*. This will ensure that trade credit experience can be shared with other suppliers and that the credit manager will be notified of any adverse changes in Company *A*'s business as soon as the agency becomes aware of them. Finally, the credit manager makes a note to check the timeliness of payment for the first several shipments of framises to Company *A*.

Company *B*, with annual sales of $10 million, applied for a credit line of $25,000 for the purchase of framis sub-assemblies, indicating that the company would be Company *B*'s principal supplier for this product. The credit manager checks and obtains the following credit history from the suppliers listed on Company *B*'s application:

Supplier	High credit	Payments	Amount owed	Rating
1	$18,000	Slow 10 days	$18,000	Satisfactory
2	14,000	Prompt	12,000	Satisfactory
3	3,000	Slow 30 days	1,500	Acceptable

The credit report from the agency shows that Company *B* has been in business for four years, and its principals were previously bankers with no experience in this industry. The credit manager then checks with Company *B*'s bank and finds that the company has borrowed the full amount under its working capital line, and there has been no clean-up since the line was established 18 months ago.

With the foregoing information, the credit manager sees a dilemma: on the one hand, he could become Company *B*'s principal supplier of framis sub-assemblies, which is a very profitable product. On the other hand, Company *B* seems to have exhausted its trade and bank credit, and may be on the brink of experiencing financial problems. There appears to be no clear preponderance of evidence pointing to rejection or to acceptance. Therefore, the credit manager is obliged to seek more information.

The credit manager contacts the controller of Company *B* to request financial statements for the most recent interim period and the last three fiscal years and credit references from banks and other vendors. He also inquires about the availability of personal guarantees of the principals. The guarantees would be demanded only if the financial statements failed to enable a clear decision to accept or reject the credit application by reflecting, for example, deficit net worth, continuous losses, deficit working capital, or a very high debt-to-net worth ratio.

Credit Scoring Systems. Once the credit manager has gathered and organized the data concerning the prospect's business, the next step is to evaluate that data. Because conflicting facts and trends may complicate the evaluation process, credit scoring systems have been devised that attempt to place relative weights on the various factors entering into the risk evaluation decision. Those factors usually include DSO calculation, payment history, analysis of various balance sheet and operating statement ratios, and a prediction as to the likelihood of the company's bankruptcy. Such models can be simple ones devised by an analyst based on a few major criteria, or computer-based models purchased commercially, including those for personal computers that take into account a number of factors.

Credit scoring systems seek to quantify certain characteristics of a credit applicant and measure those quantities against certain established values identified by the company as factors that distinguish good credit risks from poor credit risks. The key elements of an effective credit scoring system, therefore, are the definition of factors critical to distinguishing prompt paying customers from marginal or high risk accounts, and the subjective weights assigned to each.

Both positive and negative characteristics are important to a credit scoring model. Negative characteristics, such as the following, historically predict trouble in collecting payment.

- Short time in this business, possibly indicating an unproven track record in managing a business or understanding the particular industry. History shows that the business mortality rate is highest in the first two years, and that businesses that survive for five years have a strong chance of remaining viable.

- Little experience in managing any business, which could be a warning that although the principals may be experienced in making goods or providing services, their capability to lead the business to consistent profits may be in question.

- High ratio of debt to invested capital, which requires the generation of cash flow sufficient to service the debt. Otherwise, the business may be headed for a downturn or other adverse development, regardless of the length of time it has been in business and the experience of its management.

Positive characteristics, on the other hand, historically tend to predict success in collecting accounts receivable. These naturally include the reverse of the negative characteristics previously listed, as well as the following:

- Dominance in the industry (or an important niche), which can assure pricing stability and strong cash flow.

- Demonstrated good experience among trade creditors, which is an indicator that a new trade supplier would likely be treated fairly as well.

- Favorable regard for the integrity and ability of management by the firm's bankers, which is an indication that management's intentions, apart from its capabilities, are honorable.

Figure 4-2 shows how relative weight can be assigned to these factors, the score compiled, and the result compared to a norm. A technique called "discriminant analysis" is used in the assignment of relative weight to each characteristic in order to attempt to differentiate the good accounts from the bad. Typically, the credit scoring model uses two cutoff levels. Applicants scoring above the higher cutoff are granted credit; and applicants scoring below the lower cutoff are denied credit. Applicants scoring between the two cutoff levels undergo further analysis in order to make the credit decision. In this manner, a credit scoring model may incorporate the decision tree approach.

EXAMPLE: Company *M* has been in business for two years, and is operated by John Turnbuckle, who previously worked as the general manager of a competitor for 13 years. A recent balance sheet shows a debt-to-worth ratio of 1.2 to 1, and a current credit report shows that most

FIG. 4-2
Discriminant Analysis Technique in Credit Scoring Model

		Company M		
Characteristics	Range	Raw Score	Weight	Weighted Score
Time in Business	Less than 1 year = −2 More than 8 years = 5	−1	1	−1
Management Experience	Less than 5 years = 0 More than 10 years = 5	5	3	15
Debt/Net Worth Ratio	More than 2.0X = −1 Less than 0.5X = 4	0	2	0
Degree of Competition	High degree = 0 Monopoly = 2	1	1	1
Vendor Experience	Poor = 0 Excellent = 5	4	3	12
Regard for Management	Low regard = −2 High regard = 2	1	2	2
Cash Flow	< 1% of sales = −2 > 2% of sales = 5	3	3	9
			Total Weighted Score	38

trade creditors are paid promptly, while a few accounts are paid up to 30 days past due. There is no history of bankruptcy or suspicious fires in the background of either the company or its principal, and the bank says it has a favorable regard for Mr. Turnbuckle. The company's volume last year was $37 million, and the income statement showed a marginal profit, with cash flow of more than $5 million for the year before, with most of it invested in production equipment to expand the business.

In the credit scoring model, Company M achieved a weighted score of 38. From experience, the credit manager knows that applicants scoring more than 30 points (weighted) represent a strong account and an excellent credit risk. Therefore, Company M's credit application was approved for an initial credit line of $3,000. Also from experience, the credit manager knows that applicants scoring below 12 points (weighted) tend to have problems paying their bills within a reasonable period and frequently slip into bankruptcy. Consequently, applicants scoring below 12 are automatically rejected (or referred to a competitor). Applicants scoring between 12 and 30 on this scale require further analysis. Perhaps a closer examination of the applicant's financial statements and a telephone interview of the controller would enable the credit manager to make a reasoned judgement.

The credit manager also knows that companies scoring from 12 to 17 points generally are marginal and require some form of credit enhancement such as guarantees or a letter of credit. Also, companies scoring from 18 to 25 points may be acceptable customers but the credit review should be extended to obtain more information. Companies scoring from 26 to 30 points are usually good accounts but a routine review of the credit information should be made before approving the credit line.

Determining Credit Limits. Concomitant with deciding whether to extend credit to a prospect, the credit manager must decide how much credit should be granted. If the contemplated sale is expected to be repeated regularly, the credit manager can deal with the credit limit in one of two ways. The unstructured approach would be to approve the amount of the first sale and to allow subsequent credit sales up to that amount. When the aggregate amount outstanding begins to exceed the initial credit limit, or a portion of the outstanding balance is past due, the payment history can be reviewed and a decision can be made about a new credit limit.

A more structured approach would involve using preset levels of credit, such as $3,000, $7,000, and $12,000, and uniformly placing all customers into one of these limit classes. Certain criteria can be established as guidelines for qualifying for each credit limit, such as past payment history, company size, buying patterns, and financial strength.

Forms of Trade Credit

Several forms of credit are available to the seller to facilitate sales, ranging from consignment at the weak end of the spectrum, to the promissory note. Further, credit may be granted directly by the seller to the buyer or credit may be extended indirectly through a financial intermediary using devices such as a letter of credit, factoring, or a credit card.

Open Account. Open account credit is granted directly by the seller to the buyer and is the prevailing form of commercial trade credit for domestic transactions. The seller issues an invoice or statement to the buyer stating the credit terms and the amount due. A number of conventional credit terms can be granted under this account, including (in their approximate order of stringency) cash terms, ordinary terms, monthly billing, seasonal dating, and consignment.

Cash terms. In businesses where goods turn over rapidly or goods are perishable, cash terms of net 7 or 10 days are frequently used. A common example is the grocery industry, where the wholesaler makes a delivery once a week to a modest-sized store. On each weekly delivery, the driver collects a check for the amount of the previous week's delivery. For larger customers, payment may be mailed with similar short due dates. Thus, cash terms are almost like paying at the time of delivery but allows the convenience of orderly preparation of a payment.

Ordinary terms. In ordinary terms, a due date—often 30 days—is set by which time payment in full is due. Occasionally, a discount is offered for payment prior to the due date. The due date and the discount date are usually calculated using the invoice date as the benchmark because the invoice date often is the same as the shipping date. Typically "ordinary terms" might be "net 30," where payment in full is expected 30 days after the invoice date, or "2/10, net 30," where the buyer is allowed a 2 percent discount if payment is made within 10 days after the invoice date.

Monthly billing. Monthly billing is essentially a statement of transactions during the month for which one payment is due by a specified date. Discounts for early payment may be incorporated into the monthly billing method. Typical monthly billing terms may cause the statement to cut off as of the twenty-fifth day of the month, with payment due by the twenty-fourth of the following month. Notation for such terms would be "24th *prox*" (where *prox* denotes the following month). Discounts can be incorporated to encourage early payment. For example, a 2 percent discount may be offered for payment by the tenth of the month instead of the twenty-fourth, and its notation would be "2/10th, *prox* net 30th."

Seasonal dating. Dating terms are frequently used in seasonal industries where production times are lengthy relative to the selling season. For toys, for example, the main retail selling season lasts only a month or two before Christmas, while manufacturing must begin many months earlier. Toy manufacturers therefore often grant terms calling for payment around Christmas or shortly afterward instead of within a certain number of days following shipment of the merchandise. As another example, snow ski manufacturers must produce their product year-round to supply retail requirements that last only a few months. Therefore, while shipments may occur in late summer and early fall, payments are often deferred until mid-February or March, when the retailers' cash flow would normally permit payment. Seasonal dating terms are also frequently used in the apparel trade, where clothing must be produced and shipped before the start of each season.

Consignment. It is arguable whether consignment is a sale at all. A consignment transaction occurs when a manufacturer or distributor delivers merchandise to a retailer with the understanding that the retailer will not pay for the goods until the goods are sold to the retailer's customer. Because the retailer has no obligation to pay until a sale transaction has been consummated, the distributor is at considerable risk here, totally dependent on the integrity of the retailer to promote the sale of the goods. Additional considerations for the distributor are the potential risk of theft or casualty loss from fire or other peril, and the risk that the retailer will neither pay for nor return the merchandise.

Installment Accounts. Installment accounts are usually used for big-ticket sales. The buyer is granted the right to pay for the purchase in periodic payments that may stretch over several months or years. Usually, the installment terms are governed by an installment sale contract executed by the buyer and seller, which describes the rights and obligations of both parties in the transaction. In particular, the seller often retains a security interest in the merchandise sold as well as the right to sell the contract to a financial institution. In this way, the seller can recoup its sale proceeds (less a discount, of course), and the buyer can pay for the purchase over time.

Revolving Credit Accounts. A revolving credit account is considered in good standing as long as the amount of credit used does not exceed the amount of the credit limit and payments are current. The required payments are usually tied to a percentage of the amount owed, subject to a minimum monthly payment, and interest is charged on the unpaid amount. Revolving credit is more frequently used in consumer sales than in commercial sales, and can make the seller look more like a bank than a provider of products. Revolving credit accounts ease the buyer's burden of paying for purchases although they do not assure a rapid payment for merchandise purchased or sold.

Documentary Credits. Documentary credits can have several facets, including control over the release of the merchandise to the buyer, substitution of the good credit of a bank for that of the buyer, and extended financing terms.

A documentary credit consists of a bill of exchange, such as a draft drawn by the seller against the buyer, and is accompanied by other documents. These documents may include title documents, such as a bill of lading that is required by the carrier before releasing the merchandise to the custody of the buyer; insurance documents; packing and inspection certificates; certificates of origin; and any other documents that the buyer and seller may mutually agree to exchange at the time the merchandise passes from the custody of the seller to the custody of the buyer.

A simple documentary credit requires the payment of a draft before the shipper's bill of lading is released to the buyer. The documents can be directed to the buyer's bank or a correspondent of the seller's bank, with the goods consigned to the bank. In that way, the bank can control the transaction on behalf of the seller. In addition, this places the bank in the position to provide secured financing by having the buyer pledge the merchandise as collateral security.

Letters of Credit. Letters of credit are a variant of documentary credit and are most commonly used in international merchandise transactions. Letters of credit are also used domestically, occasionally as a sales tool. The seller may boost sales to marginal customers by offering to pay the letter of credit fees charged by the buyers' banks. In a letter of credit transaction, the buyer's bank substitutes its own credit for that of the buyer. The bank then becomes obligated to make the payment on behalf of the buyer, provided that the seller complies with the documentation requirements set forth in the letter of credit document.[2]

Promissory Notes. A promissory note is an evidence of indebtedness. It may be secured by the pledge of almost anything or it may be unsecured and it may arise from the sale of goods, the borrowing of money, or the settlement of some other obligation. Promissory notes are not frequently used in commercial trade credit because they are cumbersome to obtain and administer and they are not any more valid as an evidence of indebtedness than the documents typically obtained in an open account transaction (e.g., purchase order, delivery receipt, or invoice) or a documentary credit transaction. Promissory notes are frequently used to consolidate past due debts of a customer to a supplier as a recognition and confirmation of the indebtedness, but this situation arises when there are collection problems and not in the ordinary course of doing business with timely payments.

Incentives for Timely Payment

In reviewing DSO and aging schedules, it quickly becomes apparent that not all customers contribute to the slowness of collections and the variable portion of the accounts receivable asset. To improve collections and reduce the asset toward its baseline level, the financial manager should maximize the focus on the mediocre portion of the customer base to improve the overall averages. Concentration of effort on the marginal players will improve both the overall averages and, in the long run, reduce the risk of loss.

Many industries sell on open account using ordinary terms of net 30 days, which may be considered as the standard. The financial manager who wants to encourage customers to pay sooner has the following types of options:

1. Offer shorter payment terms;

2. Dun past due customers sooner and more aggressively;

3. Offer financial disincentives to pay late;

4. Offer financial incentives to pay early;

5. Offer sales financing, particularly for big ticket items, using a third-party financial services firm or bank, if necessary.

---

[2] See Chapter 16 for a detailed discussion of letters of credit.

Options 1 and 2 offer no real leverage to the financial manager and may alienate the customer in a competitive environment. Option 3 may be viable as a "negative incentive;" that is, imposition of a penalty for late payment will encourage some to pay on time, and those who pay late suffer the penalty of their own volition. A negative incentive not to pay late, however, is not nearly as powerful as a positive incentive to pay early. Option 4 is such a positive incentive that it satisfies the customer's profit motive and Option 5 may enable the expansion of business between trading partners by making available to the buyer a new source of funds that would otherwise not be available.

Early Payment Discount. Offering an early payment discount can be a powerful incentive to the customer and a considerable expense to the seller. A discount for early payment is tantamount to payment of interest and works exactly like the interest calculation on a bank loan.

To calculate the interest rate in an early payment discount, the regular payment date first must be determined. In terms of "net 30 days," payment would be due in full on the thirtieth calendar day after the invoice date. A discount of perhaps one percent of the amount of the invoice might be offered for payment made by the tenth calendar day after the invoice date. Therefore, the buyer would earn one percent of the invoice amount for paying 20 days early. In a financial manager's 360-day year, there are 18 periods of 20 days, resulting in a "yield" of 18 percent per annum to the buyer (and a corresponding cost to the seller). To be more precise, in a 365-day year there are 18.25 periods of 20 days, or 18.25 percent annual interest if the discount is one percent. If the discount rate is 2 percent, then the annual interest rate is 36.5 percent. Then, adjusting for the fact that only the lower net amount needs to be borrowed to pay the invoice, the net interest cost rises to 37.24 percent. For example, an invoice for $1,000 payable 2%/10 net 30 may be paid by day 10 in the amount of $980. The $20 discount for 20 days early payment is annualized at $365 interest per year. This interest, when divided by the amount borrowed ($980), results in a net cost—or yield—of 37.24 percent per annum.

Obviously, if the payer's cost for obtaining funds (either by borrowing or from liquidation of invested funds) is less than the yield afforded by taking discounts, the discounts should always be taken. Since in many industries the standard trade terms are 2%/10 net 30 (i.e., a 2 percent discount is allowed if the invoice is paid within 10 days after the invoice date; otherwise, the full amount is due within 30 days after the invoice date), the buyer has a powerful incentive to take the discount and pay in 10 days, even if it requires borrowing from the bank at 4 percentage points above the prime

FIG. 4-3

Annual Effective Interest Rates for Early Payment Discounts

Discount Offered	Number of Days Paid Early					
	5	10	15	20	25	30
0.5%	36.68%	18.34%	12.23%	9.17%	7.34%	6.11%
1.0%	73.74	36.87	24.58	18.43	14.75	12.29
1.5%	111.17	55.58	37.06	27.79	22.23	18.53
2.0%	148.98	74.49	49.66	37.24	29.80	24.83
2.5%	187.18	93.59	62.39	46.79	37.44	31.20
3.0%	225.77	112.89	75.26	56.44	45.15	37.63

rate. Figure 4-3 shows the effective annual yield to the buyer and cost to the seller of the early payment discount at various discount rates for various time periods.

In order to take the discount, the buyer should ask about the seller's rules because it is usually the seller's prerogative to determine the discounts allowable. Of course, it is the buyer's prerogative to attempt to negotiate those rules with the seller, since trade terms are just another component of the transaction like price, color, quality, and delivery.

Customarily, sellers allow the discount provided that the envelope containing the remittance is postmarked no later than the last day of the discount period. The seller then suffers the mail float.

Credit Line Limit as Payment Incentive. An alternative method to encourage timely payment is to grant relatively small credit limits initially to each new customer. Those customers who demonstrate responsibility in handling their accounts may then qualify for higher credit limits. This could force the customer to pay for the previous shipment of goods before the next shipment is made, thereby keeping the seller's accounts receivable current. This is a powerful incentive where the seller has no effective competitors and no product substitutes. However, this device tends to break down quickly when the buyer does not feel compelled to place another order with the seller. Credit limits are therefore considered to be a negative incentive for late payment rather than a positive incentive for early payment like the early payment discount.

Late Payment Penalties. Where an early payment discount is a positive incentive to pay early, a late payment penalty is an incentive not to pay late. Many companies print a notation on their invoices to the effect that, "a penalty of 1.5% per month will be charged on past due balances." While the intent is noble, the execution is usually lacking, and late payors frequently become aware very quickly of the seller's unwillingness or lack of ability to enforce the penalty. The cash application function in many companies is often neglected and understaffed, permitting little effort to be made to calculate and bill this penalty back to the customer for late payment.

As an example, a well-known major U.S. manufacturer invested considerable resources in its billing, collection, and cash application systems, and the results have repaid the investment many times over. This is because the accounts receivable managers use all of the features of the system to encourage discipline among the company's customers in the remittance of payments.

The company manufacturers a variety of products sold in various markets to a diverse clientele. The company's "major markets group" generates invoices that average about $25,000 and the typical industrial or commercial customer may receive two or three such invoices per month. Billing is on standard terms of 2%/10 net 30, with a late payment penalty of 1.5 percent per month on past due invoices.

While this company's terms of sale may not be unusual, its enforcement is. Using the postmark date to determine the timeliness of payment, the company disallows discounts taken improperly, and actually issues credits to customers who inadvertently neglect to take discounts. With this kind of capability, which is uncannily accurate, the company generates an unusual level of respect among its customers, which often leads to a genuine desire to pay bills on time. By encouraging customers to toe the mark and by building the 2 percent early payment discount into its pricing, customers who may pay other suppliers two or three days after the discount period are discouraged from doing so with this vendor. Customers tend to recognize that the interest cost of failing to take the discount is very high if they pay on day 30; and it is considerably higher than that if they miss the discount deadline by only a day or two. In that case, they paid early by many days but they failed to receive the discount.

With annual sales volume of $1 billion, shortening this company's DSO by one day reduces accounts receivable by $2.7 million, worth $270,000 annually at a 10 percent hurdle rate. And this company probably has shortened its DSO by two or three days through enforcement of its payment terms.

Moreover, by monitoring remittances closely, the company is able to disallow a substantial amount of discounts to which customers are not entitled. The dollars saved are probably offset by the costs of operating the system; however, the discipline that the process fosters works to the company's ultimate benefit by encouraging the payor to remit in a more timely manner.

Electronic Payments

As electronic payments gain in popularity, trading partners find it necessary to negotiate an agreement to share the mail and check clearing float. In a 10-day discount period with payment by check, the timeline for the payment may be as follows:

	Day
Check mailed by buyer	10
Check received by seller and deposited	11
Collected funds received by seller and buyer's account charged	13

Even though the buyer paid by day 10, as evidenced by the postmark on that date, the payment transaction is not actually consummated for both parties until day 13. Therefore, the frequently negotiated solution for electronic payments is to allow the discount if the electronic payment is received (and settled in immediately available funds) by day 13. If the payment terms for payment by check were "2%/10 net 30," they would become "2%/13 net 33 electronic."

MANAGING BILLINGS

The history of modern cash management is replete with devices and techniques to manage the three phases of collection and disbursing float: mail, processing, and check clearing. However, until treasury practitioners began to look at the entire cash flow time line in the 1980s, "billing float" had been ignored.

"Billing float" is the amount of time from the moment the shipment occurred, when a bill or invoice could have been rendered, to the moment a bill or invoice is actually mailed. This is an important concept, for the failure to render a bill on a timely basis will invariably result in a corresponding failure of the remittance to be received on time.

Rendering the Invoice

Management of the billing function, like any other management task, requires goals and performance standards. In billing, the performance goal might be to send an invoice on the day of shipment, or the next day at the latest.

An invoice is typically sent by mail, but other methods are available. For large transactions, the sales representative may personally deliver the invoice, particularly in nonroutine sales or in situations where the sales representative may want to assure personal attention. Alternatively, increasing numbers of companies are adopting systems for the electronic exchange of documents using Electronic Data Interchange (EDI).

Normal custom and trade practice calls for an invoice to be rendered promptly upon shipment. Any delay from this norm can result in a delay in receipt of the customer's remittance. Similarly, inaccurate invoices, even if timely rendered, also delay remittances.

Successful billing operations require close coordination among the sales and order entry function, production, shipping, and billing departments. The sales department is responsible for determining the pricing and recording of the order in the order entry system. The production department produces the product and turns it over to shipping for dispatch to the customer. The shipping department records the shipment and notifies the billing department. The billing department incorporates the details of the shipment and the pricing from the order entry system to produce the invoice; and all of this processing must be designed to occur quickly, efficiently, and accurately.

For example, suppose a marketing manager ordered a promotional item custom-imprinted with the name of the company through his purchasing department. After checking price, availability, and delivery time on the telephone, the purchasing agent issued a written purchase order to the selected vendor. The purchase order reflected the agreed payment terms of net 30 days. The materials were produced and shipped as promised, but the vendor took three weeks to mail the invoice. Obviously, the payment would not be remitted within the agreed payment terms, since the simple task of processing the payment and producing the check normally exceeds one week.

With this lack of coordination among departments, the seller's cash manager suffers the consequences. (Of course, the buyer's cash manager enjoys the countervailing benefit.) Most customers are honest to the extent that they fully intend to pay their bills, and to do so within the time period allowed by the vendor. However, there are many hurdles that a payor must overcome in order to effect a payment. In the absence of incentives, the payment will be forthcoming in ''due course'' (in other words ''the check is in the mail''). Paper must be appropriately shuffled and the omnipresent computer is always beyond control. But in fact, a typical accounts payable process often requires 5 to 10 working days from the time the invoice is received until the check is produced and ready to mail. Any accounts payable system can usually be truncated so that a "rush check" can be produced in an emergency. However, the vendor who submitted the invoice late may be unrealistic in believing that the payor will push the paper through the system without any incentive such as an early payment or prompt payment discount.

CASH MANAGEMENT SUGGESTION:

Delivery of the invoice by mail to the proper department can take an extra day or more unless the address specifies its final correct destination. In setting up the customer billing record, the sales representative should determine the correct ultimate destination, such as "Accounts Payable Department" or "J. Schmoe, Payments Supervisor." The credit department periodically should verify that the address is correct to ensure timely delivery of invoices.

CASH MANAGEMENT SUGGESTION:

The invoice should show clearly the payment terms offered. The absence of disclosure of payment terms on the face of the invoice gives the payor the opportunity to make an assumption (to the payor's benefit) of what those terms should be.

CASH MANAGEMENT SUGGESTION:

The invoice should bear a telephone number (preferably a toll-free number) for the customer to call in case of any apparent discrepancies. Incoming calls should be directed to the accounts receivable unit where the initial contact can attempt to determine the undisputed amount. Payment of that amount should be requested, with the disputed amount noted for investigation. The investigation should be conducted by the department with the greatest incentive to collect, or the greatest pain from failure to collect. For example, if the sales representative is compensated based on collections rather than sales, then the dispute should be referred to the sales representative. In the absence of any such incentives, the investigation should be undertaken by the accounts receivable department staff. The important issue, nevertheless, is to collect the undisputed amount on a timely basis, as this usually far exceeds the amount disputed.

Electronic Data Interchange

EDI uses standardized machine readable data formats to enable the transmission of electronic equivalents of paper documents, thus substantially eliminating human intervention in the process. This enables the delivery of invoices, as well as many other documents integral to the purchase/sale transaction, from the seller's billing system to the buyer's accounts payable system, substantially eliminating the errors common to manual data entry. Transactions are not just computer-to-computer, but "application system-to-application system."

Additional savings result when the buyer eliminates paper payment processing systems. Since the purchase order, receiving document, and invoice are all electronically lodged in the buyer's computer, the computer can accomplish the necessary matching to initiate payment. Many companies that have adopted EDI have found that accounts payable staffing can be reduced by half or more. Further, the level of timeliness and accuracy of payment invariably increased, effecting additional savings.

EDI is naturally connected to the payment mechanism because it enters the payment data into the buyer's accounts payable system and the seller's accounts receivable system as a direct result of the purchase/sale transaction. From that point, the accounts payable system can carry through with an electronic payment, such as an automated clearing house (ACH) credit transfer,[3] and the seller's cash application process can be virtually totally automatic.

If the buyer plans to pay electronically, the management of accounts receivable is simplified, as is the forecasting of cash receipts. This occurs because the payment, coupled with preagreed payment terms, is driven by the EDI process along the entire purchase/sale time line. With an integrated EDI system in place, knowledge of the shipping date can instantly be translated into knowledge of the electronic payment settlement date. This information is very valuable to the cash manager in planning the firm's funding or investing requirements a few weeks in advance.

Trading partners have communicated transactions with each other for many years using electronic hook-ups of various kinds. Perhaps the oldest method is for the purchasing agent of the buyer to send a teletype message directly to the seller's sales representative. This method was improved upon by a process begun in 1979 when a number of industry trade groups agreed to adopt common data formats for members of their respective industries. These data formats enabled trading partners to have their computers com-

---

[3] See Chapter 7 for a detailed discussion of automated clearing houses.

CASE STUDY

A medical reimbursements company dealing with large employers found many of its employer-clients to be delinquent in remitting funds. The subject firm's business was to act as agent for the employer in paying certain types of medical service providers. The providers submitted documented invoices to the firm and the firm issued payments in biweekly cycles. A few days prior to releasing checks to the providers, the firm sent invoices to the employer-clients for the amounts involved plus a small service fee. The objective was to receive the client's remittance by the time the checks to the providers cleared. The firm moved very large amounts of money and worked on a very small margin, relying on its highly computerized operation to restrain expenses, and on the high credit quality of its customers to avoid credit losses.

Contracts with employers called for the firm to be reimbursed within five working days after the invoice date. The firm used regional lockboxes for collection of mailed remittances, and it accepted electronic funds transfers at its concentration bank.

In analyzing its accounts receivable, the controller noticed repeated delinquency by most of the firm's clients, including major companies that are known to have excellent payment records. The controller decided to contact a number of these clients personally (the firm had no cre-

municate the data in machine-readable language. Thus, the buyer's electronic purchase order was sent to the seller's electronic order entry system, which eliminated rekeying of data and the errors and transpositions that almost always occurred.

Although numerous industry groups have developed their own distinct data formats, most companies operate across several industries. For example, the manufacturer of electrical wire harnesses that sells to the automotive industry is also a member of the electrical industry from the standpoint of procurement activities. Both the automotive and electrical industries may have their own data formats for the exchange of documents between trading partners. Meanwhile, materials are received and finished products are shipped via the transportation industry, which may use yet another set of data formats. Therefore, in 1979, the American National Standards Institute (ANSI), a voluntary organization responsible for approving national standards, sanctioned the creation of a voluntary committee to develop cross-

dit manager) and discovered some interesting and real reasons for the remittance delays.

1. The payment terms in the contracts were never explained to the payment department personnel;

2. The invoices sent by the firm did not specify the payment terms;

3. The invoices were often misdirected to the person who negotiated the contract, but who had no operational role in effecting payment, rather than to the person or department responsible for making the payment;

4. Invoices were directed to the company's main mailing address without further specific reference. This required the mail envelope to the opened in order to determine that it contained an invoice before it could be directed to the correct destination.

In meeting with the managers of the payment units of the various clients, the controller was able to explain the payment terms in the contract and discuss alternative payment methods to ensure timely remittance. As a result, cash flow improved greatly and the company's investment in accounts receivable was reduced substantially.

industry national standards for electronic business data interchange. This committee, the twelfth of its type, was named the Accredited Standards Committee X12 (ASC X12).

ASC X12 has developed standardized data formats to substitute electronic "transaction set" documents for many of their paper counterparts, and additional X12 transaction sets continue to be added to the list. Some of the more widely used X12 transaction sets are:

- Request for Quotation

- Response to Request for Quotation

- Quotation

- Price/Sales Catalogue

- Purchase Order

- Purchase Order Acknowledgement

- Purchase Order Change Request

- Purchase Order Change

- Order Status Inquiry

- Advance Shipping Notice

- Ship Notice/Manifest

- Bill of Lading

- Receiving Advice

- Invoice

- Payment Order/Remittance Advice

With these standardized formats already for use and more continuing to be developed and refined, the use of EDI between trading partners in the purchase/sale transaction has accelerated rapidly. New industry trade groups began to adopt the X12 standards, and companies began to adopt EDI as a way of doing business. Meanwhile, trade groups began to develop implementation conventions for use within their respective industries. Many of those industry groups that earlier had developed their own proprietary electronic data formats began to examine the X12 formats closely and several have adjusted their standards accordingly. Meanwhile, international counterparts to ANSI began to coalesce and to develop cross-border international standards, particularly in the European Common Market.

One of the more important driving forces for the use of EDI has been the U.S. automotive industry, which began in 1985 to seek to convert its thousands of suppliers to EDI. In this way, the auto manufacturers could place orders and track deliveries electronically to assure that parts and subassemblies would arrive just in time for assembly. Also, inventories at the assembly plant could be reduced virtually to zero, freeing millions of dollars previously tied up in working capital.

Other industries and government agencies have been jumping aboard the EDI bandwagon, including the United States Treasury Department (which acts as fiscal paying agent for many government agencies), and the Department of Defense. It is possible that a major revolution may be occurring in the way companies transact business. As of late 1988, several thousand companies were using EDI daily, and thousands more were making plans to use EDI as well.

MANAGING COLLECTIONS

The effort and resources required to manage collections depends on the nature of the business, the number of customers, and the discipline inherent in the customer base. It is probably safe to say that the larger the customer base, the more effort is needed to manage collections. A retailer that offers its customers a charge account privilege must be prepared to incur a major expense to administer the entire credit and collection apparatus. Of course, an effective charge account program should generate significant additional sales. On the other hand, a manufacturer of industrial products that has per-haps 200 active customers may not need to devote a significant amount of resources to the credit and collection function. The new customer's credit application or the occasional problem of slow payment can be handled by the controller's or treasurer's department as an adjunct to its regular duties. Whether the credit and collection functions are formalized into a credit department or carried out as additional duties in another area, it is essential to monitor the performance of the accounts receivable asset. Such monitor-ing will generate signals when the asset may be exceeding its desired size, and it will warn of trouble brewing.

Monitoring the Performance of Accounts Receivable

The accounts receivable asset is typically monitored at two levels: the total dollar value of accounts receivable is monitored using turnover statistics; and the individual accounts are monitored using an aging schedule.

Turnover Statistics. Turnover of accounts receivable measures the overall performance of the accounts receivable asset. Turnover may be measured in several different ways; DSO is perhaps as reliable as any of the statistical turnover methods.

DSO. DSO measures the aggregate average collection time at any moment; it is an average of the actual number of days of all accounts outstanding. The most accurate (but not efficient) method for calculating DSO as of any date is to add daily sales cumulatively backward from the current date until the cumulative total equals the amount of receivables outstanding. A more efficient, although less accurate, method is to use historic monthly, quarterly, or annual sales figures. The sales total of a model period is divided by the number of calendar days to derive the average daily sales figure. This figure is then divided into the amount of receivables outstanding to calculate the DSO figure. This method of calculating DSO is less accurate than the method using actual cumulative sales because it uses average daily sales rather than actual daily sales. It loses accuracy when, and to the extent that, actual daily sales are volatile and deviate from the average. For example, the subsequent collection of a large current receivable can affect the DSO figure significantly if outstanding accounts receivable are sharply reduced while the rate of sales remain unchanged.

Receivables turnover ratio. A traditional method of measuring the performance of receivables is the receivables turnover ratio. This measure is the ratio of sales for a period divided by the related accounts receivable outstanding. This measure tends to be less accurate than DSO for several reasons. Foremost of these is that it fails to define the appropriate sales period. Receivables outstanding at any moment reflect accumulated uncollected sales. To relate month-end receivables to sales over the past month may not reflect accurately those uncollected accounts relating to sales from two months ago. Likewise, to relate current receivables outstanding to sales over the past year may give an even more distorted picture if all receivables over five-months old have been collected. Accuracy also suffers when using average receivables during the period, because averages in the numerator of the fraction tend to mask reality, unless an extended time period such as a year is used.

Therefore, the turnover ratio of sales-to-receivables is useful only if consistent sales periods are used, and the ratio is monitored as it fluctuates over time. This ratio is an abstract measure and meaningless when out of context, whereas the DSO figure measures something real: the average number of days that it takes to collect receivables currently.

Accounts Receivable Aging Schedules. Most businesses use simple accounts receivable aging schedules that classify every unpaid invoice as ''current'' or ''past due.'' Current usually means the invoice has not yet matured. That is, where payment terms are net 30 days, any invoice of up to 30 days old is current and any invoice more than 30 days old is past due. Past due is usually broken down into incremental 30-day categories for the convenience of constructing the aging schedule, with a final catch-all category of over 90 days or over 120 days. The financial manager customarily tracks the aggregate dollars and percentage of total receivables in each past due category, and bases the collection effort on an analysis of each account. In large operations, staffing is often organized according to the length of time past due: part of the staff, the more personable and tactful ones, handle collection of accounts that are only slightly past due, while another part of the staff, the seasoned veterans who have heard every excuse in the book, are assigned to the longer past due accounts.

Collection Techniques. The aging schedule is indispensible to the management of receivables because it shows every outstanding receivable account-by-account and often invoice-by-invoice. With a little sensitivity, the manager can spot some of the following tendencies in the aging schedule and deal with them appropriately.

1. A new customer who slips past due. This customer might receive a polite telephone call at 10 days past due inquiring as to the intent and timing of payment. This call can benefit the seller in three ways: (a) it can serve to discover a deadbeat early; (b) it lets the customer know at an early date that the seller watches its accounts receivable closely, which tends to discourage slow payment patterns among new customers; and (c) it can uncover the existence of an incorrect billing address.

2. A customer who allows one invoice to go past due while paying subsequent invoices. This customer should receive a call inquiring whether there is a dispute involving that invoice, or perhaps the invoice in question has been misplaced. Both parties are well served to discover early that there is a dispute cooking or that an invoice has been lost.

3. Any customer who is past due to a certain point. Any customer reaching a certain point past due, e.g., 30 days, may receive a pleasant reminder that payment is past due. A sterner sounding letter may be mailed when the receivable hits 45 days past due, and a threatening letter may go out at the 60-day mark. Most collection operations have standard letters mailed at specified intervals to facilitate the collection effort. These serve to invite the customer who has been intentionally slowing down disbursements to release the particular payment to the seller.

Routine collection letters often have only limited impact, however, because they seldom get past the accounts payable clerk. A more effective method is to contact a manager, preferably personally by telephone. This method brings to the attention of management a potential personnel problem lurking among the staff, and the past due amount will usually receive the attention it deserves.

All of these contacts are designed to retain the customer's business by reminding the customer of two things: how much its business is valued, and the customer's obligation to pay on a timely basis. The letters should also encourage the customer to call to discuss the account if payment will not be forthcoming momentarily. In this game, personal contact is the key to knowing the customer's intentions and taking appropriate action.

Forms of Accounts Receivable Financing

In developing a policy on the use and size of accounts receivable, the financial manager should not overlook the financing options available. Because the accounts receivable asset is diversified and continually turns over, it represents an attractive asset with which to raise working capital financing. Many lenders have expertise in asset-based financing and offer working capital loans that grow and shrink with changes in the amount of receivables outstanding.

Accounts receivable financing is often used by companies whose growth has outstripped available capital, yet whose business is profitable and asset values are sound. The use of financing relating to the accounts receivable asset tends to inculcate some discipline to the borrower because there is an extra incentive to collect the outstanding receivables. Failure to collect on a reasonably timely basis causes the company's base of eligible receivables to erode, thereby reducing the company's borrowing power, and it causes excessive interest costs to be incurred.

Accounts receivable financing has two fundamental forms: the outright sale of accounts receivable, which is a form of financing called factoring; and borrowing secured by the assignment of the accounts receivable.

Factoring. Factoring dates back hundreds of years to the time when trading ships sold their receivables to money lenders before leaving port. The money leaders, known as factors, remained at the port and collected from the buyers after the trading ship had departed. With an intimate knowledge of the local buyers, the factor could advise the ship's captain in advance whether a particular buyer's receivable was good enough to be purchased. If the buyer's credit was know to be bad, the factor could refuse to purchase that account receivable, causing the ship's captain to refuse to sell to that buyer.

"Old line factoring" operates in much the same way today in a manufacturing environment. The manufacturer need not be concerned about checking the credit of its customers and monitoring the performance of accounts receivable, for those are the factor's tasks. The manufacturer uses the factor as a credit department: new account credit applications are referred to the factor, and if the factor approves the credit risk the sale may take place. If the factor declines, the manufacturer may sell at his own risk, which is usually considerable.

A variation on old line factoring is "maturity factoring" where the factor purchases the receivable only on its due date if it has not already been paid. If the manufacturer chooses to offer an early payment discount, then many receivables will be collected prior to maturity. But the maturity factoring arrangement enables the manufacturer to keep the receivables asset current, with the factor bearing the risk of collecting all past due accounts.

Asset-Based Borrowing. A more common and less expensive method for financing receivables is to borrow from a financial institution secured by the pledge of accounts receivable. Frequently, the lender will require the pledge of inventory as well as an assignment of the proceeds of the receivables (i.e., cash flow). This enables the lender to obtain adequate collateral security for the loan. For example, there is a very fine line between the point where inventory is transformed into a receivable and when a receivable is transformed into funds. Therefore, the lender usually will want to obtain the assignment of all three forms of the asset.

In lending against this collateral, the lender establishes a rate of advance (i.e., the lender will make loan advances up to as much as, say, 70 percent of the amount of eligible accounts receivable) to enable the amount of the loan to grow as the amount of receivables grows. The lender will usually also define eligible receivables entitled to advances by excluding all receivables past a certain due date, usually 90 days.

Finally, the lender and the borrower must agree on the matter of "notification." In notification financing, the seller notifies the buyer to remit payment to the lender rather than to the seller. Obviously, this is a signal to the buyer that the seller's financing source wants to capture the payments before they reach the seller. Notification is common and necessary in old line factoring, and factoring is common in certain industries such as apparel manufacturing. However, in most situations notification is a sign of financial weakness and may damage the otherwise good relations that a seller has with its customers. In non-notification financing, on the other hand, the buyer is not notified of any financing arrangement, and remittances are made to the seller. The seller is obliged to report the amounts billed and collected accurately and timely to the lender.

SUGGESTED READINGS

Altman, Edward I. *Corporate Financial Distress: A Complete Guide to Predicting, Avoiding, and Dealing With Bankruptcy.* New York: John Wiley & Sons, Inc., 1983.

Farragher, Edward J. "Factoring Accounts Receivable," *Journal of Cash Management,* Mar./Apr. 1986, Vol. 6, No. 2.

Hale, Roger H. *Credit Analaysis: A Complete Guide.* New York: John Wiley & Sons, Inc., 1983.

Lurie, James B. "A Profit-Based Approach to Credit Policy," *Journal of Cash Management,* Nov./Dec. 1987, Vol. 7, No. 6.

Viscione, Jerry. *Analyzing Ratios: A Perceptive Approach.* New York: National Association of Credit Management, 1983.

————. *Financial Analysis: Tools and Concepts.* New York: National Association of Credit Management, 1984.

CHAPTER 5

Depository Systems: Channeling and Accelerating Receipt of Funds

INTRODUCTION

Depository systems are designed to transfer funds from the buyer's pocket or bank account to the seller's bank account as quickly and accurately as possible. Depository systems for companies in retail and other consumer-oriented businesses differ in structure from those of nonretail businesses because of the large volume of payments received at the point of sale, and the acceptance of coin and currency and bank cards for payment in retail businesses. Nonretail businesses, on the other hand, generally make payment by check, and the vast bulk of the payments are delivered through the mail.

Nonretail businesses customarily request their customers to remit their payments to a post office lockbox, which is serviced by a bank or other processor. Lockbox remittance processing reduces mail float, processing float, and clearing float, thereby providing earlier availability of funds to the depositor. Float is the length of time a check takes from the moment it is issued to the moment it is charged to the maker's account at the drawee bank. By reducing float, the depositor gains the use of greater amounts of collected funds.

Electronic payments, both wire transfers and automated clearing house (ACH) transfers, involve no float and the value date for the payment is known in advance by both parties. This eliminates uncertainty between trading partners in the payment process.

Once a business has deposited remittances from its customers, the next challenge is to move these funds to a central bank account where the funds may be used to cover disbursements, make loan repayments, or be invested.

Small businesses are often well served by a single bank account for processing deposits and payments. As a firm grows, however, it reaches a level of complexity where there are too many transactions for easy monitoring through a single bank account. Divisions or subsidiaries may need to track their collections and disbursements individually, and the cash manager may want to separate the stream of incoming funds from the stream of outgoing funds for forecasting, tracking, and control purposes.

The firm must have a method for receiving its receipts and putting them into the bank in order to convert them into usable funds as quickly as possible. Funds are credit balances on the books of a depository. A check is merely an order to pay, addressed by the payor to its bank; it is neither money nor funds. A credit card voucher, likewise, is not funds until a bank "purchases" the ticket from the merchant and credits funds to the merchant's bank account. Even coin and currency are not funds until they have been counted, transported to a bank, and deposited. With the vast array of laws and regulations pervading business transactions, proper accounting for cash receipts dictates that coin and currency and other forms of receipts be deposited into a bank before they may be disbursed for payments.

DEPOSITORY TOOLS

Funds are received as:

- Coin and currency, received at the point of sale, usually in a retail business;
- Paper, in the form of checks, drafts and credit card charge drafts; and
- Electronic messages, transmitted through the banking system, advising that the recipient's depository account is being credited through a bookkeeping entry by order of a payor.

The method the firm uses to collect its receipts often limits the method that can be used to deposit its receipts.

There are a number of methods a bank uses to accept deposits from its customers:

1. *Window deposits.* Window deposits, often referred to as "over-the-counter deposits," are accepted at a banking office by a teller.

2. *Armored carriers.* Armored carriers are used for transporting coin and currency from the depositor's premises to a bank and are merely a means of safe transport.

3. *Unarmed couriers.* Couriers are used for transporting checks with no negotiability or intrinsic value and are substitutes for the depositor's personnel in transporting deposits to the bank.

4. *Night depositories.* Night depositories are secure bank facilities into which a customer may drop a sealed bag containing a deposit after banking hours. The bank may have authority from the customer to open the bag (under control of two people) the next day, process the deposit, and credit the customer's account for the amount of the deposit. Otherwise, the bank will hold the sealed bag for the customer to open in the morning.

5. *Credit and debit cards.* These are plastic cards that are used to generate a voucher that the card-issuing bank uses to charge the cardholder's line of credit or deposit account. Credit and debit card vouchers are deposited by delivery of the paper draft (the "hard copy" signed by the buyer) to the bank in the same manner as checks are deposited. Some banks allow their merchant customers to retain the hard copy at the point of sale, and the

merchant electronically transmits the sales and card data to the bank. In either case, the bank normally credits the merchant's account on a next-day basis and charges the same account for the merchant discount, which is based on the merchant's volume of bank card voucher deposits and the average voucher size. While the merchant may treat credit cards and debit cards similarly, it may be of interest that credit card charges are billed to the cardholder for later payment, while debit card charges are promptly charged to the cardholder's deposit account.

A variation of the credit card is the travel and entertainment charge card, such as those issued by American Express, Diners Club, and Carte Blanche, and proprietary credit cards such as Sears' Discover Card. All of these cards except the American Express card are issued by banks, although the bank may not be featured prominently on the face of the card. More important to the retailer who accepts these cards is the method by which the retailer receives payment. Generally, the retailer is required to mail the card vouchers to the card issuer, who responds by mailing a check for the amount of the vouchers less a merchant discount. Occasionally, a card issuer may make an arrangement with a bank in a region to accept charge vouchers for deposit to the merchant's account as if the vouchers were a bank card.

RETAIL BUSINESSES

The one characteristic that differentiates the banking needs of a retailer from those of a nonretailer is that the retailer usually receives payment from the customer at the point of sale. Nonretail businesses normally grant credit and receive payment after the sale.

The use of credit cards in a retail sale constitutes payment at the point of sale because the retailer can convert the credit card sale to funds virtually as easily as if it were a check or coin and currency. The only retail credit sale not equivalent to cash is a "house charge," where the customer is allowed the privilege of payment on some form of open account after the moment of sale.

Since retail sales generate payments at the point of sale, provision must be made to prepare the deposits and transport them to a bank in a timely and secure manner. Retailers with more than one outlet must further arrange to have those deposited funds concentrated into a bank account where the funds can be used for disbursements, investments, or other general purposes of the business. For a retailer with outlets located regionally or nationally, the funds concentration process becomes more complex to coordinate because it involves accounts at different banks.

Guidelines and techniques for handling coin and currency are best tailored to the specific situation in conjunction with the maintenance of physical security and controls. Security considerations require maintaining low levels of coin and currency in vulnerable areas, a low profile in cash handling procedures, dual control wherever possible, and frequent audit and surprise cash counts.

CASH MANAGEMENT SUGGESTION:

When depositing bulk coin and currency and checks, depositors usually benefit by using a separate deposit slip for the checks. If the checks are included on the same deposit slip as the bulk coin and currency, the entire deposit may be held over by the bank until the coin and currency are counted. By using separate deposit slips for cash and checks, the checks can be processed promptly and perhaps gain availability by meeting earlier clearing deadlines.

Security

Many firms prefer not to expose their employees to risk of attack when transporting money, so they use armored carrier services to pick up coin and currency deposits from the retail location and transport them to the bank. Armored carrier personnel are highly trained in security measures and procedures and are usually insured against loss from theft or robbery. The carrier's responsibility begins when it physically accepts the deposit at the retail location and ends when it makes physical delivery to the bank. The carrier normally requires that deposits be securely sealed in a bag or container, that they be clearly labeled with the identity of the sender and receiver, and that the value of the package be carefully noted.

In addition to providing these services, some armored carriers offer the service of buying and selling coin and currency to service a merchant's change funds. For example, a retailer may receive more $20 bills than it can use and run short of $1 bills and all denominations of coins. The store can often "buy" the needed coin and currency from the armored carrier by exchanging the excess currency, usually with some advance notice. Except for change funds, however, the carrier has no interest in the items being transported other than their safety and correct and timely delivery.

Coin and Currency

Carriers or banks that "sell" rolled coin and currency normally charge the buyer for this service. The price of coin is a few cents per roll, and the price of currency is usually a few cents per hundred dollars. Likewise, when depositing coin and currency the bank normally charges the customer for handling it, which has caused more than one disagreement between depositor and banker. While the retailer may argue that he should not have to pay to deposit coin and currency, the banker argues that he must count and process it before it can be used by the bank. Where large amounts of coin and currency are involved, the bank normally prevails. The retailer may well respond by installing its own coin and currency processing capability by counting, rolling, strapping, and recycling cash in-house to reduce the amount of cash deposited or purchased. Many who grant credit in the nonretail sector often wish they were in a "cash" business until retailers tell them how expensive (and filthy) it is to process, store, and maintain security over coin and currency.

Checks

Dealing with checks is easier than dealing with coin and currency, but it also may be more costly. While physical security may be somewhat relaxed, the cost of a few cents per check deposited is often comparable to depositing coin and currency. Moreover, checks that are returned by the drawee bank and charged back to the depositor constitute an additional, and sometimes substantial, burden. Thus, when a business sets up a depository system for a retail operation that accepts checks, it should anticipate a significant volume of returned checks. This requires the establishment of an appropriate policy concerning the acceptance of checks in payment for purchases, the amount allowable (if any) in excess of the amount of the purchase, and acceptable issuers and forms of identification to be required.

The necessity for accepting checks may be dictated by competition as well as local custom and practice, and the cost can be high. Nevertheless, the incidence of return checks has declined, say some retailers, because of the proliferation of automatic teller machines that have supplanted retailers as a primary source of currency for those consumers who cannot get to their banks during normal banking hours. Also, direct debit point-of-sale (POS) cards have reduced the number of checks tendered at the checkstand, thereby assuring reduced volume of returned items.

CASH MANAGEMENT SUGGESTION:

Banks often offer preferential pricing and availability for checks that are pre-encoded with the amount in the magnetic ink character recognition (MICR) line before they are deposited. Desktop encoding equipment is available to perform this task at a reasonable cost to the depositor who has a large volume of checks. In addition, further pricing concessions are offered to the customer who presorts checks by drawee bank locally, and by city, regionally or nationally.

Selection of Retail Depository Banks

In the retail business, often the first priority in selecting a depository bank is convenience. Proximity to the retail location is important if store employees are carrying the deposit. If deposits are made after hours through a night depository, then the bank's physical layout and exterior lighting are also important considerations when selecting a depository bank. The depositor should make sure that the bank assigns two employees to open and count each deposit. This dual control is important to both the bank and the depositor to assure the integrity of the deposit. However, if an armored carrier is employed, convenience is less of a factor because deposits may be carried to any bank in the local area, even to the bank's central coin and currency processing vault. Normally, banks discourage customers from depositing large amounts of coin and currency at branches because few branches usually have counting and wrapping equipment.

Before selecting a depository bank, the depositor must determine whether the bank can participate in the depositor's scheme to move funds to a concentration bank. For example, if the depositor uses ACH debit transfers to concentrate funds from the depository bank into another bank, the depositor will want some assurance that the depository bank is on-line to the ACH processor and can respond quickly and accurately to ACH debit transfer instructions. Some banks are too small to have on-line capability and can accept ACH instructions only by telephone or mail. Telephone connections are prone to error, and mail services are not timely. Although the Federal Reserve (the Fed) settles ACH transactions on a timely basis, notification of the settlement to the customer may be delayed by limited communications between the Fed and the depository bank.

Bank Card Merchant Deposits

Most banks accept merchant deposits of credit card vouchers such as MasterCard and Visa. Debit cards are becoming popular, as are "dual cards," where the cardholder may select at the point of sale whether the voucher is to be charged against a line of credit or against a deposit account. Typically, the vouchers are accepted for credit to the merchant's account at face value, and the bank then charges the merchant's account for the amount of the merchant discount. This charge may occur shortly after the deposit is made or at the end of the month. Many banks use a pricing matrix involving total dollar volume and item volume to determine the merchant discount rate. Under this type of pricing, one merchant may have a lower discount rate than another, even though their dollar volumes deposited may be similar. The fact is that the cost for the bank card system and the depository bank to process a voucher is the same, regardless of the voucher amount. Therefore, the merchant with the larger number of items will be charged a higher merchant discount rate.

Competition among banks is often keen when it comes to soliciting bank card deposits. First, a bank seeks to gain a market share on the card issuance side in order to generate retail relationships with cardholders, which leads to income from finance charges. In addition, the issuing bank receives a payment from the bank card clearing association for each voucher that is generated by one of its cards. Moreover, when a bank accepts a merchant deposit, it separates out all vouchers generated by its own cards before it sends the remaining vouchers to the bank card clearing system. The bank, therefore, gets to keep the full amount of the merchant discount. When a bank forwards vouchers to the bank card clearing system, such as Master-Card or Visa, it must pay the clearing system a fee for each voucher. Clearly there is a profit advantage to a bank that can dominate its market on both card issuance and merchant deposits since it avoids paying many of the clearing fees. That bank is in a position to keep the full amount of the merchant discount on its own cards, and it earns finance charges on those cards whose balances are not paid in full each month. These banks may be amenable to negotiating a preferred rate with merchants who generate a large amount of credit card sales.

Competition among banks for merchant deposits manifests itself in another way: electronic deposits. Some banks use POS terminals that are installed at the merchant's checkstands and connected by telephone line to a central computer. The computer may belong to the depository bank, the bank card clearing system, or a third-party service provider who has contracted with the depository bank or bank card system. The POS terminal performs two functions:

1. It obtains approval of the transaction by verifying the card. The form of approval depends on the complexity of the system that is used. It may consist simply of comparing the card number against a list of "hot cards," or it may actually check the status of the cardholder's account at the issuing bank; and

2. Upon approval, it creates and stores an electronic record of the card voucher.

An option is for the store to have its own on-site computer that maintains the "hot card" list. In this case, there is no on-line connection to the central computer. This system is somewhat riskier but a lot less expensive to operate. At the close of business each day, store personnel review and verify the day's card sales and vouchers and then electronically transmit the merchant's deposit of vouchers electronically to the bank.

In an electronic POS system, whether the system operates with a central computer or an on-site computer, the hard copy of each voucher is retained at the store for future reference. The bank receives the vouchers electronically and processes them without handling any paper, thereby holding down costs, which may be reflected in lower merchant discount rates. In an electronic environment, since all bank card sales must be authenticated (which is a relatively quick process), the merchant can minimize the number of invalid or over-the-limit vouchers returned because the store clerk did not follow proper procedures. As with a bad check, one uncollectible bank card voucher accounts for the lost profit not only on the sale it represents but also on perhaps three times the amount of that sale, or more. The merchant loses the entire revenue from the sale and must bear the cost of the product sold.

Credit Risk and Charge-Backs

The merchant who agrees to accept charge cards (either credit or debit) must be prepared to deal with vouchers that are rejected by the card issuer and charged back to the merchant depositor. Charge-backs are governed by the agreement between the merchant and the depository bank, acting as agent for the bank card system, or by the issuer of the cards themselves. For example, the depository bank may guarantee no charge-back on any transaction placed through a POS terminal and approved on-line before its completion.

The other side of the POS credit risk coin is the risk posed to the bank by the merchant itself. The laws of many states protect the consumer against unscrupulous or fraudulent practices, and they allow a certain period, often three days, for the consumer to rescind the transaction. Meantime, the bank may have paid the merchant in good faith, placing the bank in the middle of the conflict between the merchant and the consumer. This form of risk is particularly acute, for example, in the mail order business where the sale takes place without personal contact between buyer and seller, and without the purchaser actually seeing the merchandise until after the charge transaction is completed.

Another example of merchant credit risk lies in the travel business, where several different factors can cause the transaction to fail. First, the travel agent who executes the charge card transaction might not pay the carrier or tour operator, or the carrier or tour operator might not deliver the travel service as promised to the consumer. Because of some adverse experience, participants in the travel industry who have weak credit or unproven performance records may encounter difficulty in finding a depository bank for bank card vouchers. An example of low risk, on the other hand, is the restaurant business. Restaurants generally do not experience these difficulties because the nature of the charge transaction is entirely different from a travel or merchandise transaction. Usually the charge transaction is completed after the meal has been consumed, allowing any customer complaints to be settled prior to execution of the charge transaction.

NONRETAIL BUSINESSES

One characteristic of nonretail business is that the sale is normally made on credit terms whereas the retail sale is made on a cash basis and is concluded at the point of sale. This characteristic introduces a set of challenges and opportunities to wholesale, commercial, and industrial businesses that do not exist in retail businesses.

One challenge is to establish credit terms and a collection policy that encourage customers to remit their payments on a timely basis.[1] Another challenge is to channel the flow of payments so that the funds move from the buyers' bank accounts to the seller's bank account as quickly as possible. A third challenge is to have payments accompanied by appropriate data that enables the seller to record the payment in its accounts receivable records.

Nonretail businesses collect most of their receipts in the form of checks received through the mail and an increasing number of corporate-to-corporate payments are being received via EFT. Receipts are received in the mail either through a postal lockbox serviced by a bank (or occasionally by a nonbank lockbox processor) or at the company's offices. The latter receipts are transported to the bank by the firm's employees, unarmed courier, or mail, and they enter the depository bank as window deposits. The following is a list of some of the different collection methods:

---

[1] See Chapter 4 for a detailed discussion of credit and collection policy.

1. *Lockbox.* A lockbox is a post office box opened in the name of the depositor but accessed and serviced by the remittance processor. Banks and other nonbank processors that offer lockbox services usually process incoming mail and prepare customers' deposits at a time of day and in a manner that accelerates the availability of funds to the customer.

2. *Depository transfer check (DTC).* A DTC is a check often prepared by a bank on behalf of its depository or concentration customer and drawn against the customer's depository account in another bank. DTCs are deposited in a customer's concentration account to draw funds from multiple depository accounts. DTCs are also used for other purposes, including funding imprest accounts such as payroll and controlled disbursing accounts. Interestingly, DTCs may be either paper-based or electronic.

3. *Preauthorized draft (PAD).* A PAD is a draft drawn by a payee against the bank account of the payor and deposited to the payee's bank account. PADs are usually employed by insurance companies and others where the amount of the payment is fixed and the frequency of payments is repetitive. The payor must preauthorize its bank to honor the drafts, which may be in the form of either a paper draft or an electronic ACH debit transfer.

4. *ACH Transfer.* An ACH transfer is an electronic transfer of funds from one bank to another through the ACH system. Settlement typically occurs on a next day basis through the Fed clearing accounts of the two banks. ACH payments may be "credit transfers," which are initiated by the payor, or "debit transfers," which are initiated by the payee.

5. *Wire Transfer.* A wire transfer is a series of messages sent by telegraphic means between two banks—generally employing a Federal Reserve Bank as an intermediary—advising that the banks are simultaneously to make bookkeeping entries to reflect the payment of funds between their respective customers. A wire transfer typically takes the form of a sending bank instructing the Fed to charge the sending bank and to credit the receiving bank, as well as to advise the receiving bank of the bookkeeping entry. Wire transfers settle on the same day that they are initiated, thereby giving rise to "same day" or "immediately available" funds.

Whatever method is used, an open account is settled when the seller receives a check, a draft, or an electronic payment from the buyer and applies the remittance to the buyer's account. Although electronic payments are growing in volume and importance and are likely to continue doing so, checks are still the predominant form of payment, and check remittances are usually channeled to the payee through a postal lockbox.

LOCKBOX DEPOSITS

Checks are received by a seller principally through the mail at either the seller's premises or through a postal lockbox. A lockbox has several clear advantages over receiving checks at the seller's premises:

- Faster availability of funds;

- Reduced processing costs;

- Greater reliability in deposit processing;

- Greater flexibility in capturing remittance data; and

- Greater security over the remittance.

There are two types of lockboxes, wholesale and retail, which function in a similar manner. The principal difference between wholesale and retail lockboxes lies in the kinds of service required by the payee/depositor in order to capture the remittance data to apply the funds properly. A wholesale lockbox is one in which remittances tend to be in large amounts and relatively few in number; they represent corporate-to-corporate payments. The wholesale remittance processors are often required by their depositors/customers to capture the remittance data electronically, including invoice numbers and corresponding amounts being paid, as well as adjustments to invoiced amounts. Also, remittance advices usually consist of an apron or stub attached to the check stating the reason for the payment. Moreover, the payment usually must be applied to a specific open invoice rather than to an open account, which requires certain steps to capture the remittance data electronically. The data may be captured by the lockbox processor, or the processor may furnish a photocopy of each check to the customer, who can capture the data from the check copy.

A retail lockbox receives remittances that are usually small in dollar amounts and large in volume, usually involving consumer-to-corporate payments. The processor of retail lockbox remittances is often required to capture only the total amount paid and the remitter's account number without reference to individual invoices. Retail lockboxes usually serve companies doing business with consumers such as oil companies, department stores, cable television companies, and other similar operations. Retail lockboxes generally receive payments from remitters on open account, and they are usually accompanied by paper remittance advices (sometimes referred to as "coupons" or "turnaround documents") in machine-readable or optically scannable form suitable for high volume processing.

Retail lockboxes lend themselves to automated processing of remittance data because of the high volume of remittances received. The turnaround document contains a "scan line," or series of data fields that can be scanned by optical character recognition equipment to capture the data quickly and efficiently. The scan line normally contains the customer's account number and the statement amount. Where credit arrangements permit payment of less than the full amount, the minimum payment amount may also be contained within the scan line. The lockbox processor is able to capture this data automatically and retain the account number and related payment amount electronically. Some experts estimate that a firm receiving approximately 100,000 payments or more per month may find it economically feasible to process those payments in-house rather than to contract with a lockbox processor.

Lockbox Processing

The basic steps in processing remittances through a lockbox are described below and are shown in the flow chart in Figure 5-1.

1. Transport mail from post office to processing center.

2. Sort mail to individual lockboxes.

3. Open envelopes.

4. Remove and process contents.
   - Examine the check—Compare amount of the check to the remittance advice, if any, and make notation on envelope or elsewhere as to amount; verify that the payee is an acceptable name and that the check is dated and filled out properly to avoid negotiability problems.
   - Separate check and preserve envelope and other contents intact.
   - Prepare deposit of all checks.
   - Prepare batch for each customer by balancing the amount of checks with the amounts recorded on the envelopes.
   - Prepare photocopies of all checks and match photocopies back to respective envelopes (optional).
   - Prepare data file of remittances and transmit to customer (optional).
   - Prepare package of envelopes and contents and send to customer.

FIG. 5-1
Lockbox Remittance Processing Steps

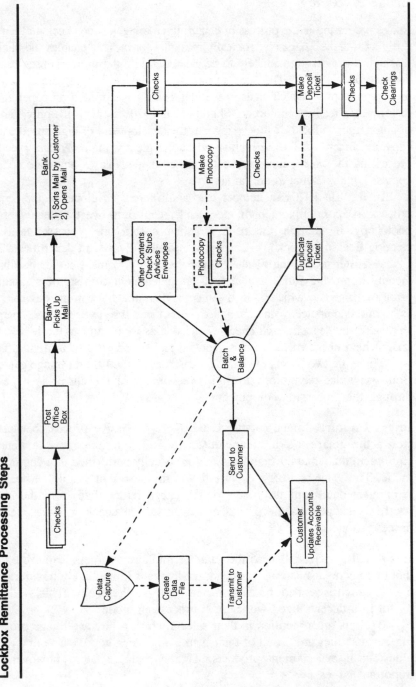

Image Processing

Image processing is the process of capturing an image of the check and temporarily storing the image electronically in digital form. This enables the bank to dispatch the check immediately to be cleared, while the image is used to process the bank's work. The bank's processing includes data capture or making the "photocopy," which actually is a digitized image printed on paper and is therefore not really a photocopy. Until the late 1970s, perhaps the only element of automation in lockbox processing was the development of high-speed photocopy machines. While the high-speed copier greatly improved the speed of processing the check, it sometimes produced unreadable or obliterated photocopies. Digitized images are far superior.

In the late 1970s, a number of manufacturers developed equipment to process lockbox items at high speed and greatly improve the quality of the photocopy. In addition, this new equipment enabled the processor to assign clearing float in the lockbox department instead of the transit department. This enables faster processing of checks and the ability to meet earlier deadlines, thereby improving funds availability. The equipment consists of a modified proof machine into which a video camera and an image recording device (such as a microcomputer with a magnetic disk) are inserted. As the operator "proves" the deposit, each check is encoded as to amount in the MICR line and a video image of the item is captured and stored on disk in digital form.

There are two forms of image processing: image lift and image capture. Both use video technology to digitize an image of the check as it passes through the processing equipment.

Image Capture. Image capture is the more expensive process because it stores the image on a computer disk. This requires more expensive equipment than image lift and is therefore usually performed in a centralized mode. The value of image capture lies in the processor's ability to capture remittance data from the image of the check rather than from the check itself, which permits the processor to release the check into the clearing process sooner.

Image Lift. Image lift uses the same technology as image capture except that there is no disk storage. Instead, the image is immediately transferred to paper, which is sent to the customer in lieu of a photocopy. This system is useful in a decentralized workstation processing mode.

Bankers often mention in their sales pitch that they use image processing because they are proud of their bank's high-tech approach to one of the oldest cash management products. To the cash manager, however, the important issues are:

- Whether the company will benefit from faster availability as a result of image processing;

- Whether the digitized paper image will be a meaningful improvement over the photocopy;

- Whether the bank will provide earlier reports on lockbox remittances and available funds; and

- Whether the bank will reduce its charges for data capture because of the scanning capability of image processing rather than manual keystroking.

Electronic capture and retention of the check image and information provide a much clearer image of the item than use of a high-speed photocopy machine. This high quality image enables the processor to separate the check from the other remittance media early in the processing stream before any data is captured for the customer. Any copies required by the customer are then printed out and returned to the processing clerk for inclusion in the package of remittance media to be sent to the customer. If the customer requires any customer remittance data to be captured, the bank does so from the video image on a screen rather than from the check or a semireadable photocopy.

Image processing entails a sizeable capital investment by the bank, often in excess of $1 million. Consequently, banks using image processing tend to charge premium prices for their lockbox service. In addition to the explicit price charged, banks using image processing may have hidden forms of compensation such as retaining the improved availability rather than passing it on to the customer.

CASH MANAGEMENT SUGGESTION:

Since availability is assigned in the lockbox department, which is usually a profit-center, the cash manager should verify that the availability assigned to the customer's deposit is at least as good as the availability assigned to items in the transit department. Moreover, if the proof operation is located within the lockbox department, that department may choose to limit the number of deposits prepared for any customer. The cash manager should verify that by holding deposits open longer, the benefits of an aggressive availability schedule are not lost by missing earlier deposit deadlines. Missing a deposit deadline for items drawn on banks in certain cities may mean the loss of a full day of availability on those items. This is clearly an additional cost to the depositor, although it is not necessarily a corresponding benefit to the bank.

Benefits of Lockbox Processing

Use of a lockbox processor (usually a bank) involves more than merely shifting the processing of remittances outside the company. Usually there is a saving in the cost of processing and there are gains in funds availability, reliability, and security as well. The benefits of lockbox remittance processing are discussed below.

Funds Availability. The principal advantage of a lockbox processor as compared to a company processing its own deposits is faster clearance of checks. This is achieved by meeting earlier deadlines for clearing checks than is possible by the depositing customer. Incoming mail is normally processed by the United States Postal Service at night. Lockbox processing units, therefore, normally begin their work in late evening, which is when the Postal Service begins to make incoming mail available to large processors. The processor picks up mail from the post office on a regular and continuing basis throughout the night to feed its processing pipeline. The processor often locates its facility close to the post office as well as close to the clearinghouse meeting location to reduce transportation time. Processing of incoming mail is normally completed by about 7 A.M., which enables the processor to exchange checks with other local banks early enough in the day for same-day settlement and to prepare its direct-send cash letters to correspondent banks and the Fed. Such early scheduling maximizes same-day availability and minimizes the amount of two-day (or more) float.

Reduced Costs. A lockbox processor can usually reduce the cost of preparing deposits (compared to a company's cost to do the job itself) through intensive staff training and supervision. This also reduces "processing float" time and clerical errors.

Reliability. Lockbox deposits are usually prepared reliably. When a lockbox processing clerk is absent, other trained processing clerks pick up the slack. When a depositor's clerk fails to report for work, on the other hand, substitute personnel are usually less well trained and often are ill-prepared. Sometimes deposits are actually deferred until the absent clerk returns to work.

Data Capture. Lockbox processors are equipped to capture data from the check or remittance advice and enter it onto electronic media (magnetic tape or disk) for transmission or delivery to the depositor. The depositor uses this data for cash application and automated update of accounts receivable.

Processors can capture virtually any kind of repetitive data desired, for which additional charges are usually applied.

Security. Greater security over remittances is provided by having checks received at a post office box where the processor handles the remittances using controlled procedures. This reduces the opportunity for a disgruntled or careless employee to compromise the integrity of the remittance process.

Post Office Selection

The lockbox processor usually studies the local postal distribution system before selecting a particular post office as its lockbox receiving point. This is important in large cities because postal distribution systems are complex, having to deal with mail coming in locally, regionally, and interregionally by truck, train, and air.

Uneven quality of mail service often exists among cities and within metropolitan areas. Thus, in one major regional city, an aggressive cash management bank is located adjacent to the main post office. This bank arranged for a window to be cut in the wall common to the bank and post office (with appropriate mutual approvals and security, of course) through which the bank receives its mail. In a much larger city, some large banks determined that several of the suburban post offices received their intercity mail as soon as the central post office did. As a result of lower mail volumes, the suburban postmasters could sort incoming mail to the large lockboxes faster. Accordingly, several banks in that metropolitan area maintain their lockboxes in suburban post offices. Postal service in another very large city has a long-standing reputation for delays in processing, and local banks have arranged to receive mail at lockboxes in nearby cities. In yet another major city, the central post office is committed to high-speed automated processing, and a major airline uses that city as a hub. As a result, incoming mail is routed to the post office speedily and sorted and made available to lockbox processors early in the evening.

Same Day Reporting

One problem that typically plagues the cash manager in operating lockboxes is that while the amounts deposited are reportable the same day, the availability associated with the deposit is not reported by the processing bank until the next day. By then, the bulk of the deposited funds are collected, which requires an expensive wire transfer to draw the funds into the concentration bank. This situation is magnified when the depositor is a government contractor because U.S. Treasury checks are usually given same-day availability at money center banks.

A solution to this problem lies in same-day reporting by the lockbox processor. Upon completion of the day's processing of lockbox remittances, the processor should be prepared to report the amount of the deposit and related availability data to the customer. The cash manager may then take steps either to invest the available funds or to move the funds to a concentration bank by initiating an inexpensive DTC (either paper or electronic) to match the availability of the deposit. The ability of a bank to report availability the same day that it processes the deposit depends on whether the lockbox department processes transit items itself and if it uses image capture systems. If so, then an availability report should be available the same day to the customer. A bank can report lockbox deposits via telephone call, direct data transmission (or physical delivery of a disk or tape), indirect data transmission via value-added network (electronic mail or electronic data interchange), or via the processing bank's balance reporting system.

Unique ZIP Codes

Processors of very large volumes of lockbox remittances may apply to the U.S. Postal Service to be assigned their own unique ZIP codes, in which case the Postal Service merely rough-sorts all items to the ZIP code and delivers this mail to the processor. The processor then performs the fine sort to individual customers or box numbers. Use of a unique ZIP code can be important because it provides quicker delivery of mail to the processor's site.

Lockbox Studies

A lockbox study is a methodical analysis, using a sophisticated computer model and data about mailing times and check clearing times between thousands of pairs of cities to determine the optimum number of lockbox sites and their optimum locations.

The objective of a lockbox study is to find those lockbox locations in which combined mail and clearing float are minimized. A lockbox study is used in conjunction with a review of a company's collection system and determines the optimum number and locations of lockbox sites based on the locations of the company's customers and their banks. A lockbox study is also used to establish a collection system or to fine-tune an existing system.

Occasionally, a lockbox study is part of a review of the company's overall treasury systems. While a lockbox study may result in small improvements of collection times, treasury reviews often find more fertile ground for accelerating collections by improving internal procedures rather than reducing float. While the cash manager is reducing float by a half day, for example, bottlenecks in the accounting function may be delaying the mailing of invoices by several days or a week.

Lockbox studies can be as simple or as complex as desired. A seller may easily determine where the bulk of its remittances originate by using the 80-20 rule: If 80 percent of the remittance dollars come from 20 percent of the customers, then only remittances from those very large customers may need to be reviewed to determine the cities of origin. On the other hand, and particularly if the 80-20 rule does not prevail, the seller may need to examine a more thorough sample of remittances. In this case, a consultant may be called in to help organize and coordinate a full-blown lockbox study.

Cash managers should ask several important questions before authorizing a lockbox study that may cost several thousand dollars and many hours of work. The following are some of the questions to ask before conducting a lockbox study:

1. Should the scope of the study be confined to remittances, or is a more thorough review of transaction processing along the cash flow time line needed?

2. Should the scope of the study encompass the entire company or only a part (division, subsidiary, or group)?

3. Is the objective of the study to fine-tune the existing lockbox system or to examine additional new sites?

4. Are there a few customers whose remittances are so large that they would dominate and add bias to the overall data? If so, should they be removed from the data and analyzed individually?

5. Will management consider using an established lockbox network or would they prefer to select their own banks?

6. Will lockbox selection decisions be based solely on cost considerations, including float and processing costs, or are there other factors such as existing banking relationships, quality of service, and credit considerations? What are the relative levels of importance of these other factors in selecting lockbox processors?

Selection of Lockbox Depository Banks

Selection of a lockbox bank begins by first determining the city in which to locate the lockbox and then by selecting the particular bank. City selection is usually based on independent studies of intercity mailing and check clearing times in which pairs of cities are selected and mail and check clearing times between the pairs are measured. Lockbox banks and other processors regularly purchase the results of these mail and check clearing studies to update the databases in their lockbox study computer models.[2]

In a full lockbox study, the company's actual remittance data are carefully sampled in order to ensure reliable results. The sample data must be selected to ensure that all large dollar remittances are accurately represented in the database and that the geographic distribution of remittances in the database is correctly dollar-weighted. To ensure the accuracy of these elements, the time when the data is collected must be chosen carefully, and the use of one calendar month is usually sufficient for most industries. Seasonal aberrations and unusual or nonrecurring sales or collections patterns might be encountered. In such cases, the period of data collection may be extended to more than one month, or data samples may be taken at different times of the year.

Once the study is organized, data collection begins by studying all remittances for the review period and by capturing the following information for each remittance:

- Amount;
- Drawee bank's transit routing symbol;
- Postmark city;
- Postmark date; and
- Date received.

This data is entered into a computer, usually at a bank or other processor that has software for a lockbox study model. The computer analyzes the mail float and check clearing float of the data sample and compares it to the databases of mail and check clearing times. The resulting statistical output is helpful to determine the optimal number of lockbox sites and the locations of those sites. This result is based solely on the pattern of remittances in the seller's data sample, and it usually requires some interpretation and analysis.

Once the number of sites and their specific cities are determined, the differences among the several banks in each city should be examined since their respective check clearing times and availability schedules will vary. Check clearing time directly affects the availability of funds to the customer

---

[2] The most widely used supplier of this data is Phoenix-Hecht, which is a subsidiary of UAI Technology, Inc., the developer of the most widely used lockbox study model.

and depends on how aggressively each bank clears checks. In looking at the array of possible lockbox banks, the following should be kept in mind:

1. Banks change their clearing schedules and patterns frequently, so a current difference among banks may change in a few months;

2. The clearing and mail float differences among different banks in the same city are real but usually not very large. Availability differences are typically measured in tenths of a day. When applied to the volume of remittances together with an interest rate factor, the amount of the difference may not be very significant.

3. Bank pricing, operating efficiency, and employee responsiveness are usually the deciding factors in selecting a lockbox bank in a particular city.

A bank evaluation should include a personal visit and guided tour of the lockbox processing department. The best time to visit a lockbox department is when it is in full operation, usually between the hours of midnight and 6 A.M. Visiting during these hours will glean much more information than observing a sea of empty desks and unused equipment in the middle of the day.

Visiting an unfamiliar paperwork processing operation for the first time, such as the lockbox department of a bank, is more valuable when some of the major factors that can differentiate one bank from another are explored. Cash managers can uncover differences by asking a few key questions, such as:

1. Are deposits prepared according to a schedule designed to meet each availability deadline? Does all mail received prior to each deadline become processed in time to meet the deadline?

2. What problems does the processor have in maintaining adequate staff at peak processing times? Does the processor scan work before critical deadlines to identify large dollar items for processing in order to improve a customer's funds availability?

3. Does the bank offer the same availability schedule that is used in the database of the computer model?

4. What is the capability of the processor in the area of automated MICR line capture and data transmission to enable the company to use automated cash application procedures?

5. Can the bank make intraday reports of lockbox activity via the bank's balance reporting system?

6. Does the bank have the capability to report electronic payments received via wire transfer and ACH together with regular lockbox remittances?

7. How are problems resolved?

8. Who is the customer's contact point?

If greater detail is desired, "The NCCMA/BAI Wholesale Lockbox Questionnaire" may be useful. The National Corporate Cash Management Association (NCCMA) is an organization representing the treasury management profession. The Bank Administration Institute (BAI) is a research organization operated by the banking industry. Together, the NCCMA and BAI developed a unique questionnaire that is annotated with explanations and reasons for each of the more than 100 questions that might be posed to a prospective lockbox bank. Some selected questions from that questionnaire are contained in Appendix 5-1.

Lockbox Networks

Lockbox processors have developed at least five types of networks to process remittances in multiple locales for a customer: intercept system, mail truncated ZIP codes (MTZs), bank alliance, *de novo* networks, and nonbank processor networks. These networks tend to spring up and die out depending on marketing success, effects of state laws, and other factors. They are all designed to enable a customer to have a number of available collection points with funds automatically concentrated and remittance data consolidated and made available to the customer in a timely manner.

Intercept System. Lockboxes operated by a single processor that services post office boxes in multiple cities constitute an intercept system. The mail is intercepted in each city and sent by courier to the processor's central processing site, where all deposits are prepared. The principal advantage is routing of mail to regional lockboxes, which reduces mail float. The principal disadvantages are the cost of picking up and transporting mail from the remote truncation points and the centralized deposit of all remittances, which increases clearing float as compared to regional deposit.

Mail Truncated ZIP Codes. A variation of the intercept system is the use of MTZs. The U.S. Postal Service has developed a feature of the national ZIP code system called Accelerated Reply Mail, in which a special ZIP code tells the Postal Service to intercept the piece of mail and send it directly to the nearest mail processing sectional centers rather than to send it on to its final destination. There, the lockbox processor picks up the truncated mail at each of the sectional centers (there were 212 such sectional centers nationwide as of 1988), process the checks, and consolidate the remittance and deposit data electronically for transmission to the customer. The funds also are remitted automatically to the customer's concentration bank account. Alternatively, the postal service will reship all such truncated mail to the customer via Express Mail for overnight delivery.

The obvious advantage of using MTZs is that both mail float and clearing float are sharply reduced. Since all mail, even local pieces, must be routed through a postal sectional center, truncating mail at the first such center cuts down on the amount of time the piece spends in the postal system. Also, since the piece is truncated close to the point of entry into the postal system, the check is presumably also close to the drawee bank, and therefore the clearing time would be relatively short. MTZs can be cost effective when processing relatively large volumes of payments so that the cost can be offset by the float savings. MTZ network service is usually more applicable to consumer payments than business-to-business payments because of the tremendously wide dispersal of originating points.

Bank Alliance. Several banks in different cities may agree to form a consortium to process lockboxes in their respective locales. The customer opens and maintains an account with each bank, which processes all remittances into that account. By prearrangement, all banks in the consortium automatically sweep all deposited funds daily to the customer's concentration bank, which may be any one of the consortium banks. All charges and fees are usually combined into a single account analysis presented to the customer by the concentration bank, which acts as the system coordinator for the customer. The principal advantage is that the customer does not need to deal with more than one bank in connection with the operation of the lockbox network, although the customer must establish and maintain a separate deposit account at each bank. The principal disadvantage is that the customer is limited to the cities served by the banks in the consortium.

De Novo **Network.** Lockboxes operated by a single bank in different cities constitute a *de novo* network. This type of network thrives where banks are allowed to operate across wide geographic areas, particularly interstate. The bank normally operates lockbox processing sites in several cities and is able to credit remittances directly to a customer's concentration account. The principal advantages of this system are that (1) control and responsibility are centralized into one processor, (2) there are no wire transfer or depository transfer charges to concentrate funds, and (3) there is no need for multiple deposit accounts. With the advent of interstate banking, particularly as state laws open up to out-of-state banks, several large banks are expected to create attractive *de novo* networks for lockbox processing.

Nonbank Processor Networks. Although nonbank processors are not in the business of accepting deposits, some do have special expertise in remittance processing. These networks have been established variously by a large insurance company, several nationwide retailers, and several nonbank service bureaus. They process remittances for unrelated companies and deposit the remittances into the client's bank accounts near each processing site. The principal advantage of nonbank processors is that they provide high quality processing. The principal disadvantage is that the processor often takes on processing for others as an adjunct to its own business, and the client's work may not enjoy as high priority as the processor's own work. Also, nonbank processors generally do not enjoy the same deadlines that banks have for check clearings, resulting in less favorable availability schedules for the client.

CASH MANAGEMENT SUGGESTION:

As interstate banking becomes the rule rather than the exception, a new element creeps into the selection of lockbox banks and networks: the bank that can service customers in many locations. As barriers to interstate deposit-taking continue to fall, superregional and nationwide interstate banks will undoubtedly position themselves to replace existing lockbox networks wherever these large banks operate. For some banks, that is expected to be in all major cities of the country.

Therefore, the cash manager should use caution in organizing any new multibank lockbox configurations for the company's use, pending developments in interstate banking that may greatly simplify the process.

Capturing Remittance Data Electronically

The foregoing description of lockboxes has dealt with the issue of finding the bank or banks most suited to the mix of customer remittances based on mailing locations. In addition, the cash manager must also consider the important matter of dealing with the remittance data. While the cash manager focuses on the timely receipt and availability of funds, the accounts receivable or credit manager is necessarily concerned with applying the funds to customers' accounts and open invoices. The cash application function can, and often does, begin in the lockbox processing area and therefore the buying decision should be shared by the cash manager and the accounts receivable manager, perhaps with input from the data processing department as well.

The data relating to a remittance, such as the payor's name, account number, invoice number(s) paid, and adjustments taken, must be captured electronically from the face of the check and from media enclosed with or attached to the check such as a payment coupon or check stub. The particular data elements required by the accounts receivable system will vary from company to company; but if the accounts receivable ledger is maintained electronically in a computer, then the remittance data must be converted from paper to electronic form sometime during the processing. The company can capture the data from photocopies of checks and the actual enclosures and attachments or from a scannable coupon or other return document, or have the bank capture the data.

Most larger companies seem to prefer having the bank capture the remittance data to handling the data capture in-house. The reasons for this include the following:

- More timely receipt of the electronic data, since the lockbox bank processes the work and captures the data in the early morning hours, making the data available for transmission to the company, usually by midday;

- Lower cost of data capture because of the differential that often prevails in labor rates;

- Processing efficiency because capturing the remittance data is the only function performed by the bank's data capture staff; and

- Reliability of the data because of redundant equipment usually available to the bank, and the lack of interference by other processing tasks in the work schedule.

Retail Lockbox Processing. The methods of data capture vary based on the lockbox customer's needs. In a retail lockbox, for example, where the company receives a large volume of relatively small remittances, usually from consumers, the company may require the payor to return a coupon or other preprinted document with the remittance check. The coupon or other document typically contains a "scan line," or a printed field containing the customer's account number, amount due, and frequently, the minimum acceptable payment. By visually comparing the remittance check to the coupon, the retail lockbox processing clerk can determine whether it is a full payment, a minimum payment, or some other amount. Full payments are processed as a group, using the scan line of the coupon. Partial payments are processed as a separate group or groups. In certain situations, such as charge accounts and credit cards, certain minimum monthly payments are required. In these cases, the coupon's scan line may have the amount of the minimum payment embedded in it, and by processing these minimum payments as a group, processing is accelerated with accuracy. Finally, those payments that do not conform in amount to the scan line must be processed separately with an operator keying the payment amount in lieu of using the scan line amount. This slows the processing and adds to the cost.

Wholesale Lockbox Processing. Wholesale lockboxes are characterized by relatively fewer payments of relatively larger amounts, usually involving business-to-business trade payments. The processing of wholesale remittances is less adaptable to automated processing because of the low volume, the number of invoices being paid by any one check, and the adjustments taken by the payor.

The capture of remittance data from wholesale lockbox remittances frequently involves a two-step process:

1. The MICR line of the check is read and captured electronically. The combination in the MICR line of the drawee bank's transit routing number and the payor's account number is a very unique set and provides a very reliable identification of the payor. To use this identification method, however, the payee must establish and maintain a database of each customer's bank numbers. This often entails maintaining a database of multiple IDs for those companies that use multiple disbursing bank accounts.

   Besides capturing the identity of the payor, the MICR line also contains the amount of the check. For payors that maintain their accounts receivable on "open account," this information may be sufficient to apply the funds.

2. Payees that apply funds to open invoices must have the additional remittance data that reflects the particular invoices being paid and details of any adjustments that the payor has taken. This data can only be obtained by a clerk who reads the check, check stub, and accompanying data, and then keys the appropriate data into the data stream. When the appropriate data has been captured, it then is moved into a computer tape in a format that the payee's computer can read. The data then is transmitted, or the tape is delivered, to the payee.

Some cash application systems use algorithms to apply payments to multiple open invoices without having to capture the detailed remittance data. Generically termed "autocash", the algorithms guide the sequential processing of the funds application system by evaluating all open invoices in a particular payor's account and seeking to identify the particular invoice or combination of invoices that add up to the exact amount of the payment. Obviously, adjustments taken by the payor prevent an algorithm from functioning effectively; and the greater the number of open invoices, the slower and less effective the algorithm. However, where there are relatively few open invoices per account and a small number of adjustments, algorithm processing represents a very cost effective way to apply cash to accounts receivable.

PACKAGE-SORT DEPOSITS

In some cities where there are clearinghouses, the banks may encourage customers depositing very large numbers of checks to perform much of the check processing themselves. Public utilities and major department stores often have sufficient check volume to justify investing in their own check sorting and encoding equipment. By encoding the amount on each check, sorting the checks by clearinghouse bank, and assembling batches of checks in accordance with the clearinghouse rules, the depository bank may be able to offer the company a very attractive price for such package-sorted deposits. The company must be aware, however, that the bank normally performs no processing of the checks other than to deliver the preassembled bundles to the other banks at the clearinghouse. This requires that the company retain photocopies of each check for research purposes and that the depository bank grant the company permission to endorse each check on behalf of the depository bank.

EFT DEPOSITS

Electronic funds transfers[3] (EFTs) involve various forms of payment. Generally, an EFT is accomplished by a bank making a bookkeeping entry on its books to debit the account of one depositor, while simultaneously crediting the account of another depositor, and advising both depositors electronically that the transaction has been made. The bank involved is usually a Federal Reserve Bank, where the depositors are two commercial banks perhaps acting on behalf of their respective customers. The bank in the middle may also be a commercial bank acting as settlement agent between its two corporate

---

[3] See Chapter 7 for detailed discussion of electronic funds transfers.

customers, or there may be two Federal Reserve banks or correspondent commercial banks that must settle with each other.

A company that receives frequent electronic payments may seek to have its bank combine the EFT remittance data (e.g., name of sender, amount, reason for payment) with similar data captured in the lockbox department from paper-based receipts. Since the important factor to the company is the receipt of funds and the data with which to apply the funds to accounts receivable, there is really no reason why the EFT data cannot be consolidated with the lockbox data. Some banks have the capability to consolidate this data and frequently call this service "electronic lockbox."

Wire Transfers

A wire transfer is a telegraphic message between two banks, usually sent through a Federal Reserve Bank, advising that a payment has been made or instructing that a payment should be made. In the case of an incoming payment, the payee's bank would be notified by its Federal Reserve Bank that its Fed clearing account has been credited for a certain amount, that the bank should further credit the payee, and that the payment is by order of the named payor. The only thing electronic about this transaction is the method by which the Fed notifies the payee's bank. Actually, no funds moved at all, except on the deposit ledgers of the Fed. Wire transfers that are moved through the Federal Reserve System are called "Fedwires".

ACH Transfers

The ACH system is a series of regional associations of commercial banks operating under the umbrella of the National Automatic Clearing House Association (NACHA) for the purpose of exchanging electronic payments without incurring the high cost of Fedwires. Each ACH typically contracts with a processor, usually the Federal Reserve Bank of the district in which the ACH is located, or a private data processor/network operator. To reduce the cost of making electronic payments, NACHA developed a series of standardized data transmission formats that are used by banks and their customers to exchange payment data and instructions.

Most ACH payments are "credit transfers" where a payor initiates a payment for credit to the bank account of the payee; however, "debit transfers" may also be initiated. From a depositor's viewpoint, the ACH can be used as a "draft" system to withdraw funds from a customer's bank account. In this respect, an ACH debit transfer functions like an electronic draft. The debit transfer form of payment is particularly useful where the amount of the payment is fixed and the frequency of payment is repetitive and regular. Most examples of its use are in the consumer sector for such payments as insurance premiums, loan payments, health club dues, cable television charges, and loan payments. ACH debit transfers are also heavily used by businesses in lieu of paper depository transfer checks to concentrate funds from multiple depository banks.

RETURN ITEMS

The bane of depository systems is the return item, which is a customer's remittance check that was deposited into the banking system and subsequently dishonored. Checks may be returned by the drawee bank for any of the following principal reasons:

- There are insufficient funds in the account;
- The check is drawn against funds that are not yet available funds;
- Payment on the check has been stopped;
- The account is closed;
- The check contains an unauthorized signature;
- The payee's endorsement is missing; and
- The amount has been altered.

The return item is the principal element of payment risk in a paper-based depository system. Every business that accepts checks from customers must expect some portion of its deposited checks to be dishonored and returned. Retail businesses experience greater volumes of return items than businesses selling to other businesses, but no company can be completely insulated from return items.

One of the more bothersome problems about return items is that they seem to take too long to be returned after they have been deposited. In retail businesses, this period often allows the maker's trail to cool off, sometimes making it very difficult to locate the maker.

This time lag exists because until recently the banking system has been ill-prepared to handle return items expeditiously. Whereas the banking system has developed advanced technology to read, process, and dispatch checks in large volumes electronically in the clearing process, return items have been handled manually and sent back along the chain of endorsements, often through the U.S. mail.

Holds

Banks traditionally have placed "holds" on the accounts of consumers and small businesses when large checks drawn on nonlocal banks have been deposited. While the bank's usual explanation to the customer is that the hold is required until the bank collects its funds, the real reason is that the hold covers the clearing time *plus* the time usually needed for the check to be returned. As banks watched the return period lengthen in the 1980s, they lengthened the hold periods to as much as 15 business days on checks drawn against distant out-of-district banks. Consumers complained to state and federal officials, resulting in legislation at both levels to place a cap on the hold periods. In 1987, Congress passed the Expedited Funds Availability Act,[4] and the Fed moved to implement the new law by issuing Regulation CC and modifying existing Federal Reserve Regulation J. These regulations now override the Uniform Commercial Code provisions to define certain types of drafts as checks and require these drafts to be subject to the same rules of presentment and dishonor as checks. Effective September 1, 1988, Regulation CC limited the hold on local checks to three days, and nonlocal checks to seven days. In 1990, these limits are reduced to two days and five days respectively. Interestingly, local checks are defined as checks drawn on banks located in the territory served by the depository bank's Federal Reserve district bank branch or Regional Check Processing Center (RCPC), which may cover a rather large territory.

In order to aid banks to comply with these maximum hold periods, the Fed developed new rules and systems for handling return items more expeditiously. Among the new rules is a requirement for all returned checks of $2,500 or more, whether cleared through the Fed or not, that the drawee bank notify the bank of first deposit of the dishonored item by 4 P.M. on the second business day after it receives the check, instead of midnight on the third business day. In addition, the Fed placed new requirements on banks that refuse payment of a check to return the check to the bank of first deposit within the same time frame that the bank would achieve for a deposited item drawn on the same bank.

Return Item Processing

One of the principal operational innovations developed to comply with the Fed's mandate to speed the processing of return items is to use the banking

---

[4] The Expedited Funds Availability Act is Title 6 of the Competitive Equality Banking Act of 1987, enacted on Aug. 10, 1987.

system's own check clearing mechanism to dispatch the return items instead of the mail. Under Regulation CC, the drawee bank must return an item to the bank of first deposit within the same time period that would occur in a forward collection to that bank. This means that if the bank's availability schedule shows the clearing time for a deposited item to be one day, then that drawee bank must clear a return item back to the depository bank in one day as well. Banks may facilitate this return process in any reasonable manner, including using a correspondent bank that may specialize in clearing return checks, or printing the routing number of the bank of first deposit in MICR characters onto a paper strip that is glued to the bottom of the return item or to a carrier envelope into which the item is inserted. This procedure is known as "qualifying" the item. The depository bank's routing number is found in the depository bank's endorsement on the reverse side of the check. In order to preserve the readability of these endorsements, a space is reserved on the reverse side of the check for the exclusive use of the depository bank. This space lies between three inches of the check's leading edge and $1^{1}/_{2}$ inches of its trailing edge. [5] The bank of first deposit must use that space to imprint its name, deposit date, nine-digit routing number, and arrows pointing to each end of the routing number. It is important to the cash manager that the company's endorsement avoid encroaching into this area reserved for the bank of first deposit. Encroachment may cause obliteration of the bank's endorsement, which could relieve the drawee bank of responsibility to return the check according to the time deadlines required.

When the return item is thus qualified, the drawee bank enters the item back into the clearing system (either Fed, direct send, correspondent, or clearinghouse), where it is dispatched quickly to the depository bank. It is important to note that any intermediate bank endorsers are by-passed in this process in order to speed the item back to the bank of first deposit, where the item would otherwise end up anyway for ultimate collection from the depositor.

Paying for Return Items

The problem of collecting from the maker of the return item is one matter. The process of the depositor reimbursing the depository bank for the item, however, often plays havoc with a depository system. When zero balance accounts (ZBAs) are used for deposits, the funds represented by the deposit of the check have already been transferred out of the depository account by

---

[5] Per letter dated April 13, 1988 from the Federal Reserve Bank of San Francisco to all depository institutions in the twelfth Federal Reserve District.

the time the return item arrives. Furthermore, if the depository bank is different from the concentration bank, then there is no available mechanism to reverse the deposit automatically so that the depository bank can recover the funds.

The depository bank must pay the presenting bank for the return item immediately, and it must simultaneously be reimbursed by the depositor. Timely recovery of the funds is very important to the depository bank. However, a problem arises if the depositor has no funds available because all the deposits flow out of the depository account automatically.

If the depository bank overdraws the customer's account with the charge-back of a return item and then proceeds to bounce DTCs because of insufficient funds, this may be interpreted by the concentration bank as a signal of a possible credit problem with the depositor. Moreover, in concentration account systems using ZBAs, the depositor typically builds in accounting controls that require the amount of the deposit and the amount transferred to the concentration account to be exactly equal. As a result, no funds are available in the depository account, not even the current day's deposits, to cover the charge-back of a return item by the depository bank.

Retail chains and others have been wrestling with the problem of how to handle redemption of return items for a long time. Some of the useful solutions to this problem, other than charging the return item back to the depository account, are discussed in the following pages.

Automatic Redeposit. Most return checks are issued by consumers and are often under $100. These return items are usually paid upon being deposited and presented a second time.

Company policies vary regarding the automatic redepositing of return items. The Uniform Commercial Code[6] allows a check to be returned for insufficient or uncollected funds and redeposited once. After being returned the second time, the check may not be redeposited again. At that point, the depositor may request the depository bank to send the item to the drawee bank for collection.

Cash Funds. The local depositing unit (e.g., a store) purchases the return item from the depository bank using coin and currency on hand. The effect of this procedure is that the integrity of the stream of current deposits is not affected by the return of a check from an earlier deposit.

Cash funds are frequently used by retailers where relatively small checks are involved. The store buys the return item from the depository

---

[6] See UCC § 4 for rules concerning redeposit of return items.

bank by withdrawing currency from the till. When money is taken out of the till, the disbursement usually is treated as paid-out and accounted for at the end of the day. In nonretail situations, an office petty cash account may be used as the source of funds. The disbursement is accounted for at the time the petty cash fund is reimbursed. However, paying for a return item depletes the limited amounts of coin and currency on hand, often making this method impractical if return items occur frequently or are greater than a nominal amount.

Depository Imprest Fund. The depository bank charges the return item back to the depository account, which is covered temporarily by the deposit float in the account and perhaps a small imprest balance. Periodically, usually at the end of each month, the account is reimbursed for the total amount of charge-backs by depositing funds from another account into the depository account. This system requires that someone in the company keep track of the cumulative amount of return items since the last reimbursement and carry out the reimbursement process.

Deposit concentration systems normally transfer out all amounts deposited. However, there are two variations involving imprest balances that are frequently employed, especially in retail situations when the incidence of return items is expected to exceed the capacity of local coin and currency. These variations are a positive balance imprest fund and variable deposit report.

Positive balance imprest fund. Normally, the depository account is operated as a ZBA. In this respect, it is actually an imprest account with an imprest balance of $0. In order to accommodate the charge-back of return items, management may decide to maintain a positive balance in the account instead of $0. Funds in the bottom of the account are therefore available to absorb the charges for return items while daily deposits and the concentration of those funds remain at the top of the account. However, there are several drawbacks to this method:

1. Accounting for return items is delayed until the imprest balance is refunded. This delay may be longer than desired within the normal accounting cycle.

2. An overt act to refund the account is required, which means that if this act is delayed, an overdraft may occur in the bank account.

3. If many depository accounts are involved, a considerable amount of funds will be tied up in the system and the administrative costs of tracking and reimbursing each bank account can be high.

Variable deposit report. Using this method, the depository account is maintained at a $0 imprest balance, and the amount of the deposit that is reported into the deposit concentration system is reduced by the amount of any return items. For example:

Starting balance in depository account	$ 0
Actual amount of deposit	1,000
Amount of return item	(150)
Net deposit amount reported	$ 850

The deposit concentration system will generate a DTC to move $850 from the depository account, leaving $150 in the account to absorb the charge-back of the return item.

The disadvantage of this system is that it breaks down the discipline often required of a field unit or store to report the exact amount actually deposited. If the amount reported is allowed to differ from the amount actually deposited, a degree of sloppiness, at best, or fraud, at worst, is introduced.

Local Check. Frequently, field operations are furnished with a checking account that draws on a head office bank to pay for miscellaneous petty cash disbursements, travel expense reimbursements, and other similar expenditures. This account may also be used to buy back any return items from the depository bank.

The advantages of this system are that it avoids the use of coin and currency and does not affect the stream of deposits. The disadvantage of this system is that there can be no effective dollar limitation placed on the field unit, which may allow the field unit to use the checking account for improper purposes.

"Collection" Item. Collection is the process, after the depository bank has funded the return item, by which the depository bank mails the dishonored item to the drawee bank free, without any requirement for payment. The drawee bank monitors the maker's bank account daily and makes payment to the depository bank only when the maker's account has sufficient funds to cover the amount of the item. The drawee bank charges the maker's account and issues and mails a cashier's check to the depository bank. Customarily, the drawee bank may hold the item for up to 10 days in the absence of any specific instructions to the contrary from the depository bank. The drawee bank is under no obligation to ensure payment and may return the item to the depository bank at any time after it has made a reasonable effort to effect collection of the amount through the bank account involved. Consequently, the payee has little leverage to use in collecting.

Return Item Drafts. Blank return item drafts (RIDs) similar to the one shown in Figure 5-2 are entrusted to the depository bank. The depository bank reimburses itself by drawing a draft against an account of the depositor, which is often located at another bank. In drawing the RID, the depository bank may be required to indicate on the face of the draft certain pertinent details concerning the return item, such as the name of the maker and the date it was originally deposited. The depository bank then endorses and clears the RID for its own account and usually forwards the return item to the depositor together with a copy of the RID for follow up and collection action directly with the maker.

The use of RIDs eliminates the need to track the cumulative amount of return items, as well as the need to take specific action to reimburse the account. It functions under the control, and at the initiation, of the depository bank. RIDs are helpful when return items are sizeable in amount. Several companies have used them to cover returns up to $5,000 or more, relying on wire transfers for greater amounts.

The RID may be either a check or a payable through draft, depending on the requirements of the depositor. RIDs differ from checks in the following ways:

- They contain space on the face to record the name of the maker and amount of the return item;

- They provide for the depository bank to draw it against an account of the depositor, usually at the concentration bank; and

- The depository bank is identified by a rubber stamp instead of an official signature in the signature area.

The depositor establishes a return item account, which may be a ZBA, at the concentration bank. A supply of prenumbered RIDs is furnished to each depository bank together with instructions as to their use. The drawee bank is furnished with resolutions or instructions authorizing it to pay RIDs when drawn by any of the authorized depository banks. Alternatively, if the RID operates as a "payable through" draft, the company would be responsible for authorizing or rejecting payment as the drafts are presented.

The RID can be printed as a multipart form, consisting of the original containing the MICR line, and two or three copies. The depository bank attaches one copy of the RID to the actual return item and makes it available to the local office or store for immediate collection processing. Another copy of the RID is mailed to the depositor's central accounting department, which normally requires separate notification that a check or draft has been

FIG. 5-2

Return Item Draft

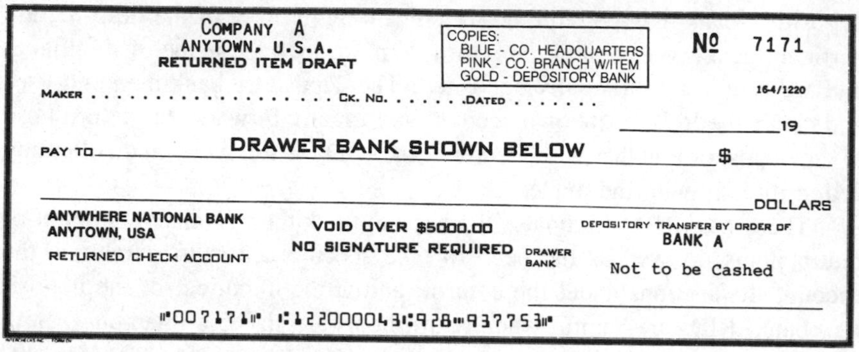

```
           COMPANY  A              COPIES:                        №  7171
          ANYTOWN, U.S.A.          BLUE - CO. HEADQUARTERS
         RETURNED ITEM DRAFT       PINK - CO. BRANCH W/ITEM
                                   GOLD - DEPOSITORY BANK              164/1220
  MAKER ..................... CK. No. ......DATED .......

                                                              _____19____

  PAY TO_____  DRAWER BANK SHOWN BELOW                 $_____

  _____DOLLARS

  ANYWHERE NATIONAL BANK      VOID OVER $5000.00      DEPOSITORY TRANSFER BY ORDER OF
  ANYTOWN, USA                                                 BANK A
                            NO SIGNATURE REQUIRED   DRAWER
  RETURNED CHECK ACCOUNT                            BANK     Not to be Cashed


        ⑆007171⑈ ⑈122000043⑈928⑈937753⑈
```

drawn against the company's bank account. This is in lieu of producing a check register. A third copy may be retained by the depository bank for its records.

The principal advantages of RIDs in remote depository situations are:

1. The depository bank controls the reimbursement funding mechanism rather than the depositor's local staff. This frees the local staff from the task of initiating the return item funding, and it usually satisfies the depository bank's need to have an immediate and reliable source for reimbursement.

2. No funds are tied up in imprest accounts.

3. No overt funding act is required by the company.

4. Accounting for each return item is prompt and accurate, occurring on a cash basis whenever an RID is paid by the head office bank account.

CASH MANAGEMENT SUGGESTION:

It is a good idea to remove the depository account number from the local unit's endorsement stamp (simply cut with a sharp blade) when RIDs are used. This will force the depository bank, when faced with a return item, to look up the correct account number rather than to debit the bank account automatically based on the endorsement. In so doing, the bank clerk should be instructed to prepare the RID instead of charging the depository account.

Notice of Protest

A Notice of Protest is a certificate prepared by the drawee bank in which an officer of the bank makes a statement recounting that the item was presented for payment and was dishonored, and is accompanied by a brief description of the reason for the dishonor.[7] If a payee wishes to take legal steps to enforce collection of a dishonored item, the payee must present, either directly or indirectly through the payee's bank, the dishonored item to the drawee bank with a demand for payment together with a request that the drawee bank protest the item if it is not paid.

The payee may then use the Notice of Protest in a court of law as proof that the item was properly presented for payment and that payment was denied. In the absence of such proof, the maker of the dishonored item may assert that the item was not properly presented to the drawee bank or that a clerical error caused the item to be returned. The fact is that a rubber stamp or a paper sticker attached to the face of a check purporting to indicate that the check was dishonored is not valid legal proof of dishonor.

---

[7] See UCC § 3-509 for legal discussion of "Protest."

Selected Questions From the NCCMA/BAI Wholesale Lockbox Questionnaire

---

Source: *Copyright (C) 1987 by NCCMA. Reproduced with permission. The complete NCCMA/BAI questionnaire and a related glossary may be obtained from the NCCMA at (203) 426-3007, or by writing to the NCCMA at 52 Church Hill Road, Newtown, Conn. 06470. There may be a small charge.*

Section 1. Mail Processing

1-1. Please describe the flow and processing of mail in your city's main (and substations if used) mail facility. Please indicate separately the post office's processing hours for incoming and outgoing mail during the week and on weekends.

Statistically, the distance from the post office to the bank's lockbox operations is already quantified in the Phoenix-Hecht mail survey. Therefore, this is not a question to quantify data. However, you do want to insure that your lockbox mail is not coming through a post office substation and that it is processed through the post office seven days a week and throughout the day.

1-3. Does your bank have a unique five-digit ZIP code assigned exclusively for receipt of wholesale lockbox items? If not, please state the number of addresses sharing the ZIP code and the monthly volume for the entire ZIP code.

It is important that your bank have a unique ZIP code specifically for the use of wholesale lockbox mail. In a large operation, it is inappropriate for retail lockbox and wholesale lockbox mail to be received in the same ZIP code. In certain cities, banks are unable to obtain a unique ZIP code solely for the use of the wholesale lockbox department. Under these circumstances, the ZIP code may be shared among bank departments, or, worse yet, it may be shared among many companies within a city. Clearly, in the latter situation, there are more opportunities for errors and delays.

Section 2. Lockbox Processing

2-1. Please describe the major components of your lockbox department's processing procedures. This should include the overall method of processing (assembly line, group, individual, etc.) and the specific processing procedures for a standard wholesale lockbox. Please highlight your quality control checkpoints and the components that are directly controlled by the lockbox manager. Please include a schematic or flow chart of the processing procedures.

This question is for general information. Pay particular attention to the work flow quality control points and which areas are directly under the control of lockbox manager. Work flow should be as streamlined as possible to avoid delays in processing, and as much of the work flow as possible should be under the control of one unit manager. If a lockbox processor uses an assembly line method, you need to verify that the bank can identify who on the assembly line handled each function for each check. Otherwise, it will be very difficult to manage output quality.

2-3. What will your weekly processing schedule be for our lockbox? Will our lockbox mail be processed on all shifts (including weekends and holidays) and receive multiple deposits (releases of checks for availability assignment) as a feature of your lockbox service?

The bank should answer this question specifically for your lockbox; general information about the department's operating hours in this context is useless. You want to be sure that your company's lockbox receives full processing since most mail arrives at night and on the weekends. Unless your box has a minimal volume (e.g., only a few hundred items a month), your objective should be to obtain a release of checks from lockbox for availability assignment at every transit deadline. A bank's continuous processing does not mean that you are receiving availability assignment continuously. It is important that the bank specify processing for your lockbox only in terms of when it is assigning availability to your company. The latest Phoenix-Hecht surveys show that just 50% of the lockboxes still receive only one or two deposits (assignments of availability) a day or that the number of deposits has to be negotiated. Do not count on the bank's best efforts.

2-4. When are the deposit times for our lockbox, and how are they determined?

You should understand when the deposits (assignments of availability) will be made for your lockbox and how these deposit times are determined. If the answer is not specific, you need to go back and negotiate what the process for your lockbox will be.

2-6. What is your ledger cutoff time for lockbox deposits? What is the latest mail pickup to be included in the last deposit? Will you process and deposit all of our payments on the same ledger day as received? If not, when are these items deposited?

In general, the later the ledger cutoff the better. The closer the final mail pickup is to the ledger cutoff the more mail you will have processed during a processing day. If your timing needs for receiving balance information or for transferring funds are prior to the ledger cutoff time, be sure that you are not causing a delay in processing by asking for an earlier deadline. You want to insure that all mail received during a ledger day will be deposited for your benefit on that same ledger day. It is unacceptable for a bank not to process all mail received on the same ledger day unless you specify an early cutoff for data transmission or information purposes. Again, remember that most lockbox models assume that mail can be processed within two hours of being received from the post office. If mail is being held past the ledger day cutoff, the results you achieve in your lockbox will not match the results reflected in the study.

2-9. Do you process both wholesale and retail payments on the same equipment? If yes, how are payments prioritized for processing?
It is preferable that wholesale lockbox be completely independent from retail lockbox. Typically, the retail application may require the machine 10 to 20 times as much during the day as the wholesale application. This can have a very negative impact on your wholesale lockbox cash flow.

2-17. Please describe your error control system for items within your wholesale lockbox department.
Once a lockbox is initiated, the most visible part of a lockbox within your company will be the number of errors that are made. Because of this, you need to understand thoroughly how the bank prevents errors, how errors are considered in the performance evaluations of managers and supervisors, and how the bank deals with processors who make errors.

2-18. Is there a formal procedure for responding to error and adjustment inquiries from lockbox customers? If yes, please describe this procedure, including the response time and bank contact area.
A bank should have a formal procedure for addressing error resolutions. This, at a minimum, should include phone numbers and contacts for routine errors and phone numbers and contacts of management in operations and for the account relationship if you have to escalate the problem to resolve it. Most errors should be resolved within 24 hours. Any time period greater than this should be addressed directly with the bank.

2-21. Do you allow night and weekend tours of your lockbox area? Can we arrange access to your lockbox department for unannounced audits of our lockbox?
With the majority of the processing at night, night shift becomes the most logical time for a lockbox tour. A bank that will not allow a tour during its primary processing shift may be trying to hide something. To obtain an unrehearsed view of your lockbox, it is necessary to audit your lockbox as your auditors do your department. This means that you have to gain unannounced access to the lockbox department to review the status of your particular box. This can be accomplished by having your relationship manager give you a letter of introduction to the guard, authorizing the guard to admit you anytime during a period of perhaps three to four weeks.

2-23. Upon request, will you provide the names, addresses, contacts and telephone numbers of three of your present lockbox customers as references? References should be companies with remittance volumes and processing requirements similar to ours.

In evaluating a lockbox, it is often a good practice to talk to other companies that are using the bank service that you are evaluating. To be meaningful, these companies should be very similar to you as far as the services that they are using in lockbox. Since companies have agreed to be references for the bank, do not hesitate to probe about areas of concern or areas where you want more clarification about the bank's capabilities and performance history.

Section 3. Check Processing and Funds Availability

3-1. Please describe the major components of the transit department's procedures and how they interface with the lockbox department. Which department encodes checks processed by lockbox?

You need an understanding of the bank's transit department because this department actually clears the checks processed by the lockbox department. No matter how efficient the lockbox department is, if the transit department does not have the ability to handle checks properly, you might lose availability. You should review the bank's controls for moving checks between lockbox and transit. Pay particular attention to where the checks are MICR encoded as this is a function that is best controlled by the lockbox department manager. If it is not, there could easily be a conflict of priorities that would negatively affect your cash flow. This is assuming availability is assigned in transit, not in lockbox. Some banks assign availability in a lockbox department to minimize the impact of these situations.

3-3. If you determine availability by individual check endpoint, please provide your bank's latest availability schedule that will apply to our lockbox (include a separate weekend schedule, if applicable). If this schedule does not pertain to checks of all dollar sizes, please explain.

An availability schedule is a good general reference when you have to validate availability assignment to a particular check or customer. Be sure that there are no qualifications on the availability schedule, such as only applying the schedule to checks over a certain amount or only to certain customers.

3-4. How many availability schedules are offered to your lockbox customers? Is the schedule you are offering our company your best, and is it the same schedule you provide to UAI (most current release) and other lockbox models? If not, quantify the difference and explain how we can obtain your best availability and the extra charge, if any.

While it is normally not advertised, there are banks who have more than one availability schedule for lockbox customers. You have to confirm that the availability schedule assigned to your lockbox is the same availability schedule in the lockbox study model you used, or the results that you achieve in practice will not be the same as the model's results. Be sure to quantify the impact on your particular endpoints that the difference in schedules will cause. Also, be aware that there is often a substantial increase in price to move to a better availability schedule.

3-6. List the times of your transit deadlines for availability assignment to our account; include both weekday and weekend deadlines.
You should understand exactly how the times of your deposit (assignment of availability) will correlate to the overall transit deadline schedule. It is preferable to have a deposit for each critical transit deadline to the extent that there is not a prohibitive surcharge for this service or to the extent that funds to be collected offset the expense of the deposit.

3-7. Is availability assigned in the lockbox area or in the transit area? If lockbox, please describe how the assignment is done and how adjustments are made to availability for delays between lockbox and transit.
Transit is the most appropriate department for availability to be assigned in that it is the last department the checks are in prior to leaving the bank. If availability is assigned in lockbox, it is possible that the items will miss the deadline and that the bank will have to absorb the float. To protect against this, the bank may have to set an early deadline in lockbox or make back adjustments when there is a problem between lockbox and transit. Economically, the funds usage liability is too great to be ignored if there is slippage in transit. If a bank is deliberately withholding availability from its customers, it may choose to assign availability in the lockbox system rather than transit because transit is a live operating system that cannot be manipulated as easily as a lockbox system. However, float assignment in lockbox might insure that the customer is not negatively impacted by any delays in item processing.

3-10. How frequently do you publish updated availability schedules? Do you routinely send the revised schedules to your lockbox customers?
While banks may refine their send programs on a daily or weekly basis, they usually only publish new availability schedules a few times each year. The only way you can review these changes is through a new published schedule. You should request that the bank send you a copy of each new availability schedule published since most banks do not do this routinely for all lockbox customers.

Section 4. Data Transmission

4-1. Please describe your procedures for the capture and transmission of remittance detail, such as account or invoice number, MICR line or other data for automated posting of accounts receivable records. Do you retain the actual check in the lockbox department until data capture is completed or send the check for collection prior to data capture? Please include the type and quality of equipment used

and whether it is managed by the lockbox department. What back-up arrangements exist should the system fail?

This question is intended to give you a conceptual overview of how the bank captures and transmits your remittance data. You need to understand how much flexibility the bank allows in permitting you to customize the information you want them to output. You also need to understand how much control the lockbox department has over this process and what the backup arrangements are. If the bank retains the check until after data capture, there will be a negative impact on cash flow. Data transmissions from outside the lockbox area should also be evaluated for control.

4-4. Can you integrate corporate trade payment (e.g., CTP, CTX, CCD with addenda formats) information in the transmission of remittance detail? If yes, how is this accomplished? If not, what alternatives do you offer?

It is important to be sure that items coming to the processor electronically can be merged with the data transmission stream for the lockbox. Today, there is not sufficient volume in electronic receivables for most processors to do this on other than a manual basis. However, you should understand the controls on movement of receivables information between the ACH area and the lockbox area to insure that you get your information on a timely basis.

Section 5. Deposit and Balance Reporting

5-2. For a given day's lockbox activity, at what time of day can you report the total amount that will be credited to our account?

If you are going to draw the funds from your lockbox system through a concentration account using either DTCs or ACH direct debits, you should understand what time the concentrating bank needs the data to execute the transfers for next-day availability. You also need to understand what time your lockbox processors will be able to provide this information.

5-6. Does your bank have the capability to provide same-day float information for lockbox deposits? If yes, at what time(s) is it available? Is it available on an individual check basis or in aggregate?; if on an individual check basis, in what form can it be delivered? Is this float information the same as is passed to your analysis system?

If your lockbox depository bank is collecting a significant portion of your checks on an immediate basis or if there are particularly large checks that are collected on an immediate basis, you may find that on a daily basis the bank generates more in collected funds than is required to compensate the bank for the account activity. In these situations, it may be necessary for you to ascertain the amount of immediate money during the day so you can wire the funds to the concentrating bank. In some cases, there may be two-day funds that offset the immediate funds. The only other way to reduce the balances to the compensation requirement level would be to have an agreement from your bank to let you draw (wire, DTC, or ACH) against uncollected funds. This would allow you to lower the average daily collected balance in the account without incurring the expense of a wire transfer. If same-day float information is available, you should be sure that it is available in time to meet the needs of your concentrating bank, to understand in what form it will be delivered and to insure that the daily balance reporting will match the input to the account analysis statement.

Section 6. Pricing and Account Analysis

6-1. Does your bank publish a fee schedule with descriptions of all your bank's activities and services? If yes, please forward a current copy. If no, please provide your standard prices for the following list of basic services. For how long are these prices guaranteed?

Basic Services

Lockbox Rental Charge
Lockbox Maintenance (Fixed)
Per-Item Processing Charges (including photocopy, attaching checks to remittance statements, etc. Please describe your charges fully.)
Notification to Customer of Daily Deposit (State assumed method.)
Wire Transfer (Outgoing Repetitive)
Account Maintenance
Deposit Ticket
Item Deposited
Item Paid—Paper
Item Paid—ACH
Return Item
Data Transmission
Data Consolidation/Pooling
FDIC Insurance Charge (or percentage)
Overdraft Charges
Uncollected Funds Charges
Return of Remittance Documentation
(Note: List other services and volumes for which you want prices.)

Pricing is the area of lockbox evaluations where most companies feel the most comfortable. It is important that you get a full picture of pricing; take the total charge by the bank/vendor in aggregate and divide it by the number of items deposited to get a true per item cost per lockbox item processed. Be sure to cover all the prices for your proposed lockbox. You should understand nonrelated charges such as FDIC insurance or perhaps even a float surcharge. Be aware of the bank's price change cycle. Many processors change prices on an annual anniversary date of the account opening while others have one set date for all cash management accounts prices to be changed. Often, you can negotiate a guaranteed period in which the processor will keep prices at the agreed upon level. Also, sometimes there is opportunity to negotiate a percentage above which the price cannot be increased during the period of the contract. If there are special processing requirements for your account or for your lockbox, be sure that you specify these instructions to the processor so that they can be included in the pricing.

6-4. By what means can you deliver to us the hard copy of lockbox remittance detail? Please provide representative rates for each delivery option based on a volume of _____, a destination of _____ and a delivery time of _____. How will these charges be passed on to us? (Volumes to be supplied by company.)

The standard method of delivering most lockbox backup detail is by first class mail. Therefore, most processor pricing models include this as the base charge for delivering hard copy. If you want something other than this, you should describe your needs to the processor and ask for a specific price for the additional service.

Section 7. Lockbox Network Supplement

7-1. Please indicate the type of lockbox network service(s) you provide. What is the name of your network?

Mail Intercept	[ ]
Nonbank Processor or Vendor	[ ]
Regional Processor	[ ]
Bank Alliance	[ ]
Single Bank Network	[ ]
Other (Please explain) _____	

This is for general information and identifies the type of network service that the bank provides.

7-2. Please list your bank's lockbox network locations. For each location, identify which are affiliate banks, independent banks that have an agreement with you, nonbank vendors, wholly owned processing facilities, and intercept points.

In order for the network to be effective in terms of improvement in mail and availability, the lockbox sites must be strategically located, especially relative to your customer base. You also want to know the network participants since you need to be comfortable dealing with any or all of the processors in the network.

Section 8. Electronic Payments Supplement

8-1. Please indicate which of the following types of electronic payments your bank is capable of receiving:

> **Wire Transfers**
> **ACH—CCD Format**
> **ACH—CCD + Format/Vendor Express**
> **ACH—CTP Format**
> **ACH—CTX Format**
> **EDI Payments—ANSI X12, TDCC, UCS, etc.**
> **Other—Please describe**

Not all banks can handle various transaction types. It is important to document which types the bank can process. There are really no universally accepted standards in this area yet.

8-3. Please discuss how the bank handles detailed receivable information and the various reporting options for receiving this information for each type of electronic payment.
It is important to determine the bank's capability to provide receivable information to its customer. Reporting options should be provided, as well as the timing and level of detail that can be obtained.

8-5. What is the bank's capability to integrate electronic payment information with the lockbox remittance detail transmission? How is this accomplished? Are there additional charges? If the bank does not provide this service, what alternatives are there?
The bank's capability to integrate the electronic payment detail with the lockbox remittance transmission can be useful to the customer that receives different types of payments. How the bank consolidates the information can also be important. The bank should identify the different standardized transmission formats it uses as well as the timing of the transmissions.

Disbursement Systems

Paper-Based Disbursements

INTRODUCTION

Checks and drafts have been an integral part of commerce for hundreds of years and developed as attractive alternatives to settling transactions by physically delivering coin and currency, precious metal, or other forms of money. A draft is a written order to pay, drawn against a payor or the payor's depository. In business, a draft is drawn against the payor (or maker) and sent through the clearing process to the payor's bank. The payor reserves the right to honor or reject the draft when it is presented to the bank. A check, which is a special form of draft, is a written order addressed to a depository instructing it to pay a certain sum to the payee or to pay to the order of someone designated by the payee. Since the check has no maturity date, it is payable on demand. The bank to which the check is addressed is the drawee bank.

Negotiability is a key element in the success of checks and drafts. If a check were written "pay to John Jones," the drawee bank could honor the written order only if and when John Jones personally appeared to present the instrument. However, most checks are not cashed or deposited at the drawee bank. Therefore, most checks are written as "pay to the order of" so that it moves quickly through the banking system. Thus, the payor allows the drawee bank to pay anyone who presents the item as long as "John Jones' " signature or endorsement appears on the item. The Uniform Commercial Code (UCC) governs the use of negotiable instruments and certain practices in commercial banking.

CASH MANAGEMENT SUGGESTION:

The financial manager should review Articles 3 and 4 of the UCC, which govern much of the cash manager's activities. (A copy of the UCC can usually be found in most law libraries.) Article 3, "Commercial Paper," deals with all common forms of negotiable instruments, including checks, drafts, notes, and certificates of deposit (CDs). Article 4, "Bank Deposits and Collections," deals with the process of collecting items through the banking system and the relationship between the payor bank and its depositor.

Under the UCC, in order to be negotiable, an instrument must:

- Be signed by the maker or drawer;
- Contain an unconditional promise or order to pay a sum certain in money and no other promise, order, obligation or power;
- Be payable on demand or at a definite time; and
- Be payable to order or to bearer.

An instrument that meets all of these requirements is negotiable and is:

- A "draft" ("bill of exchange") if it is an order;
- A "check" if it is a draft drawn on a bank and payable on demand;

- A "CD" if it is an acknowledgement by a bank that money has been received with an engagement to repay it;
- A "note" if it is a promise other than a CD.[1]

The instrument may change ownership during the check clearing process. Each successive owner, known legally as a "holder in due course," is required to endorse the item and thereby implicitly guarantee the endorsement of the previous holder. This ensures that each holder is linked to the previous holder if the instrument is dishonored. In that event, the instrument is returned by the drawee bank to the endorser who presented it to the bank. However, Federal Reserve Regulation CC, which was implemented in September 1988, requires the drawee bank to dispatch the dishonored instrument in a manner that will return it to the bank of first deposit in a quick manner. The drawee bank may bypass the intermediate endorsers and return the item directly to the depository bank. The dishonored instrument is known in banking as a return item and is commonly referred to as a bounced check.

DRAFTS

A draft is a payment order drawn by the issuer against itself or another party other than a bank. In order for the draft to clear through the banking system, however, it must be payable through a bank, which acts as agent for the issuer. As a result, a draft is often referred to as a payable-through draft (PTD). The agent bank, whose name appears on the face of the draft, facilitates clearing the item through the banking system but is not a principal party to the transaction.

Drafts are used routinely in certain industries, including property and casualty insurance (to pay claims), automobile manufacturing (used by the manufacturer to draw against dealers for cars shipped), and agriculture (to purchase items such as livestock, grains, and tobacco). Personal lines insurance companies have reduced the number of drafts they issue because of complaints by payees about the difficulty in cashing the items or obtaining early availability on them. However, in many business-to-business payment situations, PTDs are a viable alternative to checks.

Drafts behave like checks in the clearing process until they reach the agent bank. The magnetic ink character recognition (MICR) line on a PTD is the same as on a check, except that in the on-us field, where the account

---

[1] UCC § 3-104

number would appear, there is a symbol or digit that causes the PTD to be outsorted by the agent bank into a special pocket of the bank's reader/sorter.

The PTD may not be charged to the issuer's account without the issuer's prior approval. Therefore, where a company is using PTDs for regular accounts payable, the bank will typically create a data file by capturing the MICR line of all the issuer's PTDs presented that day, sort all PTDs electronically by serial number, and list the amount of each PTD in a data file. This file is then sent or transmitted to the issuer for processing, leaving the actual paper draft at the bank temporarily. (The paper drafts usually are physically delivered to the company for inspection and approval when the PTDs are issued in the field.)

The issuer creates a data file of PTDs issued. This file is updated and purged of PTDs presented and authorized for payment each day. During daily account reconciliation, those PTDs for which there is an exact match of serial number and amount are authorized to be paid. Where there is a match of serial number but mismatch of amount, the actual PTD must be checked before payment is authorized. The issuer physically scans the PTD for authenticity by examining signatures and endorsements.

In handling PTDs, the bank acts merely as agent for the issuer. The issuer bears full responsibility for paying or rejecting each item and has the same amount of time to reject an item as the bank has for a check drawn against an account with insufficient funds. Upon approval by the issuer, the bank charges the issuer's account for the total of all items being paid, rather than for each item. It should be noted that the bank must pay for the drafts when it receives them through the clearings. If the customer's account is not charged until the next day, the customer is expected to compensate the bank for the float. Alternatively, the customer may give the bank standing authorization to charge the customer's account when the drafts are received; the bank would then credit the customer's account for any drafts that may be rejected.

The bank's charges for paying a PTD may be considerably lower than for paying a check since the bank bears no responsibility for demand deposit account processing or inspection of signatures. Aside from physical presentment to the customer, the only processing performed by the bank may be data capture, electronic sorting and file creation, and electronic presentment to the issuer. These costs often are charged at flat rates or at very low per-item rates. In addition to the bank charge, the issuer bears the cost of electronically matching the paid file against the open items file and the cost of examining signatures and endorsements. These costs are usually more than offset by eliminating the expense of full account reconcilement processing provided by the bank.

Because it processes batches rather than individual checks, the bank may charge a lower price, perhaps as little as 25 percent of the price charged for paying a check. Additional savings occur from the elimination of stop payments, since the company is responsible for approving or rejecting all items. Moreover, the company matches the paid drafts against those issued to produce the account reconcilement data that banks usually provide for an additional charge. For issuers of large numbers of payments, drafts can represent significant savings in processing costs.

ELEMENTS OF A CHECK

Checks are negotiable instruments designed to move physically through the banking system in an efficient manner. The legal elements of negotiability do not affect the automated processing of checks. For example, a missing signature does not prevent a check from traveling through the system and being paid without discovery of the legal deficiency. In order for a check to be processed through the check clearing system, it must contain several specific elements: size, date, payee, amount, signature, drawee bank, and MICR line.

Size

The minimum and maximum dimensions of a check are at least 7 inches but not more than $8^3/_4$ inches long, and not less than $2^3/_4$ inches and not more than $3^2/_3$ inches wide (vertical height). These dimensions must be complied with in order for the items to be processed through standard automated check processing equipment.[2]

Date

The date on a check is significant only if it has not yet been reached. Such items are "postdated" and do not exist legally as a check. A postdated check is more like a promissory note because it is payable after some point in the future. Postdated checks often are cleared accidentally through the banking system and paid by the drawee bank because of human error in scanning the check's date.

---

[2] Specifications governing the paper, MICR quality, and format are contained in American Bankers Association Publication 147R3 (and supplement) and ANSI Standards X3.2 and X3.3.

The concept of "stale date" is more related to common custom and practice than law. Under the UCC, a bank is not obligated to its depositor to pay a check more than six months old.[3] However, the bank may pay the item and charge the customer's account as long as it does so in good faith. To invalidate a check merely because it has not been cashed within a certain arbitrary period raises the question of whether the payor is liable for the payment. If stale-dated checks automatically became invalid after six months, it might be implied that an obligation could be extinguished merely by the passage of time. Liability is discharged by the passage of value, not just by the passage of time or the issuance of a check. The bank's failure to identify a stale-dated item is generally not a basis for the payor to claim a refund against the bank unless the payor had placed a stop payment order and the bank had accepted that order.

Payee

The name of the payee, which is the party that the maker wishes to pay, is placed on the face of the item. The maker obtains proof of payment when the item is paid by the drawee bank and bears the endorsement of the payee. The maker is responsible for naming the payee on the face of the check. Failure to name a payee, or to make the item payable to "Cash" or to "Bearer," means that any person can cash the item, even if the item is stolen or fraudulently negotiated. The words, "Pay to the order of" customarily appear on the face of the item before the name of the payee. This phrase has two important components:

1. "Pay to" is the unconditional instruction given by the maker to the drawee bank, without which the drawee bank would have no authority to pay the item.

2. "The Order of" allows the item to become a negotiable instrument; that is, it permits the payee to transfer ownership of the item to another person or to deposit it to the payee's bank to collect the item from the drawee bank. Without the words "the Order of," the payee must present the item personally at the drawee bank to obtain payment.

---

[3] UCC § 4-404.

Endorsements

The endorsement on an item constitutes a legal receipt for value as well as a guarantee of all prior endorsements. For example, a check is issued by Brown payable to Green; it is then endorsed by Green to Smith, who deposits the check in the bank. Obviously, the depository bank has no way of knowing whether Brown's signature or Green's endorsement are genuine. If Green's endorsement is not genuine, Smith may have stolen it or may in some other way not be entitled to the funds. Presumably, the depository bank knows Smith's signature and is confident the check will be covered. Therefore, by accepting the check for deposit and crediting Smith's account, the depository bank is relying on Smith to accept responsibility for the item if it is returned unpaid. It then becomes Smith's responsibility to locate Green for reimbursement.

If the payee's endorsement is missing, the maker is entitled to demand a refund from the drawee bank and to return the item unpaid. A forged payee endorsement is tantamount to the absence of an endorsement. In the event that a payee claims nonpayment because of a forged endorsement, the payee must furnish an affidavit to the maker that the endorsement was forged, and the maker delivers the item and the affidavit to the drawee bank for a refund.

Federal Reserve Regulation CC specifies that the payee's endorsement must be placed within a very specific area on the back of a check. That area is the space within $1\frac{1}{2}$ inches of the trailing edge of the check, as depicted in Figure 6-1. The trailing edge is the left-hand end of the check when it is viewed from the front.

It is important that the payee confines its endorsement (the Fed spells the word "indorsement") to this area because the remainder of the check is reserved for bank endorsements. If the payee's endorsement encroaches beyond $1\frac{1}{2}$ inches from the trailing edge into the area reserved for the bank of first deposit, the check may be delayed in being returned to that bank (and, therefore, to the payee) in the event the check is dishonored. This could place the payee at a disadvantage, as it would delay the payee's efforts to collect on the bounced check from the maker.

Amount

A check or draft must have an amount indicated on its face. Customarily the amount is stated twice, both in numerals and in words. In the event of a discrepancy between the amount in numerals and the amount in words, the amount in words prevails.

FIG. 6-1

Endorsement Standard: Bank of First Deposit

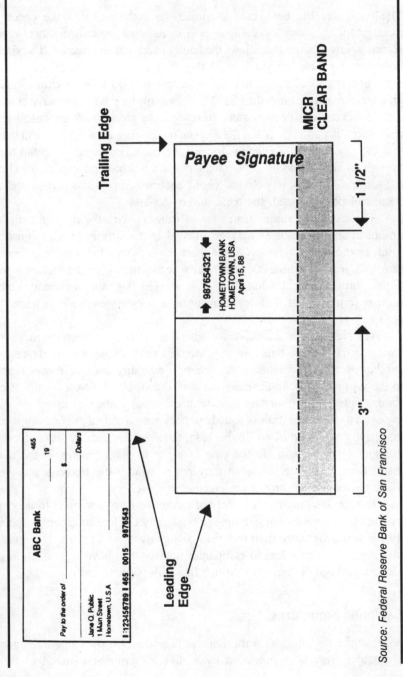

Source: Federal Reserve Bank of San Francisco

Signature

The only way the bank can determine the authenticity of the check is to examine the signature and compare it to an authentic specimen. Checks may be signed in any manner that allows the bank to verify the signature. The signature need not be legible, only unique. Although drawee banks purportedly examine signatures on all checks, some do so selectively. By spot-checking signatures on checks drawn for less than $1,000, for example, a bank can save considerable clerical costs, especially since so few checks are actually fraudulent and the risk of loss is nominal. When the account owner files an affadavit with the bank that the signature on a check is forged, the bank is obliged to refund the customer's money. In doing so, the bank pursues the last endorser of the check in the same manner as it would a forged endorsement. If the perpetrator of the fraud cannot be located, the bank suffers the loss.

The signature authenticates the instrument with the drawer's (maker's) unique mark. Signatures may be manual or facsimile, single signature or joint, or omitted altogether. Since there is no device that can read the signature line and determine its authenticity economically and efficiently for the high volume of checks that must be processed, signatures remain subject to human scrutiny and therefore constitute a major weakness in paper-based payment systems.

The signature on a check is a contractual element between the maker of the item and the drawee bank. In the case of a draft drawn by the payee against another party, the signature is the drawer's warranty that the drawer is entitled to the sum involved. In the case of a draft drawn by the payor against itself, as for example a PTD issued by an insurance company, the signature shows intent to pay at the time the draft is issued but does not provide a guaranty or warranty that payment will be made. In this case, the signature merely serves to identify the source of the item. In the case of a check, the signature is the maker's instruction (revocable though it may be) to charge the maker's account and make payment upon proper presentation of the check.

Businesses may use a variety of signature forms, subject to acceptance by the drawee bank. For example, a bank may decline to accept responsibility for verifying more than one manual signature on a check. However, this might present a problem to companies that want to have two (or more) people countersign or that want to use facsimile signatures.

Facsimile Signatures

A facsimile signature is a mechanical reproduction of a manual signature. Signatures may be reproduced by a rubber stamp or a metal plate. This method poses legal problems if the facsimile is used without authorization because the drawee bank would have no way of knowing that the facsimile was misused. Accordingly, the drawee bank normally requires indemnification by the customer before honoring a facsimile signature. Because of this liability, most companies should institute very strict measures to ensure that the facsimile stamp or plate is kept in a safe place and that access to it is very limited. Most companies using facsimile signatures place responsibility for custody and control solely with a person who is authorized to sign checks manually. This person normally exercises personal supervision over the use of the facsimile plate.

Unfortunately, some companies take shortcuts in securing facsimile signatures, perhaps believing that if all other aspects of check production are tightly controlled, the signature will not be a problem. If a facsimile signature is misused, however, the amount of potential loss is more than offset by the savings achieved elsewhere in the check-issuing process. Banks sometimes follow this policy as well when they choose not to examine signatures on checks that are less than a predetermined figure.

For example, a company may be confident that its procedures and controls for issuing checks are so strong that its accounts payable computer software is programmed to issue and "sign" the check at the same time. Accordingly, the check-issuing computer's printer produces a unique set of characters that are peculiar to that configuration of computer, printer, and software. These characters must be unique and consistent in order for the drawee bank to recognize them.

Drawee

Checks. The drawee on a check is the bank that is being unconditionally ordered by the maker of the check to pay the sum of money. Some high-volume check issuers print the entire face of their checks, including the MICR line, on blank safety paper. Firms using this method of issuing checks typically use several drawee banks in different geographical regions, selecting one for each check based on float characteristics. The selection of the particular drawee bank for each check is made by the computer based on a database containing mailing times and check clearing times. The objective is to maximize disbursement float.

Drafts. Placing the name of a bank on the draft preceded with the words, "Payable through (name of bank)," only facilitates clearing the item. In this case, the drawee is the company whose name appears as the issuer of the item. Some drafts, particularly those created in documentary trade

FIG. 6-2
Sight Draft

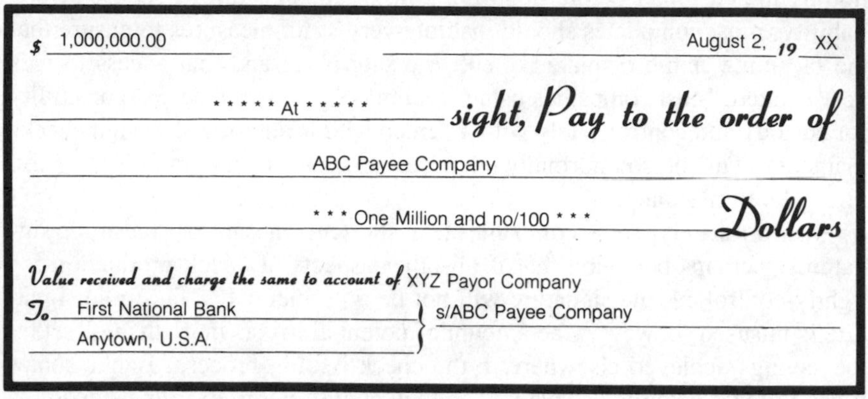

$ 1,000,000.00   August 2, 19 XX

* * * * * At * * * * * ——— *sight,* $\mathcal{P}$*ay to the order of*

ABC Payee Company

* * * One Million and no/100 * * * ——— $\mathcal{Dollars}$

Value received and charge the same to account of XYZ Payor Company

$\mathcal{J}_o$ First National Bank   } s/ABC Payee Company

Anytown, U.S.A.

---

transactions, are drawn by the seller against the buyer (who is the drawee) and addressed to the buyer's bank, as shown in Figure 6-2. In this case, the seller requests payment from the bank, suggesting that the payment amount be charged to the account of the buyer. Of course, the bank would be obliged to obtain approval from its customer (the buyer) before paying the item. The value of this form of draft is that documents evidencing title or ownership to goods are not placed into the buyer's hands until the draft is paid (or accepted, if it is a time draft).

Warrants. In a warrant, the drawee is the maker itself, and there is no reference to any bank. A warrant is the commitment of the entity to make payment out of its treasury and is frequently used by government units.

Alternate Drawee Bank

A company may want to draw its checks on a bank in one locale and have the check readily cashable at a bank in a different locale. For example, a company may have multiple business sites in two states and may be subject to laws that require payroll checks to be cashable in the respective states. These local laws can play havoc with a company's centralized payroll system. One solution is to use a drawee bank in one state and to print on the face of the check, in addition to the name and location of the drawee bank, the name and location of a different bank in the payee's state, which then becomes an alternate drawee. The name of the alternate drawee bank would be preceded by the words, "Payable if desired at (alternate drawee bank)." Bankers often refer to this as a PID arrangement.

Alternate drawee bank arrangements are also used in controlled disbursing, particularly by banks in the Pacific time zone. These banks are at a competitive disadvantage to East Coast banks in notifying western-based customers of the amount of their daily clearings. Therefore, some western banks offer controlled disbursing to their customers using a correspondent bank in an earlier time zone as the drawee bank. The western bank handles all customer-related arrangements and the daily funding, and its name usually appears on the face of the check as an alternate drawee, as is shown in Figure 6-3.

While the check remains drawn on the bank whose routing and transit numbers appear in the MICR line, the alternate drawee bank stands ready to cash the check for the payee. When these situations occur, the alternate drawee bank would be out of pocket by the amount of funds disbursed for the length of time it takes to clear the item. In addition, the alternate drawee bank must take steps to notify all of its banking offices of the PID arrangement. Therefore, most alternate drawee banks are paid for these services. In addition, most alternate drawee banks require a written indemnification agreement with the check issuer. Under such agreements, the alternate drawee agrees to use care in checking identification and other procedures in the encashment process. However, the alternate drawee bank normally cannot track stop payments or authorized signatures since it is not the holder of the account on which the check is drawn.

MICR Line

The MICR line was introduced in 1958 and was made mandatory in 1964 by the Federal Reserve (the Fed). The MICR line is used for sorting and routing checks through the banking system in the clearing process. It contains all the information necessary to move the item from the depository bank to the drawee bank, and it usually holds sufficient information to allow the drawee bank to process the item internally and charge it to the maker's account. All of the fields of the MICR line except the amount are imprinted when the checks are manufactured. The amount is encoded by the depository bank when the check is first deposited.

The MICR line lies in a band one-half inch high along the bottom edge of the check and consists of a series of machine readable numbers and sym-

Fig. 6-3

Components of a Check

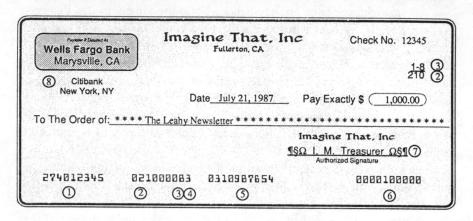

(1) Auxiliary or On-Us Field
(2) Routing Symbol
(3) Transit Number
(4) Check Digit
(5) On-Us Field
(6) Encoded Amount
(7) Signature (depicting computer-generated "signature")
(8) Drawee Bank (Citibank); Alternate Drawee Bank (Wells Fargo)

Source: Reprinted with permission from The Leahy Newsletter.

bols. The first MICR character must be at least one-quarter inch from the left edge of the check. The MICR characters are printed with a special ink containing magnetic material that enables scanning equipment to "read" the printing.

Figure 6-3 shows the component fields of a check's MICR line. These components are discussed in the following paragraphs.

Auxiliary On-Us Field. This optional field, often located at either the left end or the center of the MICR line, may be used by the drawee bank or the maker. Usually, the serial number of the item is repeated here to enable the drawee bank to capture that number electronically for account reconcilement purposes. Companies that employ MICR printers to issue checks may add the issue date (usually in Julian form) to facilitate disbursement float studies; they may also use a prefix before the serial number to identify a division or operating unit of the company that has issued the item.

Routing Number. The routing number is the same as the "denominator" of the set of numbers that usually are shown in the upper right-hand area of the check. The routing number is a four-digit number used to direct the check through the clearing system to the Fed office that services the drawee bank. The first two digits identify the Federal Reserve district of the drawee bank. The next digit identifies the Federal Reserve office (head office or branch) that services the drawee bank. The fourth digit shows the drawee bank's state or indicates that there is a special clearing arrangement. The routing number on the check in Figure 6-3 is "210": thus, the first digit indicates the second Federal Reserve District; the second digit, "1," indicates that the Fed office servicing the drawee bank is office No. 1, or the second Federal Reserve District Bank's headquarters office in New York. If the maker's account were domiciled at a drawee bank serviced by the Buffalo branch of the New York Federal Reserve Bank, the routing number would be "220" instead of "210"; the last digit, "0," indicates that no special clearing arrangements exist.

Transit Number. The transit number, also known as the "ABA Number," identifies the drawee bank. The system for assigning such numbers was adopted by the American Bankers Association in 1911 and is operated by Rand McNally & Co., which assigns transit numbers to new banks and keeps track of all previously issued transit numbers. In Figure 6-3, the transit number 8 represents Citibank. The transit number is preceded in the "numerator" of the "fraction" printed in the body of the check by a one- or two-digit number called the prefix. Numbers 1 (the digit "1" is New York City) through 49 indicate specific cities, and numbers 50 through 99 indicate states. This prefix number is not printed in the MICR line because it is a vestige and not used in the automated clearing mechanisms of the banking system.

Check Digit. The check digit is the ninth digit in the field containing the check routing number and transit number. This number is the result of an algorithm involving the preceding eight digits to verify the accuracy of the routing number for the benefit of the automated routing process. The algorithm used in Figure 6-3 is called Modulus 10 Straight Summation. This algorithm uses weights of 3, 7, and 1. The algorithm is applied to the transit and routing numbers in the check in Figure 6-3 as follows:

Transit/Routing No. 2   1   0   0   0   0   8

$$\frac{2}{3} \quad \frac{1}{7} \quad \frac{0}{1} \quad \frac{0}{3} \quad \frac{0}{7} \quad \frac{0}{1} \quad \frac{8}{3}$$

Multipled by

$$6 + 7 + 0 + 0 + 0 + 0 + 24 = 37$$
$$\frac{3}{40} = \text{check digit*}$$

* The number needed to raise the total to a multiple of 10. Thus, the routing and transit number contained in the MICR line on the check is 021000083.

Account Number. This field, also known as the "On-Us" field, usually contains the maker's account number at the drawee bank. It may also contain the branch office number of the bank where the account is serviced.

Amount. The dollar amount of the item is printed or encoded in this field by the bank when the item is first deposited. This field is always located at the far right end of the MICR line.

HOW CHECKS CLEAR

To understand paper-based disbursements requires a knowledge of how checks clear through the banking system.[4] Each bank uses different methods and routings, depending on where the check is deposited and where the drawee bank is located. Virtually all checks accepted by a depository institution begin their journey through the clearing system in the depository bank's "Proof and Transit" operation. They may then be routed to a clearinghouse association of local banks, delivered to a Fed check processing center, sent to a correspondent bank in another city, or any combination of these.

This routing process is significant to the corporate cash manager because depository banks differ in the time it takes to clear checks received as deposits and in the resulting availability they grant to their customers' deposits. It is easy for a bank to deposit all out-of-town items with its Federal Reserve regional check processing center (RCPC); however, the more difficult and expensive path of sending the items directly to a correspondent or distant Federal Reserve Bank results in improved funds availability. Clearly, a company benefits from selecting a depository bank with an availability schedule that most closely matches the company's pattern of deposited items.

For example, a company whose deposits consist mostly of checks drawn on local banks would often benefit from using the largest local bank

---

[4] See Chapter 3 for detailed discussion of how checks clear through the banking system.

as its depository. In this way, many items will be on-us items and will be accorded immediate availability upon being deposited. Checks drawn on other local banks will be cleared through the local clearinghouse and will be accorded next-day availability. Using a small local bank for a depository, on the other hand, results in few on-us items and increases the likelihood that the bank may not be a member of the clearinghouse. This would result in more clearing float (and less available funds) for the depositor.

Another example of bank selection is the company whose deposits consist of checks drawn on banks all over the country. A large bank will have developed more "direct send" arrangements with correspondents in other cities than a smaller bank. Consequently, a larger bank may be able to offer faster availability on those deposits as well.

The converse is also true. A company could theoretically take advantage of differences in bank check clearing patterns on the disbursing side by using a drawee bank that is small, located away from a major city, and not a member of any clearinghouse.

Proof Operations

"Proof" is the process by which the depository bank examines each deposit it receives to make sure that the sum of the checks and coin and currency received from the depositor equals the amount shown on the related deposit slip. The proof operation is conducted by a machine operator who reads and keys in the amount of each check in a deposit, then keys in the amount shown on the deposit slip. When the sum of the items deposited equals the amount on the deposit slip, the deposit is balanced and said to be "in proof." If the amounts do not agree, the operator is instructed either to examine the deposit and correct the error or to reject the deposit for research and further processing. Normally, the amount of the deposit is adjusted to conform to the contents actually received by the bank, and the depositor is notified of the adjustment.

During the proof operation, the proof machine encodes the amount onto each check in the amount field of the MICR line, "reads" the routing symbol and transit number on each check, and sorts the checks into a few "pockets" within the proof machine.

Transit Operations

The physical sorting of checks according to their respective transit routing numbers is the first step in the "transit," or check clearing, process. Small banks may sort checks into only three or four check-clearing categories, such as:

- "On-us," which are then processed by the depository bank the same way as incoming checks from other institutions;

- On other local banks, for checks that are exchanged with those banks in the local clearinghouse; and

- On out-of-town banks, for checks that may be sent to the Fed's RCPC or a large correspondent bank that services the small bank's clearing operations.

Large banks often sort checks into dozens of pockets. Instead of using the proof machine for sorting, the checks are sent from the Proof Department to the Transit Department (also referred to as Item or Check Processing Department), where they are sorted on large reader/sorter machines. It is not unusual for a bank to use one or more reader-sorters, each equipped with up to 36 pockets representing either an actual end point or a group of end points that require further fine-sorting.

For example, a large Los Angeles bank may set up its reader/sorter with 36 pockets to sort as follows:

Pocket Number	Bank Category
1	On-us
2–9	California clearinghouse members
10	District #12 nonmembers of clearinghouse
11–21	Eleven other Fed District Banks
22	New York banks
23	Chicago banks
24	Dallas banks
25	Boston banks
26–34	Banks in nine secondary cities
35	Rejects
36	Miscellaneous

The reader/sorter contains a computer that uses table-driven software to interpret the transit routing number and then direct each check to a particular pocket. The computer tables are established by the bank to reflect the bank's current check clearing arrangements with correspondent banks and the Fed.

For example, all checks drawn on Boston area banks would be directed to Pocket No. 25, and checks drawn on banks outside Boston but within the first Federal Reserve District (in which Boston is located) would be directed into the 1st Fed District pocket, which might be Pocket No. 11. Checks landing in Pocket No. 25, all drawn against Boston area banks, are destined to be sent via direct cash letter to the bank's principal correspondent bank in Boston. If the Los Angeles depository bank decides, for whatever reason, that it wishes to discontinue sending checks directly to its Boston correspondent, it simply alters the table in the software to direct all 1st District checks, including items drawn on Boston area banks, to Pocket No. 11, which directs all checks to the Boston Federal Reserve Bank.

In this way, the depository bank sorts all of the checks daily into batches to be deposited to the bank's own accounts around the country. Large banks find it economically feasible to send cash letters directly to each of the Federal Reserve Banks and to a number of correspondent banks. Smaller banks, however, may find this too expensive and therefore deposit most of their out-of-town items with their local Fed, perhaps sending one or two cash letters directly to correspondents in large cities.

Regional Check Processing Centers

The Fed operates some 48 check processing centers that handle more than 57 million checks each business day. These processing centers include the 12 Federal Reserve Banks, their 25 branches, and 11 other locations called "regional check processing centers" (RCPCs). A bank wishing to deposit checks with the Fed may do so not only at its "home" Federal Reserve Bank but at any branch or RCPC in the country by directing a cash letter to the Reserve Bank, branch, or RCPC. Each of these 48 check processing centers has its own availability schedule based on the time it normally takes to present items to the drawee banks. This clearing time is usually same day or next day and seldom exceeds two days.

Cash Letters. A batch of checks sent by the bank to the Reserve Bank or a correspondent bank is called a "cash letter." A cash letter is one or more bundles of checks with tape listings, together with a cover document that summarizes the contents of the bundle(s) and contains the dollar total. The cover document functions like the deposit slip used by a company or that an individual would use in making a deposit.

A bank typically sorts the checks it has taken in during the day into direct-send cash letters of several check classifications. For example, the Los Angeles bank may sort the checks in Pocket No. 25 (checks drawn on Boston-area banks) into additional categories in preparation for sending these checks directly to its principal Boston correspondent bank. In so doing, the Los Angeles bank might separate the checks in Pocket No. 25 into batches of checks drawn on:

Pocket No. 1—The Boston correspondent bank

Pocket No. 2—Other members of the Boston Clearinghouse Association

Pocket No. 3—Nonmembers of Boston Clearinghouse located in the Boston metropolitan area.

Checks resorted into Pocket No. 1, all drawn on its Boston correspondent, would be bundled into a cash letter, labeled "Boston correspondent—On Us." Checks in Pocket No. 2 would be bundled into a cash letter labeled "Boston correspondent—Mixed." The bundles from Pockets No. 1 and 2 would be sent directly to the Boston correspondent for deposit to the account of the Los Angeles bank. Checks in Pocket No. 3 would be bundled into a cash letter labeled "Boston—Mixed" and sent to the Boston Federal Reserve Bank if the dollar value were large enough to justify the costs involved. Otherwise, the bundle would become part of the cash letter delivered to the Los Angeles branch of the San Francisco Reserve Bank, which services the Los Angeles depository bank.

Federal Reserve Float. Federal Reserve float is the dollar amount of checks that the Fed has credited to its bank depositories but that has not yet been charged to the drawee banks.

Upon receiving a cash letter from a depository bank, the Fed prepares to credit that bank's account according to its availability schedule. The Fed then sorts the items by drawee institution and makes presentment to the drawee, at which time the Fed charges the drawee bank's account. The system is designed so that the depository bank's account is credited on the same day that the drawee bank's account is debited. Although the credit to the depository bank is almost always made on a timely basis, occasionally the physical presentment of the item to the drawee bank is delayed, creating Fed float. During this period, the funds represented by the check are on deposit in the accounts of both the depository and drawee bank.

Fed float develops whenever mechanical failures or transportation delays occur in the check clearing process. This float constitutes an interest-free loan to the banking system, although it is arguable whether the depository bank or the disbursing bank is the beneficiary. In 1980, Congress, which had become alarmed at the amount of Fed float that was building in the system, enacted the Monetary Control Act (MCA) of 1980. The MCA mandated that the Fed curtail Fed float and charge interest on the amount of Fed float that continued to exist. Figure 6-4 shows the magnitude

Fig. 6-4

Federal Reserve Float
(annual averages of daily float in $ millions)

1950	$520	1960	$1,160	1970	$2,931	1980	$4,470
1951	1,016	1961	1,317	1971	3,039	1981	3,202
1952	930	1962	1,591	1972	3,339	1982	2,523
1953	820	1963	1,744	1973	2,739	1983	1,785
1954	737	1964	1,885	1974	2,301	1984	760
1955	902	1965	1,831	1975	2,116	1985	808
1956	1,138	1966	2,090	1976	2,648	1986	738
1957	1,152	1967	1,636	1977	3,762	1987	988
1958	993	1968	1,913	1978	5,443		
1959	1,051	1969	2,571	1979	6,526		
Decade Average	$926		$1,774		$3,484		$1,909

Source: Compiled by The Leahy Newsletter *from various editions of* Banking and Monetary Statistics *and from the Federal Reserve Bank of San Francisco. Reprinted with permission.*

of the Fed float problem, which peaked in 1979. By then the average annual amount of Fed float was $6.5 billion; the peak month was January, with an average of $9.9 billion. This peak reportedly was caused by a midwestern snowstorm that closed Chicago area airports for three days, preventing the transport and presentment of checks drawn on Chicago banks. Consequently, for those three days, depository banks enjoyed the credit for those funds while the Chicago banks had not yet been charged.

Two factors were largely responsible for the dramatic reduction in Fed float after 1980 to an average level of below $1 billion: improvement in transportation systems and the addition of second presentment. As a direct result of the MCA of 1980, the Fed reorganized its transportation schedules and routings to reduce the possibility of transportation delays. This involved supplementing its use of scheduled airlines with air charters and couriers. Of course, airline deregulation and the resulting instability of flight schedules was counterproductive to the Fed's efforts in this regard.

The Fed also initiated the practice of making a second presentment during the day for those banks with a large volume of checks, generally $10 million or more per day. This practice, the Fed's "High Dollar Group Sort" program, sharply reduced the amount of Fed float by reducing the amount of checks held over to the next day. Historically, the Fed's check processing facilities sent checks out to its members in time to be received by 6–7 A.M. each day. Any checks that were processed by the Fed after the deadline were held over to the next day. However, by having a second cutoff and presentment in the same day, the number of items held over—and the amount of the Fed float—was substantially reduced.

Clearinghouses

Depository banks clear checks drawn on distant banks by sorting and packaging them into cash letters. Cash letters sent to correspondent banks and to various offices of the Fed for further routing to the drawee banks are used to clear checks drawn on distant banks. However, checks received by depository banks that are drawn against local institutions are usually cleared through local clearinghouse associations. The number of banks in a clearinghouse association depends on the local rules and desires of its member institutions. If only a few banks are involved, they may simply deliver checks to each other several times a day and make a net settlement at the end of each day. If many banks are involved, they may exchange checks several times a day at a central location. These exchanges usually occur at designated times during the day. Typically, each bank delivers bundles of checks to each of the other member banks and receives bundles of checks from each of the other banks during these meetings. At the conclusion of the final meeting of the day, net settlement amounts are calculated for each bank, and payments are made through the Federal Reserve accounts of each bank.

In large cities, it is often not possible for all banks to be members of the local clearinghouse association. Banks that are not members must use member banks to clear checks on their behalf. This arrangement is often facilitated by the fact that the back office check processing operations (i.e., proof and transit operations, presentments, and demand deposit accounting) are occasionally performed for smaller banks by their large local correspondent banks. Economies of scale provide a strong influence in decisions regarding check processing because of the considerable investment required for equipment and staffing.

DISBURSEMENT FLOAT

Components of Disbursement Float

The cash management function was developed in part on the premise that a company could increase its working funds by increasing its disbursement float. Disbursement float is the amount of time that elapses from the moment an issuer releases a check to the moment the check is charged to the issuer's account. Disbursement float consists of the aggregate of the following:

1. *Mail float*—Elapsed time the check spends in the mail while traveling from issuer to payee;

2. *Processing float*—Elapsed time taken by the payee to open mail, process, endorse, and deposit the check; and

3. *Clearing float*—Elapsed time taken by the banking system to move the check from the depository bank to the drawee bank and for the drawee bank to charge the check to the maker's account—

   • If the depository bank is the same as the drawee bank, clearing float is nominal; or

   • If the Fed clears the item and makes presentment to the drawee bank in accordance with the Fed's availability schedule, there is no Fed float. Fed float, if any, is part of clearing float.

Remote Disbursing

Remote disbursing is the attempt to delay the presentment of checks by drawing them on a bank that is located outside a major city and not well served by airlines. The ideal remote disbursing point is located in a rural area whose only access is a 50-mile bumpy dirt road. The bank's remoteness contributes to the difficulty (and slowness) of physically presenting the checks drawn against it. When the checks are finally presented, the bank telephones the issuer to advise the amount, and the issuer covers the checks by initiating a wire transfer.

As remote disbursing proliferated in the 1970's, largely encouraged by sophisticated cash management banks that made remote disbursing arrangements with small affiliates or correspondent banks, the Fed became concerned about this practice, especially about the large risk to the drawee bank. Specifically, the Fed was concerned about the drawee bank's limited capital resources and the large dollar amounts of the checks presented for payment. If the funding for even one day's disbursements was delayed, the bank's capital would be impaired. This easily could lead to the bank's failure and possible losses by other customers. With the passage of the MCA of 1980, the Fed was finally able to persuade banks not to do business with companies practicing remote disbursing.

Controlled Disbursing

Controlled disbursing is the practice of drawing checks against a bank that has the capability to inform the issuer early enough each day to permit funding in an exact amount the same day. Controlled disbursing differs from remote disbursing in that the drawee bank usually is reasonably large and well capitalized and is often located in a major city. This early notification of the amount needed to clear the day's checks was extremely helpful to corporate cash managers struggling daily with the cash flow forecast. This information enabled the cash manager to set the company's cash position early enough in the day to invest or borrow in the money markets.

Controlled disbursing had such a powerful attraction that most cash managers moved their disbursing business to large regional banks and to banks in Federal Reserve cities after remote disbursing was banned. They willingly dropped their efforts to extend clearing float in favor of receiving early notification. The larger banks in the big cities were considerably better equipped (with capital, expertise, and credit lines) to handle the disbursing activity of even the largest corporations.

Controlled disbursing is a descendent of remote disbursing and is accepted reluctantly by the Fed as a valuable and competitive banking service. There are still some small banks located far from Federal Reserve check processing facilities that are involved in remote disbursing. However, most of these banks are affiliated with large banks through common ownership or strong correspondent relationships.

In 1984, the Fed initiated the high dollar group sort (HDGS) program, in which the Fed makes a second daily presentment of checks to drawee banks that have more than $10 million of checks being presented from outside their Fed district. This second presentment, and other efforts by the Fed to make later presentments during the day, have two implications for companies that use controlled disbursing:

1. Later presentment delays the time of notification of the amount of checks clearing for the day until after the last presentment is received and processed. This delays the cash manager's daily cash planning and the initiation of borrowing or overnight investment transactions.

2. Those banks with a high dollar volume of check presentments often have highly automated systems and can offer attractive per-item pricing.

CASH MANAGEMENT SUGGESTION:

> A controlled disbursing strategy that developed as a result of HDGS is to use a drawee bank having less than $10 million in average daily present-ment of out-of-district checks. The banks that meet this criterion and offer controlled disbursing services are generally relatively small and are often affiliated through common ownership or strong correspondent ties with larger banks that are subject to HDGS. A company may have a modest disbursement float advantage by selecting a drawee bank that is not subject to HDGS. Cash managers may find a number of banks that contract out their check processing to their large affiliate, thereby extending disbursing float and providing attractive pricing.
>
> In a survey conducted in late 1987, Phoenix-Hecht identified 277 sites where controlled disbursement is offered, compared to 240 sites a year earlier and 176 sites in 1984. The survey noted that nearly half the sites (128) in 1987 had daily presentments of less than $10 million. [5] Clearly, there is ample opportunity for controlled disbursing with extended float. Selecting a bank for controlled disbursing involves evalu-ating a number of factors including clearing float, HDGS, processing efficiency, funding alternatives, proximity to the issuer, and pricing. The Bank Administration Institute's Controlled Disbursement Questionnaire, in Appendix 6-1, will help cash managers select a bank for controlled disbursing service.

Remote Mailing

Remote mailing is the mailing of checks from a location far from both the drawee bank and the payee. Some companies that process their accounts payable centrally have installed remote check printers in their plants and offices around the country. The central computer determines on which bank to draw each check and which check printer will print the checks. The com-puter-originated decision is based on a database containing mail times between the locations of each printer and each payee and check clearing times between payee locations and drawee banks. The computer seeks to maximize the amount of time it takes for both legs of the trip.

Disbursement Studies

When float was the dominant playground for cash managers, disbursement float studies—and their depository counterpart, lockbox studies—were

---

[5] Reported in *Corporate EFT Report*, Vol. 8, No. 6, (Mar. 16, 1988) p. 6.

designed to take maximum advantage of remote banks and mail times. The general rule was to pay east coast vendors with checks drawn on west coast banks, and vice versa. Disbursement studies sought to select banks optimally located to increase mail and clearing float. Despite the stigma now associated with remote disbursing, disbursement studies are nevertheless useful for identifying drawee banks to be used for controlled disbursing with or without extended float characteristics. Inefficiencies in the check clearing system will continue as long as paper checks are moved from depository banks to drawee banks. However, to design a disbursement system based on taking advantage of these inefficiencies is risky as long as the Fed continues to reduce float by increasing the efficiency of the check clearing system.

STOP PAYMENTS

A stop payment is an order to a bank by the maker of the check to refuse payment of that check when it is presented. Stop payment orders are issued for many reasons, most often because a check was issued in error or there is a dispute between the maker and the payee. Under the UCC, banks are only obligated to honor a verbal stop payment order for 14 days.[6] During that time, a written stop payment order may be issued to the bank in any acceptable form, which is effective for six months unless it is renewed in writing. A bank usually notifies the customer of this time limit when the bank accepts the order. While it is the customer's responsibility to renew the stop payment order when it expires, some banks make it a practice to notify their commercial customers (and sometimes their retail customers) when stop payment orders are about to expire. This gives the customer the opportunity to renew the written stop payment order and incur the usual fee or allow the order to lapse. If the stop payment is allowed to lapse and the check is subsequently presented for payment, the bank may pay the check.

Banks cannot avoid paying a check because the check has a stale date. The UCC allows, but does not obligate, a bank to reject an item more than six months after its date; the bank is not liable to its customer, however, if it paid such an item in good faith.[7] Therefore, customers may attempt to persuade their banks to carry stop payment orders until cancelled rather than relying on the item becoming stale and therefore being automatically rejected.

---

[6] UCC § 4-403.

[7] UCC § 4-404.

Stop payment orders apply only to checks and not to drafts, since a check is an unconditional order to pay issued by the maker to the drawee bank. Payment of a draft, on the other hand, must be overtly approved or rejected by the payor rather than the bank at the time of presentment, in which case the decision to pay lies solely with the payor.

ORGANIZING BANK ACCOUNTS FOR DISBURSING

Any system must be properly organized in order to run efficiently. An automobile engine that suffers from fouled spark plugs may propel the car down the street, but it will not move very quickly and will guzzle gas in the process. Likewise, a corporate disbursing system may suffer bottlenecks, gaps, and delays, and cost altogether too much to operate if it is not well organized.

There are several elements that characterize a well-planned disbursing system:

- The disbursing function should be controlled by the financial manager;
- Disbursements should be drawn against bank accounts used solely for these disbursing activities;
- There should be a systematic flow of funds to cover authorized disbursements; and
- There should be a flow of funds only when permission is obtained to cover a special disbursement or when a request is made by field personnel.

Other elements of a well-planned disbursing system include well-defined, systematic, and accurate procedures for authorizing, generating, and accounting for payments.

It should be noted that none of these elements has a bias toward either paper-based or electronic disbursements. Indeed, the principles should be the same regardless of whether checks or electronic funds transfers (EFTs) are used; in fact, many systems employ both forms of payment.

Control of Disbursing Activities

Disbursing activities should be under the control of the financial management of the organization. Financial managers have primary responsibility for conserving the firm's assets. This role requires effective accounting, auditing, and controls, as well as adherence to budgets and funding forecasts. At the same time, financial managers must be responsive to the needs of the organization. Therefore, the function of managing disbursements usually becomes a task of balancing competing forces. The disbursement manager must balance funds disbursements with available resources and requests for disbursement against fully-expended or nonexistent budgets.

In most small- or medium-sized organizations, reponsibility for managing disbursements resides at the corporate headquarters and may be found in one person: the controller. As firms grow and become more complex, the controller's functions are expanded and typically are divided into separate areas: accounts payable, accounts receivable, and general ledger accounting. As the volume of disbursements grows, the following circumstances arise:

- Vendor complaints about slow payments increase;

- Decentralized business units clamor to have their own disbursing systems;

- Review and control over payments diminish as the volume increases; and

- Data processing overhead increases.

Thus, it is the controller's task to maintain control as the situation becomes more complicated.

Separation of Duties and Decentralization

The controller's training as an auditor dictates that the system have a separation of duties and checks and balances. Sometimes this requires an increase of overhead expenditures, which leads to the painful decision of whether to spend money the firm may not have or to make an investment in the growth and future viability of the firm. Assuming the latter path is followed, the firm undoubtedly will use modern computers and software to handle its payroll and accounts payable function. In addition, a limited amount of decentralized control may be permitted, particularly if subsidiaries or major divisions operate with some autonomy and maintain their own accounting functions. In effect, the decentralized unit functions as a clone and extension of the headquarters controller.

Accounts Payable Function

The accounts payable function has one principal objective: to initiate payment of the firm's legitimate obligations on a timely basis. To accomplish this function, the accounts payable system must have mechanisms to verify the legitimacy of the obligations, to verify that they are the firm's obligations and not someone else's, and to know when to pay the obligation—not too soon or too late.

Most accounts payable systems recognize that there is an essential difference between paying for tangibles, such as goods, materials, merchandise, or equipment, and paying for intangibles, such as services. The purchase of tangibles may be controlled through the issuance of a purchase order (or a material release order under a blanket purchase order). When the tangible goods are received by the firm, a document is created internally to evidence receipt of the goods, which is followed up with an invoice sent by the seller to the buyer. The accounts payable function then takes over and attempts to match the three key documents: purchase order, receiving document, and invoice. When they match in all respects (i.e., merchandise description, quantity, and unit price, as well as other agreed items such as freight, insurance, duties, and handling charges), the invoice is approved for payment. As a result of this paper processing, the typical accounts payable department becomes a swamp of paper. There is hardly a manager of a paper-based accounts payable department who does not complain of having too much paper, too many vendor complaints of slow payment, too many instances of lost discounts, and too many audit criticisms.

The purchase of intangibles, such as services, is handled differently from tangibles by the accounts payable system because there is no receiving document and often no purchase order. In this case, the accounts payable department must rely on the approval noted on the face of the invoice by an authorized person. This requires knowledge by the accounts payable clerical staff of the levels of authority of each person in the company who has authority to approve expenditures. While these grants of authority are often made informally and remain undocumented, the financial manager with responsibility for disbursements is well advised to document in writing the de facto approval authorities.

Electronic Data Interchange

A solution to the paperwork bind in accounts payable is electronic data interchange (EDI). EDI is a process of doing business that embraces the entire purchasing/procurement/materials management area, feeding into accounts payable and then into the payment mechanism itself. EDI is the exchange of business transaction information electronically in standardized machine readable format. It replaces paper documents with the electronic equivalent of documents that can be sent, received, read, and manipulated by the computers and application systems of the trading partners in a transaction. Since most companies have many trading partners, EDI is based on standard data formats. Many of these standards have been developed and are continually improved under the auspices of the Accredited Standards Committee X12 of the American National Standards Institute (ANSI), a voluntary coordinating organization for the United States' national standards system.

By using EDI, a company acting as a buyer can obtain quotations, place orders, record receipt of materials, receive invoices, and match purchase orders, receiving documents and invoices electronically. In fact, many companies have begun to eliminate invoices altogether, relying instead on electronically matching the electronic purchase order with the receiving document to authorize payment. This process has been termed "evaluated receipts settlement" (ERS). ERS works well when the trading partners have prenegotiated payment terms, (e.g., payment is due X days after date of receipt or after shipping date). Just as EDI enables a buyer's transaction to flow from the quotation to the payment, ERS enables a seller's transaction to flow from order entry, to shipment, to invoice, to cash application upon the receipt of funds.

One EDI transaction set—the electronic equivalent of a paper document—is the advance shipping notice (ASN). The ASN is sent by the seller to the buyer electronically to state the actual shipping date and contains the description and quantity of materials being shipped. The ASN therefore establishes the date that the invoice would otherwise have been issued, which would have determined the payment due date. Accordingly, the accounts payable operation can be converted from paper documents to electronic documents through EDI, thus reducing the number of paper documents involved.

Types of Bank Account Structures

The design of a company's bank account system, like the design of a building, must incorporate function and structure. A well-designed banking system must first handle the immediate banking needs of the company. The system must also be able to adjust to the future growth of the company. Thus, a configuration of bank accounts and services must be developed that provide the required functionality, information reporting, and control that the company needs.

An important objective of a disbursing system is to isolate disbursing from depository activities by moving these distinct functions into separate bank accounts. By separating these funds flows, the tasks of monitoring and forecasting funds flows and balances are enhanced, reconcilement of the bank account to the general ledger is facilitated, and control is improved by keeping the functional responsibilities for disbursing and collecting funds separate.

A logical and important extension of this concept is to separate disbursing into its basic components of accounts payable and payroll. Since these two functions are usually performed separately within a firm, accountability and control are improved by assigning separate disbursing accounts to them.

Once the basic separation of collections from disbursements has been achieved and disbursing activities have been separated by functional organization, the cash manager can then focus on the matter of operating the bank account system. In particular, the question of funding the disbursing accounts becomes critical. The particular method of funding that is selected may dictate additional elements of structural design. For example, using funded imprest accounts would not require any structural changes, while using zero balance accounts (ZBAs) would require such changes.

Imprest Accounts. An imprest account is a demand deposit account (DDA) for which management has preselected a fixed general ledger balance. As disbursements are made out of the account, the general ledger balance is restored by funds from another account. Imprest accounts are most frequently used in situations where the disbursing function is not under direct control of financial managers who need to maintain close review and control over the disbursements being made.

A typical situation in which an imprest account could be used might be a branch office that needs to make local disbursements for postage, petty cash, and salesmen's expense reimbursements. The head office normally pays all occupancy and payroll expenses, but the branch office needs to make modest disbursements on a recurring basis. Accordingly, an imprest bank account would be assigned to the branch, certain branch office personnel would be designated as authorized signatories, and the account would be funded by an initial deposit from the head office. The amount of the initial deposit is normally based on the anticipated dollar volume of disbursements and the frequency of funds replenishment. For example, if the branch is expected to disburse approximately $1,000 per month and the funds are replenished monthly, the imprest balance should be $1,000. Alternatively, if the frequency of funds replenishment is weekly, then the imprest balance should be $250.

The branch initiates the request for funds replenishment and keeps track of its checkbook (general ledger) balance. Typically, the branch would prepare a report, perhaps in the form of a check register that is annotated to indicate the reason for each disbursement, showing the total amount of disbursements made since the last funds replenishment request. The request is sent to the head office financial manager who reviews the reported disbursements and approves the funding request, which is made either by check or EFT. The key to the successful operation of an imprest account is to review closely where the disbursements are going and make the branch office overtly request replenishment of funds. Making perfunctory reviews without challenging the disbursement requests defeats the purpose of an imprest account.

Zero Balance Accounts. A ZBA is a special form of imprest account in which the bank balance is maintained at $0 (or a pegged amount) while the checkbook (general ledger) balance fluctuates as a lower or negative balance. In order to maintain the bank balance at $0, the bank must have a funding source on which to draw automatically to restore the ZBA to a $0 balance daily upon clearing all checks. Normally, this funding source is the concentration account within the same bank, although a ZBA may be funded from an account at another bank.[8]

The main advantage of a ZBA with automatic funding is the ease with which disbursements can be monitored, especially if there are several such ZBAs. The cash manager merely monitors transfers out of the concentration account rather than checking on transactions in each disbursing account.

A "true" ZBA is one that is automatically funded by the bank on the same day the check clears. In order to accomplish this, the bank must post all charges to the account and draw a total before making the transfer; the transfer must occur before the books are closed for the day.

An alternative to a true ZBA occurs when the bank permits the disbursing account to become overdrawn and then makes a manually-generated transfer the next day to cover the overdraft. This system works, but it is not nearly as efficient as the true ZBA.

It should be noted that banks generally charge a small premium for the maintenance of each ZBA. This premium, which covers the cost of daily transfers to the ZBA, is not required with nonZBA DDAs.

A multitiered disbursing ZBA is used when a granddaughter subsidiary's ZBA is funded by its parent's ZBA (the daughter subsidiary), which is

---

[8] See Chapter 8 for a detailed discussion of how the concentration account is funded.

funded in turn by the parent's concentration account. Only a few banks offer multiple tiered ZBAs, but this service can be very helpful.

General Accounts. A general account is a DDA that combines the collection and disbursing functions into a single bank account. No special bank services need be involved, and no special operating techniques are required. Aside from the small additional monthly maintenance charge to maintain separate accounts for collections and disbursements, the use of a general account has no particular advantages. However, because a general account involves more than one type of transaction, reconciling it to the general ledger is often very difficult. Therefore, using a general account is discouraged except when there is a heavy volume of one type of activity (e.g., deposits) and a very light volume of the other type of activity (e.g., disbursements).

Special Situation—Purchase Order Payment Vouchers

Finding uncommon solutions to common challenges is the mark of a creative financial manager. The list of such uncommon solutions to disbursing challenges is probably endless, but the purchase order payment voucher is noted for its general usefulness to a wide range of businesses.

The biggest challenge to large companies is the large volume of small checks needed to pay amounts due to vendors for accounts payable. The "80-20 rule" typically prevails in large companies. The 80-20 rule is where 80 percent of the dollars are paid to only 20 percent of the vendors. Thus, the converse is also true: only 20 percent of the dollars are paid to 80 percent of the vendors, with the average payment being comparatively small.

Several companies have reduced the costs of issuing checks and the frequency of complaints about slow payment by using a "purchase order with payment voucher attached" (POPVA). The payment voucher is actually a blank draft that is attached as a tear-off stub to the purchase order form. The payment voucher states that the draft is valid only if drawn for an amount less than a given limit (often $1,000). Upon receiving the order and executing the shipment, the seller detaches the payment voucher, fills it out for the amount of the sale, and deposits it in payment for the sale. The seller has virtually no accounts receivable and need not even render an invoice.

Buyers generally offer this arrangement only to regular vendors who are proven to be trustworthy and reliable. The buyer typically establishes a file of open purchase orders and compares the amounts of the open purchase orders as the payment vouchers are paid. Payments made within preestablished ranges of dollar amounts are accepted, while payments for more or less than these limits are examined and perhaps discussed with the vendor. The buyer's control is exercised by reviewing the payment voucher drafts as they are presented and immediately terminating any vendor who abuses the system. The loss from any vendor is confined to the limit on the face of the payment voucher. The buyer's savings include reduction of the number of accounts payable checks issued and bigger discounts by putting the payment under the seller's control. These savings generally outweigh any fraud losses, lost payment float, and lost payment terms.

ACCOUNT RECONCILEMENT

No control system can prevent a defalcation by a dishonest person who simultaneously knows how the system operates and has access to the funds. Therefore, reconcilement of all disbursing bank accounts to the general ledger is very important to the cash manager to verify that all of the company's funds are intact and accounted for. Reconciliation of a bank account to the general ledger begins with matching checks paid by the bank against records of checks issued to determine the dollar amount of checks outstanding. For accounts handling a large number of checks (many accounting managers believe the threshhold is 500 to 1,000 checks per month), the matching process is best handled by matching computer files of paid checks against issued checks to determine the amount of outstanding checks.

Many banks provide full Account Reconcilement Service (ARS) in which the company furnishes its checks-issued file to the bank and the bank matches that file against its file of paid checks to produce a file of checks outstanding. In partial ARS, the bank furnishes a computer file of paid checks to the company and the company's data processing department handles the matching process.

SUMMARY

The system of check disbursements has been refined over the past 200 years to enable banks to process the physical paper rapidly, electronically, and efficiently. The system requires that the physical movement of a piece of paper from the payee's depository bank to the payor's drawee bank be very fast. Disbursement float arises from the time a check is placed in the mail until the check is paid against the payor's bank account. The cash manager's task is to orchestrate all of the elements of checks, bank services, and the check clearing process to monitor and control the outflow of funds.

APP. 6-1

BAI Disbursement Questionnaire (Abbreviated Version)

Source: Reprinted from "Controlled Disbursement Questionnaire" (abbreviated version), June 1987 p. 2-5, with permission from the Bank Administration Institute. The full version can be obtained from the BAI at 60 Gould Center, Rolling Meadows, Ill. 60008-4097, telephone (312) 228-2343.

I. Background

   1. Do you offer controlled disbursing? If so, how long have these services been available?

   2. Through what means do you provide controlled disbursing services: main office, branches, affiliates, correspondents, other?

   3. How many locations do you use for controlled disbursing? Please provide the name and location of the institution that appears on the check and its transit routing code for each controlled disbursement facility. Is this a city point, RCPC, or country point?

   4. What measures are you willing to take to minimize or eliminate any potential exposure arising as a result of using an affiliate or correspondent?

   5. What is the capitalization level of your bank, affiliate, or correspondent used for controlled disbursing?

   6. Please provide the number of active customers to whom you provide controlled disbursing services and the total number of accounts used by those customers.

   7. Please provide the average daily dollar and item clearing volumes and the number of accounts (and/or subaccounts) used by your largest controlled disbursement customer. (Based on controlled disbursement item volume.)

II. Presentation

   1. For each controlled disbursement site, how many presentments are made by the Fed? When are the first and last presentments made (EST)? What percent of the dollars are received at each presentment? What percentage of items are received at each presentment? What is the average daily total dollars and items at each controlled disbursement site?

   2. For each controlled disbursement site, does the facility also receive a presentment from the local clearinghouse? At what time is it received each day? What is the latest time that an item can be presented and still charged to the account on the current day?

   3. Do you accept over-the-counter presentments after the notification of cut-off hour? If yes, how is this handled?

4. As a matter of policy, does your controlled disbursing facility accept direct sends from correspondent banks? If not, do you accept any direct sends on an exception basis? If direct sends are accepted, what is the presentment deadline? When must your bank be notified that a direct send will be presented?

5. Please specify any days (regular or holiday) on which the disbursing location(s) would be closed or would not receive cash letters.

6. Has your controlled disbursement point(s) been designated as a High Dollar Group Sort (HDGS) endpoint? If so, how has this affected your controlled disbursing service? If not, do you expect this to happen, and when?

7. Is your controlled disbursement endpoint surveyed by Phoenix-Hecht's Continuous Check Clearing Study? If you have made more than one point, which points are surveyed? Please provide your own bank's specific Phoenix-Hecht clearing times from the most current survey available.

8. What options for notification and funding exist in the event of a second presentment?

9. What internal or external factors might have a significant impact on your controlled disbursement services over the next two or three years?

III. Processing

1. What is your capacity in terms of dollar and item volumes for each of your controlled disbursing facilities? At what percent of dollar volume capacity do you currently operate? Of item volume?

2. Are damaged and/or rejected items re-entered into the system manually or automatically? When are they re-entered? Once reprocessed, are reject items included in the morning notification call?

3. Where is the processing of disbursement items handled, and who does the processing? What is the title and physical location of the individual who will interface with us on the notification call and on any problems that may arise?

4. How long does it take you on average to process the checks presented for your controlled disbursement customers?

5. What equipment do you use to process (sort) disbursement checks?

6. What back-up arrangements exist in case of system failures?

7. Is the operations area that supports your controlled disbursing activity separate and distinct from the bank's main operations center?

8. Are any outside service bureaus used for any portion of your controlled disbursement services?

9. Where are accounting and reconcilement functions performed?

10. How does your operations area assign priority to timely processing?

IV. Notification

1. At what time do you normally notify customers of their daily clearings? What is the earliest you are able to make the daily notification? What is your latest deadline? How many notifications are made to each customer?

2. On average, what percent of the dollars and items are included in the notifications?

3. If you have more than one controlled disbursement location, are there different deadlines for each point?

4. How many times have you missed notification deadlines and by how much in a recent 90 day period? Please specify the dates of the 90 day period.

5. Is your Federal Reserve office able to provide you with electronic notification of the cash letter to be presented each day? If so, do you take advantage of this? What level of detail is available? At what time is the information provided to you? Does the transmission represent 100 percent of all items presented including reject/damaged items?

6. By what methods can you notify your customer of the amount of the checks to be charged to their account? Does the method selected affect the notification time? What is the preferred method by the majority of your customers?
   Telephone ....
   Automated Balance Reporting...............
   Telex or TWX ....
   Other (please specify).....................

7. Do you anticipate any changes occurring that will affect your notification times?

8. What type of detail is available on same-day notification (e.g., total debits)?

9. Does notification of daily clearings (or funding requirements) include both check and Automated Clearing House debits?

V. Funding Methods

1. What options do you give to your customers for funding their controlled disbursement accounts? Explain each method.

2. Which method of funding do the majority of your customers use? How many customers and accounts are funded by each method? Which method do you prefer?

3. For those funding mechanisms which result in next-day funds, do you require compensation for the availability delay? If so, please explain.

4. Do you guarantee coverage of disbursement requirements through your flagship bank should a funding problem arise?

5. Must a master account be maintained at the flagship bank for funding purposes?

6. Do you offer multitiered zero balance subaccounts that may be funded automatically from a single master account? Is there a limit to the number of subaccounts for each parent? Where is the master account located and what transfer mechanism funds the subsidiary account? How many tiers of accounts can you provide?

7. Do you request that customers maintain imprest balances in their controlled disbursement accounts? At what levels? Can these balances be used to pay for services?

8. If rejects and damaged items are not re-entered into the system in time to be included in notification, how is the resultant overdraft handled?

9. What procedures are used to resolve overdrafts caused by funding failures as a result of improper funding from your customers? As a result of the bank's error or delay in notification?

10. If interest on overdrafts is assessed, what rate is used?

11. Does your bank automatically transfer funds to cover checks clearing the controlled disbursement account, or does the customer make the transfer?

VI. Disbursement Services

1. Do you offer Account Reconciliation Service (ARS) to your controlled disbursement customers? Is it optional?

2. Do you offer both full and partial account reconcilement plans?

3. Do you offer the following service options?
   Data Transmission ....
   Magnetic Tape Output ....
   Diskette ....
   High Order Digit Break ....
   Numeric Sorting of Checks ....
   Check Retention or Destruction ....
   Same Day Advisement of Stop Payments ....
   Automated Balance Reporting of Disbursement Debits ....
   Float Analysis Reports ....
   Microfiche Reports ....
   Microfilm of Paid Checks ....
   Customer Selected Cut-Off Dates ....
   (If not, what cut-off dates are allowed?)
   Please provide sample account reconciliations and account statements.

4. Do you provide special cutoffs as requested? How much notification time is required?

5. What is the normal statement cut-off date? How soon after the cut-off date would we receive our bank statement, cancelled checks, and reconcilement?

6. Is the turnaround time for account reconciliation increased if checks are fine sorted?

7. Does your bank offer "on-line" (terminal entry) stop payment capabilities? What are the methods by which we can input stop payment requests? How is confirmation of a stop payment request transmitted back to us?

8. Can you provide clearing information by both master and subaccount on a daily basis? Can this be effected through an automated as well as manual method? By what method of communication? What time is this information available?

9. Do you offer check retention and storage services? What is the monthly minimum volume?

10. For what length of time are the cancelled checks stored by the bank on-site?

11. For what length of time are the cancelled checks stored by the bank before they are destroyed?

12. Upon customer inquiry, what is the average turnaround time for providing a check copy?

13. What other disbursement services do you offer to your controlled disbursement customers?

14. Do you provide the opportunity for automatic investment of any excess balances left in the controlled disbursement account? If so, does this service move excess balances same-day (the day the excess is created) or does it only move the previous day's excess funds?

VII. Implementation

1. Do you allow controlled disbursement accounts to be used for any other purpose (such as deposits or outgoing wire transfers)? If so, please specify.

2. Do you offer controlled disbursing for consumer-oriented payments, payroll or dividends? If so, please specify.

3. Do you require companies to meet any special operating constraints in order to open controlled disbursement accounts, such as financial and/or operating presence in your area or a prior relationship with your bank? Please be specific.

4. Would new accounts have to be established in order to switch regular disbursing accounts at your bank to controlled disbursing accounts?

5. Is an account required at your flagship bank even if funding is made to your affiliate or correspondent offering controlled disbursing?

6. Do you have an established maximum dollar value limit that may not be exceeded by an individual check? Do you have any restrictions regarding individual check amounts?

7. Do you examine the creditworthiness of prospective controlled disbursement customers?

8. Do you require a back-up line of credit for controlled disbursement customers? Will controlled disbursing activity at your bank infringe upon our ability to borrow under our current line of credit?

9. What lead time is required to open a controlled disbursement account?

10. What formal agreement would we have to sign to institute this service?

11. Are controlled disbursement customers required to purchase other services?

12. Please provide names, addresses and telephone numbers of four references for your controlled disbursement service.

VIII. Pricing

1. Please provide prices for your controlled disbursement service including but not limited to the following:
Flat Monthly Fee
Minimum Service Fee
Account Maintenance
Check Paid
Funding Charge
Daily Clearing Notification
Input to Balance Reporting Systems
Full Reconciliation
Flat Monthly Fee
Minimum Service Fee
Per-Item Reconciled
Partial Reconciliation
Microfiche of Reports
Microfilm of Paid Checks
Fine Sort of Paid Checks
Stop Payment
Archival Storage of Paid Checks
Archival Retrieval of Paid Checks
Data Transmission of Output Reports
Disbursement Float Summary

2. Are there any significant elements of your fee structure that have not been addressed in this section? Please detail.

3. Please provide a pro forma account analysis for the following volume of items, dollar volume and processing requests: (customer to provide)

4. Do you accept both fees and balances and combinations thereof as compensation for your services?

5. If fees are accepted, do you use a different price schedule for fee compensation than for balance compensation?

6. How do you calculate your earnings credit rates? What have those rates been for the past six months? Is the earnings credit applied to the collected or investable balances?

7. Do you deduct Federal Reserve requirements when calculating compensating balance levels? Are they implicit in your earnings credits or explicitly deducted? What are the current Reserve requirements at your bank?

8. Does your bank require balance compensation for uncollected funds?

9. Can excess balances for other relationship services at the same or a different location be used to support all or part of the controlled disbursement service?

10. Please provide the formula for converting service charges to balance requirements.

11. Do you guarantee prices? If yes, for how long?

12. Do you assess a charge for FDIC insurance? What is the assessment?

13. How many days after the month ends are account analyses sent to customer?

Electronic Payment Systems

INTRODUCTION

An electronic funds transfer (EFT) is the transmission of an electronic message to a depository institution instructing it to make a book entry reflecting the transfer of ownership of funds from one depositor to another. Electronic forms of payment have been used for many years because they are faster to effect and settle between payor and payee, cost less to process, and lend themselves to modern technology.

    The cash manager must understand the EFT mechanisms and processes for two principal reasons: to select the most appropriate and cost-effective method of moving funds for each type of business situation, and to initiate the transfer properly in order to ensure its timeliness, accuracy, and reliability.

The form of the message, the electronic medium used, and the resulting advice from the depository to the payee varied. The medium may be a public or a private telecommunications carrier. The message itself may be in structured or unstructured format, it may be encrypted or fully readable, and it may carry authentication or be untested. In initiating an EFT transaction, the cash manager first determines the form and timing of settlement that is most appropriate to the transaction, then initiates the transaction in the transmission mode that achieves that settlement goal. An EFT system is merely a settlement system in which the participants initiate and receive electronic notification of transactions. The important considerations to the cash manager are speed of notification and settlement, and the cost of the transaction. The EFT transaction that must be completed and the recipient notified within a matter of hours is more expensive to process but may be more useful to the parties involved than the EFT transaction that will be settled at the end of the day. Further, single transactions are more expensive to process through the banking system than batches of like-type transactions.

Various EFT systems were developed to improve upon the Federal Reserve's (the Fed's) wire transfer system, which functions as the baseline for all EFT systems. Bankwire, Bankwire II, and Cashwire were three such systems, the last of which discontinued operations in 1986. Fedwire and automated clearing house (ACH) transfers are the only such systems available to all users. Other proprietary systems are available to members of certain groups, such as Clearinghouse Interbank Payments System (CHIPS), operated by the New York Clearinghouse Association, and Petro-Clear, operated by a Houston bank on behalf of a small group of large oil companies for monthly settlement of bulk petroleum transactions. Some may argue whether systems such as CHIPS and Petro-Clear are EFT systems or simply settlement systems.

Settlement Methods

As previously mentioned, an EFT transaction involves the electronic notification of the parties concerning a transaction on the books of an intermediary, usually a bank. Settlement occurs when both sides of the bookkeeping transaction have been completed; that is, when the payor's account has been charged and the payee's account has been credited. The timing of these two steps varies, depending on the EFT method used.

There are three fundamentally different EFT settlement methods available:

1. Immediate simultaneous settlement, such as Fedwire;

2. Delayed settlement, such as CHIPS; and

3. Value-dated settlement, such as in ACH transactions.

Immediate Simultaneous Settlement. In immediate simultaneous settlement, such as the Fed's Fedwire system,[1] the depository institution reduces the balance in the account of the payor and increases the balance in the account of the payee immediately upon receiving instructions from the payor. In a Fedwire transaction, for example, the depository institution is the Federal Reserve Bank, or two Fed district banks that hold the reserve accounts of the payor and payee depository institutions. When the Fed makes these entries to the books and notifies the payor and payee banks, the entry is irrevocable and settlement is therefore said to be final. The cash manager who needs to effect a payment with immediate and final settlement, as in the purchase of real estate or other assets, repayment of debt, or a corporate acquisition, would most likely use a Fedwire or similar transfer.

As shown in Figure 7-1, the simultaneous settlement/immediate availability transaction, usually referred to as a wire transfer, is initiated by the payor instructing its bank to pay the payee's bank for the account of the payee. The payor's bank, in turn, instructs its Fed district bank to charge the payor bank's account and to credit the payee bank for the account of the payee.

Delayed Settlement. In delayed settlement, payment transactions involving pairs of payors and payees are accumulated during the day. At the end of the day, the net position of each participant is calculated and settled with a central depository. The central depository will make either a charge or a credit to each participant's account, with the total amount of charges equaling the total amount of credits. Examples of this type system are CHIPS, in which the participants are banks with offices in New York City and the central depository is the New York Federal Reserve Bank, and Petro-Clear, in which the participants are oil companies and the central depository is a designated commercial bank. The cash manager usually does not have access to such systems, although many corporate payments are routed through these systems by the payors' banks. The disadvantage to a corporation in having its payments routed through a delayed settlement EFT system is that the actual moment of final settlement, that is, knowing

---

[1] For a further discussion of Fedwire, see "Wire Transfer Systems," this chapter.

FIG. 7-1

Simultaneous Settlement/Immediate Availability

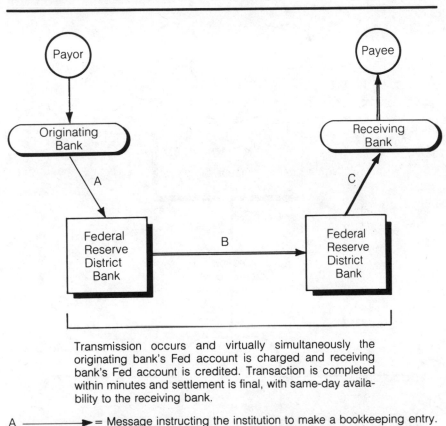

Transmission occurs and virtually simultaneously the originating bank's Fed account is charged and receiving bank's Fed account is credited. Transaction is completed within minutes and settlement is final, with same-day availability to the receiving bank.

A ————▶ = Message instructing the institution to make a bookkeeping entry.
B ════▶ = Message advising that a bookkeeping entry has been made.
C ————▶ = Message advising that a bookkeeping entry has been made and instructing an additional bookkeeping entry be made by addressee.

exactly when the payment has irrevocably been made, is not communicated to the payee.

In the absence of specific instructions from the customer, the payor's bank usually selects the payment method. The customer initiating the payment may specify, however, that a CHIPS transfer is desired rather than a Fedwire transfer if delayed settlement is acceptable and there is a lower bank charge for this type of transfer. Figure 7-2 is a flow chart of a typical delayed settlement transaction.

FIG. 7-2

Delayed Settlement/Same-Day Availability

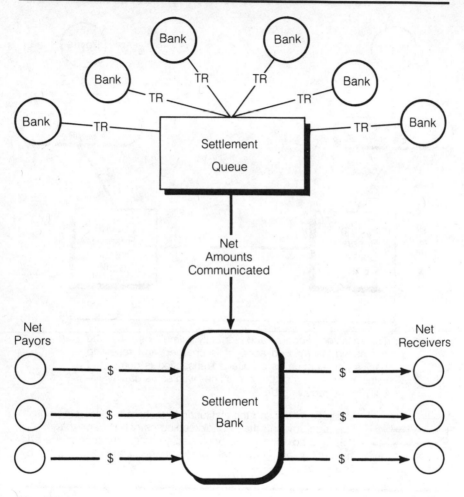

TR = Transaction reports by payors are communicated to central settlement queue throughout the day.

$ = At the end of the day, net amounts are transferred among accounts at Settlement Bank. Net payors are charged and net receivers are credited, with total charges equalling total credits.

Value-Dated Settlement. Value dating is the notation in the payment message that specifies the date on which the bookkeeping entries are to be passed, regardless of the settlement timing and transmission mode. In the absence of a specified date, the presumption is that settlement is to occur on the same date as the initiation of the message. In fact, Fedwire and CHIPS settle the same day. ACH transfers always settle one or more days in the future,[2] and a value date is therefore necessary in the message format. It is a good idea to specify a value date to avoid an incorrect presumption on the part of anyone handling the transaction, even if the intended settlement date is "today."

Value-dated settlements are used in foreign exchange transactions where normal settlement occurs two business days after the contract date (for spot transactions). The payor of dollars may initiate a value-dated transfer on the contract date for settlement two days later. Value dating may, and should, be used in any wire transfer instruction so that the timing of the payment is absolutely clear.

CASH MANAGEMENT SUGGESTION:

Many funds transfers initiated by the cash manager are known at least one day in advance of the transaction. The cash manager should consider using value-dated transfer systems such as ACH to effect these transactions, because the transaction charges are usually considerably lower than for immediate settlement systems such as Fedwire.

Disbursement account funding, especially in controlled disbursing or imprest account situations, is a good example of where value-dated transfer systems are appropriate. Other such examples include payments that must have certainty of settlement, which rules out the use of checks, but where the payment amount and date are known in advance. These would include many types of contractual payments, debt service (principal and interest) payments, and dividend funding.

Transmission Modes

Apart from the settlement method used, there is a significant difference among the different EFT services in the transmission modes, batch or one-at-a-time, that are used. Fedwire, CHIPS, and the Society for Worldwide Interbank Financial Telecommunications (SWIFT) carry payments one-at-a-time. ACHs, on the other hand, carry multiple payments in batches. Of principal concern to the cash manager is the fact that batch transmissions are

---

[2] Several ACHs and their bank and corporate clients seek to enhance the technology and rules to achieve same-day settlement of value. This has not been achieved as of 1988.

considerably less expensive per payment but final settlement is more highly defined in the one-at-a-time mode.

The Fed charges less than $1 to each bank (sending and receiving) that handles a Fedwire transfer. Each payment transaction is carried separately, is fully traceable, and settlement occurs and is final when the receiving bank accepts notice that its Fed district bank is crediting its reserve account.

In ACHs, on the other hand, while both the originating and receiving institutions settle on the same day, the two ends of the actual settlement may occur at different moments. This leaves open the question about precisely when settlement becomes final. The moment of finality is important to the participants in the transaction, including the payor and the payee, in the event that one of the financial institutions or the payor or payee fails during the process. Fortunately, no bank failures in recent years have tested this question, but the Fed and others recognize the potential problems that can arise.

WIRE TRANSFER SYSTEMS

A wire transfer system is characterized by the electronic movement of funds one payment at a time. Three wire transfer systems handle the bulk of the corporate-to-corporate EFT dollar volume: Fedwire, CHIPS, and SWIFT. A fourth payment system, the ACH, also handles a considerable volume, but it is not generally considered to be a wire transfer system because it moves funds in batches of payments, as opposed to the one payment at a time, as in true wire transfer systems.

Fedwire

Fedwire, or the "Federal Reserve Communications System—80," is a communications network linking the Fed's 37 district and branch banks. Fedwire is used to transfer funds and U.S. government securities in book entry form. In a Fedwire transaction, a Fed district bank receives an instruction from one of its depository banks to pay another depository bank by charging the payor's Fed account and crediting the payee's Fed account. If the payment is being made on behalf of a customer rather than for the bank's own account, the message would also state the identity of the depository bank's customer, the identity of the payee bank's customer, and give perhaps a brief message explaining the reason for the payment.

Member banks and nonmember depository institutions with accounts at the Fed may initiate and receive Fedwire transfers. High volume users—those institutions with more than 600 transfers per day—usually use direct computer-to-computer telecommunications links with their nearest Fed Bank or branch. Several hundred financial institutions are on-line with the Fed. Institutions with smaller volumes use dial-up communication links, micro-computers or human-to-human contact over the telephone, or make arrangements with correspondent banks to handle Fedwire transactions for them.

The volume of Fedwire transfers during the 1980s has grown markedly, principally for the following reasons:

- It is a reliable system and is the only way to achieve same-day availability of funds without settlement risk;

- The U.S. government began to make vendor payments of $25,000 or more via Fedwire in 1984; and

- The Monetary Control Act of 1980, which required all depository institutions (including banks, savings and loans, and credit unions) to maintain reserves in accounts with the Fed, gave thousands of depository institutions access to Fedwire.

Initiating Fedwire Transfers. A Fedwire transfer of funds from one depository institution to another via the Fed can be initiated by a cash manager in several different ways, which are best categorized as nonelectronic and electronic notification to the originating bank.

Nonelectronic initiation of a wire transfer occurs when the cash manager telephones the originating bank with payment instructions or delivers payment instructions in a letter, facsimile transmission, or telex. Although facsimile and telex are indeed electronic transmissions, they are not in structured machine-readable formats. Therefore, upon receipt of the messages by the originating bank, the messages must be handled manually.

Electronic initiation of a wire transfer occurs by using a terminal or personal computer to send an electronic message in a structured data format via a modem to the bank, where the message is received on a computer and reviewed, edited, stored, and routed without manual handling. Many cash management banks permit the corporate customer to initiate repetitive funds transfers via a terminal, and some accept instructions via a terminal for non-repetitive funds transfers as well.

Repetitive funds transfers. Cash managers frequently must transfer funds to the same destination bank and bank account. Such situations include funding of local payroll and petty cash accounts, payments of open accounts to large suppliers, or any other large payment to a repetitive end point.

Repetitive funds transfer systems usually use a "line number" approach for their origination. A line number is selected from a "line sheet," which is a paper document properly authorized by company officials that shows all of the pertinent information for each repetitive end point. The line sheet may be used manually for verbal instructions, or can be built into the database of a cash manager's treasury workstation for terminal-initiated wires. As shown in Figure 7-3, the data contained in a line sheet includes

- Name, address, and transit routing number of each receiving bank;
- Name and account number of beneficiary;
- Name and account number of account to be charged by the originating bank.

Each end point is then assigned a number corresponding to the respective line on the form, making the task of communicating with the bank simple by merely referencing a line number instead of having to repeat all of the details of the transfer's destination. Many banks and their customers prefer line sheets because of improved security.[3]

CASH MANAGEMENT SUGGESTION:

When it is necessary to use verbal instructions for repetitive wire transfers, financial managers who want to maintain security as well as flexibility of staffing may authorize the bank to accept instructions from a clerical staff member by reference only to a line number. In this way, management may be assured that the clerk can move money routinely only to certain preauthorized destinations and may do so without involving supervisors or managers. This technique is particularly useful for funding payroll accounts or moving funds from one account to another within a company, where disbursements from the destination bank accounts are adequately controlled. The necessity of repeating all of the data each time for repetitive transfers in a manual mode too often leads to transposition of digits or other errors. Moreover, by merely referring to a line number and stating an amount, a modicum of security is introduced.

Repetitive funds transfers are increasingly being initiated by cash managers using "dumb" (interactive) or "smart" terminals, or personal computers that use funds transfer software. In these cases, the user initiates the

---

[3] For a more detailed discussion of providing security for electronic funds transfers, see the section on security, in this chapter.

FIG. 7-3

Line Sheet for Repetitive Funds Transfer

First National Bank

Customer: This Company, Inc.

Account # 01-1234567-8

Line Number	Destination Bank	Bank Location	TR* Number	Debit or Credit	Account Name	Account Number	Max $ Amount
001	First National Bank	Chicago, Ill.	07100001	CR	This Company, Inc.	52379680	$ 25,000
002	Peoples Bank	E. Overshoe, Kan.	10110047	CR	This Company, Inc.	2134806	10,000
003	New York National Bank	New York, N.Y.	02100946	DR	This Company, Inc.	6497235	100,000
004	New York National Bank	New York, N.Y.	02100946	CR	This Company, Inc.	6497241	100,000
005	New York National Bank	New York, N.Y.	02100946	CR	This Company, Inc.	6497248	50,000
006	Goober State Bank	Rome, Ga.	06130087	CR	ABC Construction Co.	30479206	30,000

*Transit Routing number of destination bank

Approved for use by:
This Company, Inc.

By:_____   Date:_____
Title:
Authorized Signer

By:_____   Date:_____
Title:
Authorized Signer

transfer by making reference to the appropriate line number and inserting an amount. Upon successful completion of certain verification dialogue, the message is transmitted through a modem to the bank's computer, where the transfer is reviewed for accuracy and then entered into the bank's Fedwire terminal. Depending on the level of sophistication of the bank's system, the user may be furnished with confirmation of the completion of the transaction in the form of a Fedwire number or a bank trace number.

Most banks that offer repetitive funds transfer initiation through terminals or personal computers offer price discounts on such transactions of up to 25 percent off the bank's price for nonautomated initiation of wire transfers. This discount is justified because of less human intervention by bank staff and the substantially lower error rate in the completion of transactions. In addition to the transaction price, banks frequently have a fixed monthly charge that covers the cost of maintaining the line number data in a database.

Nonrepetitive funds transfers. Nonrepetitive funds transfers are those that occur only once or too infrequently for the user to set up the account party (payee) on a line sheet, or when management is unwilling to allow the routine payment of funds to a given end point. An example of this is when management lacks confidence in a vendor requiring payment by EFT and is skeptical about recovering an erroneous payment. In such cases, management may insist on using a nonrepetitive technique for initiating the payment in order to assure control over the payment.

Internal auditors have struggled for many years with the question of how to control the initiation of nonrepetitive EFTs. Cash managers typically have been able to give verbal telephone instructions to the bank to move virtually unlimited amounts anywhere in the world, while a check for a few thousand dollars may require the manual signature of one or more corporate officers. A few years ago, a concerned internal auditor at a major Hollywood entertainment company was motivated to suggest that the cash manager be joined on the telephone by another authorized person so that they could speak in unison when ordering a funds transfer. Of course, this suggestion was impractical, but the company used the terminal-based line number method as soon as the bank made it available.[4]

There are alternative methods for providing security over nonrepetitive EFTs, such as telephone call-back and written authorization.

---

[4] Id.

Telephone call-back. In an effort to verify the authenticity of verbal instructions, banks often require that the company designate a second person in the company whom the bank may call to verify the details of the transaction before the transaction is executed. However, there are three problems with this method of security:

1. The individual designated to receive the verification call may not be available to respond;

2. If available, that individual may not have been informed of the transfer details by the time the verification call is received from the bank; and

3. With "call forwarding," the bank cannot be assured of reaching the designated person if a fraud is being perpetrated and the designated person's telephone has been set to forward calls to an accomplice in the fraud.

Written authorization. The use of facsimile transmission ("FAX") has greatly improved the viability of furnishing written authorization to a bank to initiate an EFT. Without FAX, it is usually impossible or impractical to deliver written and signed transfer instructions to any bank that is not located close to the company. FAX enables a cash manager to furnish authentic written instructions immediately to a bank located virtually anywhere in the world.

Moving U.S. Treasury Securities. In addition to funds payments, Fedwire is used by financial institutions to transfer ownership of U.S. government securities. This is one of the services the Fed provides to the U.S. Treasury as the Treasury's fiscal agent. Since 1977, the U.S. Treasury has issued Treasury bills (T-bills) in book entry form; that is, in the form of a credit to an account on the books of the Treasury for each holder of T-bills. The purchase and sale of all Treasury securities (except for those old paper certificates still in the hands of investors) settles by charges and credits to the holders' accounts communicated by the respective financial institutions via Fedwire.

Under a program called Treasury Direct, the Treasury maintains accounts in which investors hold their Treasury securities. The delivery and payment for these securities upon a sale in the secondary market is accomplished over Fedwire. The Treasury pays interest on the notes and bonds via an ACH credit transfer. This program was implemented by the Treasury's Bureau of Public Debt and the National Automated Clearing House Association (NACHA) in 1986. By the end of 1986, the Treasury Direct system had opened some 78,000 investor accounts; this continued at a rapid pace in 1987, as the Treasury added the monthly offering of 52-week T-bills and weekly offerings of 26- and 13-week T-bills to this program.

CHIPS

CHIPS is a computerized telecommunications network owned and operated by the New York Clearinghouse Association for the private use of approximately 140 members with offices in New York City. Members include domestic and foreign banks with agencies and branches in New York, and subsidiaries of U.S. banks with offices in New York that are engaged in international transactions, known as Edge Act companies. CHIPS provides delayed same-day settlement of funds to its participants and handles settlement of roughly 90 percent of all Eurodollar transactions and foreign exchange transactions settled in dollars. It also handles the settlement of foreign trade transactions and domestic transactions. CHIPS' daily volume exceeds 150,000 interbank transfers valued at more than $600 billion.

The CHIPS member banks act for themselves and for their correspondent banks in handling interbank settlements and foreign remittances. As depicted in Figure 7-4, a CHIPS transaction is initiated when a member, Bank A, uses its CHIPS computer terminal to enter a payment order directed to another CHIPS member, Bank B. The CHIPS computer system then:

1. Prepares a record of the transaction;

2. Charges the CHIPS account of the paying member and credits the CHIPS account of the receiving member; and

3. Transmits notice of the transaction to the receiving member.

At 4:30 P.M. (eastern time) each day, the CHIPS computer produces a report showing the net settlement position of each member. Each member will have either a net debit (amount due to the clearinghouse) or a net credit (amount due from the clearinghouse) and is allowed time to review the report. Members with debit balances must pay the clearinghouse by 5:45 P.M. Payment is effected by a Fedwire transfer to the CHIPS settlement account at the New York Fed. When the debit balances are all settled, the clearinghouse transfers funds by Fedwire from the CHIPS settlement account to the members with net credit balances. These payments are usually completed by 6 P.M., and the settlement is final when the receiving institutions are advised of the Fedwire transfer.

FIG. 7-4
CHIPS Payment Transaction

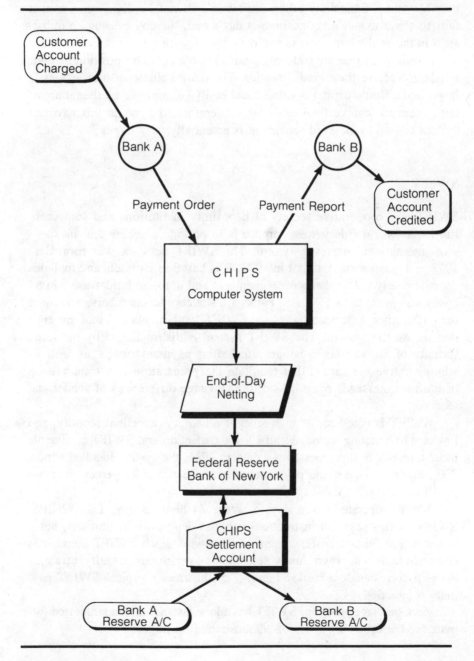

Thus, CHIPS effects transfers with same-day availability, although settlements are delayed until the end of the day. Because of this delay, it is possible that a financially ailing institution will not be discovered until it fails to cover its net debit position at day's end, thereby causing an imbalance in the settlement process and possibly triggering the collapse of other weak institutions that are suddenly plunged into a net debit position by their failure to receive their credit transfer. The daily volume of transactions is huge, and a firm's capital position could easily be impaired by the failure of the system to achieve final settlement. Therefore, the risk in this payment system caused by delayed settlement is potentially very large.

SWIFT

SWIFT is a cooperative society of depository institutions and some central banks worldwide whose purpose is to provide a secure and inexpensive international message system. The SWIFT network was formed in 1973 and became operational in 1977. It is based in Brussels and includes approximately 2,250 shareholder-members and nonshareholder users in 54 countries. More than 150 U.S. banks are shareholder-members, and more than 100 other American banks are SWIFT "submembers" that are entitled to use the system. The SWIFT system is distinguished by the fixed formats of its various messages, including payment orders as well as administrative messages, that facilitate the preparation and transmission of uniform messages regardless of the language differences of sender and receiver.

SWIFT is noted for its high level of reliability, excellent security, and low cost of handling message traffic and payment orders. SWIFT can handle more than one million messages a day. In 1986, the system handled almost 200 million messages and payment orders, reflecting a 22 percent increase in volume over 1985.

SWIFT operates seven days a week, 24 hours a day. Like CHIPS, SWIFT carries payment instructions between depository institutions, but it is not a true funds transfer system like Fedwire. Each SWIFT member is responsible for its own funds settlements, which are usually arranged through correspondent banks. Figure 7-5 illustrates a typical SWIFT payment transaction.

As a message medium, SWIFT has adopted standardized structured formats for the following types of administrative messages:

FIG. 7-5
SWIFT Payment Transaction

European Company's Remittance to U.S. Company

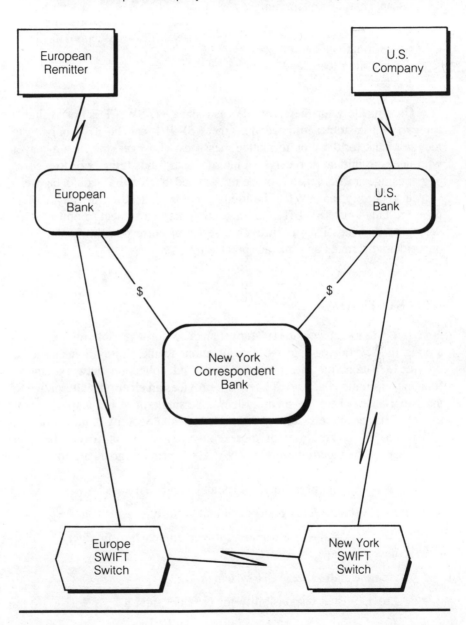

- Funds transfers for customers
- Funds transfers for the bank's account
- Confirmations of foreign exchange transactions
- Confirmations and advices concerning loans and deposits

- Collection advices and payment acknowledgements
- Letters of credit
- Balance reports
- Advices and confirmations of securities transactions

Unfortunately for the corporate cash manager, SWIFT is not available for carrying customer-initiated messages. SWIFT can be used only by a member bank for these preformatted messages. However, the cash manager who needs to initiate or receive an international funds transfer or to receive any message traffic capable of being handled by SWIFT would be well-served to specify that SWIFT be used. If the bank sending the payment or message fails to use SWIFT, the transaction may be subject to unnecessary delays as its winds its way through a series of correspondent banks using unstructured formats and manual processing.

ACH SYSTEMS

NACHA was organized in 1974 by banks to form an interregional link among the several regional ACH associations in the United States, and to provide a nationwide electronic payment and collection network among financial institutions. The ACH network provides an electronic alternative to the paper-based check payment system. The single most influential user of the ACH has been the federal government's Social Security Administration, which was in the forefront of those converting payments from check to direct deposit by electronic means. NACHA's primary goals are to:

1. Establish and promulgate rules and standards;
2. Establish standards for control and security;
3. Act as a catalyst for a market-driven approach to product development;
4. Commercialize the ACH system;
5. Provide fiscal responsibility for NACHA; and to

FIG. 7-6

Annual Volume of ACH Transactions

Year	Number of Transactions (in millions)	Percentage Increase
1983	399.2	12.7%
1984	486.5	21.9
1985	586.0	20.5
1986	743.4	26.7
1987	936.0	25.9

6. Strengthen communication between NACHA and government regulators and legislators, service providers, key trade associations, and industry groups.[5]

In early 1987, NACHA approved the formation of 10 additional ACHs, all owned by individual large banks. As of the end of 1988, there were 29 regional ACHs and 13 private ACHs owned by individual banks and chartered by NACHA. The private ACHs were chartered because of the volume of transactions that these banks generated. Together, the 42 ACHs represent some 17,500 financial institutions, including commercial banks and thrifts, which serve approximately 40,000 companies and government agencies, and millions of consumers. Bankers argue whether the advantages of operating a proprietary ACH, such as greater operational controls and more advantageous cutoff times, outweigh the disadvantage of smaller overall volume, leading to higher fully-burdened costs per transaction. To the company, however, the issue of cost is largely inconsequential. For example, for a company with 10,000 transactions per month, a price difference of one cent per transaction amounts to only $100, hardly a deciding factor compared to the issues of better service, accuracy, and reliability.

The volume of ACH transactions has grown steadily, as shown in Figure 7-6.

Of the 936 million ACH transactions in 1987, 529 million (56.5 percent) were commercial transactions, and 407 million (43.5 percent) were payments involving the Treasury, such as direct deposit of Social Security payments, federal retirement benefits, and other similar credit transfers.

---

[5] NACHA press release, Mar. 16, 1987.

This reflects continued rapid growth in commercial volume, for government volume in 1986 represented 54 percent of the transactions compared to 46 percent commercial.

In addition to these volumes of ACH transactions, uncounted millions of additional transactions were completed without leaving the originating bank because the originators and the receivers of the transfers used the same bank.

As impressive as these volumes and growth rates are, the volume of ACH transactions is small compared to the estimated 45 billion checks written annually in the United States. However, the growth rate of check issuance is slowing, while the growth rate of electronic forms of payment remains high.

Each ACH in the United States[6] is authorized by NACHA to process payments in standardized formats. The processing of substantially all ACH activity (except Calwestern and New York) is handled by the Fed. Calwestern ACH, in California, Nevada, Utah, and Idaho, contracts with a private sector service provider rather than the Fed, and the New York Clearinghouse operates the ACH processing mechanism itself.

It is important to understand the proper use of ACH terms in order to avoid confusion when setting up instructions with banks and others involved in the ACH transaction. The terms "payor" and "payee" are generally not used when discussing ACH payments. The terms "originator" and "receiver" are substituted, and the type of transaction, whether it be a credit transfer or debit transfer, is described. The elements critical to ACH are the routing sequence of the electronic message and the direction in which the funds move. Therefore, if Company A wants to make a payment to Company B using the ACH system, Company A is the originator, the transaction type is a credit transfer, and Company B is the receiver. The originator, Company A, requests its bank (Bank A) to pay Bank B for the account of Company B. Bank A in this transaction becomes the Originating Depository Financial Institution (ODFI), and Bank B becomes the Receiving Depository Financial Institution (RDFI). If the ODFI and the RDFI are each served by different ACHs, then the ODFI's ACH becomes the originating ACH and the RDFI's ACH becomes the receiving ACH. Such is the acronymistic world of ACH. Figure 7-7 depicts how a typical ACH credit transfer takes place.

A different situation might involve an insurance company that initiates an electronic draft (using an ACH debit instead of a paper draft) against the bank account of a policyholder. The insurance company is the originator and

---

[6] See Chapter 3 for listing and locations of ACHs.

FIG. 7-7
ACH Credit Transfer

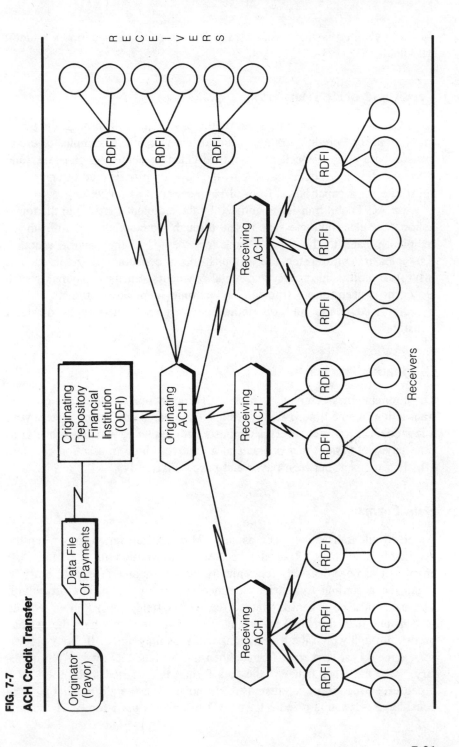

the policyholder is the receiver, and the type of transaction is a debit transfer.

Credit and Debit Transfers

An ACH credit transfer is initiated by the payor and sent through the banking system for "credit" to the account of the recipient. Examples of credit transfers are direct deposit of payroll, dividends, annuities, pensions, and payment of trade accounts payable by the buyer. An ACH credit transfer is a substitute for a paper-based form of payment such as a check.

An ACH debit transfer is initiated by the recipient of funds in the transaction. The electronic message is sent through the banking system from the recipient's bank to the payor's bank for "debit" to the payor's account. Examples of debit transfers are various forms of consumer payments such as insurance, utility, mortgage, and rental payments. Business payments such as cash concentration transfers (electronic depository transfers) and preauthorized dealer and distributor payments are also types of debit transfers.

Origination Process

The company may originate a single ACH transaction or thousands of ACH transactions at one time. ACH is designed as a batch processing system with a low cost per transaction. This contrasts with Fedwire, which is a one-at-a-time payment system that operates at a relatively high transaction cost and effects settlement between payor and payee differently.

Data Formats

An electronic transaction, such as an ACH credit transfer, begins when the originator assembles all of the necessary information in a manner that enables it to be processed electronically by a computer. The data must be organized according to a strictly defined system of syntax and procedure. The data must be organized into discrete data fields (also known as data records and data elements) according to specifications to which the various parties through which the transactions will pass may agree. If those processors agree to use a private format, then the format is known as "proprietary." On the other hand, if the data format is designed to be used by a broad cross section of interested users and made generally available, it is considered a "standardized" format. Data formats used for ACH transactions are standardized under the auspices of NACHA for use by all banks and companies involved in originating, processing, and receiving payment transactions through the ACH system. ACH transactions are originated by a company and processed electronically by as many as two banks and two ACHs. Without standardized data formats, the payment and its related data could not be processed by any party other than the originator.

A company originates an ACH payment by setting up the transaction details in a standardized data format prescribed by NACHA and then communicating that NACHA-formatted transaction to the ODFI. There are five NACHA formats for corporate use:

- Prearranged Payments and Deposits (PPD)

- Cash Concentration or Disbursements (CCD)

- Corporate Trade Payment (CTP)

- Corporate Trade Exchange (CTX)

- CCD Plus Addenda

Prearranged Payments and Deposits. The PPD format is generally reserved for consumer-oriented credit and debit transfers. The bulk of corporate-initiated ACH transactions are for the direct deposit of employee payrolls, in which the data necessary to travel through the banking system is organized according to the PPD format, and for the "automatic bill paying" services of utilities, lenders, and retailers. PPD transactions normally settle two days after initiation, compared to next-day settlement for all other ACH transactions.

Cash Concentration or Disbursements. Cash management funds concentration systems use the CCD format to create electronic depository transfer checks (DTCs).[7] The CCD transfer is settled next-day, and is a relatively simple and straightforward data format. While relatively few companies pay their trade payables electronically, the CCD format is increasingly used for intercorporate ACH payments because of its simplicity and the ability of virtually all financial institutions to initiate and receive it.

Corporate Trade Payments. The CTP format was introduced in 1983 as a pilot involving a few large companies that transacted a considerable volume of business among themselves. Since that time, the CTP format has been

---

[7] See Chapter 5 for a detailed discussion of funds concentration systems and depository transfer checks.

released by NACHA and is available for use by any company whose bank can process it. The CTP format can be used to make a payment (theoretically either a credit or a debit transfer, although very few actual debit transfers in CTP format are originated) with as many as 4,990 addenda records (roughly comparable to invoices). An addenda is a structured data format containing the details concerning the payment, such as the invoice number being paid, invoice amount, and credits and other adjustments. The CTP-formatted transaction settles next-day. The CTP payment format does not have a high volume usage, mainly because of the following problems:

1. Relatively few banks, perhaps not more than 200, can originate or receive the CTP format;

2. CTP lacks the capability for encryption and authentication, which are considered important by many companies and government agencies;

3. The CTP format is rigid, with data fields of fixed lengths, and is therefore an inefficient use of data storage and transmission capacity; and

4. Few companies are willing to develop the interface and translation capability to handle the CTP format, usable only with the bank, when they already use other standardized formats for communicating with their trading partners.

Corporate Trade Exchange. In 1987, NACHA authorized the use of the CTX format, which modifies the CTP format to overcome the previously described drawbacks. Some banks began almost immediately to develop the capability to handle the CTX format because they perceived that it would be more acceptable to companies effecting corporate trade payments than the CTP format.

CTX retains the parts of the NACHA format that enable the message to travel through the banking system: the file header and trailer records that form an electronic envelope surrounding the data being transmitted. CTX has replaced the NACHA format for the payment message with a standardized ANSI X12 format used by increasing numbers of companies in their normal dealings with their trading partners (both suppliers and customers), not merely their banks. The use of cross-industry standardized formats for business data interchange is called Electronic Data Interchange (EDI), of which the NACHA formats for payment transactions are a subset.

In EDI, the standardized formats for data exchange are developed by the Accredited Standards Committee X12 of ANSI. NACHA borrowed the

X12 standardized electronic document called the "payment order/remittance advice" (transaction set 820), incorporated it into NACHA's CTP communications envelope, and named the result the CTX format.

CTX has an advantage over CTP in that it can still flow through the banking system; increasing numbers of companies are capable of reading and translating from the X12 format to their own internal formats for automatic processing and updating of the payment data; the X12 format uses variable length data fields; fields that are not needed in the particular transaction can easily be suppressed; and the X12 format is capable of being encrypted and authenticated.

CCD Plus Addenda. The U.S. Treasury, which is the disbursing agent for hundreds of U.S. government bureaus, departments, and agencies, had been using EFT (principally Fedwire) since 1983 to make large payments to vendors. In 1987, the Treasury expanded its "Vendor Express" program for paying vendors and reduced its costs by introducing the use of ACH payments. The Treasury selected the CCD format because virtually all financial institutions can accept it, whereas few institutions can receive the CTP format, and the PPD format is reserved for consumer payments.

The standard CCD format uses a structure of 94 characters, of which up to 80 characters may be used free-form to describe the transaction. This limited amount of space, however, is not in a "standardized machine-readable" format. In seeking a flexible way to expand its use of EFT in paying vendors, the Treasury adapted the CCD data format by inserting an addenda record into the free-form space in the CCD and terming it "CCD Plus Addenda." The Treasury created the addendum by borrowing a data segment from the X12 payment order/remittance advice called the RMR ("remittance advice") data segment. The Treasury then advised its vendors that henceforth (after July, 1987, subject to the phasing-in of this program over a period of a year or more) it would send the payment through the banking/ACH system (originating through the New York Fed) using the CCD format, with the RMR data segment in the addenda. This addenda contains up to 80 usable characters of machine-readable data and is flexible, yet structured. It enables a computer with EDI translation software to read and interpret the message, and then feed the remittance data into the funds application function of the vendor's accounts receivable software.

In introducing CCD Plus Addenda, the Treasury made it clear that it was relying upon the banks and their customers to work out methods for passing remittance data contained in the addenda from the banks to the customers. Some banks have complained that they do not care to be in the data transmission business, and that the CCD Plus Addenda data is not in the banking system's NACHA format. Bank customers who are the vendors to the government sometimes complain that their customer, the government, is being cavalier about providing the payment data.

Many expect, however, that following an initial transition period the banks will routinely begin to capture and pass on the RMR data segment; and those customers to whom it is important will become able to receive, read, and interpret that data and feed it automatically into their funds application programs for the automatic update of accounts receivable.

With the advent of the CCD Plus Addenda and the CTX formats, companies that had not previously been involved in electronic payments have now become exposed to the possibility of receiving ACH payments. As technology leaders in the banking and corporate communitites begin to embrace EFT, an increasing number of companies will be asked by their customers to receive trade payments through ACH. Some additional factors that encourage the use of EFT for the payment of trade accounts include:

- Sharp reductions in disbursing float relating to paper-based disbursements since 1980;

- Increases in postage and labor rates for paper-based disbursements;

- The evolution and proliferation of EDI in the procurement and selling processes that drive the accounts payable and accounts receivable functions; and

- The advent of relatively inexpensive and effective EDI management software to control the data flows between trading partners and manage and translate the payment flows between the company and its bank.

Data Transmission

The corporation's data processing department is usually responsible for building or buying a system that automatically generates a data file in the appropriate NACHA format from the company's internal payroll, accounts payable, accounts receivable, or funds concentration application software. The data file is then delivered or transmitted to the bank via telecommunications.

For many companies, this is the first—and perhaps the only—application of data communications, and some are reluctant to rely on data transmission for fear of having the integrity or confidentiality of the data breached. Instead, they prefer to deliver a magnetic tape or disk by hand, risking delay and failure to meet delivery deadlines, and loss or physical damage to the tape or disk enroute to the bank's processing center.

While a cash manager need not be fully conversant with data processing or other technical terminology, evidence indicates that the cash manager's future involvement in data systems, telecommunications, and computers will be increasing fairly rapidly. Therefore, it is desirable that the cash manager have a basic level of understanding of certain terms and concepts.

Data communication from the company's mainframe computer to the bank's computer can be achieved at a high speed (4,800 or 9,600 baud (described in the following list) in synchronous (also known as bisynchronous) mode, which tends to safeguard the accuracy and integrity of the data. Many banks also offer the facility to receive transmissions from the customer's personal computer at 1,200 or 2,400 baud. This computerspeak may be defined as follows:

- "Baud" is a unit of measurement of the rate of information transfer. One baud is approximately one bit per second.

- "Bit" is the smallest unit of information recognizable by a computer, and is derived from the contraction of the words "binary digit." A bit is not to be confused with a "byte."

- "Byte" is a character of information that is normally composed of eight bits and usually encoded in the ASCII format.

- "ASCII" is the acronym for American Standard Code for Information Interchange, developed by the ANSI accredited Standards Committee X3. Another standard form of code is EBCDIC, for Extended Binary Coded Decimal Interchange Code, which is used internally in a mainframe computer and converted to ASCII before being transmitted to most networks and mini- and microcomputers.

- "Bisynchronous" (also known as "synchronous") mode is more a protocol than a type of transmission, in which a defined block of data is sent in a burst. The receiving computer awaits the block of data, receives it, tests it to see that all data elements are intact and undisturbed from their original configuration, and either accepts the data block or returns a message to the sender that the data has been altered in transmission (a negative acknowledgement). Therefore, synchronous data transmission affords a high degree of integrity to the data being sent.

- "Asynchronous" transmission is the mode used by personal computers to transmit data and is relatively slow (300 to 2,400 baud). Speed is retarded because each byte, or character, is transmitted individually, and the receiving computer acknowledges the receipt of each one. However, there is no way for the receiver to verify whether the data has been altered in transmission, so the accuracy of the transmission needs to be controlled by some other means, principally through the use of accounting controls such as hash totals. Personal computer communications use this transmission mode almost exclusively.

Prenotification

To ensure that the data files are formatted correctly, and that the ODFI, ACH, and RDFI can read and accept the files, NACHA rules require that in using certain types of transactions, the originator must "prenotify" the receiver at least 10 calendar days in advance of the first "live" transaction. Those transactions that require prenotification are PPD credits and debits, CTP debits and CTX debits, and certain types of point-of-sale (POS) transactions that use the ACH. Prenotification involves initiating the intended transaction, such as a credit transfer for a payroll, for a zero-dollar amount. If any party along the route (ODFI, ACH, or RDFI) is unable to process the transaction, that party is obligated to notify the originator. A common occurrence in "prenotes" is for the originator to receive no negative responses, indicating that the transaction could have been completed if it had carried funds. However, when the first live transaction is initiated, it may not be completed. Investigation often reveals that the RDFI is a small bank that receives its notification of credit by mail from its Fed district bank, and that notice is received days after the payday. Consequently, the payee believes that the employer/originator failed to effect payment on a timely basis. This type of problem unfortunately has no easy resolution other than for the RDFI to find a more timely way to receive notices of credit from its Fed, or for the payee to find a bank that has already solved this problem.

Routing

Upon receiving the transmission from the originating company, the ODFI verifies the file header and control records, and then strips the on-us payments (i.e., those payments in the file that are destined for accounts within that bank) from the file. These payments are held in a queue until the value date. The remaining payments are immediately transmitted to the regional ACH serving the bank. The regional ACH then sorts the payments into files destined for RDFIs in its region and for other ACHs, and then transmits the payment data files to those RDFIs and to the other ACHs that serve the other RDFIs for which there are payments.

Timing

NACHA rules require that PPD credit transfers be originated at least two business days prior to the value date. That is, for a Friday payroll, the originating company must furnish the payment data file to the ODFI by Wednesday. In fact, the ODFI may specify that the file be received no later than noon or 1 P.M. Wednesday. This allows the ODFI time to read and process the file, to contact the originator to resolve any errors, discrepancies, or readability problems before the close of business on Wednesday, and to strip off the on-us payments. On Wednesday night, the ODFI passes the payment data files to its ACH. On Thursday, the ACH processes the file and transmits payment data file to the RDFIs and the other receiving ACHs, which in turn, process and transmit payment data files to the RDFIs in their respective regions.

NACHA rules further require that a PPD credit transfer reach the RDFI the night before settlement. This allows the RDFI time to credit the deposit to the receiver's account as of the opening of business on the value date. It is important that the consumer/payee have the credit available as of the opening of business in order to enable the teller to cash the payee's check or the ATM to dispense cash on payday. Although this is a marketing rather than a technical issue, it is one that every bank must face. Therefore, NACHA has attempted to create a "level playing field" with this rule, and it is up to each financial institution to decide whether to take advantage of the rule.

RDFIs have the option of making an actual credit posting or a memo posting on the night preceding the value date for a credit transfer. The memo posting fools the bank's ATMs and teller terminals into believing that the money is actually in the account first thing in the morning. If the RDFI makes an actual posting, then it is technically making an advance to its customer by crediting the customer's account one day before settlement. Despite the cost of doing this, however, a memo posting may be even more costly for the RDFI—software may be needed to make and control the memo posting. And to do neither—to wait until the evening of the value date to post the credit—will unnerve the customer who needs access to his payroll deposit on payday.

The failure of the receiving bank to post the deposit or otherwise to make it available to the customer is a matter between the customer and the bank. However, if the customer is an employee of the cash manager's company, and the employee complains about a late payroll, the company suddenly becomes involved.

CASH MANAGEMENT SUGGESTION:

When implementing direct deposit of payroll, which NACHA calls "SurePay" and many banks have renamed with their own proprietary names, the employer should warn employees that many small banks and thrifts may not have the capability to reflect direct (ACH) deposits into their customers' accounts until after the close of business on payday. The employer should point out that this is dependent solely upon the capabilities of the employee's bank and is beyond the control of the company and the originating bank

NACHA rules are less stringent in business-to-business transfers than in business-to-consumer transfers. Transactions using the business formats (CCD, CTP, CTX, and CCD Plus Addenda) may settle as early as the next day, or may be warehoused by the ODFI or ACH for up to 30 days. Same-day settlement was not yet a reality as of the end of 1988, but the Fed and NACHA were developing rules and technology to accomplish them. Same-day settlement would significantly reduce risk in the ACH payment system, but would present a threat to the volume of Fedwire transactions. Since the Fed operates nearly all of the ACHs, however, the Fed's attitude toward same-day ACH settlement remains to be seen. Officially, the Fed expects sometime in the future to see 24-hour, round-the-clock processing of ACH transactions, which would require mechanisms to settle ACH transactions the same day they are originated, probably at the end of the day. But this is not expected to occur in the near future. [8]

For next-day settlement, the ODFI sets a receiving deadline early in the afternoon of the day preceding settlement and then uses the rest of the afternoon to strip off on-us transactions and send the remainder of the payment data file to the regional ACH by that evening. During the night, the ACH prepares payment data files for its members and other ACHs, and these are transmitted early the next day and retransmitted by receiving ACHs to the RDFIs later in the day. The RDFIs then credit or debit the receiver's accounts that evening.

---

[8] From a speech by Bruce J. Summers, senior vice-president of the Federal Reserve Bank of Richmond, Va. at the National Corporate Cash Management Association Annual Conference, Atlanta, Ga. (Nov. 16, 1987).

Pricing

While the ODFI is free to set its own charges for originating an ACH transfer, it is constrained to certain minimums because it must pay for each transaction that it transmits through its regional ACH. It is also constrained by its internal processing costs. OFDIs often charge a few cents per transaction plus a flat fee per transmission. The cost to a bank of acquiring and installing modern mainframe ACH processing software can run in excess of $1 million. Banks that have invested in the most modern ACH processing software are usually the most cost-efficient, and they generally seek high volumes of transactions over which to amortize their software costs. To encourage these high volumes, banks often shave prices to less than $0.10 per transaction, and frequently quote prices to hundredths of a cent.

A bank's cost of processing ACH transactions is a function of its share of the market and its own internal processing efficiency. Since ACH transactions are measured in terms of pennies with banks seeking high volumes, pricing differences among competing banks typically do not amount to much. Moreover, upon negotiation, banks can often meet a competitor's lower price. While price, therefore, is not often a critical factor to the cash manager in selecting a bank to originate ACH transactions for a company, it may be useful to review some of the underlying costs and economics of a bank's ACH operations.

EXAMPLE: Two banks are competing for the same PPD formatted direct deposit payroll of Company *A*, located in Los Angeles. Bank No. 1 is a California-based bank with approximately a 30-percent share of the California market. Bank No. 2 is a New York bank that can accept deposits only in New York. Company *A* has no employees located in New York; 5,000 employees are located in California and 7,000 employees are located elsewhere in other states. The respective ACHs serving Bank No. 1 and Bank No. 2 charge their ODFIs $0.02 per transaction. Both banks use similar modern systems to process the incoming transactions at an internal cost of $0.01 per transaction. Therefore, both banks have a cost of $0.03 per transaction.

Bank No. 1, in the company's home market, enjoys a cost advantage over Bank No. 2 because of its involvement in the same market as its depositors. Bank No. 1 pays its ACH for only 10,500 transactions compared to the 12,000 transactions that Bank No. 2 turns over to its ACH, because some 30 percent of the 5,000 California employees' payments are "on-us" when originated through Bank No. 1; that is, they go to employees' accounts in Bank No. 1. Bank No. 2 is at a

FIG. 7-8

Comparative Costs of ACH Transfers for Bank in the Market and Bank Outside the Market

	In the Market (Bank No. 1)	Outside the Market (Bank No. 2)
Total ACH payments	12,000	12,000
Less: On-us (30% of California employees)	1,500	-0-
Payments passed to ACH	10,500	12,000
ACH charge per payment	$0.02	$0.02
Total ACH charge	$210.00	$240.00
Effective ACH charge per payment*	$0.0175	$0.0200
Internal charges per payment	$0.0100	$0.0100
Total cost per ACH payment	$0.0275	$0.0300

*12,000 payments/Total ACH charge

disadvantage because it has no accounts from employees of Company *A* and must therefore clear all 12,000 payments through its ACH.

In processing the 12,000 transactions it would receive from Company *A*, Bank No. 1 would first strip off the 1,500 or so (30 percent of 5,000 payments) on-us transactions. In this case, Bank No. 1 is both the ODFI and the RDFI. Bank No. 1, therefore, has an effective cost of only $0.0275, compared to Bank No. 2, which has a cost of $0.03. For Bank No. 2, or a smaller bank in the company's home market, to compete effectively on price with Bank No. 1, it must reduce its price. Figure 7-8 depicts the comparative cost structures of the two banks.

Bank No. 1 has a further advantage. By being located in a time zone further west than Bank No. 2, Bank No. 1 can usually offer a later cutoff time for receipt of the data transmission to initiate the payroll transaction. This could be more important than price to Company *A* in managing the production schedules in its payroll and data processing departments, particularly when a quarter-cent difference on 12,000 transactions per month is only $30.

Settlement

Settlement of an ACH funds transfer occurs on the value date. In a credit transfer, the originator's account with the ODFI is charged and the receiver's account with the RDFI is credited. The opposite occurs on the value date in a debit transfer. The ODFI and the RDFI settle with their respective ACHs through their Fed clearing accounts.

A considerable payment risk exists in the ACH system because of its need for future settlement. Because settlement occurs one or more days after the transaction is originated, there is a risk (in a credit transfer) that either the originator or the ODFI could fail to pay on the value date.

> EXAMPLE: A company's payroll is payable on Friday, for which it gives its originating bank the related payment files Wednesday at noon. That evening, after stripping off the on-us payments, the originating bank transmits the remaining payments to its ACH with the contractual commitment to settle in available funds on Friday. The RDFIs accept the payment orders on Thursday and prepare to credit their customers, the employees, on settlement day, Friday. Meanwhile, as the payment orders are flowing through the ACHs and banks on Thursday, the employer files a petition in bankruptcy and fails to fund the ODFI on Friday. By that time it is probably too cumbersome and too late to recall all of the payments, particularly if there are hundreds or thousands directed to banks all over the country.
>
> To safeguard against this possibility, most ODFIs review their customers' financial condition and approve the credit of their originating customers. Other ODFIs insist on receiving payment or cash collateral at the time of origination of the ACH transfer.

CASH MANAGEMENT SUGGESTION:

> The cash manager should be alert to any instance where the ODFI requires the premature funding of an ACH credit transfer, and should endeavor to avoid any such prefunding requirement if the company's credit standing is good. The bank is entitled to be satisfied as to the credit risk involved, but it is not entitled to prefunding unless the transaction pricing is adjusted to reflect the benefit derived by the bank from the prefunding. A company that prefunds its ACH credit transfers should attempt to negotiate the payment of interest by the bank on the amount of funds for the time period involved.

Receiving Process

NACHA has no specific requirements covering notification by an RDFI to its receiver/customer that funds have been received in a credit transfer; therein lies a problem. The internal computer software systems used by most banks, including major cash management banks, have lacked the capability to spin the amount and data relating to an incoming ACH payment to the bank's balance reporting system. Consequently, many of the larger banks began in 1987 to invest substantial sums to upgrade their software to overcome this challenge to notify their customers of incoming ACH transactions on a timely basis.

Most of the 17,000 financial institutions that belong to regional ACHs joined in order to be able to receive Social Security deposits and federal retirement payments. With a modest investment in software, a bank can run the PPD formatted data directly into its demand deposit accounting (DDA) system to post the credit to the customer's account. That same software usually also accommodates the receipt of credit transfers in CCD format; however, few software installations are capable of providing notification of the CCD or PPD payment to the customer except at the end of the month in the bank statement. Since this is unacceptable to most corporate cash managers, banks have had to develop systems—often makeshift—to generate same-day notification of the receipt of an ACH credit transfer. Such notice, together with information as to the identity of the originator and the reason for the payment, is critical to the cash manager and the credit manager.

This data typically has not been nearly as important to the consumer, for the payments are expected on a certain date and in a certain amount and the receiver usually needs to know very little administrative information about the payment. The amount of the Social Security or federal retirement payment, or the amount of the payroll deposit is anticipated, and the customer merely wants to receive confirmation that it has been credited to the customer's account. Business firms, on the other hand, receive remittances from many different sources with unpredictable timing, and the particular invoice or contract number to which the funds are applied must be identified. Furthermore, business-to-business payments often reflect adjustments and allowances taken by the remitter, and these must be identified along with the payment.

The RDFI in a business-oriented credit transfer clearly must deliver the complete data in an accurate and timely manner to the receiver. By now, many banks have developed the capability to deliver this data electronically via their balance reporting systems. Other banks with relatively small CCD or CTP volumes simply notify their customers of the data by telephone or printed advice. While this may be an inefficient way to end a high-tech ACH payment transaction, it may be cost-effective for both parties in a low volume environment.

SIMULTANEOUS MOVEMENT OF DOLLARS AND DATA

As described earlier in this chapter, the NACHA formats are designed to enable payment dollars to flow through the banking system together with the related payment information. The receiver of the funds must have the data in order to know the source and reason for the payment. In business transactions, the CCD format that was designed for limited application has limited space for the data. The CTP format, on the other hand, was designed to carry a considerable amount of data, but is not widely accepted.

The CTX format allows the company the flexibility to keep the data together with the payment as it travels through the payment system. The company has the option of wrapping the X12 formatted data in the NACHA-formatted electronic envelope and transmitting the data package to the bank; or it can transmit the unwrapped data in X12 format to the bank, which can then wrap it in the electronic envelope.

Of course, the bank must be capable of handling this enveloping function. Also, as an RDFI the bank must be able either to pass on to its receiver/customer the wrapped package or unwrap it and pass on the X12 message, depending on the customer's needs and capabilities. The receiver accepts the data, unwraps it from the NACHA envelope if necessary, and enters the X12 payment data into its own accounts receivable funds application system. Companies capable of handling X12 data first run the data through a translator (computer software that translates from the X12 format to the company's own internal data format), and then into the accounts receivable funds application software system.

Some banks choose not to acquire the technology and systems to handle the data. This is somewhat shortsighted and unfortunate because today's payment system is a data transmission and processing system, even if paper checks still form its base. Banks are linked to the Fed by computers and use data transmissions throughout the day. Banks electronically capture payment data from the magnetic ink character recognition (MICR) line of the check and the deposit slip, and use computers rather than quill pens to post entries to accounts. It is also possible that as EDI gathers steam, it may cause an explosion of demand for electronic payments that neither the banks nor the corporate financial managers had expected.

Some players adopt the electronic transmission technology but choose not to link the data and the dollars together. If the dollars and data are separated and travel different routes from payor to payee, then they may not arrive at their destination at the same time. Sometimes the dollars will arrive before the data, pleasing the cash manager but keeping the credit manager in the dark. Since the funds cannot be applied to update the open accounts receivable without the available data, the customer/payor may suffer delays in the shipment of goods. If the remittance data arrives first, the credit manager has a dilemma; this is tantamount to the customer saying, "Trust me, the EFT is in the ACH."[9]

Nevertheless, companies often find it simpler to separate the dollars from the data. They send the dollars through the banking system and ACH using the CCD format for the payment, merely making reference to a message that has been placed into the receiver's electronic mailbox.

An electronic mailbox is an electronic repository for information that eliminates the need for two trading partners or a bank and its customer to coordinate data transmission schedules. Electronic mailbox service is provided by a number of value-added networks (VANs),[10] that allows a user to send to multiple receivers in one session, and to receive and consolidate messages from multiple senders.

In separating the dollars from the data, the payor simultaneously originates an ACH credit transfer and transmits a remittance advice to the payee's electronic mailbox using a standardized format such as X12 or other standards used in certain industries. This keeps the payment mechanism simple, and virtually all banks can handle the CCD formatted payment. The data, which is translated from the payor's native in-house format to the standardized format, is transmitted to the payee's electronic mailbox without having to be wrapped in some other envelope. Moreover, for security purposes, the data can be encrypted and authenticated, or both.

The receiver/payee (in a credit transfer) logs onto the VAN periodically during the day and extracts the messages from its electronic mailbox. This presents a challenge, however. Because the payment and the data traveled separate routes, they must be reconciled by the receiver/payee before being used. The receiver must be assured that the amount of the payment traveling through the banking system agrees with the amount reflected in the data that traveled a different route. Otherwise, the receiver/payee's funds receipts and funds applications may be out of balance.

---

[9] Presentation by Jack Shaw, EDI Strategies, Inc., at the Cash Management Association of Southern California's INFO/EXPO '87, Los Angeles, Cal. (May 5, 1987).

[10] Some of the larger value-added networks that routinely handle X12-formatted message traffic and offer electronic mailbox services are: General Electric Information Services (GEIS), Rockville, Md.; McDonnell Douglas EDI Systems Company, Hazelwood, Mo.; IBM Information Network, Tampa, Fla.; ORDERNET division of Sterling Software Corp., Columbus, Ohio; REDINET division of Control Data Corp., Lakewood, Ohio; Kleinschmidt, Inc., Deerfield, Ill., Transettlements, Inc., Atlanta, Ga., CompuServe, Columbus, Ohio.

A possible solution to this dilemma lies with a few major banks that may provide the VAN and other value-added services necessary to make the system work as previously described, while sparing the originator and the receiver from the need to gear up technologically.

Standardized Formats

There is little disagreement on the need for, and value of, standardized machine-readable formats for the communication of information among trading partners and banks. This is true for buyers and sellers using X12 or other industry-specific formats to carry out the purchase/sale transaction; for banks using NACHA or Bank Administration Institute (BAI) formats to transmit data among themselves concerning payments, collections, and funds concentration; and for banks and companies to communicate with each other as the terminal points in the payment/ collection timeline. Many industries have developed proprietary standard formats for data communication among their members, including the NACHA formats for the banking industry; TDCC formats for the transportation industry; UCS formats for the grocery industry; WINS formats for the public warehousing industry; and the EAGLE formats for hardware and housewares.

The NACHA standards relate solely to the payment mechanism. BAI, a banking industry research and trade association, has developed standards for communication and transmission of banking data among banks. Principally because the BAI standards have no specified data dictionary, they have been subjected to differing interpretations by banks, which tends to diminish their effectiveness.

Recognizing these different industry-specific standards, ANSI in 1979 sanctioned the Accredited Standards Committee X12 to set cross-industry standards for electronic business data interchange involving companies rather than just bank-to-bank communication. Those standards began to be widely accepted in 1986 when the first group of electronic "transaction sets" (the electronic equivalent of a paper document, such as a purchase order or invoice) in standardized cross-industry format was approved by ANSI. Earlier, ANSI had sanctioned Accredited Standards Committee X9 to set data standards for bank-to-bank and bank-to-customer data transmissions. Much of the work of identifying the need for particular transaction sets and for developing the data formats falls to the ASC X12 Finance Subcommittee, which is a standing task group composed of members from both the banking and the corporate world who work on a voluntary basis. The Finance Subcommittee's scope of responsibility encompasses "EDI projects relating to invoicing, financial transactions, and implementation issues involving banks and corporations."[11]

Over time, differences between the X12 formats and those predating X12 tend to be reduced. It is speculation, however, whether the NACHA and X12 standards may migrate closer to each other, so that a single set of standards may ultimately exist.

SECURITY

Banks have attempted to protect the security of fund transfer instructions by various means, including tape recording verbal instructions, using "line numbers" for repetitive transfers, and making verifying phone calls to other authorized persons regarding nonrepetitive transfers. The tape recording method is faulty because it does not prevent error or fraud; it serves only to verify after the fact that the instructions were given; and there usually is no positive voice identification mechanism associated with this device. The call-back technique is faulty because frequently the person sought by the bank for verification is unavailable; or that person may not be informed about a completely legitimate transaction.

Companies may seek further security measures, such as the following:

1. Severely restricting the number of individuals authorized to give EFT instructions to the bank;

2. Limiting the number of EFT transactions each authorized individual may initiate per day; and

3. Limiting the maximum dollar amount of any one EFT transaction by each authorized individual.

These restrictions should be communicated in writing to the bank and signed by a senior manager who is also an authorized signer on the bank account involved. Further, as a follow-up measure, the manager should obtain written acknowledgement and acceptance of these instructions from the bank.

Banks require accurate transfer instructions furnished by an authorized person. Unfortunately, verbal communication does not offer much protection against error or fraud to either the bank or the company. Therefore,

---

[11] Constitution of Finance Subcommittee of ANSI ASC X12 (draft January 1989).

bankers and cash managers alike have sought and developed other solutions that are more reliable yet flexible in protecting them both.

Since written instructions signed by an authorized person are too cumbersome and slow to be useful, companies and banks have found that the interactive terminal or desktop computer can solve the problem nicely. These are particularly good for nonrepetitive funds transfers where all of the information regarding the destination of the transfer must be supplied along with the payment instructions. The system requires two authorized people on the company's side, each having a secret password, to initiate and verify funds transfer instructions before the bank will act on them. The system operates by having the first authorized person (usually the junior partner) use the secret password to access the bank's funds transfer system and set up the details of the transfer. This entails inputting the name, address, and transit routing number of the destination bank, the name and account number of the beneficiary, and the amount of the transfer. The bank's computer accepts this data and stores it in a queue awaiting verification by another person with a higher level password. Subsequently, the verifier logs onto the system with the secret password, accesses and reviews the payment instructions lodged in the queue in detail, including the destination bank's name, name and account number of the payee, and account number to be charged, and signifies the appropriate action for each payment order. Such actions may be approval, rejection/cancellation, or deferral in the queue for later action.

In this manner, the system affords the security of having two people independently involved in the transaction and the flexibility of timing to accommodate them both. A refinement of this system can usually be accomplished during implementation with the bank. Instead of authorizing just two people, the company may authorize two groups of people. People in the junior group may be authorized only to set up the payments, while people in the senior group either may set up the payments or approve them.

Of course, the security aspects of this system are totally compromised when authorized people tape their passwords to the sides of the terminals for easy access, a not infrequent occurrence. Security is preserved by periodically changing the passwords; security experts suggest that passwords be changed monthly, or more frequently—for instance, whenever a person's authorization is rescinded.

Security over EFT message traffic is also effected through encryption and authentication.

Encryption

Encryption is the scrambling of a message to make it unreadable by an unauthorized person. The sender scrambles the message prior to transmission using a predetermined algorithm. The receiver, who must have the algorithm, or encryption key, decrypts the message at the receiving end. In computer-originated messages, the sender and receiver, using pairs of "black boxes," handle the encryption/decryption process, which may actually be only program boards inserted into their desktop computers designed to operate under an encryption algorithm.

An encrypted message that travels through a telecommunications network such as Fedwire or ACH must nevertheless be wrapped in an electronic envelope bearing the address of the receiver. While this may sound obvious, some parties such as the military may be concerned that even the unencrypted destination of the message can be sensitive information in the wrong hands.

In 1981, ANSI adopted a data encryption algorithm[12] called the Data Encryption Standard (DES). The National Bureau of Standards has authorized its use to protect the data transmissions of all federal agencies except the Department of Defense, which uses a different (proprietary) encryption algorithm. DES enables a sender and receiver to exchange cryptographic keys, and for the sender to scramble and the receiver to decipher messages sent between them.

Authentication

Authentication of a message is used to verify the identity of the sender, and to preserve the integrity of the message from tampering or other alteration during transmission. Authentication can take different forms, and it involves the prior exchange of "test keys."

A test key is an algorithm used by the originator to prepare a code number, referred to as a message authentication code (MAC),[13] that is inserted into the body of the message. The receiver reconstructs the MAC from the contents of the message using the test key; if successful, the message is deemed to be authentic. Bank test key algorithms typically use the value date or date of transmission, the corresponding day of the week, month of the year, payment amount, a message sequence number, and a

---

[12] This standard is formally catalogued as ANSI X3.92-1981.

[13] For construction of a MAC, see p. 7-42.

unique customer number. The unique number is changed periodically to preserve the security of the test key.

An authenticated message can be read by anyone coming into contact with it. However, if the amount or value date of the message is altered, either by transmission error or by tampering, the receiver's calculation of the MAC will generate a different result from the MAC contained in the message. This difference alerts the receiver that the message may not be authentic.

CASH MANAGEMENT SUGGESTION:

> The cash manager concerned about security in passing funds transfer instructions to the originating bank should consider authenticating the message with a test key. Due to custom and tradition, the bank may be reluctant to allow the use of its standard test key, which many banks somehow believe should be reserved solely for use by correspondent banks. In this case, the cash manager might then construct a proprietary algorithm and request the bank to honor it in authenticating funds transfer instructions from the cash manager's company.

LEGAL ISSUES

The cash manager should recognize that some legal issues exist in the EFT environment. These issues relate to the acceptance of verbal instructions by a bank to make payments from a customer's account, and to the failure of the EFT system to complete a transaction in a timely and accurate manner.

There is no statutory law governing EFTs, and limited case law leaves many open questions. In the absence of a clear legal framework, written agreements regarding EFTs between the customer and bank provide the only substantive basis for defining the parties' respective responsibilities and liability. The Uniform Commercial Code (Articles 3 and 4) addresses issues concerning only paper-based payments. Only Federal Reserve Regulation J addresses Fedwire payments. The National Conference on Uniform State Laws, in recognizing the inadequacies of existing laws, is in the process of developing a new Article 4A of the Uniform Commercial Code, "Wire Transfers," which could become statutory law on a state-by-state basis, probably not before 1990. The principal issue needing resolution relates to the question of liability. As Article 4A was drafted, most damages resulting from a delay or failure by a bank along the route of the transfer would not be the responsibility of the bank, but would rest with the initiating company.

ANATOMY OF A MAC

A MAC is created by the sender in the form of a compiled number based on certain elements of data contained in the message. The MAC is included in the body of the message. The sender and receiver obviously must exchange the test key before the MAC can be used. While every organization's MAC code structure is different, many similarities of construction permit the generic description of a MAC. The MAC structure described here by way of an example is very simple; firms wishing to improve the degree of security may add more elements to the structure.

The basic elements of a MAC are the payment amount and identity of the sender. The MAC will often add a third element: a consecutive number to ensure that no payments are duplicated and that none is missing.

Payment Amount

The payment amount is broken down into its arithmetic components without regard for the particular currency involved. For example, 4,369,259 (dollars, yen, pounds—it does not matter) would be broken down as follows:

$$
\begin{array}{r}
4,000,000 \\
300,000 \\
60,000 \\
9,000 \\
200 \\
50 \\
\underline{9} \\
4,369,259
\end{array}
$$

The sender would refer to the MAC key to determine the random number that pertains to each component. A MAC key using randomly selected numbers for the amount might be:

9,000,000	209	900,000	12	90,000	214
8,000,000	56	800,000	630	80,000	507
7,000,000	817	700,000	399	70,000	849
6,000,000	5	600,000	417	60,000	492
5,000,000	27	500,000	79	50,000	413

4,000,000	539	400,000	2	40,000	288		
3,000,000	985	300,000	387	30,000	116		
2,000,000	216	200,000	862	20,000	46		
1,000,000	400	100,000	931	10,000	9		

9,000	286	900	247	90	110	9	812
8,000	519	800	780	80	509	8	120
7,000	416	700	525	70	612	7	776
6,000	892	600	59	60	632	6	301
5,000	13	500	98	50	820	5	919
4,000	510	400	130	40	7	4	447
3,000	774	300	151	30	162	3	691
2,000	303	200	333	20	15	2	28
1,000	725	100	681	10	46	1	8

The amount element is then compiled as follows, using these random numbers:

4,000,000	539
300,000	387
60,000	492
9,000	286
200	333
50	820
9	812
4,369,259	3,669 = amount element

Identity of Sender. The sender is assigned a fixed number that is always used in compiling the test code number. The sender's fixed number should be changed periodically, with the initiator of the change taking particular precautions to ensure the security of the new fixed number during transit to the proper recipient. To accomplish this, the initiator of the change could mail a letter to the recipient advising him that he will be assigned a new fixed number that will be sent under separate cover. Then, the number should be clearly printed or typed on a plain sheet of paper containing no information other than the identity of the sender. This should be mailed to the recipient a few days later. This will ensure that the cover letter and the new number do not travel together but will nevertheless arrive close together.

Continuing the example of the construction of the MAC, the fixed number is incorporated into the compilation. The sender's fixed number in this example is 1024. The fixed number element is then added to the amount element:

Amount element	3669
Fixed number	1024
Total	4693

Consecutive Number. Each message sent is assigned a two digit consecutive number beginning with 01 for the first message and increasing consecutively to 99. The one-hundredth message reverts to

Corporations have had a problem with this refusal by banks to accept responsibility for the transfer's accurate and timely completion.

In conducting EFT business, banks usually request their depository customers to execute two different agreements: a wire transfer agreement and an agreement governing ACH transactions. Bank-prepared wire transfer agreements generally absolve the bank of any liability for damages for their failure to execute a transaction properly. Banks can sometimes be pushed to exclude gross negligence from the reasons for avoiding liability, but simple negligence is generally not sufficient to convict a bank. Also, banks are wary of accepting liability for any consequential damages—those damages suffered indirectly as a consequence of the primary cause.

EXAMPLE: A 1982 legal settlement illustrates how consequential damages can arise from a failed funds transfer transaction and serves to show why banks must try to limit their legal exposure.[14] In 1973, a Chicago firm instructed its Chicago bank to transfer $27,000 by wire to a Swiss bank for an installment payment on a ship charter. The instructions were properly issued to the Chicago bank two days in advance of the due date. The Chicago bank dispatched the message via telex (SWIFT was not yet operational) to its Swiss correspondent bank, which acknowledged receipt of the message. The Swiss bank, however, failed to make the payment to the shipowner, who immediately cancelled the charter. Since ship charter rates

---

[14] Evra Corp. f/k/a/Hyman-Michaels Co. v. Swiss Bank Corp, No. 73-C-2643 (ED Ill.) filed May 12, 1981.

01 and the sequence is repeated. The consecutive number is appended as a prefix to the compiled number rather than added to the compilation.

Assuming that the message for which we are compiling a MAC is the thirty-seventh message sent to the particular recipient, the resulting MAC is 374693.

This MAC is usually inserted at the beginning of the message, as:

"Test 374693. Pay Unicorn Bank, Barcelona, pesetas 4,369,259 for account España Widgets SpA for value December 12. Regards. Company A, N.Y."

To improve the security of the MAC, some banks add to the compilation additional random number elements for the day, date, and month of the value date.

had risen dramatically from the time of the original charter contract, the Chicago firm suffered damages when the charter was cancelled. The court agreed that the amount of the damages was $2.1 million, based on the cost to recharter a ship at the then-current rates.

The Swiss bank's failure to act was apparently caused by the fact that its telex machine ran out of paper, so no actual copy of the message was created. The court later reversed the damage award after determining that the Swiss bank had acted properly except for the missing paper in the telex machine, which was determined not to have happened very often.

The failure to complete a wire transfer of $27,000, for which the Chicago bank charged its customer a fee of about $5, resulted in consequential damages of more than $2 million.

For ACH services, the bank agreement typically covers all the ground covered by the wire transfer agreement and more, including an acknowledgment that the customer has received a copy of, and understands, the *NACHA Operating Rules* (available from the bank, the regional ACH, or NACHA),[15] the rules of the regional ACH, and the rules and operating procedures of the bank. Such agreements should be

---

[15] *Nacha Operating Rules* is available from NACHA, 607 Herndon Parkway, Suite 200, Herndon, Va. 22070, (202) 659-4343. The price is approximately $14 for ACH members ($27.50 for nonmembers).

reviewed by legal counsel and discussed or negotiated with the bank before being executed.

SUMMARY

The basic electronic payment systems available to businesses are the Fed's Fedwire and the nationwide ACH system. In addition, CHIPS, operated by the New York Clearinghouse Association, is used to settle payments—generally originating from foreign exchange and other international payment transactions—among some 140 major U.S. banks. The SWIFT network of over 2,000 banks worldwide is a message system that among other messages, carries payment instructions between correspondent banks.

Fedwire carries payments one at a time, and settlement between the sending and receiving banks is immediate. CHIPS effects transactions one-at-a-time as well, but settlement is delayed until after the close of business each day. ACH payments are made in batches of multiple transactions and settle next day (or later). ACH payments are transported through the banking system using standardized structured data formats.

The cash manager must understand how the electronic payments systems operate to effect the payment in accordance with the timing required by the underlying transaction and at an optimally low cost.

Security measures to protect the integrity and confidentiality of EFT are available, principally through use of computerized initiation of transfers, line sheets, and test code authentication.

SUGGESTED READINGS

Cesario, Frank A. "Innovation and the ACH." *Journal of Cash Mgmt.* Vol. 7, No. 6 (Nov./Dec. 1987), pp. 45–48.

Cesario, Frank A. "Vendor Express Lights Up the ACH." *Corp. Cashflow* (Mar. 1988), pp. 28–34.

Gage, Theodore J. "Increased ACH Use Presents Challenges Few Banks Can Meet." *Corp. Cashflow* (June 1988), pp. 16–18.

Hill, Ned C., and Daniel M. Ferguson. "EDI and Payment Terms; Negotiating a Positive Sum Game." *Journal of Cash Mgmt.*, Vol. 7, No. 5 (Sept./Oct. 1987), pp. 21–26.

Lipis, Allen H., et al. *Electronic Banking.* New York: John Wiley & Sons, Inc., 1985.

Monhollon, J.R. and B.J. Summers. "The Role of the Federal Reserve in the Electronic Payments Evolution." *Journal of Cash Mgmt.*, Vol. 7, No. 3 (May/June 1987).

Penney, Norman and Donald I. Baker. *The Law of Electronic Funds Transfer Systems.* 2d ed. Boston: Warren, Gorham & Lamont, Inc., 1988.

Poje, Richard J. "Who's Holding Up Your Wires?" *Corp. Cashflow* (Aug. 1988) pp. 29–33.

Vergari, J.V. and V.V. Shue. *Checks, Payments and Electronic Banking.* New York: Practising Law Institute, 1986.

White, George C. "Electronic Payments Commentary: U.S. Treasury's 'Vendor Express' Is Key 1980s ACH Development." *Journal of Cash Mgmt.*, Vol. 7, No. 4 (July/Aug. 1987) pp. 56–58.

White, George. "Electronic Payments Commentary: CCD, CTP or CTX—Which Corporate Format to Use?" *Journal of Cash Mgmt.*, Vol. 5, No. 6 (Nov./Dec. 1985).

Woo, Benson K. "Viewpoint: Why Corporate America Has Not Embraced Electronic Corporate Trade Payments." *Journal of Cash Mgmt.*, Vol. 5, No. 6 (Nov./Dec. 1985).

PART IV

Funds Management Systems

CHAPTER **8**

Designing and Managing the Funds Management System

OBJECTIVES

The objective in designing an effective funds management system is to enable funds to flow into the firm unimpeded and unassisted by human intervention to the place where they can be used and to provide the information and control systems necessary to manage the funds. Effective funds management systems are designed; they do not just happen. All too often, as a company grows and evolves, bank accounts are added as needed without any strategic plan to support new business units and special purpose needs as they arise. Without a master plan, the resulting bank account configuration will probably defy logic and require excessive manpower to operate.

A well-designed system operates effectively and efficiently, with the cash manager having no involvement in moving funds from the point of first deposit to the point where funds are concentrated and invested or used to cover loans and disbursements. The system should also facilitate the routine functioning of the disbursement systems while retaining adequate controls to avoid unauthorized disbursements. Overlaying the bank account configuration is a bank balance and transaction reporting system that tracks funds flows and serves to monitor the flow of funds in relation to the short-term funds forecast.

In achieving these objectives, it is necessary to be prudent when incurring hard dollar expenses to reduce clerical and managerial involvement. Such expenses are incurred by buying services from banks and other service providers and acquiring computer software to assist in the treasury management function.

GUIDELINES FOR DESIGNING A FUNDS MANAGEMENT SYSTEM

With these objectives in mind, the following guidelines can be used to design a funds management system that operates with minimum manual intervention and optimum controls, and generates the kind and quantity of decision support data necessary to manage the system.

Separate Bank Accounts for Receipts or Disbursements

A funds management system should be designed to keep funds moving in only one direction through each bank account. By using separate zero balance accounts (ZBAs) for deposits and disbursements, the bank account reconcilement function is greatly simplified, aberrant transactions are highlighted, and the forecasting of funds flows is greatly facilitated. In contrast, the use of a general account to handle two-way flows of funds prevents the highlighting of aberrant transactions because they are masked by other transactions, and makes the reconciling of the bank account to the general ledger a nightmare. In addition, funds forecasting is nearly impossible since the net funds flow in a general account is the result of the opposing streams of deposits and disbursements, neither of which can be readily forecasted using a general account.[1]

Concentrate Deposits to a Central Point

By centralizing the function of funds management and concentrating funds into a central point, the firm is able to operate on a lower level of funds overall and maintain better controls. Instead of a small amount of funds in each business unit, the firm should attempt to pool the funds of all its business units where liquidity can be centrally managed. This enables the firm to borrow less or invest more, and respond quickly and efficiently to the liquidity needs of any one of its business units. Moreover, the task of managing funds and liquidity is centralized in the hands of trained and supervised treasury staff instead of being dispersed among operating units that may be less capable in liquidity management.

Move Funds in Bulk

The movement of funds costs money. Transaction charges are levied both by the bank sending the funds and the bank receiving the funds, and the amount of the charges is independent of the amount of funds moved. Therefore, there is a tradeoff between the frequency and the amount of the transaction. The cash manager should seek ways to accumulate small amounts into a bulk transfer to save transaction charges without leaving too great an amount of funds idle awaiting transfer. Often, companies with remote deposit locations making small or infrequent deposits may find that the charges for moving funds from the depository accounts to the concentration account outweigh the time value of the funds. Therefore, it would be more profitable to defer the movement of funds to the concentration account until a sufficient amount has accumulated in the depository account to justify the transaction cost. For example, if each transaction to concentrate funds costs $0.50, and the time value of the funds is 10 percent (either as an investment or reduction of debt), then daily deposits of a minimum of $1,800 would be required for daily transfer ($1,800 $\times$ 0.10/360 = $0.50 per day). If daily deposits average only $600, then transfers should be made every three days instead of daily. A tracking system would be needed to monitor the accumulation of funds in each depository account to determine when the transfer should be made.

---

[1] See Chapter 12 for a detailed discussion of short-term funds flow forecasting.

Avoid Using Wire Transfers

Processing checks is inexpensive; automated clearing house (ACH) transfers are even less expensive. However, wire transfer charges are steep, ranging upward from $7 to send a Fedwire plus a slightly smaller amount levied by the receiving bank. Wire transfer capability must be part of any funds management system, but it should be reserved for nonroutine transfers absolutely requiring same-day settlement. ACH transfers, by contrast, cost pennies per transaction but usually settle on a next-day basis. Therefore, the funds management system should be designed so that payments can be anticipated at least one day in advance whenever possible, and ACH transfers can be initiated and received. Paper checks will remain an integral part of the United States' payment system long after the cover has fallen off this book, although electronic payments will gain in importance at the expense of checks. Businesses in certain industries, however, such as automobile manufacturing, freight, petroleum, and pharmaceuticals, among others, can expect the volume of electronic payments to surpass checks.

Make Optimum Use of Float

Float will exist in the payment system as long as paper checks must be moved physically from the depository bank to the disbursing bank. The game of extending disbursing float and compressing collection float will persist, but its level of importance will continue to decline. As companies adopt electronic data interchange (EDI) and ACH payments, the economies of electronics will begin to outweigh the benefits of float management. Nevertheless, float is still not to be ignored.

Use Electronic Funds Application Systems Whenever Possible

A funds management system should take advantage of electronic funds application systems wherever electronic payments are used. The concept of moving funds from bank account to bank account should be expanded whenever possible to encompass application-to-application transfers. That is, the payor's accounts payable system and the payee's accounts receivable system are linked by a payment mechanism that transfers value from one company's application system (accounts payable) to another company's application system (accounts receivable), not just to effect payment between two bank accounts.

Provide for Forecasting and Tracking Capability

The system should be designed with a view toward facilitating forecasting of funds receipts and disbursements. The system design should strike a balance between too much and insufficient detail on the transactions flowing through the system. Detail is increased by the use of specific-purpose bank accounts. While generating historic data for use in forecasting short-term funds flows, this structure adds only modest cost to operating such a system.

Use Computers for Performing Routine Tasks

Prior to the advent of desktop computers cash managers toiled with columnar pads and pencils with erasers performing routine mind-numbing tasks. Today, many of these tasks are performed quickly and more accurately on an inexpensive desktop computer. In addition, computers enable the cash manager to use infinitely more permutations of data than he could manually.

Spend Money Prudently in Replacing Manual Effort

Computers and related software are available in virtually all price categories. Thus, appropriate investment decisions should be made to ensure that technology is cost-effective and actually replaces manual effort, not just compounding a problem somewhere else. For example, an investment of $8,000 in a treasury workstation (TWS) to replace a 30-minute daily clerical task may not be very wise, particularly if it requires extensive retraining and special expertise to operate the new system.

Use the Funds Management Function as a Decision Support System

The funds management function should be recognized for what it is: a decision support system. The end result of the bank account structures, devices, and techniques is a system to enable the improved management of a firm's liquidity. This is reflected in daily decisions about borrowing to cover funds shortfalls and investing surplus funds. This set of decisions is still best performed by the human being. One should be aware, however, of the rapid development of software that resembles artificial intelligence that is being employed in the development of expert systems.

FUNDS CONCENTRATION SYSTEMS

A funds concentration system is any methodology employed to transfer funds to a central point where they may be employed to fund disbursements, pay down loans, or be invested. The details of a firm's bank account configuration and the cash management devices and techniques used depend on too many factors to prescribe a particular structure for any one type or size of company. However, it is possible to identify some basic elements of a prototype funds concentration system around which the configuration can be customized to meet the needs of virtually any firm.

Companies often collect their customer's receipts "in the field," at retail locations, regional offices, and plants. However, the company's bills and payroll often are paid out of a central location. Consequently, it is necessary to develop a system to move these collections regularly, systematically, and efficiently to the central location. In a well-designed funds management system, that central location will use a single bank account to concentrate all collection proceeds. Large companies organized into operating groups may have a concentration account for each group with excess funds at the group level being concentrated to the parent or corporate level. Whether the structure consists of a single concentration account or a more complex structure of multiple concentration accounts, the principles, devices, and techniques employed to marshall the funds are largely similar.

OBJECTIVES OF FUNDS CONCENTRATION

The objectives of a funds concentration system are to channel and accelerate the movement of funds from the point of first deposit to the central concentration account, and to provide accountability for those funds. The tools to accomplish funds concentration are depository transfer checks (DTCs) and their electronic counterparts, ACH debit transfers, as well as Fedwire transfers and deposit consolidation techniques. In addition, the balance reporting services provided by the concentration bank are an indispensible tool in linking the components of the system together and monitoring and accounting for the movement of the funds. Balance reporting services, discussed later in this chapter, provide critical information about transactions and balances in the firm's bank accounts on a daily, and sometimes intraday, basis.

The well-designed funds concentration system functions like a trap: it allows, even encourages, funds to come in but it requires a deliberate act to allow funds to be released. In this way, control is maintained over disbursements while receipts flow in and are accumulated automatically. A concentration system that requires an overt act to move funds into a concentration point is not a well-designed system. The following case illustrates this point.

A soft drink bottling company with franchises across six states in the upper midwest maintained its disbursing accounts at a large bank in the downtown business district of a major city, about 10 miles away from the company's bottling plant and offices. In that particular state, banks were not permitted to have branches, which required that any checks received in the company's offices had to be transported 10 miles to the bank. The company received many large checks from major customers, such as grocery chains, through a lockbox operated by the bank. In addition to the main plant, the company operated nine other depots throughout its franchise territory. The depots were dispatch points for trucks serving their regions, and the drivers brought in checks, coin, and currency each day. Each depot made a daily deposit to a local bank and reported the amount of its deposit to the treasurer at headquarters via telephone.

After the nine depots reported their deposits each day, the treasurer's secretary drew checks for the respective amounts on each of the nine depository bank accounts, had them signed by the treasurer and counter-signed by the general manager (all checks required dual signature), and then had a clerk drive 10 miles to the bank to deposit them. Because of the company's location in the north central part of the United States, the trip to the bank was often perilous and occasionally postponed due to winter weather, resulting in no deposit funds flowing into the company's concentration account for that day. This company obviously needed a better funds concentration system.

A consultant showed the treasurer that cash flow did not have to suffer with inclement weather or the absence of the secretary, and that funds could be transferred automatically from the nine depository banks to the headquarters concentration bank account without intervention by anyone at headquarters. A funds concentration system was recommended in which the deposits were reported to the concentration bank, which prepared DTCs drawn against the nine depository accounts. This process was initiated by the bookkeeper at each depot, who would make a toll-free telephone call and report each deposit made. This triggered a computer and telecommunications system that moved the funds efficiently and reliably to the concentration bank and simultaneously made the deposit data available to the treasurer at headquarters.

Whether a system involves 9 soda pop depots, 237 retail stores, or 28 plants and sales offices that collect from customers, the cash management principle is the same: Move the funds promptly and quickly to a concentration point and make the data concerning the funds movements available to those who need to know.

Funds concentration systems satisfy two principal objectives of cash management: control and earnings enhancement.

Control

"Control" in cash management occurs when the funds arrive at a point in the company's system where they can be used by the financial manager for disbursement, repayment of debt, or investment. Until that time, the funds are either uncontrolled or are subject to control by others who may have other than approved corporate objectives in mind. This may include field sales staff who have other priorities such as making sales calls, or plant managers who may want to retain high balances in the plant's bank account to compensate the depository bank for personal loans. Uncontrolled funds may also tempt the occasional dishonest employee who commits a defalcation and juggles funds to conceal the theft.

Placing the control of funds in the hands of key financial managers through a concentration system is effected in several ways. Funds are moved from under the control of local and regional personnel and placed in the hands of centralized corporate staff where fewer people handle greater sums in a more structured and audited environment. Particularly in a business where coin and currency are received at the point of sale (POS), but in other types of businesses as well, the company is exposed to increased potential loss as more people have access to the funds. The task in any funds management system is to deposit the collections into a bank account as quickly as possible and then use or move the funds under the control of a select number of people.

Prompt movement of funds from the depository point to a central concentration account also decreases the firm's exposure to risk of failure of the depository bank. In large funds concentration systems that use many depository banks, this can be an important objective because smaller and less well-known local banks may be used for depository purposes with greater confidence because funds are continually siphoned away from those banks.

By channeling deposits toward a concentration account, unanticipated changes in the individual components of the incoming stream of funds can be noted quickly and investigated in a timely manner. For example, with the stream of receipts undisturbed by offsetting disbursements, an unusually large funds receipt would become highlighted.

In firms with multiple divisions or subsidiaries, the flow of funds from each unit may be tracked independently of the others. There are several methods, techniques, and devices used to channel the receipts to the concentration account. Selection of a particular method, technique, or device depends on the distances involved, the availability of branches of the concentration bank, the size of deposits made, the capability of the concentration bank to provide the necessary services, and often the overall business strategy of the company itself.

Accuracy in short-term forecasting is improved by maintaining the purity of the incoming stream of funds undisturbed by offsetting disbursements. Improved accuracy in short-term forecasting enables the firm to reduce borrowings or increase investments, and reduce the frequency of borrowing or investing transactions. Forecasting a series of expected events, such as deposits and disbursements over a period of time, is based on a combination of historic patterns and expected future patterns. Forecasting these events and then monitoring the actual events as they occur gives the financial manager a quick signal when events are not happening as planned. This enables management to react and take remedial steps sooner.

Earnings Enhancement

A well-designed funds concentration system enhances earnings by making larger sums available for investment or debt repayment. Larger investment sums can result in improved yields. For example, relatively small sums in several different depository accounts may result in no meaningful amount of available investable funds. By concentrating these small amounts, a sufficiently large pool of funds may be generated that can be invested in short-term money markets to produce an acceptable market rate of return.

Likewise, a company borrowing at the corporate level to support the operations of its subsidiaries and divisions can produce significant reductions in short-term loans resulting in reduced interest costs by pooling its funds. Some companies have operating units that are cost centers and net consumers of funds and other business units that produce positive funds flows. By pooling funds through a corporate funds concentration system, the company's overall funding position becomes more balanced through the central concentration account.

Another earnings enhancement benefit of funds concentration is that the inefficiencies of the paper-based system—float and slippage—can play to the benefit of the company rather than to the bank.

Float. In a typical concentration system using checks to concentrate funds, the float associated with the transfer check allows dual balances. Dual balances are created when a transfer check is deposited in the concentration account, but there continues to be a balance in the depository account until the transfer check clears. If deposits to the depository account consist of coin and currency or local checks, there will be significant amounts of collected balances in the depository account, and these balances produce credits to offset the bank's activity charges.

The existence of dual balances in both bank accounts while transfer checks clear through the banking system enables the company to compensate both banks with the same funds.

Slippage. Slippage occurs when a transfer check takes longer to clear than anticipated by the concentration bank's availability schedule, thus increasing the amount of the dual balances and adding to the depository bank's "free" compensation. As previously noted, float is a natural phenomenon in a paper-based payments system; slippage causes an exaggeration of the effects of float. For example, the concentration bank may provide for next-day availability on a DTC, although it may actually take two days for that check to clear the depository bank. This situation results in the company having dual collected funds for one day in both the depository and concentration bank accounts. Slippage is sometimes traceable to external influences, such as inclement weather, which cause delays in air traffic and, hence, in presentment of checks to drawee banks. Since many checks are physically carried through the nationwide clearing system aboard commercial aircraft, delays of even a few hours at an airport may cause a one day delay in the clearance of millions of dollars of checks. Meanwhile, the concentration bank has allowed available funds to its customer in anticipation of the normal clearing of the check. Banks and the Federal Reserve (the Fed) have considered various methods to track actual clearings and to charge back such additional float. Such procedures are expensive, cumbersome, and inconsistent, and generally do not work for large volumes of checks. However, while the Fed can charge slippage back to the depository bank for large identifiable items, and those banks may make an adjustment to the customer's float calculation in the account analysis, this is not a regular occurrence. Therefore, the customer's earnings allowance on balances may indeed be enhanced through slippage and the dual balances that may result.

FUNDS CONCENTRATION STRUCTURE

The basic structure of a well-designed bank account configuration consists of depository bank accounts to receive collections from customers, mechanisms to move the deposited funds to a central concentration point, and disbursing accounts. Separating the depository and disbursing functions is crucial to an effective funds management system because separation enables the forecasting, tracking, and control over the funds flowing through the system. The nature of the firm's business and location of its customers usually dictates the company's collection and depository system structure. The degree to which a company is decentralized often dictates the structure of the disbursing system.

Deposits

The two most significant depository elements are whether the firm customarily collects from its customers at the POS, as in a retail business, or at some time after the POS, as in most business-to-business transactions. POS transactions require that a bank account be available locally for immediate and convenient deposit. Aside from those states that allow extensive branch banking, this requires a large number of depository bank accounts, as depicted in Figure 8-1, and a mechanism to transfer funds automatically to the concentration point. Where customers remit checks by mail or electronically, on the other hand, fewer bank accounts, or perhaps only one, are needed to receive payments.

Firms whose subsidiaries collect funds are usually required by their legal advisors to establish at least one depository account for each subsidiary. This requirement is imposed because a subsidiary is a separate legal entity and is responsible for receiving its own funds. Technically, in order for a check payable to one corporation to be deposited to the bank account of another corporation, a resolution of the board of directors of the payee would be required to authorize the endorsement. Moreover, such endorsement would enable creditors to "pierce the corporate veil" of the payee corporation in the event of its bankruptcy and invade the assets of the endorsee. Once the funds are deposited and accounted for by the subsidiary, the subsidiary is usually free to pool funds with the parent to take advantage of economies of scale in the management of funds.

Whereas subsidiaries are required to have separate depository accounts by virtue of their separate legal status, divisions usually are not so required. However, the accounting structure of the firm may dictate a separate depository bank account, and the cash manager may prefer a separate account as well. Very often, a division has its own billing and accounts receivable system that stands alone. This dictates that the funds application function be independent of all other divisions as well. To preclude the misapplication of funds of one division to accounts receivable of another division, companies frequently stratify the flows of incoming remittances through a series of lockboxes, one (or more) assigned to each division. The lockbox operating procedure may credit all proceeds to a single common bank account, as long as it first isolates the remittance data for each division. Figure 8-2 shows a flow chart for stratifying incoming funds.

FIG. 8-1
POS Depository System

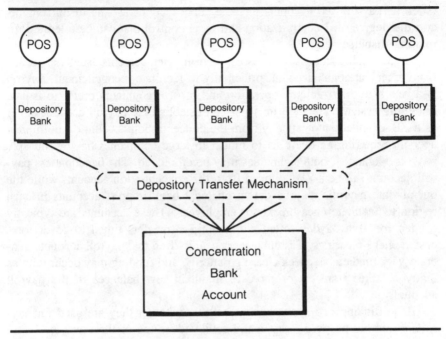

FIG. 8-2
Stratifying Receipts Through Multiple Lockboxes

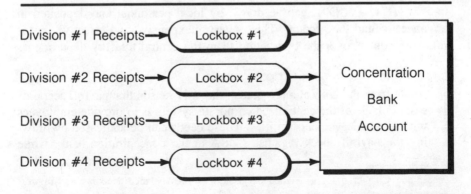

Disbursements

The critical disbursing elements to be considered are the application systems (such as payroll and accounts payable) that account for the disbursements and the degree of decentralization and local control that can be tolerated for making disbursements.

In all but the smallest businesses, payroll disbursements usually are made from a separate bank account, principally to facilitate reconcilement. Payroll is a relatively high volume operation and most accountants prefer to isolate the entire system. The cash manager can establish the payroll account either as a ZBA funded automatically from the concentration account or an imprest account requiring an overt act to fund.[2] In large companies having multiple payroll operations, both techniques may be employed. The headquarters payroll account can be a ZBA funded from the concentration account, while the out-of-state payrolls may be drawn on local bank imprest accounts in each region to facilitate encashment for employees. These accounts are typically funded for each payday, often with multiple transfers timed to cover forecasted check clearings. Cash managers usually find that payroll accounts generate very predictable check clearing patterns, and funding may occur with as many as three transfers or more to maintain low balances in the payroll account.

The funding of imprest bank accounts, whether they are used for payroll or another purpose, is typically achieved in one of three ways:

1. *Wire transfer*—A Fedwire transfer is used only where the amount is not known until the date of funding and where same-day settlement is required. Fedwire transfers tend to be expensive.

2. *ACH Transfer*—An ACH credit transfer, usually in the cash concentration or disbursement (CCD) format, is initiated at least one day prior to settlement and is inexpensive.

3. *DTC*—A DTC can be drawn by local personnel and deposited in advance to fund the account. This is very inexpensive and effective, but it removes control over the transaction from the central treasury department.

CASH MANAGEMENT SUGGESTION:

Aside from the laws of a few states, the only reason that payroll accounts exist outside of the centralized corporate system is to provide employees with local encashment facilities. These needs can be addressed by drawing the payroll checks against a ZBA at the concentration bank, while

---

[2] See Chapter 6 for a detailed discussion of zero balance accounts and imprest accounts.

having printed on the face of the check the name and address of a local bank as an alternate drawee. Figure 6-3 in Chapter 6 shows an "alternate drawee check" that is drawn on Citibank in New York, but is "Payable if Desired at Wells Fargo Bank, Marysville, Cal." Of course, the maker must have made a prior arrangement with the alternate drawee bank, Wells Fargo, in which case this form of check will normally solve problems relating to local encashment in Marysville. By keeping the check drawn on a ZBA at the concentration bank rather than a local bank, the cash manager avoids transaction costs for funding the payroll account and avoids tying up even a small amount of funds in the bottom of the payroll account.

Decentralized accounts payable systems similarly can issue checks drawn on ZBAs at the concentration bank funded by the concentration account. These checks do not normally need the alternate drawee feature. It should be noted, however, that to draw checks against a ZBA that is funded directly from the concentration account is tantamount to giving the drawer a key to the vault. Any check drawn for virtually any amount will be paid promptly and automatically as it is presented through the ZBA. Therefore, management must have the utmost confidence in those personnel who manage the decentralized payment operation.

In the absence of such a high level of confidence, it may be possible to use an imprest account that is funded only by an overt act after prior disbursements have been approved. Such situations are common where the disbursements are made without involvement of a financial manager, such as reimbursement of travel expenses in a field sales office, but where promptness in issuing checks is desired.

CASH MANAGEMENT SUGGESTION:

Occasionally, a financial manager may attempt to limit the dollar amount of checks issued from decentralized locations by preprinting a dollar limitation on its face. However, the cash manager should not rely on the drawee bank to honor such a legend. A preprinted legend is more of a psychological enforcement technique because a payee of a check issued for an amount in excess of the legend limit could be reluctant to accept the check. Moreover, the person in the field who issues the checks could undoubtedly break the payment down into multiple checks, none of which exceeds the legend limitation. If the legend limit is employed on checks drawn on a ZBA, then the system should provide for an audit of the check register to spot situations where multiple checks have been issued to the same payee to circumvent the legend limit.

Completing the optimum bank account structure is controlled disbursing. Generally, the controlled disbursing account is domiciled at a bank a distance away from where the company does business to avoid checks being presented for encashment over the counter. Controlled disbursing enables a company to know precisely how many dollars are needed each day. The controlled disbursing account is operated as an imprest account—usually a zero balance imprest account—that requires daily funding for the exact amount of checks presented. Controlled disbursing has become popular because cash managers can be certain of the flow of funds going in and out of the account. This stream is usually the firm's largest single disbursement stream, and it is much more volatile than payroll. Therefore, the cash manager is attracted to controlled disbursing as an aid in forecasting short-term funds flows.[3]

Concentration System Configuration

To meet the objectives of funds concentration, it is necessary to design a bank account's physical configuration and to implement the configuration at a bank that can provide all the necessary services. The basic architecture of a funds concentration system consists of a concentration bank account (which is nothing more than a normal demand deposit or checking account) into which all incoming funds flow. These funds flow into the concentration account through many different sources and conduits, including:

- Lockboxes at the concentration bank;
- ZBAs at the concentration bank receiving deposits over-the-counter and from lockboxes;
- Electronic funds transfers (EFTs) from customers and from the company's accounts at other banks;
- DTCs (paper or electronic) initiated by the concentration bank;
- Maturing investments; and
- Loan proceeds.

Smaller banks may offer one or more of these services as well, but they may lack the complete systems and telecommunications capability necessary to provide some of the more sophisticated services such as automated ZBAs, automated DTCs, initiation of electronic DTCs through the ACH, and same-

---

[3] See Chapter 6 for a detailed discussion of controlled disbursing.

day reporting of transactions. The full range of these services is provided by only a limited number of banks.

The use of ZBAs to channel the flows of funds from different sources facilitates the accounting for these funds movements by keeping the streams separate as they reach the concentration account. As they enter the concentration account, each source is immediately identified so that the funds may be properly credited. For example, in a company using intercompany general ledger accounts with its subsidiaries and divisions, the use of ZBAs assigned to each unit greatly facilitates the issuance of intercompany credit to the unit that is the source of the funds into the concentration account.

Similarly, lockboxes can be assigned to particular business units. The proceeds of each lockbox flow directly to the concentration account, with the source business unit easily identifiable through a report generated by the bank's lockbox department.

Funds deposited into outlying banks can be transferred via DTCs (paper or electronic), and deposited to the concentration account. Either the concentration bank or a third-party service provider would provide a report to the cash manager showing deposits by location (and nonreporting locations as well).

Similarly, where branch banking is permitted, and branches of the concentration bank are available to depositing units of the same corporation, interbranch deposits may be made directly to the concentration account using deposit slips pre-encoded with the identification number of the depositing unit. The bank then captures the coded identification number data, such as store or location number, and reports the deposit data by location to the company.

All of the data concerning the funds transferred or deposited to the concentration account are reported to the cash manager daily via the bank's electronic balance reporting service. The cash manager obtains a report from the bank each day showing all deposits to the concentration account. This report is used to monitor the actual flows of funds compared to the forecast, which enables the cash manager to respond quickly to trends and unexpected events, and also to provide the data necessary to prepare the bookkeeping entries to credit the appropriate sources of the funds properly. Through the daily balance report on the concentration account, the cash manager has a complete and accurate view of the entire cash management system, because all funds are flowing into the single concentration account with no funds (other than float) in any other bank account in the company's system.

Figure 8-3 depicts a typical funds concentration system. Note how deposits enter the system through the depository banks' lockboxes and flow to the concentration account directly or indirectly through a regional concentration bank identified in Figure 8-3 as Subsidiary #1.

FIG. 8-3
Typical Funds Concentration System

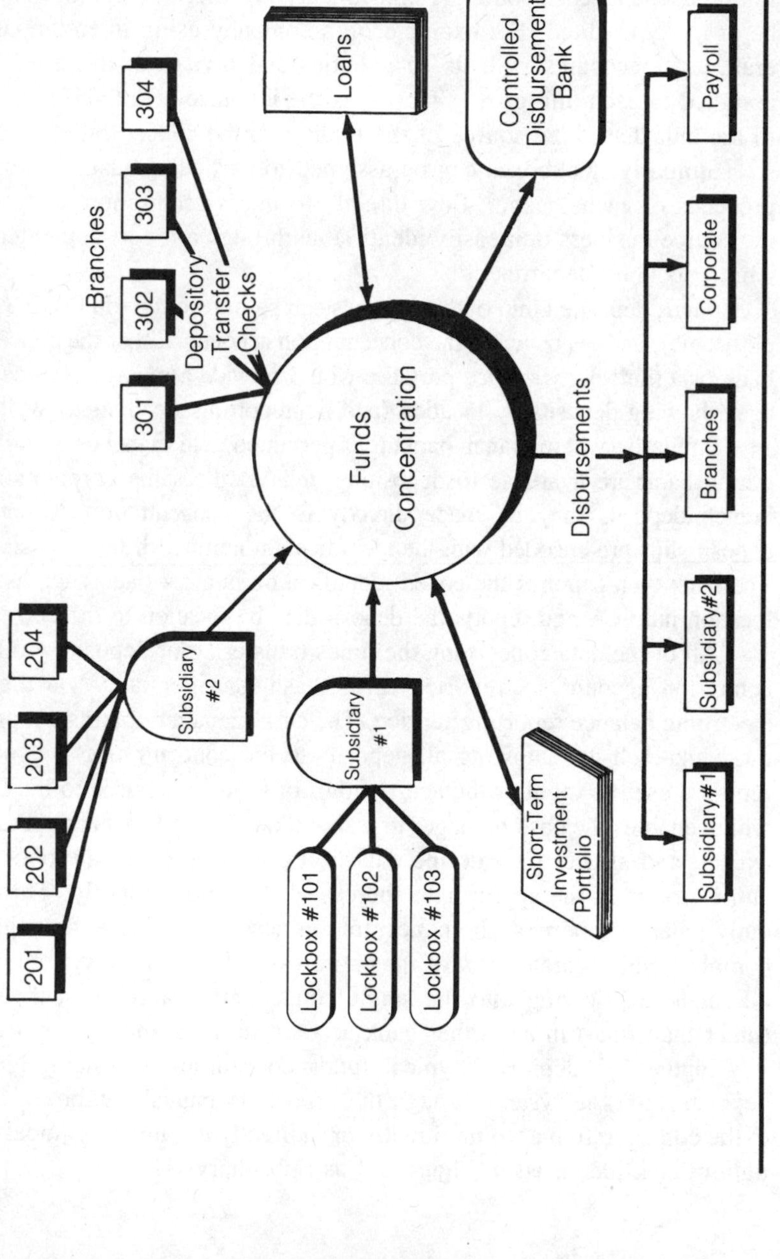

Regional Funds Concentration

Regional concentration banks often are helpful in reducing clearing times—and increasing the amount of funds available for use—by pooling funds from depository banks within a single Fed district before moving them to the master concentration bank. Regional concentration is based solely on the location of depository banks serving a corporation. Confining the regional concentration system to one Fed district may allow same-day, or at least next-day, availability of funds. Upon collection, the funds are moved to the master concentration account by EFT for credit on the day the funds became available in the regional concentration account. In this way, all funds are concentrated nationwide with same-day or next-day availability, compared to a mix of same-day, next-day, and two-day availability achieved through direct concentration from all points nationwide. While this adds a layer of concentration bank accounts to the system, and the expense and control features attendant to them, the increase in available funds can be significant.

Figure 8-4 illustrates how regional concentration banks might improve the collection float for a company by accelerating availability, thereby increasing the amount of available funds and enhancing earnings.

By installing a regional concentration bank in District C, for example, float would be reduced from 1.2 to 1.0 days. With average deposits of $400,000 per day in District C, float would be permanently reduced or, more importantly, available funds in the master concentration account would be increased by $80,000 (0.2 days × $400,000 average daily deposits). At a rate of return of 10 percent, this would yield earnings (or reduced expenses) of $8,000 per year, less the small additional costs of operating the regional concentration account, compared to concentrating the funds directly from banks 7, 8, 9, and 10.

If the results in this example seem marginal, the cash manager must realize that the benefit from this system becomes more apparent with larger sums. For example, if District C deposits averaged $1 million per day, the increase in availability of 0.2 days would amount to $200,000 one time to be held permanently, and this would yield earnings (or reduced expenses) of $20,000 per year. The one-time acceleration of collection from 1.2 days to 1.0 days generates this one-time increase in available funds of which the company has permanent use to generate earnings.

FUNDS CONCENTRATION METHODS

In a multibank configuration, there are three methods for transferring funds from the depository bank to the regional or master concentration bank: DTC,

FIG. 8-4

Comparison of Regional Concentration and Master Concentration Accounts ($'000 omitted)

Fed District	Bank	Average Daily Deposits	Days Float to Master Concentration Bank	$ Float	Days Float to Regional Concentration Bank	Revised $ Float
A	1	$30	2.00	$60	1.00	$30
	2	40	1.00	40	1.00	40
	3	57	1.00	57	1.00	57
		127	1.24	157	1.00	127
B	4	12	2.00	24	1.00	12
	5	53	1.00	53	1.00	53
	6	28	1.00	28	1.00	28
		93	1.13	105	1.00	93
C	7	75	1.00	75	1.00	75
	8	105	1.00	105	1.00	105
	9	80	2.00	160	1.00	80
	10	140	1.00	140	1.00	140
		400	1.20	480	1.00	400
	Total	$620	1.20	$742	1.00	$620

ACH debit transfer, and wire transfer. Each method presents its own characteristics regarding performance and cost, and the cash manager must carefully select the particular method or combination of methods to optimize the balance between cost and benefits.

Depository Transfer Checks

Background. Paper checks are probably the most commonly used method for concentrating funds. Until the 1960s, a common method for concentrating funds in many retail operations was for each store to make its deposit locally, then draw a check against the depository account and mail it to a lockbox at the concentration bank. As telephone rates decreased and interest rates increased, cash managers shifted the task of drawing the transfer checks to company headquarters and relied on a telephone call from each store reporting the amount of that day's deposit. The funds represented by the transfer checks were too valuable to entrust to the postal service. This eliminated the mail float that arose when the store mailed the transfer check to the concentration bank lockbox.

In the late 1960s, a high-tech system of telecommunications and computers was developed that has modified this scheme. Several such systems are in operation and involve the use of nationwide toll-free telephone networks and telecommunications centers connected to computers. The system operator may be an independent service bureau or a bank. The depositor's concentration bank maintains a computerized database that contains each store's identification number and the details concerning each store's depository bank. This includes the name and address of the bank, the bank's transit routing number, and the store's depository account number.

Operation of the System. The system operates as follows:

1. During the day, each remote depositing location uses the telephone network to report the amount of its daily deposit to the system operator.

2. As deposit reports are received, the system operator enters the depositor's location identification number and deposit amount into the computer.

3. At a predetermined cut-off time, often about 4 P.M. eastern time, the system operator cuts off the file for the day and transmits the day's data to the concentration bank. All deposit reports received by the system operator after the cut-off deadline become the next day's business.

4. The data is transmitted from the system operator's computer to the concentration bank's computer via telephone lines.

5. The concentration bank receives the data transmission and matches the location-by-location deposit data with the bank's data base of depository bank routing information to produce either an ACH debit or a computer-printed DTC. To produce the paper DTC, the bank uses blank safety paper and a special kind of printer to print the magnetic ink character recognition (MICR) line of the check. Furthermore, the following legend is printed in the signature area of the check: "Depository Transfer Check—No Signature Required. Not to be Cashed."

6. The bank produces all of the DTCs required for the day and prepares a deposit to the customer's master concentration account. This deposit often is made as late as 7 P.M. local time, with the actual timing designed to meet clearing and bank posting deadlines.

7. The system operator makes available to the customer a report showing deposits by location for use by the headquarters accounting department in distributing credit for the aggregate concentration deposit. Depending on the system's capabilities, the system operator may also make available a report of nonreporting locations for the cash manager's follow up.

Anticipatory Transfer Checks

The anticipatory transfer check (ATC) is a subset of the DTC. Where the DTC is drawn after the deposit has been made and the deposit amount is precisely known, the ATC is drawn before the collections and deposit are made. Therefore, the amount of the ATC is a forecasted—often "guestimated"—amount. This device continues to be particularly popular in retail businesses where sales and, therefore, deposits are somewhat predictable. Typically, headquarters maintains a runnning log of each store's actual deposits and transfer checks drawn and the resulting balance in the depository account. Then, on a set day each week, an ATC is drawn against each store's depository account to cover most of the amount anticipated to be deposited through the next business day. As actual sales and deposit data are received, a "clean-up" transfer check is then drawn to transfer the actual amount remaining in the bank account. This system of anticipatory transfers can be fine-tuned by anticipating and drawing more frequently, by being more aggressive in estimating the amounts that are expected to be deposited, by depositing the transfer checks locally for next-day clearance, or by using overnight courier service to deposit the transfer checks to a distant concentration bank. Many sophsticated retailers use computers to forecast store deposits based on historic data and algorithms to predict current activity.

There are several advantages of the DTC over the ATC:

1. There is no guesswork as to the amount of the DTC transfer. The amount transferred is the exact amount reported by the depository location to the system operator.

2. There are virtually no staff requirements for the DTC, so operating costs are low. The combined charges of the system operator and the concentration bank are on the order of $0.50 to $1.00 to report the deposit and create the DTC. The company typically needs no staff to operate a third-party DTC system.

3. There are lower balances in depository banks because of more frequent (daily) transfers. While both the DTC and ATC methods

will transfer the same amount of funds, the DTC system usually operates daily, keeping a steady stream of funds flowing.

4. Overdrafts in depository accounts from DTCs should signal a system problem rather than sloppiness in forecasting. An ATC system, however, can easily overdraw a depository account through a forecasting error. An overdraft in a DTC system indicates a problem in reporting or depositing or that an unidentified charge has been made to the depository account.

5. There is tighter control over depository bank accounts, resulting from immediate identification of nonreporting locations. The cash manager will be able to discuss the necessity for making and reporting deposits on a timely basis, and this tends to bring some discipline to the system.

The advantage of an ATC system for retailers is that store deposits often consist of coin and currency and local checks, most of which are immediately available funds. By anticipating weekend sales and the usually large Monday deposit, the ATC can concentrate the large amount of deposits more quickly.

Electronic DTCs

Another method frequently used for concentrating funds is the ACH debit transfer, which is sometimes referred to as an "electronic DTC."[4] The process described for paper DTCs can produce ACH debit transfers as well as paper checks, although there is a significant operational difference between paper and electronic DTC systems. In the paper DTC system, the concentration bank maintains the database of the depository banks' transit routing information. In an electronic DTC system, the database of depository bank transit routing information can be maintained by either the company or the telecommunications system operator. The system operator or the company matches the deposit reports against the database and produces a data file in a standard format suitable for ACH processing. This data file is then transmitted to the concentration bank, which acts as the gateway into the ACH system by originating the ACH debit transfer.

ACH debit transfers can have a lower cost per transfer than paper DTCs if there are a large number of transfers. Pricing of the ACH transfers often includes a combination of low charges per transfer plus a fixed charge for

---

[4] See Chapter 7 for a detailed discussion of electronic payments.

each transmission. Therefore, the cash manager must be careful in comparing costs of an ACH-based concentration system with a paper-based system. To implement a paper-based DTC system, the most tedious element is to furnish each depository bank with authority—through a new deposit resolution or an authorization letter—to honor DTCs without a signature. While most banks now frequently handle these paper DTC transactions, many banks are still learning how to handle electronic ACH transactions, and many are not equipped technologically to do so or are prepared only to handle credits, not debits. Therefore, in implementing ACH debit transfers, the cash manager should make certain that each depository bank is willing and able to handle ACH debits routinely and timely. Many companies and their bankers have learned that ACH debit and credit transfers are particularly viable substitutes for paper checks in transferring funds among a company's bank accounts for operational purposes.

The particular ACH data format used as an electronic DTC is the CCD format. This data processing format identifies the originating depository financial institution (ODFI); the receiving depository financial institution (RDFI); the account number at the RDFI that is to be charged; the amount to be charged; and the value date for settling the transaction. In addition, the format contains an 80-character field for unstructured data or a message, such as the location number and deposit date for which the CCD transfer has been issued.

The CCD debit transfer is initiated by the concentration bank, which sends it to the ACH serving the concentration bank, and the transaction settles on the value date. The value date is usually specified as the next day, and slippage occurs only when technical problems arise that delay the transmission of the CCD.

Wire Transfers

The third method for concentrating funds is wire transfer. Wire transfer is the generic term for a transfer of funds from one bank to another that is initiated through a Federal Reserve bank for same-day settlement. Wire transfer involves the settlement between banks through their respective Fed accounts and is initiated and advised over the Fed's Fedwire telecommunications system. An ACH transfer, on the other hand, is transmitted between the originating and receiving financial institutions involved in batch files containing many funds transfers at once, and these transactions all settle one or two days following transmission. ACH transfers are inexpensive because many transactions are contained in a single transmission. Wire transfers are expensive because they are processed and settled one at a time. Because of its high cost, a wire transfer should be used only for very large amounts

FIG. 8-5

Wire Transfer Cost/Benefit Trade-Off Matrix

	Interest Rate		
Amount	10 Percent	8 Percent	6 Percent
$300,000	$83.33	$66.67	$50.00
200,000	55.56	44.44	33.33
100,000	27.78	22.22	16.67
50,000	13.89	11.11	8.33

requiring same-day availability. Wire transfers for funds concentration purposes should be used only if and when the size of the transfer and the interest rate are both large enough to generate more revenue than the cost of
making the wire transfer. A simple trade-off calculation matrix such as the
one shown in Figure 8-5 incorporates the time value of money to determine
whether it is worthwhile to pay the premium price of a wire transfer to move
funds for immediate use.

EXAMPLE: Assume that a wire transfer costs $22, including charges
made by both the sending and receiving banks. Also assume that by
receiving available funds in the concentration account one day sooner,
the funds can earn interest for that day at a market rate. Figure 8-5
shows transfers by size and at different interest rates and the resulting
income that can be earned on the respective amounts for one day. Some
amounts will not earn $22 in interest for one day, so it is not worth-
while to use a wire transfer for these amounts. For example, $200,000
earning interest at 8 percent earns $44.44 per day. Therefore, to con-
centrate $200,000 by wire transfer would be economically sound at a
transaction cost of $22 in order to invest those funds same-day. On the
other hand, $50,000 earning interest at 8 percent earns only $11.11 per
day, only half the cost of the transfer. Therefore, the cash manager
should avoid using wire transfer for such a small amount, relying
instead on a less expensive transfer method. For a $50,000 transfer to
be economical at a wire transfer price of $22, the interest rate obtaina-
ble on such funds would have to rise to 15.84 percent.

Intrabank Deposit Consolidation

Consolidating deposits within a single bank is often simpler and less expensive than concentrating funds from multiple banks. In situations where one

bank may operate many branches in a geographical region large enough to service multiple depositing locations of a single business, interbranch deposits may be made into a central bank account. These deposits may be made directly into the master concentration account, a regional concentration account, or ZBAs that feed into a concentration account. Deposit consolidation is achieved entirely within one bank, eliminating the need for funds transfer devices involving paper or electronic DTCs or wire transfers. Each operating unit is assigned a unique identification number by the company. This number would be the store number in retail applications, or a location or unit number, and can be used to identify the unit making the deposit. Each depositing unit's location identifying number is preprinted on the deposit slip in the auxiliary field of the MICR line.

Figure 8-6 depicts a deposit slip and highlights the auxiliary field of the MICR line. The auxiliary field may be used for any purpose, but it most often contains the location identifier, such as a store number, of the depositing unit. The bank then captures the location identifier and deposit amount electronically as it processes the deposit and creates a deposit report for the customer's cash manager and accounting department. If the consolidation bank is unable to use the auxiliary field of the deposit slip, then the customer can usually employ a DTC system to move deposits within the bank from depository accounts to the concentration account. In this event, the customer must arrange with the bank for immediate availability of funds in the concentration account.

INFORMATION AND CONTROL SYSTEMS

The principal function of the cash manager is to manage the funds flows and balances of the firm. Information reporting systems provide the data concerning those flows and balances that enable the cash manager to perform this function. The principal source of this data is the company's concentration bank and other banks that conduct a large number of the company's transactions and hold a significant amount of the company's funds. Control systems are based on the bank's information reports provided through an electronic interface, which enables the customer to initiate certain kinds of bank transactions over a terminal.

Balance Reporting Systems

An indispensible tool to the cash manager is the "Balance Report" furnished by the concentration bank. The daily balance report provided by the

FIG. 8-6
Bank Deposit Slip

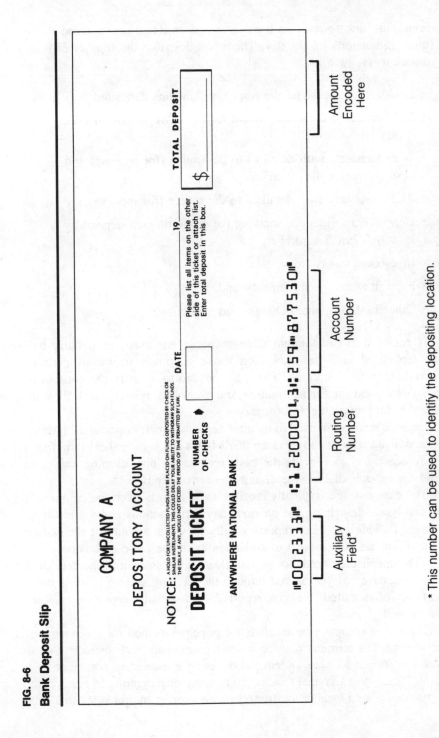

* This number can be used to identify the depositing location.

concentration bank focuses on the master concentration account and shows all funds transactions for the day. The report describes the sources of funds in various ways, such as:

- Lockbox numbers and the respective amounts deposited;
- Remittance Banking department for the aggregate of all DTCs deposited;
- Wire transfers, with detail as to the source (for receipts) and destination (for disbursements);
- ACH transfers, with detail as to the source (for receipts);
- Deposit consolidation, showing the origin of each deposit by location identifier number;
- Investment transactions;
- Foreign exchange settlements; and
- Other bank-originated charges and credits.

If regional or subconcentration accounts are used, then daily balance reports should be drawn on those accounts to monitor funds received from these sources. These are needed to identify the sources of deposits by location for accounting and control purposes, as well as to make the data available for forecasting.

Balance reports are used to monitor deposits, float, concentration transfers, and disbursements; to measure funds flows against the short-term funds flow forecast; and to provide the basis for making bookkeeping entries to record the receipt, disbursement, and transfer of funds.

The cash manager typically receives daily reports from the company's principal banks describing the previous day's transactions and the resulting balances. In addition, these reports usually show the amount of the ending balances that are still subject to collection as of the close of business that day. (The uncollected funds, or deposit float, is the amount of the deposited checks that have not yet cleared through the banking system.) While these reports are often called "balance reports," they actually report on transactions as well.

The use of computer terminals is the principal method for receiving balance reports. The terminal may be a desktop computer with memory that is driven by program software, a terminal driven by a mainframe computer, or a "dumb" interactive terminal that has no memory or programs. In either case, the customer dials a local or toll-free telephone number and provides an identi-

FIG. 8-7

Information Available Through Balance Reporting Modules

Account balances
- Ledger balances
- Collected funds
- Funds available next day
- Funds available in two or more days

Credits to the account
- Summary of total credits to an account
- Detail of individual credits

Debits to the account
- Summary of total charges to an account
- Detail of individual charges

Remittance data
- Funds concentration transactions
- Lockbox receipts

Electronic funds transfers (EFTs)
- Fedwire debits and credits
- CHIPs debits and credits
- ACH debits and credits
- Foreign remittances

Intraday reports
- EFT transactions
- Funds concentration
- Lockbox receipts
- Daylight overdraft status

News information
- Financial headlines
- Money market interest rates
- Foreign exchange rates

Control modules in the bank's information and control system may include:

EFT transaction initiation
- Repetitive funds transfers (Fedwire and ACH)
- Nonrepetitive funds transfers (Fedwire and ACH)

Paper-based transaction initiation
- Funds concentration initiation
- DTC initiation
- Preauthorized check initiation

Money market investments
Stop payment initiation
International account balances

fication code and a password through the terminal. The customer selects the balance reporting service module and requests a particular report from that module. The report is "downloaded," or sent from the bank to the terminal, where the information is either stored in memory (in a smart terminal) or printed out (in a dumb terminal). For companies with only limited information needs, banks often can deliver balance reports via voice, synthesized voice, facsimile (FAX), TWX, or Telex communication.

Balance reports usually are available 365 days a year, 24 hours a day. Cash managers typically elect to receive them early each morning for balance and activity information pertaining to the previous business day. Figure 8-7 shows the kind of information often available to cash managers through bank balance reporting modules.

Report Delivery Systems

Most banks use similar methods to deliver balance reports to their customers. When bank balance reporting services were developed in the mid-1970s, most banks created a report file for each customer and transferred that file to a third-party service provider. The third-party provider usually is a computer service bureau that allows authorized access to a company's files via a public data network (PDN), which is a network of dedicated telephone lines that connect "nodes" (or electronic gateways into the system) in major cities to the computer center of the service provider. This enables the bank's customer in a node city to make a local telephone call into the node (or a toll-free call into the PDN from outside the node city) to access its bank information files.

This type of system is still widely used by banks as their information delivery system. However, in the late 1980s, a number of important cash management banks shifted from third-party service providers to bank-owned computers, and a few banks developed their own proprietary networks to replace the PDNs. These shifts were motivated by economics; the banks wanted to control the escalating telecommunications and third-party computer costs of delivering critical information to their customers.

It is important to note that in either case, the customer does not have access to the bank's demand deposit accounting system or the bank's general ledger. This ensures the security and integrity of the bank's internal files. Instead, the customer has access to the report files that reside in a separate computer.

Report Formats

Most bank reports are sent and received in a layout dictated by those who designed the bank's system or by the designers of the computer software used by the bank. Consequently, the layout of the data varies considerably among banks. This complicates the cash manager's task of setting the company's daily funds position; the transactions and balances for each account at each bank must be analyzed before the company's funds position can be established. Moreover, the transmission of a report is expensive compared to the transmission of a data file.

Corporate demand for data file transfer instead of information reports has generally been lacking, perhaps because the typical low-tech orientation of treasury departments may have prevented cash managers from understanding the technology and, therefore, from requesting data file transfer. Moreover, treasury departments do not usually have the software available to receive and reformat the data into a meaningful layout.

However, in the late 1980s, inexpensive PC-based software was developed for use in electronic data interchange (EDI). Then the ANSI Accredited Standards Committee X12 developed an EDI format for transmission of balance reports. EDI involves the exchange of many different types of routine business transactions in standardized machine-readable formats. The acquisition and use of EDI management software became much more feasible for treasury departments because it can be used for multiple purposes, including receiving and translating data files on balances and transactions from banks.

Using EDI management software as a front end to the company's treasury management system enables the cash manager to translate the data from X12 syntax and to parse the elements of the data file into reports laid out in a way that is meaningful to the cash manager, using a database management system or an electronic spreadsheet. There, the data is available for immediate use by the cash manager as a decision support tool. The X12 balance reporting formats are expected to be adopted by principal cash management banks beginning in 1989, and the use of data file transmission will be demanded by the more sophisticated corporate treasury managers instead of preformatted balance reports.

Multibank Reports

Some service-minded banks seek to meet the needs of the customer who deals with more than one bank by offering multibank reporting. In one transmission this service, within the balance reporting module, delivers the account balances and transactions of the reporting bank as well as the reports of the customer's accounts at other banks.

Although most cash management banks are prepared to offer this service, there are some limitations. Multibank reporting is achieved technically through the process of "data exchange." In exchanging data, the participating banks transmit, or instruct their third-party service providers to transmit, the customer's report or data files to a bank that consolidates the information and prepares the report to be forwarded to the customer. This file transfer process is relatively easy and straightforward; however, it may not be completed in time to send to the customer the same day. This is especially so if the files must be transferred between third-party processors.

Secondly, few reporting banks have been able to deliver consolidated detailed debit and credit data to their customers. This inability is the great mystery of multibank balance reporting. The consolidating bank usually claims that it can handle the reporting of detail information and blames the other participating banks or third-party service providers for their inability to transmit the required detail data. Those parties vehemently deny that they lack the capability, claiming that the consolidating bank is unable to handle the detail. This usually leaves the customer groping for a solution.

The fact of the matter is that the transfer of such detail information is indeed technically feasible. However, some banks are reluctant to have their data reported to their customer through another bank, so they often do not provide this capability in designing their internal systems or in their contract with the third-party service provider. Where banks do have this capability, very often those file transfers occur after the file transfers relating to the bank's direct reporting relationships have been completed. This delays the receipt of the detail data by the consolidating bank and may prevent that bank from including the detail data in the customer's balance report on a timely basis.

Finally, multibank reporting is usually priced such that the cash manager should not expect a significant cost saving compared to obtaining the information reports directly from each bank.

CASH MANAGEMENT SUGGESTION:

In situations where information is needed from more than one bank, the cash manager should carefully determine the company's data requirements and assess the delivery capabilities and costs involved before purchasing multibank balance reporting service from a bank. Some important considerations to make in this process are how to determine where the failure occurred when a bank's data is missing from the report, how that data will be recovered, and within what time frame will it ultimately be made available.

Intraday Reporting

As banks' information systems became more sophisticated, banks no longer needed to wait for the close of business and the final posting of transactions in order to report the customer's account activity. Intraday reporting of transactions is now common among the more sophisticated cash management banks, although incoming funds transfers via ACH and the Clearing House Interbank Payment System (CHIPS) are usually reported as being provisional rather than final credits. This is because ACH transactions are processed in batches and the moment of final payment may not be clearly defined. The CHIPS system makes final settlement at about 6 P.M. New York time, although transfers among banks are effected and advised throughout the banking day. Fedwire transfers are usually given final settlement on an intraday basis.[5]

Lockbox deposits are often reported intraday, usually in the morning after the processing has been completed, although the lockbox deposits are posted at the end of the day with all other deposits. Therefore, intraday lockbox deposits may not have been processed through the bank's proof function by the time they are reported to the customer, making such deposits still subject to error corrections. Also, if remittance data is being captured from the checks, this process usually goes on throughout the day, thereby delaying the reporting of remittance detail.

Until banks change their system of posting all debits and credits after the close of business and begin to have intraday final postings, intraday reports will usually be subject to adjustments and corrections. These potential adjustments effectively prevent the cash manager from relying on intraday data. Nevertheless, the data contained in these reports is usually very useful to the cash manager attempting to monitor the company's funds position and transactions closely throughout the day.

International Balance Reporting

When receipts and disbursements in a foreign country are managed from the United States, international balance reporting is as necessary as domestic

---

[5] *Id.*

balance reporting. The U.S.-based cash manager must monitor the receipts and disbursements and make decisions regarding borrowing, investing, and repatriation of funds in the absence of a financial staff located in the foreign country.

The manner in which international balance reporting is provided varies among banks. Some banks require structural changes in the company's banking operations, including establishment of concentration accounts in either London or Brussels, and a periodic sweep of excess funds from each country into the concentration account. The concentration account may have subaccounts denominated in each currency to avoid unnecessary currency exchange transactions. The international balance report would contain balance and transaction information on each subaccount. Other banks are able to report a customer's balances and activity in accounts maintained at the bank's branches in several key countries.

Still other banks simply send the balance and transaction data of the company's accounts to the reporting bank via the message network of the Society for Worldwide Interbank Financial Telecommunications (SWIFT). In this case, the international balance report may occasionally be incomplete when one of the company's banks fails to report. It should be noted that the concept of reporting balances other than through the traditional monthly bank statement currently is not as universally accepted among foreign banks as it is in the United States. Therefore, the financial manager may have to use an extra measure of persuasion to gain the cooperation of some foreign banks to report balances and transactions daily.

In situations where a company's foreign operation manages its own receipts and disbursements, the use of international balance and transaction reporting would have little value to the U.S.-based financial manager.[6]

News Information

Some banks include financial news from world markets in their information reporting systems. This is very helpful to financial managers because it is available first thing in the morning and supplements the financial manager's morning newspaper, which may not have the latest headlines and financial news from European and Far Eastern markets.

The news module also may contain current indications of interest rates and foreign exchange rates to give the financial manager an early glimpse of where those markets have moved overnight. Some banks even allow cus-

---

[6] See Chapter 15 for a detailed discussion of managing funds internationally.

tomers to conduct investment and foreign exchange transactions of limited size at those rates, particularly overnight investment transactions, which the financial manager may execute via the terminal.

Treasury Workstations

A treasury work station (TWS) is a series of desktop computer programs that assist the cash manager in keeping track of data concerning funds flows, balances, borrowings, investments, and bank account maintenance, and it often performs other significant decision support functions.[7] TWS software may be purchased readily off-the-shelf from banks and software vendors for use on personal computers for prices ranging from under $5,000 to as much as $50,000. Some large companies have developed proprietary TWS software for their mainframe computers, which is accessed by the cash manager via remote terminal.

A TWS, like any other computer application, performs the work that a person could do but does it quicker and more accurately. In cash management applications, the TWS typically dials automatically into the bank's balance reporting system and retrieves the balance report (in either report or data file format) and other authorized information. The TWS then manipulates the data into a format that enables the cash manager to set the firm's daily funds position. The TWS stores the daily transaction and balance data as well as the short-term funds forecast, and it can be programmed to update the forecast and build an historical data base.

The TWS also maintains databases relating to the company's borrowing and investing activities and usually integrates these transactions into the short-term funds flow forecast. Some TWS systems can interface with the company's general ledger for the automatic uploading of journal entries, but many companies encounter hardware compatibility problems and a reluctance on the part of auditors to allow "unregulated data" to enter the general ledger.

The decision to acquire a TWS should not be dependent on the company's size or sales volume; rather, the decision should be based on the number of banks and bank accounts employed and the complexity involved in monitoring the transactions. A company with one bank and a simple system of one concentration account and a few ZBAs can probably survive quite well by obtaining daily balance reports over a terminal (smart or dumb) and manipulating the data manually for both funds management and

---

[7] See Chapter 9 for a detailed discussion of treasury workstations.

accounting purposes. The company with many ZBAs, and perhaps concentration accounts at several banks, may find the use of a TWS to be very cost effective.

One company, operating in over 40 states with 33 business units organized into five groups (not to mention 29 different payroll centers and two accounts payable operations), used four regional banks, one of which was the principal concentration and disbursing bank. The other three banks held accounts that had a significant number of transactions and needed to be monitored on a daily basis. Prior to buying a TWS, the cash manager used a dumb terminal to dial each concentration bank and obtain the balance reports on a total of 94 bank accounts; the manager then manually selected key data from each balance report to summarize transactions for the day and merged this data into a top-view summary reconciliation of all transactions and balances for the day. This process took an average of about two hours each day, which delayed the cash manager's access to the money markets when investments were warranted. Making the time factor even more critical was the fact that the cash manager is located on the West Coast, three hours behind New York's money markets, which often put the company at a disadvantage in having a favorable selection of investments. When the company installed a TWS (cost: about $5,000), the two-hour process was compressed into about 10 minutes of the cash manager's time because the TWS automatically accessed the banks and retrieved the bank data prior to the cash manager's arrival at the office. Then, after a brief visual edit by the cash manager, the TWS performed all the necessary data manipulations and made available in a matter of minutes the summarized data ready for decision-making by the cash manager.

DESIGNING THE OPTIMUM SYSTEM

The goal of cash management, of course, is to maintain the liquidity of the firm on a daily basis using a variety of forecasting, tracking, borrowing, and investing tools to achieve the precise level of funds desired to cover disbursements and to compensate the banks. It is important for a cash manager to have in place a well-planned bank account structure that facilitates the smooth operation of the collection, concentration, and disbursing systems; and to have an optimum information and control system in order to orchestrate the funds management system in an efficient and effective manner. As a decision support system, the required data will be available with the timeliness and level of detail required to make informed and timely decisions.

The cash manager achieves this goal by forecasting the amount of funds required to cover the day's disbursements and arranging to have that amount on deposit. In addition, the cash manager may be required to place additional collected funds on deposit to compensate the bank for loans and operating services and make up for any cumulative shortfall of balances required to reach the target balance level. The principal tool for planning and monitoring achievement of this goal is the target balance schedule.

Target Balance Schedule

The target balance schedule is customarily prepared and updated daily and cumulated throughout a one-month period. This period coincides with the period covered by the bank's account analysis statement, which contains the account activity and balances required by the company.[8] The target balance schedule, as shown in Figure 8-8, records and cumulates the daily collected balances and calculates the cumulative average daily collected balance. Using this figure and the number of days remaining in the month, the cash manager can recalculate the average daily collected balance required (the target balance) to be maintained during the rest of the month in order to achieve the overall monthly target balance. For example, in Figure 8-8, through April 17, the cumulative average daily collected balance is $93,000 compared to a target for the month of $100,000. Accordingly, in order to reach the overall monthly target balance of $100,000, the cash manager will be required to maintain an average balance of $109,000 during the remaining 13 days of the month. This is calculated by finding the remaining number of dollar days required to the end of the month and dividing that by the remaining number of days in the month.

1. Total dollar-days required for April	$3,000,000
2. Accumulated dollar-days through April 17	1,587,000
3. Additional dollar-days required by April 30	$1,413,000
4. Number of days remaining	13
5. Average balance per day required April 18 through April 30 ($1,413,000 ÷ 13)	$ 109,000

---

[8] See Chapter 10 for a detailed discussion of account analysis statements.

FIG. 8-8
Target Balance Schedule

ABC CORP.

Month: April, 19xx   Target Balance: $100
                    Target Dollar Days (30 X 100): $3,000

(Amounts in $ thousands)

Date	Day	Ledger Balance	Less: Float =	Collected Balance	Cumulative Dollar Days	Average Collected Balance
1	Mon	$174	$67	$107	$107	$107
2	Tue	163	42	121	228	114
3	Wed	138	36	102	330	110
4	Thur	112	25	87	417	104
5	Fri	96	10	86	503	101
6	Sat	96	2	94	597	100
7	Sun	96	0	96	693	99
8	Mon	130	86	44	737	92
9	Tue	147	62	85	822	91
10	Wed	185	74	111	933	93
11	Thur	245	120	125	1,058	96
12	Fri	100	14	86	1,144	95
13	Sat	100	5	95	1,239	95
14	Sun	100	0	100	1,339	96
15	Mon	129	64	65	1,404	94
16	Tue	125	37	88	1,492	93
17	Wed	140	45	95	1,587	93
18	Thur	102	29	73	1,660	92
19	Fri	135	20	115	1,775	93
20	Sat	135	7	128	1,903	95
21	Sun	135	0	135	2,038	97
22	Mon	130	44	86	2,124	97
23	Tue	134	19	115	2,239	97
24	Wed	124	32	92	2,331	97
25	Thur	132	26	106	2,437	97
26	Fri	135	9	126	2,563	99
27	Sat	135	2	133	2,696	100
28	Sun	135	0	135	2,831	101
29	Mon	120	37	83	2,914	100
30	Tue	108	22	86	3,000	100

The cash manager, therefore, must adjust the daily funds flow forecast to leave a slightly larger collected balance in the bank account in order to achieve the target balance goal.

Forecasting

Forecasting short-term flows of receipts and disbursements is essential if the firm is to make its way through the liquidity minefield. Even with careful forecasting, funds flows are subject to many exogenous forces; without forecasting, however, those forces could cause embarrassment and, at worst, a crippling blow. Therefore, if the firm is to be managed by its managers rather than being buffeted by outside forces, forecasting of receipts and disbursements is necessary.

Basically, short-term forecasting attempts to predict receipts and disbursements as separate streams over a time horizon of a few weeks. Usually, the cash manager prepares a schedule of anticipated receipts and disbursements in daily intervals for the next one or two weeks and in weekly intervals thereafter. This funds schedule becomes an essential tool during the first five days and it provides a queuing, or tickler, system, for keeping track of expected transactions during the later periods. The daily forecast is updated daily and extended weekly based on the actual transactions that have occurred.[9]

Tracking

Tracking and monitoring the actual streams of receipts and disbursements as they occur is essential to validating the accuracy of the forecast. Tracking also affords the opportunity to develop a database of historic funds flow that is useful in predicting future funds flows. Cash managers frequently summarize the actual flows into weekly aggregates for ease of storage and use this information to identify patterns and trends that may be helpful in future forecasts.

The principal source of the data used in tracking funds is the daily bank balance and transaction report described earlier in this chapter. The data for the previous business day is retrieved from the bank early the next day, summarized, and manipulated into a format that corresponds with the format of the forecasted schedule of receipts and disbursements; it is then juxtaposed with the forecast for analysis of variances from forecast to actual. The process of summarizing, manipulating, and analyzing may be accomplished manually if there is a moderate amount of data or by a TWS if there are a number of bank accounts involved.

---

[9] See Chapter 12 for a detailed discussion of short-term funds flow forecasting.

Managing Liquidity

With the forecasting system in place, the cash manager begins to experience the ebbs and flows of the firm by projecting funds flows forward in daily and weekly intervals and receiving daily reports of the actual results. Despite claims to the contrary from academicians and statisticians, there is a definite visceral aspect to managing a firm's liquidity. Every cash manager who has ever returned from vacation can attest to the period of adjustment—usually only a day or two—required to restore one's feeling for the rhythm and tempo of the funds flows.

The decisions concerning management of the firm's liquidity can be made only after the functions of forecasting and tracking of funds flows have been completed. Therefore, the firm needs a suitable bank account structure and effective systems for making these forecasts and handling the monitoring tasks. This will ensure that the cash manager does not become mired in the mechanics of the process, and will have adequate time and energy to make the strategic considerations necessary to optimize liquidity and income.

The cash manager is concerned with the collected bank balances, not the company's general ledger balances. The daily funds objective is based on the need to achieve a prescribed target level of balances in the bank accounts. That target level is designed to cover disbursements as checks are presented for payment and EFTs are required, as well as to maintain a predetermined level of compensating balances. In some cases, particularly where fees are payable, the financial manager may set the desired level of compensating balances (over and above amounts needed to cover disbursements) to zero. Then each month, and perhaps even daily, the target level of balances is adjusted to account for the amount by which the firm has actually fallen short of, or exceeded, the target.

To the extent that the firm experiences a shortfall of funds to cover disbursements, it must borrow. To the extent that the firm has enough funds to cover disbursements but not enough to fund the additional level of compensating balances, the cash manager may defer borrowing for awhile in anticipation of a period of excess funds that may restore the actual average balances back to the target level. When the targeted level has been achieved and excess funds still remain, the cash manager should then take steps to invest the excess, either in interest bearing instruments or in repayment of existing debt.

Borrowing and investing (or debt repayment) transactions have certain administrative costs and potentially real costs if not timed correctly. The timing of these transactions is aided greatly by the use of the short-term funds forecast. The following are some examples of how timing of borrowing and investing transactions can affect liquidity and profits:

1. The funds forecast predicts a shortfall that needs to be covered for only a few days, making the trend in interest rates inconsequential. The cash manager's options are to:
   - Borrow for the period involved with an option to prepay the borrowing prior to maturity; or
   - Enter into a reverse repurchase agreement in which the firm agrees to sell securities out of its investment portfolio, with a simultaneous agreement to repurchase those same securities from the counterparty at a certain date and price in the future.

2. The funds forecast predicts a surplus of funds for a few days with the excess being used at that time. The cash manager's options are to repay short-term loans temporarily or invest in overnight investments, such as repurchase agreements, and roll them over until the funds are used.

3. The funds forecast predicts a shortfall that needs to be covered for several months.
   - If interest rates are rising, the cash manager liquidates sufficient securities in the firm's investment portfolio to cover the shortfall. This limits a decline in value of the portfolio arising from increasing interest rates and permits the investment of surplus funds later at a higher interest rate.
   - If interest rates are falling, the cash manager draws on the firm's bank line of credit. The interest rate on this line of credit either floats or is fixed, and the maturity of the borrowing is kept short.

4. The funds forecast predicts a surplus of funds for several months.
   - If interest rates are rising, the cash manager would invest in money market instruments with short maturities (30 days or so) and renew them at maturity at higher yields; repaying existing borrowings, selecting the shorter-term maturities or debt carrying higher interest rates for prepayment are also options available to the cash manager.
   - If interest rates are falling, the cash manager would invest in money market instruments with longer maturities, perhaps timed to mature coincident with the forecasted runoff of the excess funds. If the cash manager is in a position to speculate on

interest rates, investing in longer term money market instruments might be considered, perhaps one-year Treasury bills, with a view to selling the instruments when funds are required. With interest rates in decline, the cash manager may realize a profit in excess of the initial yield.

Alternatively, the cash manager might consider repurchasing some of the company's outstanding debt in the open market, particularly any sinking fund debt that may be trading at a discount and where a sinking fund payment is due in the approximate time frame of the forecast.[10]

SUMMARY

In developing a smoothly functioning funds management system, the design of the bank account configuration to receive, concentrate, and disburse funds is critical. Overlaying the bank account structure is an information delivery system that enables the cash manager to monitor the funds flows throughout the system. The information delivery system is tied to a principal bank of the company and often depends on electronic manipulation of information through TWS software in a desktop computer.

With the information regarding actual transactions flowing into the treasury department and being manipulated to facilitate the cash manager's decisions, an effective daily funds flow forecasting system is the final critical link. A funds flow forecast showing receipts and disbursements as well as balances enables the cash manager to monitor the actual funds flows against a benchmark forecast.

Therefore, the effective management of the firm's liquidity depends on bank account structure, receipt of information, and the effective use of that information.

---

[10] See Chapter 11 for a detailed discussion of liquidity management.

CHAPTER 9

Treasury Workstations

Robert J. Leahy

OVERVIEW

The most exciting treasury management product today is the microcomputer-based treasury workstation. The micro-based workstation performs many time-consuming calculations that a corporate treasurer or treasury manager would otherwise perform manually each day.

A workstation consists of a special set of computer software programs—or modules—that operate on a microcomputer. A module is a software program that works and shares information with other programs. A typical complete workstation consists of

1. A microcomputer;

2. A modem, which links two computers by telephone line; and

3. A computer software program usually furnished by a bank or other vendor. (These banks and other vendors will subsequently be referred to as vendors.) This program tells the computer and the modem what to do and when to do it.

The modem automatically telephones each bank's balance reporting system at a preset time each morning to obtain account information. The software program then consolidates this information on an electronic worksheet. The format of the worksheet may vary, but it usually shows bank ledger balances, float, collected balances, debits, and credits. The work-sheet can also show target balances and adjustments in collected balances necessary to achieve these target balances.

If the debt or investment modules have also been purchased, the effect of any maturing debt or investments is added to the worksheet. Estimates of any other receipts and disbursements may then be added manually by the treasury manager. The result is the forecasted net cash position for the day. If the net cash position is positive, then the company has money to invest that day. If the position is negative, then borrowing may be required.

EVALUATING THE NEED FOR A WORKSTATION AND SELLING IT TO MANAGEMENT

The workstation does nothing that a person cannot do manually, but does it earlier, faster, more accurately, and with far less human effort. The treasury manager no longer needs to phone the company's banks upon arriving at the office because the workstation can call the bank's computer before the office opens. The only limiting factor is the need for the banks' reporting systems to have the data ready by the time the workstation calls. With this benefit provided by the workstation, the treasury manager can reach a final decision on funding actions for the day within 15 minutes after arriving at the office. The workstation will not make the transposition errors that may occur when amounts are handwritten. Workstations can also reduce timesharing charges by calling each bank's balance reporting system directly, instead of requiring that a central timesharing facility consolidate all of the balance reports. Such a feature can save a company thousands of dollars in monthly timesharing bills. Furthermore, a workstation may reduce long-distance phone charges by calling during nonpeak hours.

While workstations can reduce some treasury managers' workloads considerably, they are not for everyone. If a treasury manager uses only one bank, or does little investing or borrowing, it may be easier to keep records manually on a columnar pad. Therefore, a treasury manager should consider carefully whether the purchase of a workstation can reduce the workload or increase company profits significantly.

A treasury manager can easily sell a workstation to management if the company manages a large debt or investment portfolio. In such a case, it is easy to calculate how much extra income the company can earn if it knows its cash position several hours earlier, when the more attractive investment opportunities are available. The moment the market opens, investment managers start to call their brokers to purchase more attractive investments. As the morning passes, the only investments that remain are those with lower yields. Thus, the earlier a company knows exactly how much money it can invest, the earlier it can enter the investment market to purchase more attractive investments. The same is true when a company continually borrows money in the marketplace.

It is much more difficult to sell the concept of a workstation to management if a company does not manage its own large debt or investment portfolio. Undeniably, a workstation will save the treasury manager (or the treasury staff) time in consolidating bank balances and determining the company investment/borrowing position. Unfortunately, this savings of time is a "soft dollar" savings, but it enables the company to redeploy the person(s) who had previously called each bank to other, perhaps more profitable, tasks. The only financial change is the extra money spent on streamlining a task that had previously been done at no *additional* cost.

DEVELOPING A WORKSTATION IN-HOUSE

Custom-Made Systems

Some companies use their own data processing department to develop an in-house workstation. By designing and building a workstation in-house, the final product can be tailored exactly to the company's requirements. This eliminates the possibility that a purchased workstation will be so inflexible that the treasury manager cannot address special needs but must follow the program.

Custom-designed software is not cheap. A highly paid data processing person must be trained for several months in treasury department functions, workstation requirements, and workstation functions. During that training period, the treasury manager and others in the treasury department will be diverted from their duties. After eight months, a workstation program may (or may not) be produced. With rare exceptions, there will be little training of additional personnel and no documentation. All changes or revisions must be made by the same data processing personnel—if they are still available and have the time. Therefore, the advantages and disadvantages must be weighed carefully before the decision is made to custom design.

Component Systems

An alternative to custom design is the assembly of a workstation from readily available components. This can be accomplished by a combination of the following items:

- A microcomputer. Any modern microcomputer will do.

- A spreadsheet program. A spreadsheet program is essentially an electronic columnar pad. Lotus 1-2-3® is one popular spreadsheet program that allows a large table to be rearranged quickly and easily. Other perfectly adequate spreadsheet programs can duplicate the functions of Lotus® at a fraction of the cost.

- A modem. A modem is a device that allows two computers to communicate with each other via a telephone line. The modem allows the treasury department's computer to "talk" to the banks' balance reporting computers. Currently, general purpose modems communicate at 300, 1200, or 2400 baud. (The term "baud" loosely refers to the speed of the communication in words per minute.) A 2400 baud modem works eight times as fast as a 300 baud modem but is more expensive.

- A modem software program. This program tells the modem when to operate and how and when to make phone calls. The modem cannot operate without such a program. The program must have a feature called auto-originate, which allows the computer to make telephone calls automatically at preset times. The telecommunications portions of Symphony® or Framework® have this feature, but are expensive to purchase for this purpose alone.

The spreadsheet program, modem, and modem software program may be purchased at almost any computer store for less than $600.

To set up a component system, information must first be entered into the modem software program. This information includes when to call, what phone number to call, what password to use, which account numbers to give, and gives instructions to save the balance information on disk. This information must be entered for each bank. It can be difficult to operate modems and modem software programs, but almost all companies selling these products offer phone assistance.

The modem plugs into the phone system with the same small clear plastic phone connectors used in home phone systems. Since most office phones use the large multiline metal connectors, special adaptors must be purchased from major electronics stores.

The computer's internal clock must be set with the correct time, and the computer and modem software program must be kept operating at night. The modem program monitors the time during the night, and when it is time for the first phone call to be made, the computer will call the first bank's reporting system. Using the passwords and other previously stored information, the computer will ask the reporting system for the balance information on the desired accounts. The computer will take this information, store it, and then hang up. When it makes subsequent phone calls, it will repeat this process. Each call takes about 30 seconds for a 2400 baud modem, or four minutes for a 300 baud modem.

When the treasury manager arrives in the morning, all of the information will have already been received by the modem and stored in the computer. The modem program can display the result of each of these calls on the screen, or print the results if desired.

The next step is to "parse" the data, which means extracting the relevant information from the complete balance reports. While most treasury workstation software can handle this task, no commercial parsing programs are adequate to convert multiple bank reports into a common format reliably. Therefore, the treasury manager must scan the bank reports and manually extract the relevant information. The treasury manager must then design a worksheet on an electronic spreadsheet program, and enter the relevant information onto the worksheet for analysis.

Some integrated spreadsheet programs, such as Symphony,® do have a rudimentary parsing ability, but will function correctly only if the balance report is transmitted exactly as expected. If an extra character is accidently received during transmission, the parsed information may be meaningless or misleading to the user. An extra character can cause a disbursement account requiring $121,000 in funding to be misparsed as requiring $210,000.

Disadvantages of Component Systems

The assembly of components off the shelf does not provide the integration of a true workstation. This type of system does not have any debt and investment modules exchanging information with the cash forecast report. With the integrated workstation, the vendor provides the technical expertise in the areas of microcomputers and treasury management. In the case of a component system, the designer must supply that expertise. With a home-built workstation, the designer must ensure that the system operates correctly, all the banks have been called, current information is being used, all relevant information is on the worksheet before a decision is made, and duplicate records are made as a backup.

This takes a considerable amount of effort and skill. Since several workstations are available for less than $5,000, and some vendors accept increased compensating balances of about $81,000 a year (with balances worth 7 percent) in lieu of cash payments, the treasury manager must determine whether the increase in savings is worth the effort of assembling and maintaining the component system. Unless there is absolutely no other way to obtain the benefits of a workstation, the answer should be "no." A treasury manager is paid to save money for the company. In almost any company, there are easier ways to save $5,000.

PURCHASING A WORKSTATION

The selection of a workstation should be based on individual needs. There is no one best workstation. Some treasury managers want an inexpensive, bare-bones system to use with purchased Lotus 1-2-3® software, setting up all the worksheets themselves. Other treasury managers want a system with pre-programmed reports.

Workstation prices are also difficult to compare because there is no typical workstation. Some vendors offer debt and investment modules as part of their standard workstations. Other vendors do not offer these modules at all, or offer them as options. To complicate matters further, some vendors sell their systems for cash only. Some vendors accept either cash payment or compensating balances. Others sell workstations at a lower price, but they require a higher monthly service charge. Some workstations are less expensive, but may have a high installation charge. Others are low-priced because the workstations are less complex and require additional monthly timesharing charges. Aside from the difficulty of comparing such prices, if the need for a workstation is great, the price may not be of major concern early in the negotiation. Generally, workstations are priced from $3,000 to $40,000. With customization, the price of a workstation can easily exceed $100,000.

Evaluating Needs

The treasury manager should not have to think about hardware or software, but rather should ask what information is required to do the job. These needs should be divided into real needs (essential features) and preferences (nonessential features). A real need might be the ability to initiate automated clearing house (ACH) transactions, while a preference might be the ability to generate margin investing reports. The real needs should not be made too restrictive, since this will eliminate potential workstations.

Service and Support

For as long as a workstation is used, the treasury manager will have to depend on the vendor. For that reason, support is the *most* important factor to consider. The treasury manager will need a vendor with an ongoing ability to train the treasury manager or his employees, furnish documentation, modify the workstation program, and provide updated versions of the workstation. An average product that is well supported is preferable to a superior product that is poorly supported.

Flexibility

The treasury manager should look at the consolidation or cash forecasting module. Do the reports in this module give all of the needed information? Must internal reports be changed to match workstation reports? Or can the workstation report format be changed to match current reports? How easy is it to make *any* changes to reports? Some workstations require that all report changes be implemented by the vendor—at an additional cost. Other workstations allow the user to make report changes. It is clearly more desirable for the workstation user to be able to make changes directly.

A treasury manager should not spend a large amount of time evaluating the communications or debt or investment modules of a workstation. Differences between vendors in these modules may not be that significant for the *average* user.

Integration

The term "integration" is used in two ways in the world of treasury workstations.

1. Information on maturing debt should be *integrated* automatically into the cash forecasting worksheet. All workstations *should* be this integrated. The cash forecasting worksheet will be worthless if $5 million in maturing debt is not reflected on the cash forecasting worksheet.

2. Some workstations can *integrate* funds transactions and balance records with the company's accounting records on the mainframe computer. It is easy for a workstation to send these records to a mainframe computer. It is very complicated for a company's data processing staff to integrate the records into the company's accounting system.

Corporate References

The treasury manager should require each potential workstation vendor to furnish the names of two paying corporate customers as references. Only paying corporate references actually using the workstation should be used because they can be extremely vocal if a workstation or its vendor does not live up to initial promises. It would be preferable for these references to be using the same modules that the treasury manager intends to buy. At the very least, each reference should be using the modules that phone each bank to get the balance information, and that consolidate this information into a cash forecast.

Given two references, a treasury manager should not necessarily assume that the two furnished references will be positive references. Both references should be called and asked if they like the workstation, what kind of service and support they have received from their vendor, and if they would buy that product again. The treasury manager should listen to the answers very carefully. If a reference enthusiastically says "excellent product, extremely responsive vendor, couldn't live without it," that should be considered a positive reference. The treasury manager should be wary if a reference says "some modules are not as bad as others."

Experiment With Inexpensive Workstations

No matter how much money a treasury manager is planning to spend or how complex a workstation is desired, the treasury manager should start off by purchasing an inexpensive workstation. Despite the best planning in the world, six months after purchasing the workstation the treasury manager may realize that the wrong needs were identified and the wrong workstation purchased. This can cause difficulties if the company has spent $60,000 purchasing a customized workstation. The problem is not nearly so difficult if a $5,000 workstation had been purchased specifically as an experiment.

This advice will be difficult to implement if a treasury manager wants a heavily customized workstation. In such a case, no inexpensive workstation may have the same features. However, an inexpensive workstation is still a worthwhile purchase. After using such a workstation, a treasury manager will quickly be able to identify which functions are necessary. This knowledge will be invaluable in ordering a customized workstation. In order for this to be a valid experiment, the treasury manager should consider only those inexpensive workstations that contain all of the desired modules.

The treasury manager should use the workstation for six months. At the end of that period, the treasury manager should know *exactly* what is required in a workstation. No study or survey could ever have provided this knowledge. With this knowledge, the treasury manager will know exactly what questions to ask when shopping for a more sophisticated workstation, or whether the inexpensive workstation is appropriate. The $5,000 investment may very well save many times that amount.

SECTIONS OF A WORKSTATION

The following paragraphs give a detailed description of the different modules of a workstation. The points following each module should be used to determine real needs and preferences. The real needs should be used to determine which workstation to purchase.

Data Gathering Module

This module is used to obtain bank account information. ("Module" is a buzzword for a software program that is intended to work and share information with another program.) At a predetermined time, the module will call the banks' balance reporting computers. To do this, the module uses a modem activated by a clock-timer built into the computer. Using passwords and other information stored in the computer, the module will ask each bank's balance reporting computer for the information on all accounts and then store this information for later use. With a vendor-designed workstation, the polling of the balance reporting systems should take about one minute per account. If the company has 30 accounts in 30 banks, it should take 30 minutes to call them all and store the information.

Some unsophisticated banks may not be equipped to allow a computer to call and get account information. These banks may require that the treasury manager call and speak with a bank employee. Most workstations allow information to be input manually for these banks. However, if the treasury manager continues doing business with such banks, the treasury manager will have to input information manually *every day*.

The following are several points to consider:

1. *Parse standard balance reports.* Can the module take standard bank balance reports and convert (parse) them to a common format? If the module cannot parse, then it must obtain the balance reporting information either by receiving ANSI X12 or Bank Administration Institute (BAI)-formatted information, or by having a central computer timesharing system receive and parse all balance reports at an additional cost.

2. *Accept BAI- or ANSI X12-formatted information.* Some workstation designers have avoided the problems involved in parsing by accepting only balance reporting information formatted to the BAI or ANSI standards. This approach may not always work for all bank balance reporting systems because there is enough leeway in the BAI standards so that one computer sending information to another computer may be misunderstood. Also, not all balance reporting systems can send information in the BAI or ANSI formats to corporate customers.

3. *Make unattended telephone calls.* Can the module automatically call each bank's balance reporting system or a central timesharing service? The choice depends on the vendor that designed the module. Can the module initiate the phone calls by itself, or does the treasury manager have to direct its activities?

4. *Redial busy phone numbers.* If the balance reporting service's phone line is busy, will the module call again at a later time to get the missing account information? Some workstations allow an alternative phone number to be stored that will be called if the workstation cannot get through on the primary number. Some workstations are programmed to omit calling when a bank is closed for a holiday.

5. *Require timesharing for information consolidation.* Some workstations do not call each bank's balance reporting systems. Instead, the treasury manager must arrange for each bank to send the balance reporting information to one central computer timesharing vendor. This requirement makes for a less complex module because the module need accept pre-parsed information from only one source. But this also means that the treasury manager will have to pay additional timesharing charges for this consolidation service. The treasury manager will also be at the mercy of the bank that requires the timesharing of information for the workstation it developed. This service—and the usefulness of the workstation—may disappear if the bank stops marketing a workstation.

Consolidation and Forecasting Module

The typical consolidation and forecasting module puts account information it has received into a common format. With few exceptions, each bank's balance reporting system may provide information in a different format. Each of these formats must be parsed to a common format by the microcomputer. After the information is converted to a common format, it will be stored in a database. The data will be used on various worksheets for target balance management and intracompany funds analysis.

The consolidation and forecasting module is the heart of the workstation. Information on debt, investments, and bank balances is combined there. The resulting worksheet shows consolidated bank balances, daily receipts and disbursements, maturing investments (a source of funds), and maturing debt (a use of funds). The bottom line reflects the amount of money to invest or borrow for that day. Most workstations also have a funds forecasting worksheet that helps predict what the company's funds needs will be in the near future. It is now up to the treasury manager to temper this forecast with information that the module does not have in order to reach a final decision.

Points to consider include:

1. *Funds requirements forecasting.* Most modules allow the treasury manager to forecast funds for a specified time horizon (weekly, monthly, quarterly, or other). The "other" option would be useful if the company uses a lunar cycle, or a 4-4-5-week accounting period.

2. *Funds flow projections comparisons.* How did the treasury manager and the module do last week in forecasting funds requirements? By reviewing and compensating for variances, treasury managers may improve the accuracy of their projections.

3. *Information output.* The treasury manager will want to review the funds consolidation and forecasting report later. A module that prints the information on paper will therefore be needed. Not all workstations have this feature.

4. *Report layout determination.* Can the treasury manager alter the standard report layout to conform to reports that are now being produced? The answer to this may vary from module to module within the same workstation.

5. *Information transfer to mainframe computer.* While this is a worthwhile goal, the treasury manager should ensure that the company's data processing department can and will implement this feature before making this a real need. The data processing department will have to do a significant amount of programming before the data can be transferred.

The integration of workstation information with the company's mainframe computer must be discussed with the company's auditors. Who will be responsible for the integrity of the data being transferred? The vendor's answer to this point may vary from module to module.

6. *Timesharing requirement.* Some banks offer many workstation features via their own terminal-based timesharing system. In order to implement these same features quickly on a workstation, some banks require that the workstations call their timesharing computer to accomplish a given feature. In this instance, the workstation is acting as a terminal. Naturally, there will be a timesharing charge each time this service is used. Again, this timesharing requirement may vary from module to module.

Bank Analysis Module

This module is used to make long-term analyses of bank account information. It is less concerned with the immediate question of "What are the collected balances?" than with performing such tasks as managing target balances or comparing various banks' account analyses.

Points to consider include:

1. *Target balance management.* Can the treasury manager compare target balances with actual balances? The worksheet should show what the incremental additional collected balances should be in order to achieve a target level by month-end (or the end of any other time period).

2. *Account analysis comparisons.* To use this feature, the treasury manager may have to enter information manually from each bank's account analysis to compare what is being paid (in balances) at different banks for a similar service. Manual entry can be extremely time-consuming. Several banks provide customers with a floppy disk containing monthly account analysis information. Although this information is already in a computer-readable format, it can be used only if the vendor has programmed this ability into the workstation.

3. *Earnings credit rate analysis.* This feature would use the account analysis information entered above. The module would take the earnings credit rate and the reserve requirement used on each bank's account analysis and put them on a common basis for comparison purposes.

4. *Intracompany funds analysis.* This would allow the treasury manager to operate a single investment or debt pool while separately tracking balances for each division or subsidiary.

5. *Disbursement or check clearing reconciliation.* Can the module reconcile the checks that have cleared and those that are still outstanding? The treasury manager may need to enter information manually on the checks that have been written and their amounts (unless the mainframe computer can be persuaded to provide this information in the right format). The module would also need detailed information from the bank on which checks have cleared. The module compares the two lists and reports any discrepancies and outstanding checks. Again, it can be extremely time-consuming to enter all of this information each month.

Investment Module

This module monitors all short- and long-term investments. The investment module should also feed data into the consolidation or forecasting module described in a previous section. If company management requires this information, the choice is for the module to make the calculations, or have the treasury manager manually make the calculations. Considerable time can be saved, and accuracy improved, if the module can make the calculations. If a company has no investments, or a simple investment portfolio, then the following questions are not relevant.

1. *Daily accruals.* Can the module calculate daily accrued income on each investment, or must the treasury manager make the calculation manually?

2. *Month-end accruals.* Can the module calculate the accrued income on each investment for the month, or must the treasury manager make the calculation manually?

3. *Portfolio yield.* Can the module calculate the portfolio yield, or must the treasury manager calculate these yields manually?

4. *Confirmation letters.* If desired, will a confirmation letter be printed for the treasury manager to mail to the investment dealer for each transaction? Some investment dealers require a confirming letter for each transaction. Since each of these letters differs only slightly, considerable time can be saved if the module can generate a form letter for each transaction.

5. *Adjusted book value or market value analysis calculations.* Each money market instrument has unique characteristics that should be taken into account by the module. Considerable time can be saved if the module can make the calculations for: adjustable floating rate preferred stock; foreign investments; money market securities; and floating rate instruments.

6. *Amortization of discounts or premiums.* Can the module amortize discounts or premiums on investments, or must the treasury manager make the calculation manually?

7. *Swap opportunities determination.* Given current yield curves, can the module identify opportunities to sell certain investments and reinvest the proceeds in other instruments of a longer maturity or perhaps of a different type? Or must the treasury manager do this manually?

8. *Total portfolio statistics.* Can the module calculate performance statistics for the entire portfolio, as opposed to a single investment, or must the treasury manager make the calculation manually?

9. *Broker statistics.* Can the module calculate the yield or accrued income for all investments purchased through a single dealer, or must the treasury manager make the calculation manually? This feature would allow the treasury manager to evaluate the investment advice of one dealer, as compared with another.

10. *Multiple portfolio management.* This feature would allow the treasury manager to segregate the investments of a division, subsidiary, or client by keeping separate portfolios and separate statistics for each.

11. *Income projections.* Can the module calculate investment income in two, three, or six months if the present portfolio is kept, or must the treasury manager make the calculation manually? Such calculations can help the treasury manager make income projections to management.

12. *Margin investing.* Can the module compare the expense and income resulting from investing on margin, or must the treasury manager calculate these amortizations manually?

13. *Investment portfolio activity reconciliation.* Can the module reconcile the starting and ending portfolios by showing all additions and sales during the period, or must the treasury manager make the calculation manually?

14. *Subsidiary interest income or expense allocation.* Can the treasury manager operate one centralized investment pool while maintaining separate accounting records for each company subsidiary, or must the treasury manager make the calculation manually? This may be a legal requirement if each company subsidiary is a separate corporation. The module should keep track of subsidiary funds used to purchase investments, and should allocate the resulting income to that subsidiary.

15. *Target vs. actual comparisons.* Can the module remember what income was expected from an investment and compare it with what was actually realized, or must the treasury manager make the calculation manually?

16. *Rate reporter information reception.* Can the module receive rate information on money market instruments from outside companies providing this information?

17. *Maturities forecasting.* Can the module forecast and keep track of maturing investments, or must the treasury manager make the calculation manually?

18. *Investment information integration.* If a $2 million investment will mature tomorrow, this investment should show up on the funds forecast as a source of funds. If it does not show up, then the investment will mature and the funds may remain idle.

Debt Module

This module monitors all long- and short-term borrowings. The borrowing information should also feed into the consolidation or forecasting module described in a previous section. If company management requires this information, the choice is for the module to make the calculations, or have the treasury manager manually make the calculations. Considerable time can be saved, and accuracy improved, if the module can make the calculations. If a company has little or no debt, then the following questions can be ignored.

1. *Adjusted book value or market value calculations.* Each debt instrument has unique characteristics that must be taken into account by the debt module. Considerable time can be saved if the module can make the calculations for acceptances, commercial paper, financial futures, floating rate notes, and master notes.

2. *Bank line activity.* Is the module able to keep track of borrowings, repayments, and interest accruals under a bank credit line, or must the treasury manager calculate this activity manually?

3. *Debt service projections.* Can the module calculate the cost of servicing outstanding debt, or must the treasury manager calculate these projections manually?

4. *Maturity schedules.* Can the module forecast debt maturities and show exactly when funds will be needed, or must the treasury manager make the calculation manually?

5. *"What if" analyses.* Can the module forecast the effect of alternative conditions and maturities, or must the treasury manager make the calculation manually?

6. *Optimum mix of financing instruments.* Given various factors and constraints, can the module calculate the best method for borrowing additional funds, or must the treasury manager make the calculation manually?

Wire Transfers

This feature would allow the treasury manager to consolidate funds and to implement investment decisions directly by having the workstation call the bank to authorize wire transfers. It would eliminate the need to phone the bank and give the same information verbally.

While only some workstations advertise this Fedwire transfer capability, almost all workstations can do this. When a workstation phones a bank for account information, it calls a phone number that has been provided. The number could just as well be a wire transfer phone number. The workstation then talks to a bank's computer, and step-by-step, tells the bank computer what the treasury manager has told it to say. To get balance information, the treasury manager would give the workstation one set of commands. To initiate a wire transfer, the treasury manager would give it a different set of commands. The workstation cannot tell the difference between the commands. (Remember that in order to use this feature, the bank must be capable of accepting computer-generated wire transfer instructions.)

Workstations that specifically allow the treasury manager to initiate wire transfers also have security features that limit access to this wire transfer function. Many workstations offer levels of security, so that one person may initiate a wire transfer, but another person is required to approve the wire transfer before it can be transmitted to the bank. The real security, however, resides with the bank's system, which requires a password (or other security techniques such as encryption or authentication). A person having the necessary information can sit down at the nearest terminal and initiate a wire transfer. The solution to this security problem is to have a written agreement with the bank specifying the banks and account numbers to which money can be transferred via wire transfers. This should be implemented regardless of whether a workstation is purchased. For the sake of security, *never* put the bank passwords in a preformatted set of commands. The passwords should be entered manually each time a wire transfer is made.

Some modules can generate a standard confirmation letter *automatically* each time a wire transfer is initiated.

Corporate Trade Payments

The treasury manager could (through a bank) initiate ACH corporate-to-corporate trade payments by using this feature. All of the invoice information sent with a corporate trade payment would have to be manually entered into the workstation, or downloaded from the company's accounts payable system.

Bank Relationship Management

This feature is an electronic rolodex file (technically a database management system program) that keeps track of individual bank accounts, approved signers, their authorized dollar limits, and the names and addresses of banks and bank contact persons. This feature can be invaluable if the treasury manager has a large number of bank accounts, although any database management system program can do this. Many workstations will also generate form letters to inform all necessary banks when valid signatories change. Some bank workstations even allow the treasury manager to indicate that an officer of the bank is on the company's board of directors—presumably to prevent the inadvertent closing of a bank account.

Electronic Mail

The treasury manager can send and receive electronic mail if a third computer acts as a central mailbox.

Letters of Credit

The treasury manager can initiate letters of credit and check their status through the issuing bank only if the bank that issues the letters of credit offers this initiation and status information in an electronically accessible format.

Word Processing

Some vendors have included a word processing program with the workstation. This is usually a commercial program that may also be purchased separately.

Other Features

Back-Up of Data Files. The workstation should prompt the treasury manager to back-up history files (make a duplicate copy on a floppy disk or tape of all balance, debt, and investment information). The back-up media should then be stored in a safe place far away from the workstation. The treasury manager should back-up all history files at least once a week. A good rule of thumb is to back-up files whenever so much new information has been added that the treasury manager would not want to reenter the information if it were lost.

Graphics. If the workstation uses a combined spreadsheet and graphics program, information from the workstation can be passed to a graphics program. The graphics program itself is not necessarily included in the price of the workstation. A graphics program is an excellent way to convert numbers quickly into a pie, bar, or line chart for easier comprehension.

Help Messages. Some workstation vendors have specified one key as the help key. When this key is pressed, the workstation tries to identify the problem and produce an appropriate help message. This feature can almost eliminate the need to refer to the instruction manuals.

Remote Diagnostics. With this feature, a vendor can diagnose a workstation problem directly—and from great distances. The treasury manager simply calls the vendor's phone number and relinquishes control of the workstation. The vendor then can operate the workstation over long distance phone lines to find the problem. Remote diagnostics is the ultimate in troubleshooting. No on-site service calls are needed for software problems. The treasury manager should be certain that this remote diagnostic feature can be initiated only by the workstation operator. Otherwise, a computer hacker could access the workstation at night and instruct the workstation to erase programs and data files.

OTHER CONSIDERATIONS

Software Payment

Some banks allow the buyer to pay for the software by increasing bank balances. This would avoid the need to obtain internal company approval for the purchase of the workstation. To pay for a $10,000 program, a buyer may have to increase bank balances by about $162,000 for one year, where funds are valued at 7 percent.

System Installation

Some vendors charge for setting up the workstation at the buyer's location. Some vendors have a low selling price and a high installation charge. In theory, the installation (not operator training) of a workstation on a computer should consist of giving the treasury manager the program disks and documentation. However, the process is more complicated because the workstation program has to be transferred to the treasury manager's hard disk, and the computer start-up program may need to be modified. A technician should be able to install the workstation onto a computer hard disk in an hour (excluding travel time).

A hard disk is a nonremovable storage device that is permanently mounted in the computer. Hard disks have become so inexpensive that they have virtually become mandatory options on business microcomputers. All workstations require hard disks for program operation.

Computer Requirements

The IBM standard has become the de facto business microcomputer standard. Workstation software programs should run on IBM or clone computers. A "clone" is a non-IBM computer that meets the IBM/MS-DOS standard. Such computers are less expensive and often offer more features than actual IBM computers. However, a treasury manager should check with the workstation vendor just to be sure that a specific clone computer is acceptable.

Several vendors have developed workstations that run on Digital Equipment Corporation (DEC) microcomputers and minicomputers. These workstations have proved popular with insurance companies, which have adopted DEC computers as an informal industry standard.

VENDOR SERVICE AND SUPPORT

A treasury manager must consider more than just features when purchasing a workstation. A vendor's service and support can be more important than the features offered by that vendor's workstation. A lack of service and support can make a good workstation unacceptable. At the other extreme, outstanding service and support can make an average workstation the best choice.

Points to consider include:

1. *Vendor customization.* Some vendors offer a standard product in order to sell to the mass market at a low cost. Others cater to the other end of the spectrum and offer full customization. A third group offers a standard product, but will customize it upon request. A typical charge for customization is $1,000 a day for programmer and designer time.

2. *User groups.* An easy way to learn more about using a workstation is to get together with other treasury managers who use the same workstation. Such groups are invaluable to a vendor because of the useful feedback. However, if a vendor has only 10 corporate customers scattered throughout the United States, it is unlikely that many members will show up at a meeting. The treasury manager should ask how many times the user group has met, and how many users actually attended.

3. *Monthly service or support charges.* Someone will have to pay for the ongoing relationship with the workstation vendor. That someone is the buyer. Some vendors sell the system for a lower price but require a higher monthly service charge. Monthly service charges range from one percent to

2 percent of the total workstation price. A $10,000 workstation would typically have a service charge ranging from $100 to $200 per month.

4. *Corporate references.* Corporate references are an extremely valuable source of information. In fact, they are a must. (See "Choosing a Purchased Workstation" in this chapter.)

5. *Training at buyer's or vendor's location.* The difference in location may be important to the buyer. If the training is done at the vendor's location, there will be fewer distractions. There will be the additional expense of travel and lodging and the difficulty of finding someone to perform the absent treasury manager's duties. If the training is done at the buyer's location, the expense is less, but the treasury manager may have to interrupt training sessions constantly in order to carry on normal day-to-day activities. The treasury manager should also ask each vendor about the support available to train new employees and the resulting costs.

6. *Program updates.* Vendors should be upgrading their products constantly. What will happen six months after the treasury manager buys a workstation? Will the latest release of the purchased modules be provided at no cost? If the latest release will cost extra, how much will it be?

7. *Contracts and technical support.* With whom does the customer sign a contract? Who provides the ongoing technical support? Will the treasury manager sign with the bank that marketed the workstation, or with the original developer of the workstation? Is the bank only a sales representative, or is the bank truly a franchiser that is prepared to support the workstation? If possible, it is better to buy the workstation from the original developer—or, at the very least, from a bank that will provide technical support.

8. *Workstation sales.* Is the vendor selling directly to corporations, or only to banks? There is no point in trying to buy from a vendor that sells only to banks.

9. *Developer of workstation.* Some of the systems on the market were developed by a vendor and franchised to a bank. This is an excellent way for a bank to get into the workstation marketplace quickly, but franchising raises questions about the bank's ability to provide technical support for a product it did not develop. This point has become increasingly important as more and more banks have franchised workstations from private developers.

OTHER QUESTIONS

A workstation purchase should consist of more than just the floppy disks containing the program. However, exactly what else should be considered part of the workstation purchase? It is entirely natural that the treasury manager should want as much as possible for his money. It is also entirely natural that the workstation vendor should want to limit its exposure as much as possible. With this in mind, all potential areas of conflict should be discussed before the workstation purchase. The final agreement should be made part of the purchase documentation.

Points to consider include:

1. *Agreements.* Are agreements verbal or written? A treasury manager should get all agreements in writing, especially if there are provisions that extend beyond the delivery of the workstation itself.

2. *Documentation.* The documentation should consist of a manual (preferably in everyday, nontechnical language) telling how to operate the workstation.

3. *Help availability.* Whom should be called when there is a problem? There should be a phone number to dial for help. A workstation vendor may not be responsible for hardware problems, but the vendor should help isolate the problem to either a software or hardware fault.

4. *Telephone numbers.* How many different telephone numbers (different bank balance reporting systems) can the workstation call each morning? If required, how much will it cost to have that number increased?

5. *Adding new bank balance reporting systems.* Every time a new account at a different bank is opened, someone will have to tell the computer how to parse the information. Some workstations allow the treasury manager to do this task. Other workstations require that the vendor do the addition. How much will this cost?

A workstation that requires the vendor's help to add new reporting systems should not be purchased. If the vendor goes bankrupt or stops supporting its product, the workstation can become obsolete overnight. No new reporting systems can be added. The treasury manager should insist that the workstation documentation explain exactly how to add or delete bank balance reporting systems. Such documentation would allow the treasury manager (or the company's data processing department) to continue to make changes to the workstation.

6. *Information transfer to a spreadsheet.* Can the workstation transfer information to an electronic spreadsheet program? This may not be an important point if the workstation program itself uses an electronic spreadsheet.

PLANNING FOR SYSTEM FAILURES

Although workstations—and microcomputers—are extremely reliable, sooner or later they will fail. Failures fall into two areas: hardware and software.

Hardware failures occur when the machine itself no longer works. This failure can be caused by anything from a power surge destroying an AND gate in a ROM (compuspeak for a damaged chip), to a treasury manager accidentally spilling the morning coffee on the keyboard. Generally speaking, components with the most moving parts will fail first. This means that the printer and the disk drives (floppy and hard disk drives) will usually be the first to fail. When this happens, the computer will not work until it receives expert repairs. Since the workstation vendors are in the business of selling software, a hardware problem (whether in or out of warranty) is really not their problem. The hardware warranty—if the equipment is still in warranty—is offered by the hardware vendor and not the workstation vendor. In the interim, equipment failures become the treasury manager's problem. It is up to the treasury manager to plan for this failure. Before a failure happens, the treasury manager should ask two questions:

1. *How soon can I get the computer back?* Some companies offer on-site maintenance, carry-in, and mail service for microcomputers. If on-site maintenance is required, all arrangements must be made *before* the equipment fails.

2. *What do I do in the meantime?* The treasury manager should make sure that the current system (or a workable copy) is kept intact for the foreseeable future. Perhaps a treasury manager at a nearby corporation, who is known through a regional treasury management association, may allow a workstation to be used in an emergency. Or a second computer should be purchased just as a backup. Clone computers have become so inexpensive that a complete microcomputer can be purchased for under $2,000. The treasury manager could also ensure that the next computer installed in the company has the same accessories as the workstation computer. There could be an understanding that this computer may be used as an emergency backup. For this last alternative to work, the treasury manager will need a duplicate copy of the workstation program and a current set of historical records.

Software failure means that there is a bug in the workstation program. (The term "bug" originated in the early 1950s when a two-inch moth flew into a military computer, short-circuited the high-voltage power line, and caused the entire computer to fail. The moth died.) The workstation softwarc vendor will have to remedy the problem. There may be some delay while the vendor determines exactly what is causing the problem. In the interim, the workstation will probably not function. A software failure is not necessarily a sign of a poorly written program. A workstation program is so complex that it is possible that a user may go down a pathway via a route that the vendor had not anticipated. Again, the treasury manager should keep a backup system ready.

The treasury manager should plan ahead. All workstations will fail. The only question is when, and how well the treasury manager will be prepared.

CONCLUSION

To corporations, information has become as important as cash. There can be no movement of cash without information tracking that cash—determining the amount available, its location, and where it may be needed. This information can come from literally hundreds of banks, at different times, and in different ways. The information must be gathered, consolidated, analyzed, and comprehended. In a large corporation, the treasury manager can be overcome just by the flow of information.

The treasury workstation can manage this flow of information. It can perform the clerical tasks of gathering, consolidating, and storing information. By performing these clerical tasks, the workstation frees the treasury manager to concentrate on the primary job: making decisions about the corporation's cash.

Workstations will not solve all of the problems of the treasury department. Workstations are also not for every company. Workstations require that a company invest a significant amount of time in the training of treasury personnel, and also require technically sophisticated people to run and maintain them. But for treasury managers with a complex banking structure, or a large debt or investment portfolio, workstations can make life easier and better.

Managing the Banking Relationship

OVERVIEW

A successful banking relationship is one that builds over a long period and that is profitable to both parties. A relationship in which one of the parties is continually squeezing the other is not a good one and will end at a time that is probably inconvenient for the customer. Like a sound marriage, a strong banking relationship requires continual attention, good communication, development of mutual trust and confidence, and latitude for both sides to "spread their wings."

Developing a banking relationship strategy is important, regardless of whether a company chooses to develop relationships or to purchase banking services competitively on a transactional basis. A well-developed strategy directs the company's financial managers and staff in managing the daily banking activities. Without a strategy, financial managers might very well implement uncoordinated, even conflicting, banking operations and services.

Many large companies do not believe it is necessary to develop close relationships with their banks, especially where the only services being provided are for routine depository or disbursing accounts. In fact, many large companies often eschew relationship banking altogether, preferring to buy their banking services on a competitive basis.

Historically, bankers cultivated relationships with both large and small customers. The large companies provided the balances that were the mainstay of the bank's lending operation, and they borrowed the large blocks of funds that generated much of the bank's profits. Since the early 1970s, however, the trend among large companies has been to keep the funds balances at a minimal level, and to borrow from sources other than banks, such as commercial paper markets. Smaller companies were always courted actively—and they still are—because of the profitability of most of these relationships. Smaller companies often have fewer choices for banking sources and are therefore more dependent on their principal, and often only, bank. Moreover, the interest rate on their loans is generally some increment above prime rate, making the interest rate spread, or the difference between the rate on the loan and the bank's cost of money, attractively large.

For most companies, managing a banking relationship in the past often meant nothing more than looking at the bank's balance sheet, observing a few ratios, noting that deposits, loans, and total assets had increased, and pronouncing that the bank had a good year. The fact is that if companies managed themselves as poorly as banks managed themselves, companies would not be entitled to any credit at all.

Until Congress adopted the Depository Institutions Deregulation Act in 1980, banks could often survive with only caretaker management staffs. Creativity and aggressiveness were not often exhibited and were not needed to ensure a profit. With the rise of stiff competition in regional and national markets following the 1980 Act, many bank management teams found themselves to be inadequate to the task.

The severe credit crunches in 1967 and 1970, and the 1980 Act, have done much to awaken bankers to the need for tighter management of their businesses. The credit crunches demonstrated clearly that the most important resource for banks—deposits—is a scarce commodity, that deposits ebb and flow in a worldwide arena, and that a bank's capital structure has a bearing on its ability to generate and maintain deposits.

Until the 1967 credit crunch, bankers managed their balance sheets through the loan/deposit ratio. When the ratio of loans to deposits exceeded the magical level of 70 percent, bankers felt they had to be more discriminating in approving credit. There was little competition for deposits because of the ceiling placed on the interest rates banks could pay on interest-bearing accounts. This practically guaranteed a favorable spread between loan rates and deposit interest rates. As interest ceilings and other regulatory constraints were eliminated, banks needed to find ways to protect their interest rate spreads. This was a difficult task in the high interest rate environment of the 1970s and early 1980s because the cost of funds often rose faster than banks' abilities to increase loan interest rates. Instead of the traditional loan/ deposit ratio, banks now use the capital-to-loans and capital-to-deposits ratios and the interest rate spread between the cost of funds and average loan rates to manage their balance sheets. Also, noninterest income has come to play a major role in banking, particularly in large regional and money center banks.

Bank management capabilities continue to be spread thinly, with some 15,000 commercial banks and thousands of additional thrift institutions. As interest rates rise, spreads often narrow, thereby pressuring earnings. As investment banks move into areas that were once the exclusive domain of commercial banks, some of the more profitable services, such as short-term loans, are being drained off. With the deregulation of banking mandated by the 1980 Act, bank management teams are no longer sheltered from competition. As the competition grows, particularly as barriers to interstate banking disappear, and as bank mergers create new "super-regionals" and nationwide banks, the competition will continue to heat up.

In the past, loans were priced at prime rate or some increment above prime. The amount of the increment was strictly subjective, often depending solely on the strength of the relationship. Today, loan pricing is often an integral component of a complex calculation in which the bank seeks a target risk-adjusted rate of return from each customer. In calculating the rate of return, all factors are taken into account, including the bank's cost of funds, loans committed and outstanding, fees charged, deposit balances and activity, other services provided, relationship management costs, and bank overhead. A customer who needs favorable terms in one area may negotiate favorable treatment in that area in exchange for less favorable treatment in another area. For example, a financial manager may need to have the interest rate on the company's loans reduced to a relatively small spread above the cost of funds. The banker may agree to an unusually low interest rate in exchange for increased compensation in other areas, such as loan commitment fees or compensating balances.

Bankers themselves often only pay lip service to developing relationships as they organize to sell more transaction-based services. In fact, in the late 1980s, a number of large money center banks began to shift responsibility for account management from the traditional lending area to the cash management product sales area. This move recognized that cash management sales representatives often have much more continuing contact with customers than do the credit officers. The other effect of this shift, however, is that the cash management sales representative must focus on retaining existing business while at the same time developing new business.

Managing the Banking Relationship—Philosophical Viewpoint

How a company manages its banking relationships is as much of a philosophical matter as it is a business decision. The potential benefits that can arise from a well-managed relationship are not easily quantified; the costs of managing well, and the costs associated with the failure to manage them well, can be significant and sometimes devastating.

Bankers pay greater attention and provide greater support to those customers they perceive will offer greater profitability. Bankers often have the foresight to perceive profitability in ways other than merely interest rate spreads or large balances. For example, a small but highly promising company can present long-range prospects for profits as its demands for credit and other banking services increase; a law firm can present long-range prospects for profits by referring clients as new bank customers.

In addition to being able to perceive long-term profits, the banker needs to understand the customer's business. This is a defensive need since the banker has to understand the customer's vulnerabilities in order to anticipate potential credit losses. Nevertheless, it is a real need and may, in fact, take precedence over long-range profit goals. Consequently, for a company to manage its banking relationships successfully requires the careful release of information in order to create and build an accurate picture of the company's current situation, its progress, and its future prospects. The overriding rule in this regard is to avoid surprises since even positive surprises may indicate that management somehow lacks control over the business. Surprise is a negative signal, even if the surprise is higher than expected earnings. The credibility gap that can result from this can be expensive in terms of onerous loan covenants and pricing, or it can even lead to the bank's termination of the relationship at an inopportune time for the company.

Guidelines for Managing the Banking Relationship

Whether the cash manager consciously sets out to have well-managed bank relationships or not, there are several overriding principles that can be suggested that have been adopted and successfully implemented by at least one company.

Cash managers who can substantiate their operations with written documentation and good communication with their banks may have little to fear from government intervention. However, as the case of the now defunct E.F. Hutton Group illustrates, the government has fought to curb abusive tactics by businesses.

As a direct result of a disastrous encounter with the U.S. Department of Justice over alleged abuses in their cash management policies, Hutton adopted a highly sophisticated system for managing banking relationships. This system, established in 1986, may be used as a model for large multibank situations because it fosters sensitivity in the company to the needs of the banks and it encourages competition and incentives among the banks to perform well, and thus, to receive more profitable business from the company.

Hutton, then one of the largest financial services firms in the United States with some $2 billion in credit lines and more than 500 banking relationships, developed a rational strategy for dealing with its banks.[1] Although Hutton was acquired in 1988 by another financial services firm, its banking organization and relationship management structure was a classic lesson in bank management.

First, Hutton managed its banking system from a central location, despite its many branches and businesses located throughout the world. The banking operations were centralized for control and optimal use of funds.[2]

Hutton established a four-tier system for its banks, placing each bank in a particular tier. The assigned tier determined the type and volume of business that the bank enjoyed, as well as its level of compensation. In the first tier, for example, were the firm's most important banks for supplying credit and noncredit services. A distinguishing characteristic of this tier was that these banks were expected to be proactive in offering new ideas, products, and services for improving Hutton's financial operations. Hutton compensated first tier banks according to a somewhat complex arrangement that recognized performance in addition to transaction charges. Thus, a tier-one bank was generally well compensated.

Banks in the lower tiers were all important to the company in providing credit and noncredit services; however, they were not as closely drawn in to

---

[1] Beehler, Paul J., *Hutton's Strategy for Managing Bank Relationships*, Journal of Cash Mgmt., Vol. 7, No. 1, at 16 ff. (1987).

[2] See Chapter 8 for a description of bank account configurations and systems that provide for centralized control with decentralized operations.

the company as the first tier banks, and their compensation was clearly defined and negotiated in advance.

Like many other large companies, Hutton's bank relationship policy called for maintaining good communication with all of its banks. This included holding an annual meeting for bankers, providing routine periodic reports to shareholders and the Securities and Exchange Commission (SEC), and giving advance notice of significant news releases. Of course, first tier banks were kept better informed and given information on a more timely basis.

Rounding out the overall bank relationship policy was a periodic comprehensive review of its relationship with each bank. This review, conducted internally, included both qualitative and quantitative evaluations, a review of the compensation required and paid, and an overall rating of the bank. Other companies evaluate the quality of bank services as frequently as monthly, and some even prepare performance report cards. This device informs each bank currently and promptly as to how well or poorly it is performing in the eyes of the company.

The Hutton case sent out some clear messages from the Justice Department for companies in managing their banking operations. The Department focused on seven specific areas of Hutton's cash management operations, which may become the basis for future debate among cash managers, and possibly with the government as to the acceptability of certain cash management practices. According to the precedent of the Hutton case, a cash manager is now obligated to

1. Disclose the firm's cash management practices to the bank;

2. Explain the firm's funds concentration procedures and how uncollected funds may arise;

3. Obtain prior authorization from the bank to use uncollected funds;

4. Prove that overdrafts occur only to adjust balances to agreed levels and to recapture float created by system delays;

5. Justify on the basis of legitimate business operations the firm's formulas for anticipatory drawings against accounts and for any chaining that may occur in the process of concentrating funds;

6. Restrict kiting or cross-checking;

7. Restrict creating disbursement float by disbursing from regional banks.

While these guidelines apply only to Hutton, they nevertheless reflect the government's desire to curb abusive tactics by business.

DEVELOPING A STRATEGY

A banking strategy articulates the company's goals with regard to its banks and banking relations. These goals may be committed to writing, and may be long-term or short-term. Short-term goals may be incorporated into a financial manager's annual planning and become personal objectives as well as company goals. A crucial part of a company's banking strategy is deciding whether to spread business among many banks or to concentrate it among a few banks, or even one. However, concentrating the company's banking business carries the danger of putting all of a firm's eggs into one basket, while spreading the business tends to dissipate the clout that a good customer has.

Whether a banking strategy is formalized in writing or just discussed among the senior and middle levels of financial management, it must be communicated to those who have daily contact with the bank's operations personnel. In addition, the strategy should clearly identify who will make decisions and who will make recommendations; who will negotiate agreements with the bank and who will maintain operational contact with the bank.

CASH MANAGEMENT SUGGESTION:

As part of a continuing dialogue, the cash manager might ask the bank's relationship manager at what size relationship the customer begins to carry importance with the bank. The relationship manager should respond with a clear idea as to the levels of deposit and loan balances and the amount of fee income that become interesting to the bank. When the company begins to exceed these threshholds, it may be time for the company to consider adding another bank relationship. In this way, the company can conduct a sufficient amount of business with one or several banks to be an important customer of each without dissipating its clout.

The Players for the Company

The chairman of the board of a large retail chain once reminded his assistant treasurer never to forget that "there is only *one* manager of bank relations in this company." The chairman clearly relished using his position to meet with the company's bankers and make them squirm as he presented requests

FIG. 10-1

The Hierarchy for Managing Bank Relationships

Company		Bank
	(Senior Management)	
Chief Executive Officer, Chief Operating Officer, CFO	_____	CEO, Executive-Vice President
	(Upper-Middle Management)	
Vice-President Finance, Treasurer	_____	Senior, Vice-President Group Head
	(Middle Management)	
Assistant Treasurer, Cash Manager	_____	Vice-President, Assistant Vice-President
Supervisory/Clerical	_____	Supervisory/Clerical

for what often seemed to be unusual forms of credit. While the chairman met with bankers only infrequently, leaving the treasury staff to handle the ongoing banking arrangements, he was nevertheless a clear force in the process of managing the company's banking relations.

In addition to the chairman, the other key players in most large companies are the chief financial officer (CFO), the treasurer, the assistant treasurer, and the cash manager. Smaller companies have fewer players, but the various tasks associated with managing the banking relationships are very similar. Daily transactions must be initiated, monitored, recorded, corrected, and reconciled. Credit requirements and nonstandard operating services need to be requested and discussed.

In large-scale relationships, a certain "ladder"-type arrangement develops in which each player interfaces with the other side according to his position in the order; players seldom stray more than one rung away from their position. Figure 10-1 depicts this hierarchy.

The Players for the Bank

On the bank's side at the middle management level is the account officer or relationship manager assigned to the customer who, together with an array of operations personnel, opens accounts, provides the various operating services of the bank, resolves problems, fixes errors, and stands ready to execute routine transactions. The account officer who performs properly takes time to understand the client's business, organizational structure, financial strengths and weaknesses, key players and their motivations, and business plan. The account officer's job is to marshall the bank's resources, both financial and personnel, to place them at the disposal of the client. This often requires that the account officer sell in two directions at the same time: The bank's senior management should be made aware of the existence of the client and the overall agenda being prepared for the client, and the client firm should be introduced to the operating services of the bank. Too frequently this is limited to the obvious services because these are the easiest to sell.

The account officer who goes beyond the routine sale is particularly valuable to both the client and the bank. This account officer generally has an unusually detailed understanding of all of the bank's products and internal operations, and a keen interest in understanding the operations, motives, and objectives of the client company. Thus, the account officer truly must be involved in both sides. In this way, the account officer can go beyond the routine and perhaps synthesize services that not only address the needs of the client but earn the bank a fair profit as well. This becomes a "win-win" proposition for both sides, and results in a solid relationship that can endure the myriad errors and unfortunate encounters that too often occur.

In addition to the account officer, the other key players on the bank's team include the account officer's boss who, in a large bank, probably heads a unit of several account officers specializing in a particular industry or geographical territory. The unit head's superior officer, in turn, may be responsible for several such units, or may be in charge of all lending activities in the bank. It is reasonable to assume that these three people are oriented toward, and highly trained in, credit rather than the operating services of the bank.

Some larger banks have altered this traditional orientation toward credit after realizing that larger companies often no longer rely on banks as their principal source of working capital funds. These companies very often use the commercial paper markets for their day-to-day funding requirements, leaving their banking needs clearly oriented toward transactional operating services such as paying checks, executing wire transfers, and receiving deposits. Several banks have recognized this trend by assigning an officer from the cash management department to manage the relationship whenever there is no credit facility involved. (The credit aspects of various cash management services, such as in ACH credit transfers and controlled disbursing, usually are approved by a liaison officer trained in both credit and operating services.)

BUYING BANKING SERVICES

Once the banking strategy has been defined and the players for both the bank and the company have been identified, the next step is to approach the task of contracting for bank services. Banking services are purchased much like other goods and services, although financial managers do not customarily think of it in those terms. Small- and medium-sized companies that use only one bank often feel like a captive audience of their banks; large companies frequently do not allow themselves sufficient latitude to purchase banking services competitively as they do other goods and services.

The first step to improving the process of buying banking services is to realize that it is a purchasing process. The next step is to define how the process should take place, and the final series of steps is the execution of the process.

The Purchasing Process

The purchase of banking services may involve only one banking product, the complete replacement of a company's banking system, or any combination of services and new banks. In either case, some of the principles and methods used in deciding what bank products to purchase, such as a request for proposal (RFP) and conformance with a master plan, are the same.

Developing the Master Plan

Defining how the buying process will take place requires developing a master plan for the company's banking system. However, this does not need to be a major project. Rather, it entails reviewing the existing configuration of bank accounts and services presently being used and determining if it is an optimal system. If it is not, the financial manager should develop an optimal conceptual configuration for that company. After all, there is little sense in adding new services to a system that is fundamentally inadequate or unsound. Following this, the financial manager should devise a dynamic plan to change the system to the more sensible configuration and decide the best time to implement the new system.

As an example, a sizable regional healthcare provider had grown rapidly and outstripped its general ledger accounting, accounts payable, and banking systems after previously replacing its patient accounting (accounts receivable) system. The healthcare provider decided to replace its general ledger and accounts payable systems. At the same time, management decided to redesign and implement a new system for cash concentration and disbursements. The decision was made to implement the new banking configuration in time to accommodate the implementation of the accounts payable system which, of course, relied on an effective disbursing bank account.

In the case of this company, management seized the opportunity to wipe the slate clean and start over because it deemed the existing configuration to be totally inadequate and not worth trying to improve.

Another company, a multidivisional manufacturer, had a banking structure that was fundamentally sound but that needed some fine-tuning. For instance, the cash manager was able to explore the use of direct payroll deposit services when the company decided to implement a new payroll system that centralized the payroll function into regional hubs. This reduced the number of payroll payment centers from 29 to 7. Also, the cash manager discovered that by isolating large accounts payable disbursements into a separate bank account cash forecasting became more accurate.[3] She then began exploring the possibility of using centralized controlled disbursing.

Although the healthcare company and the multidivisional manufacturer had very different needs, the process for effecting change was basically the same. The financial managers determined the scope of the required change, defined the requirements, and then sought sources from which to obtain the required services.

As in any other purchasing situation, the buyer can use either a competitive or noncompetitive (negotiated) approach. Both approaches can be effective, although the use of competitive bidding in buying banking services is a relatively recent development. Competitive bidding has grown in popularity as relationship banking has given way to transactional banking, and as compensating balances have disappeared and fees-for-services have become the norm.

Frequently, companies use the competitive bidding approach to narrow the field of prospective banks down to one or two and then negotiate with the finalists to make their selection. Government units often use competitive bidding down to the very end. As a result, they usually obtain the required services at the lowest price. However, banks often withhold extra service and attention from government customers because of the low pricing and because there is little hope of improving the relationship owing to the cold and calculating methodology of the competitive bidding process.

In a 1986 survey of corporate cash management practices, Greenwich Associates[4] noted the continued strong influence of three major trends:

---

[3] See Chapter 12 for a detailed discussion of short-term cash flow forecasting.

[4] Greenwich Associates is a market research firm specializing in monitoring corporate use of banking services. This survey involved interviews of 1,692 companies with annual sales ranging from $250 million to $5 billion.

1. The consolidation of noncredit services into fewer banks;

2. The responsiveness of many companies to aggressive pricing by the banks; and

3. The importance of the bank's performance, in terms of quality and responsiveness, operating performance, and attentiveness to the client's overall needs in selecting and maintaining the banking relationship.

These trends reflect a rather complex series of pressures affecting the banking industry that in turn affect the delivery of banking services. For example, if the quality in the delivery of services by one or more of the company's banks deteriorates, the financial manager will seek price reductions or consolidate its activities into those banks that demonstrate competence and quality. Overlaying this process is the perception, if not the reality, that bank relationship managers tend to be less experienced and perform at lower levels of competence than financial managers may perhaps desire.

Noncompetitive Buying

Negotiated purchasing of banking services sometimes lacks the professionalism exhibited by procurement professionals. This may be attributed to the fact that many treasury managers are steeped in relationship banking, and transactional banking is a new experience. This inexperience is exhibited in three popular buying methods: the Impulse Buy, the Directed Buy, and the "Cold Sales Call" Buy.

Impulse Buy. The impulse or "knee jerk" method of buying banking services occurs when the financial manager suddenly decides a particular service is needed, and the purchase is made on the spot. A young banker-in-training some years ago carried signature cards and resolution forms as he went on his daily business development calls. He was not as naive as some people thought, for there were a few knee-jerk buyers that he was able to sign up on the spot.

Directed Buy. The financial manager may consult with a superior and be directed to buy a particular service from a certain bank, perhaps one of the company's existing banks. This direction may arise from a sense of loyalty for past favors or any other motivation that is best described as "relationship banking." It may also arise because the bank's relationship manager is the boss's brother-in-law.

Cold Sales Call Buy. The opposite of relationship banking, interestingly, is not transactional banking based on competitive bidding. At least relationship banking and competitive transactional banking are rational approaches to purchasing banking services. However, there are those unfortunate times when the financial manager buys a banking service for no particular reason other than to diversify. "Let's try Joe because he has called on us and he is a nice guy" is about all one can say about this particular method of buying banking services.

Competitive Buying

Buying bank services on a competitive basis yields the best results of all motives and methods, to a point. There must be a final negotiation period after the competitive bidding process has taken place. Seeking competition for a company's banking business causes the firm's existing banks to sharpen their focus and attentiveness to the firm's needs and produces lower prices, at least where there is a high volume of the desired service and flexibility in the price of the services. The financial manager who believes in treating banks fairly may adopt the attitude that an existing bank will lose its position only if another bank can demonstrate superior price/performance characteristics.

Competitive bidding takes place in a two-stage process. There is the RFP, followed by a runoff involving those who present the two or three most attractive proposals.

Request for Proposal. The RFP process entails preparation of the written RFP document, identification and selection of banks to receive the RFP, and analysis of the ensuing proposals. Preparation of the RFP should include the following elements of information about the company and its requirements:

1. General description of the company, nature of its business, and configuration of its existing banking system;

2. Description of the service desired and expected results from implementation of the service;

3. Estimated transaction volumes, loan balances, deposit balances (as appropriate);

4. Definition of time frames required (e.g., deadline for submission of proposals, desired date for implementation of service); and

5. Disclosure of any special requirements.

The RFP should explain what services the company wants, not merely solicit a list of the services the bank can provide. The RFP should enable the financial manager to evaluate the proposals and to confirm the bank's ability to perform. The RFP should require each bank to include the following in its proposal:

1. A description of how the bank's service operates, together with functional and technical specifications;

2. Price quotations for the services to be provided;

3. Evidence that the bank is capable of providing the services offered (e.g., how many paying customers use the service today? How many one year ago? How long has the bank provided this service?);

4. Evidence of the bank's commitment to provide and support cash management services (e.g., who is the person in charge of cash management and what other responsibilities does that person have? What has been the employee turnover rate in the cash management or operations department during the last 12 months? How has the department headcount changed from one year ago?).

It is usually very useful to request that the bank describe its pricing in the format of a pro-forma account analysis statement, to show pricing not only in terms of a fee but also in terms of equivalent balances. This will ensure that the bank will include all direct and indirect charges in the proposal; it will also enable the financial manager to make more effective comparisons among the several proposals received. A corollary question to ask in the RFP is whether the bank will accept payment either in fees or balances, and to require that the pro-forma account analysis clearly show how both methods of payment would be calculated. This will flush out any hidden surcharges. In addition, the RFP should ask if the bank would be willing to guarantee the pricing for some period, usually one year from the date of the proposal. This provision will discourage a bid that is too low.

Bank Selection. In selecting banks to which to send the RFP, the financial manager should consider banks presently furnishing services—operating and credit—to the company, other local banks, banks that have exhibited interest in the company's business by calling on the company; referrals by friends already using the service (personal contacts made through regional cash management associations are particularly helpful in this regard), and referrals by an existing bank that is known not to provide the desired service. While all of these banks should be considered, they should not all be sent an RFP, since the cash manager does not want to raise the banks' hopes of doing business with the firm. This is where relationship banking can temper the competitive transactional banking approach. Depending on the size of the proposal the company is making, initial telephone contact might be made to screen those banks truly interested in submitting competitive proposals. On the other hand, being too selective may result in omitting a potentially viable candidate. RFPs might be sent to at least 3 and perhaps as many as 10 banks, and the deadline for responses should be clearly indicated in a cover letter. It is also a nice courtesy to inform the banks of the time frame within which the company expects to make its selection decision.

Analysis of Proposals. The first consideration in analyzing the competing proposals is to make note of who failed to respond. Failing to respond not only is discourteous, but also demonstrates the level of interest that the bank has in doing business with the company. A failure to respond should not be confused with a response that says, "We are unable to make a proposal." There are many reasons for this response, such as the bank does not offer that service, the company is not in the bank's defined market at the present time, or the bank does not have the capacity to take on this additional business at this time. A bank responding in this way usually is disappointed in its own inability to make a proposal, but it should be respected for its position.

One method of responding to an RFP for unattractive new business is to price it extraordinarily high and/or with conditions that are virtually impossible for the customer to accept. This technique is often used in responding to companies whose credit is weak and where the bank would truly prefer not to be exposed. This approach is preferable to simply declining the business without offering a reason or to providing the real reason for the negative response.

In analyzing the valid proposals, the financial manager may find a great diversity in product features and pricing. In addition, some proposals may be more responsive to the specific points in the RFP than others. Generally, those proposals that directly address all of the points in the RFP display greater care in preparation and may exhibit the bank's attitude toward quality of service. At this point it is easy to reject those proposals that do not address all of the points in the RFP. Many times banks send out standard responses to these requests and give little thought to what the company is actually requesting.

As for those proposals that address the RFP and that appear to be serious, the task is to compare service features, each bank's capability to deliver the service reliably, and the price for the services requested. If each proposal has indeed included a pro-forma account analysis to illustrate pricing and has used the correct volumes and balances as called for in the RFP, then comparing prices should be a relatively easy task. The financial manager must carefully review the service features of each response to discern any differences among the banks. When differences in service features are discovered, the financial manager needs to ask two questions:

1. Are the differences real or were some features merely omitted from the description of the service?

2. To the extent that there are real differences, how important are those differences to the company?

For example, in proposals for lockbox service, one bank may tout its video image processing while another bank may not mention it. If the company did not specify that it wants a photocopy of each check received through the lockbox, the method the bank uses to capture check images is irrelevant.

Using a spreadsheet matrix may be helpful in sorting out the features claimed in each proposal. For example, a matrix can be created with all of the service features listed on the vertical axis and the banks listed across the horizontal axis; features should be indicated for each bank with a check mark, or yes/no, or a brief comment. When preparing the matrix, it may be helpful to assign a relative value to each feature. The relative value of the feature could be expressed on a scale from 0 to 4, where 4 is "absolutely necessary," 0 is "absolutely unnecessary," and values of 1, 2, and 3 are relative gradations in between. After summing up the scores for each bank, the proposals can be evaluated numerically, and the first cuts can be made in narrowing down the number of proposals.

Final Runoff. After the field has been narrowed down to a few proposals that are viable and relatively close in price, the cash manager must hold a runoff among the finalists. By this time, the financial manager has probably developed some detailed questions for each bank concerning the services discussed in the proposal or recognized the need for clarifying any vague or ambiguous points in the proposal. It is entirely appropriate at this juncture to prepare a set of questions to be directed to all of the finalists and to meet with these banks to generate a two-way dialogue.

The new round of questions may be in the form of a supplemental RFP in which the following issues are addressed:

- A detailed discussion of the quality, reliability, and accuracy of the services quoted in the original RFP;

- Any aspect of the service that the bank may have omitted from the initial proposal;

- Possible revisions to service specifications and features; and

- Possible revision in pricing based on changes in the company's requirements, if any. Any pricing changes should be reflected in a revised pro-forma account analysis.

Financial managers are well-served by promptly informing each bank of the status of its proposal. The financial manager may delay implementing the service but should not delay making the final decision since this could impair the company's credibility and could make the bidding process more difficult (i.e., expensive) the next time around.

Another strategic consideration is to encourage bidders to offer their best and final price in the initial proposals. If one bank feels that it can reduce its price later to meet the competition, then others may feel the same way and not offer the best price in the initial proposal. Rejecting high bidders early will encourage more price-sensitive proposals in the future.

Service Contracts

A bank usually seeks service contracts for most of its cash management services in order to protect itself in an increasingly litigious environment. No longer will a bank settle only for a depository agreement on the back side of the signature cards. Now banks demand written service agreements for balance and deposit reporting service, account analysis, electronic funds transfers (EFTs) with different agreements for Fedwire and Automated Clearing House (ACH) transfers, lockbox service use of alternate drawee bank on checks, and many other services. These agreements occasionally are fair and balanced; however, they should always be reviewed by corporate counsel and changes negotiated as required.

In most cases, it is a good idea to have a written agreement—one that is clearly written and understandable by a layperson—in order to define the parameters of the services to be provided. The cash manager should recognize, however, that a contract must have the mutual agreement of both parties, and the company should not feel intimidated or coerced into accepting conditions that seem onerous or unreasonable just because the bank requests it. Virtually everything is negotiable, and the company's prospect for success depends on the strength of its bargaining position vis-à-vis that of the bank.

Evaluating Credit Quality

It is important to assess the credit quality of banks supplying operating and credit services to a corporation. Federal regulators maintain "watch lists" of banks that may be encountering financial problems, but these lists are not made public. Therefore, users of bank services are left to their own devices to evaluate the soundness of the banks with which they do business.

A bank failure can play havoc with a company's operations, not to mention the depositor's potential losses, if the amounts on deposit are in excess of federal deposit insurance limits. Even if a company is only borrowing from the failed bank, all "understandings" with the bank are wiped away, and the borrower must deal either with a bank that has taken over the old bank or with a federal regulator whose only mission is to obtain repayment or sale of the loan. Moreover, while federal deposit insurance is available for limited amounts, the federal agencies that provide this insurance have been overburdened in the 1980s from bank failures to the point where the Federal Savings and Loan Insurance Corporation (FSLIC) admitted its own insolvency in 1987. Many feel that Congress has a moral responsibility to bail out the federal deposit insurance agencies, despite the fact that there is not legal requirement for it to do so.

When evaluating the credit quality of a bank, the cash manager must first distinguish between the bank and the bank's holding company. The bank is usually the better credit risk because its assets are diversified and mostly liquid, whereas the assets of the holding company consist of stock ownership of the bank and other subsidiaries, and perhaps loans advanced to the bank. Consequently, the asset mix and liquidity of the two entities are very different. The credit quality of the holding company is of interest only to the investor in the holding company's stock or debt, including any commercial paper that the holding company may issue.

The bank, as a regulated entity, publishes a considerable amount of data concerning its asset and liability mix, reserves, nonperforming loans, and its revenues and expenses. This data is available to the public through the periodic "call reports" in which each federally chartered or insured bank reports its required information to the Federal Reserve. Much of the call report information is usually undecipherable to the lay financial analyst, or at least requires considerable time to analyze. Therefore, most financial managers rely on credit analyses performed by rating organizations that use computer systems to crunch the call report data and compare a given bank's asset quality, mix, and liquidity with other banks of a similar size.

Rating agencies often approach evaluation of bank credit quality from different angles. For example, some agencies simply organize the call report data into meaningful ratios and compare the ratios for a given bank with those of a peer group of banks. Some agencies take the process a step further and apply a rating, in the form of an alphabetical letter, to the bank. Other agencies add some periodic interviews with the bank's management to the process in order to obtain explanations of past performance as well as to obtain insight into the future direction and performance of the bank. The reporting procedures of the rating agencies vary from merely listing a letter grade for a bank, to periodically sending subscribers a major report on the bank, to keeping subscribers informed daily via facsimile transmission of any event involving the bank that might have an impact on its liquidity or profitability. Of course, the prices charged by the rating agencies reflect the level of attention paid to an institution and the frequency of updates.

In evaluating the credit risk of banks, the financial manager should establish an initial screen in the form of the minimum acceptable credit rating and then should make credit decisions independent of the agency ratings. Rating agencies should be used to provide the information necessary for the financial manager to make the credit decision; but the agencies should not be relied upon to make that decision for the company.

There are four principal elements involved in evaluating the credit quality of a bank:

1. Asset composition and quality;
2. Funding sources;
3. Capital adequacy; and
4. Profitability

Asset Composition and Quality. The composition of the bank's assets determines its liquidity and capability to survive a period of financial stress. A high proportion of money market instruments, such as U.S. Treasury securities, indicates a very safe and liquid asset portfolio. Assets that are invested heavily in loans are less liquid; commercial and industrial loans to corporations are more liquid than real estate construction loans. Assets invested in real estate, whether for the bank's own operations, repossessed collateral held for resale, or investments in income-producing properties, are not very liquid.

Funding Sources. Banks obtain funding from many sources, including customer checking accounts, time deposits and savings accounts, money market certificates of deposit (CDs) and banker's acceptances, borrowings from the bank's holding company parent, "purchased funds" in the form of Fed Funds loans (the borrowing of excess reserves from another bank), long-term debt such as bonds, notes, and debentures (both senior and subordinated), preferred stock, and common stock. Banks attempt to "match fund" their assets by seeking funds having maturities that match the maturities of the bank's assets. Therefore, the amount of long-term debt should approximately equal the bank's investment in fixed assets, and its demand deposits should approximately match the amount of its "cash and due from banks" and short-term securities portfolios.

Banks that cater to consumers are often able to obtain low cost "core deposits" that remain with the bank in times of financial stress and are not particularly sensitive to changes in interest rates. These banks often have extensive branch systems that reach into suburban and rural areas to do business in the retail markets.

Banks that cater primarily to large businesses, known as wholesale banks, often have lower levels of core deposits and higher levels of purchased funds, since they often rely on large CDs as a principal source of funds. These banks, which tend not to have extensive branch banking systems, are more vulnerable to cyclical economic changes, and they rely on conducting business in large volumes to compensate for the thinner interest margins.

Capital Adequacy. Capital in any business is the cushion against erosion of assets and lack of profitability; that role is no different in banking. While federal regulators prescribe several minimum capital adequacy ratios, and carefully define the required calculations, corporate financial managers need to look beyond these simple ratios.

The primary concern of the corporate financial manager is how able the bank is to withstand the write-off of nonperforming loans. (Nonperforming loans are loans for which the bank is not accruing interest because of delinquent payments.) If the level of nonperforming loans is low in relation to capital, then the potential for problems is low. However, some banks with large loans to less-developed countries and failed real estate developers have large levels of nonperforming loans in relation to capital. If banks were required to recognize their losses on those nonperforming loans, their capital would be severely impaired. While that event is merely an accounting recognition rather than a real event, analysis of the capital adequacy ratios is a key element in determining whether the bank has already suffered the real event but not recognized it yet for accounting purposes.

Profitability. Profitability of a bank is sometimes not easily determined because unusual conventions relating to taxes and recognition of income sometimes mask the real results of a bank's operations. However, many banks publish indicators of profitability such as their net interest margin, which is the interest rate spread between the yield on loans and investments and the cost of funds. Tracking this margin over time for the bank and against other banks is very helpful in this regard. Another key indicator of profitability is the proportion of noninterest income in the revenue accounts. A high level of noninterest income indicates that the bank is able to charge fees for many of its services and this revenue stream is usually independent of interest rate fluctuations. Banks like to develop and enhance their noninterest income.

THE BANKING ENVIRONMENT

The Banker's Objectives

To manage the banking relationship successfully, the corporate financial manager must understand the forces that motivate the banker. The objectives of account relationship officers vary from bank to bank. In the past, the objective was principally to generate increases in loans and deposits. With the deregulation of banking and the need to achieve certain profit goals, the relationship manager's new objective is to realize a target level of profit on each relationship.

Bankers began to realize that profits lie in executing transactions rather than in generating deposit balances and loans. Loans made at a thin spread above the cost of funds must be very large in order to generate a gross profit sufficient to cover the account officer's salary and all of the overhead and credit support activities of the bank. But those large loans are increasingly scarce due to the lower cost of nonbank commercial paper financing and other sources of short-term funding. What remains are medium-sized and small commercial and industrial loans that often cannot generate sufficient net interest income to result in a decent return on assets or on equity for the bank.

Most bankers have realized that it is more profitable to charge for certain operating services than it is to provide these services free in order to attract the thinly profitable loan and deposit business. However, this shift in emphasis initially caused some friction with customers who were used to receiving these services free. Thus, during the 1980s, larger banks began organizing along merchant bank lines; they generate short-term loans and immediately sell them to investors, while at the same time retaining a spread. Meanwhile, in another department, they offer the cash management services.

The Banker as Marketer

Through the 1960s, bankers were strictly relationship oriented, seemingly taking the attitude that if they ended each year with higher loan and deposit levels, and if they didn't violate the sacred loan-to-deposit ratio of 70 percent or so, they must have had a good year. At the same time, they monitored each relationship to make sure that the requisite compensating balances of 20 percent of outstanding loans (or the later variation of 10 percent of the line plus 10 percent of the loans) was maintained. The errant customer who slipped beneath these hallowed levels was reminded that his relationship with the bank was deteriorating, but that he could easily assure the bank's continued goodwill by simply restoring balances to the required level.

This system of focusing on loan and deposit balances often ignored the operating services activity for which the bank was woefully unable to price properly and for which the bank seldom got paid. During the 1980s, banks went to great expense to understand the true and full costs of providing operating services. As a result, they eliminated some services, streamlined the delivery of others by developing more effective operating systems using more sophisticated computers, and instituted more aggressive pricing policies. Moreover, many banks have taken a hard look at their long-term goals and altered their marketing plans accordingly.

With nationwide interstate banking on the horizon and approaching rapidly, money center and regional banks have been faced with the question of how to define their markets. The market question has at least three dimensions: **1.** Geography; **2.** Size of Company; and **3.** Types of Services.

The geographical aspect has been relatively easy to settle. A few of the largest banks want to serve substantially all of the country; others want to serve a specific region; and still others prefer to confine their activities to a small, local area.

The marketing aspect has to do with company size and is a bit more complex because banks do not want to drive away existing business that may not fit the new strategic target market. Nevertheless, different banks operating in the same region have decided upon different strategies. Some banks focus on middle market companies, which generally includes companies with sales of $10 million to $200 million. These companies generally do not have access to commercial paper markets, and are willing to pay interest on loans at an attractive spread above the cost of funds.

The third dimension of bank marketing, the types of services to feature, may be the most difficult marketing decision because it is based principally on theory. Some banks focus traditonally on making the relationship with the client grow. This is usually measured in terms of loans and deposit balances. Other banks do not seek to develop relationships, preferring instead to generate a high volume of transactions and the fees that go along with these transactions. Of course, there is a middle ground for banks wishing to blend the traditional banking relationships while at the same time encouraging increased transaction business that is priced to be profitable at each turn.

The current phase of the banking relationship cycle has banks clearly directing their efforts to marketing transaction services. This places the cash management department in the position of being the marketing and customer service department of the bank, fronting for those operating departments that were earlier scorned. Banks now actively recruit college graduates for operations as well as credit, and attactive compensation is no longer the privilege of only the lenders. Of course, loans remain the main source of income for banks, especially those that lend to small- and medium-sized businesses where interest rates may be quoted in terms of an incremental spread above the prime rate. But in the large banks, where the traditional focus has been on lending to Fortune 500 companies, the proportion of the bank's net income from lending has shrunken considerably. It is not unusual for a large creditworthy corporation to borrow from banks at a spread of only one-quarter to one-half percent (25 to 50 basis points) above the bank's cost of funds. On a $50 million loan, that spread would generate a gross profit to the bank over one year of $125,000 to $250,000, which must cover all of the bank's direct and indirect costs, and provide some profit. Unfortunately for banks, the large, creditworthy company that needs to borrow $50 million can do so at an interest rate near the bank's actual cost of funds in the commercial paper markets.

Figure 10-2 illustrates the relationships among various borrowing costs in August, 1987, when interest rates were relatively low and stable. According to Figure 10-2, the large borrower with clout, who could borrow for three months at 35 basis points above the bank's cost of funds (as measured by CDs of a like maturity), would borrow from the bank at an interest rate of 7.3 percent. Alternatively, the same company could theoretically borrow in the commercial paper market at a rate of 6.81 percent with fees of perhaps an additional 15 basis points, for a total commercial paper borrowing cost of 6.96 percent. This is 34 basis points less than the cost of borrowing from the bank and would amount to saving more than $42,000 in interest on a three-month loan of $50 million. Alternatively, a bank and a borrower could enter into a "loan sale" arrangement in which the bank would lend at a rate near

FIG. 10-2

Selected Interest Rates, August 1987

	Discount Basis	Interest-Bearing Basis
Federal Reserve Discount Rate	5.50%	5.52%
Treasury Bills—3 months	6.02	6.11
Fed Funds	—	6.69
Commercial Paper—3 months *	6.69	6.81
Finance Co. Commercial Paper—3 months	6.48	6.59
Bank CDs—3 months	—	6.95 **
Bank Prime Rate	—	8.25

* Industrial companies rated AA.
** Adjusted for 3 percent reserve requirement. Quoted rate was 6.74 percent.

Source: Federal Reserve Statistical Release, "Selected Interest Rates," (Sept. 1, 1987).

the commercial paper rate and then turn around and sell the loan to investors. This allows the bank to earn a spread with no investment and enables the borrower to borrow at a low rate. Loan sale programs were developed by a few major banks in 1987 as a way for banks to retain lending business that otherwise would have been diverted to the commercial paper markets. Loan sale programs are normally reserved for large companies with good credit ratings.

For smaller companies, banks would charge the prime rate (8.25 percent according to Figure 10-2), which is 137 basis points higher than the rate that the larger company obtained by selling commercial paper and 95 basis points above the bank's marginal cost of funds. Most companies that borrow based on prime rate do so at a spread ranging from 50 to 200 basis points *above* prime rate.

It becomes abundantly clear, therefore, why banks have been courting middle market companies rather than large companies for loan business. At the same time, the banks have been aggressively soliciting the large corporate marketplace for transaction rather than loan business.

ACCOUNT ANALYSIS

Background

For many years banks had an internal profitability measurement device called "Customer Account Analysis." The account analysis was usually a manually prepared monthly schedule listing the number and types of transactions occurring in the customer's account, together with a summary of the collected balances maintained by the customer. The transaction volumes were assigned unit prices to arrive at the cost of providing the services. The cost figures were generally standard costs based on an outdated and usually less-than-scientific review of operating costs. The bank would apply a standard bank-wide float factor to reduce the average ledger balance to a figure approximating average collected balances. The float factor reflected the bank's overall check-clearing experience. The bank would then apply an earnings credit rate to the collected balance figure to obtain the rate of return the bank could achieve by investing these balances in U.S. Treasury bills (T–bills) to generate revenue to offset the activity charges.

This early form of account analysis is primitive by current standards for several reasons: the cost of providing the bank's operating services was crudely obtained, the float factor reflected the bank's overall average position rather than the specific customer's actual position, and all costs involved in servicing the customer's account were not included. There are still problems in this regard in even the most sophisticated account analyses today. Primitive though it may have been, the account analysis statement was useful for bankers concerned about the bank's profitability and the rate of return on its investment and assets.

It was not long before bankers began to show these internal account analyses to their customers in order to nudge them into maintaining deposit balances in excess of the required credit levels to compensate for operating services. At the same time, banks began to tack on a margin for profit. When this happened, the account analysis reflected a unit price rather than a unit cost. Some larger banks went another step further: they decided to market these operating services apart from the lending activities of the bank. What then occurred would have been a natural development for Proctor & Gamble but not for a bank: the advent of the product manager who seeks to deliver profits from a product or service by managing the features of the product and providing information about the product and training to the marketing staff.

The Account Analysis Statement

The account analysis statement, which is rendered monthly by the bank, usually lists the average balances maintained by the customer, provides the total volume of transactions that took place during the month, and describes other services rendered in connection with a particular demand deposit account (DDA). An earnings credit is attributed to the balances, and the fees for the transactions and services provided during the month are deducted from the earnings credit to arrive at a result that is either positive or negative. A precise break-even result is theoretically possible but rather unlikely. An account analysis statement is prepared for each DDA in the relationship. Interest-bearing accounts are excluded on the theory that they are fully compensated on a self-contained basis and provide no additional compensation to either the bank or the customer.

The account analysis statement is also an invoice from the bank to the customer, with the customer expected to pay the bank the amount of the deficiency (the negative result previously described, if any). In the event of a positive result, the amount is either lost or carried forward to the next period, since the bank is prohibited by Federal Reserve Regulation Q from paying interest on demand deposits. However, there is a possibility that this regulation may be modified or even dropped in the early 1990s.

The account analysis statement is one of the cash manager's most valuable tools, along with the daily transaction and balance report and the daily cash flow forecast. The account analysis statement is used retrospectively to verify the volumes of transactions for which the bank is charging fees, and it is used prospectively to project volume trends and the need for additional bank services and compensation.

The cash manager can use the account analysis statement to review the bank's compensation. A strong long-term banking relationship demands that the bank be fairly compensated; but no more than that. A company's management may decide that "fair" includes only those services shown by the bank on the account analysis statement; or it may elect to include additional compensation for "intangible" services, such as the bank's assurance that it will continue to make credit lines available during a credit crunch, an extra effort expended by the account officer, or guaranteed access to the bank's senior management.

The cash manager uses the account analysis statement to analyze transaction volumes to see if the bank is counting (and charging for) the correct number of transactions. The cash manager may use actual volume statistics if they are readily available internally, or a reasonable estimation of the volume to compare to the activity claimed by the bank. By tracking the volume of each type of service from month to month, the cash manager can quickly spot an aberration, which may be merely a counting error by the bank, or a signal that a trend is changing.

The cash manager also uses the account analysis statement to review the actual lineup of services being purchased by the company to determine if certain services are unnecessary or new services may be needed. For example, the statement may show that account reconcilement service is being purchased at a cost of $100 per month for an account that clears an average of 150 checks per month. Barring other significant factors, clearly this is more expensive than having an accounting clerk handle the reconcilement manually. A lockbox receiving only 50 checks totalling $10,000 per month may not be worth the $150 per month that the bank charges for the service. Likewise, the new subsidiary's disbursing bank account clearing 1,000 checks per month worth $10 million clearly is a candidate for controlled disbursing.

Another important use of the account analysis statement is to compare pricing among different banks. Cash managers can monitor price trends, including changes in both the scheduled prices and the offsetting earnings credit rate, by analyzing the account analysis statements of the respective banks.

Structure of an Account Analysis Statement

Many banks attempt to differentiate their account analysis statements from the statements of other banks by altering the terminology, reconfiguring the order of calculations, showing activity charges in terms of required balances and deficient balances in terms of fees, and combining categories of expense. Part of the motivation for this practice is to disguise the real costs and prevent accurate comparisons with other banks.

In 1987, the National Corporate Cash Management Association (NCCMA) published a standardized account analysis statement format, which is designed to promote bank-to-bank comparisons. The standard includes a glossary of terms and a layout of data that any bank could choose to embrace. The standard is based on considerable research conducted by the NCCMA and involved input from a large number of corporations and banks. Use of the NCCMA's standardized account analysis will grow slowly because banks must alter (or replace) the computer software that generates the account analysis statement. Later in 1987, the American National Standards Institute, through its Accredited Standards Committee X12, took up the task of reducing the NCCMA's prototype to a standardized data format for electronic transmission by banks to business clients. Electronic transmission of the data in standard X12 format enables a business to receive its account analysis data from each of its banks, all using a common data format, and to arrange the data in whatever layout the cash manager desires. This is particularly effective because the X12 standard for the account analysis statement uses common terminology as defined by the NCCMA.

The NCCMA's standard account analysis is a composite of the best features of account analysis statements used throughout the banking industry. It is not a fundamentally new concept, but rather a distillation of existing paper-based layouts. Therefore, it is useful to examine its generic features as a proxy for many other formats presently in use.

As shown in Figure 10-3, the account analysis statement identifies the account and the period covered by the statement, and shows the top level summary of balances and income (or deficit) for an account relationship. If the relationship consists of only one account, this section reflects that one account only; otherwise it summarizes all accounts in the relationship. For each month, the statement begins by disclosing the average ledger balance, average float, and average collected balance. Since float is a function only of the dollar volume of checks deposited and the mix of drawee banks, there

FIG. 10-3

Balance and Compensation Information

Bank Account Analysis Statement
Account Detail

Section I. Customer information
Bank name: Gotham Trust

Statement date: 9/20/86

Customer Name and Address	**Account Title**	**Account Number**
N. C. Ceema 7001 Boxwood Drive Oldtown, Conn. 12345	Division A Lockbox	001-7895-115

Bank Contact (Name & Phone)	**Analysis Period**
I. M. Gridley (212) 123-4567	8/1/86 to 8/31/86

Section II. Current and Historic Balance and Compensation Information
Balance Information (Part A)

Month	Average Ledger Balance	Average Float	Average Collected Balance	Net Adjustment	Adjusted Collected Balance	Earnings Credit Rate	Earnings Allowance
1/86	300,000	275,000	25,000	0	25,000	8.65%	184
2/86	175,000	125,000	50,000	0	50,000	8.75	336
3/86	205,000	150,000	55,000	0	55,000	8.42	393
4/86	110,000	79,000	31,000	0	31,000	8.22	209
5/86	140,000	85,000	55,000	0	55,000	7.75	362
6/86	100,000	90,000	10,000	0	10,000	6.90	57
7/86	140,000	98,000	42,000	9,600	51,600	7.20	316
8/86	259,750	66,500	193,250	0	193,250	7.15	1,174
9/86							
10/86							
11/86							
12/86							
YTD	179,371	121,315	58,057	1,225	59,281	7.87%	3,030

10-29

Section II. Current and Historic Balance and Compensation Information
Compensation Information (Part B)

Month	Collected Balance Required	Excess/ (Deficit) Collected Balance	Total Service Charge	Excess/ (Deficit) Allowance	Fees Paid	Net Compensation Position
1/86	29,946	(4,946)	220	(36)	0	(36)
2/86	61,082	(11,082)	410	(74)	0	(74)
3/86	62,926	(7,926)	450	(57)	0	(57)
4/86	74,747	(43,747)	505	(296)	0	(296)
5/86	49,376	5,624	325	37	0	37
6/86	126,075	(116,075)	715	(658)	0	(658)
7/86	71,953	(20,353)	440	(124)	0	(124)
8/86	109,780	83,470	667	507	0	507
9/86						
10/86						
11/86						
12/86						
YTD	73,162	(13,881)	3,732	(702)	0	(702)

Source: © National Corporate Cash Management Association. Reprinted with permission.

is no connection between the average ledger balance and either float or average collected balance. Of course, if a company deposits the same amount of checks, and the mix of drawee banks does not change very much, the amount of float will be constant as well. If the company's ledger balances are maintained at a constant level by the cash manager, then the ratio of float to ledger balances will also be stable.

Average Ledger Balance. The average ledger balance amount is a daily average and can be verified by the cash manager from the monthly bank statement, provided that the bank statement and the account analysis statement cover precisely the same period. However, this is often not the case because account analysis statements are often based on the calendar month while bank statements often coincide with the company's fiscal month-ending date. Although the cutoff dates of the two statements may differ, causing the average ledger balance and amount of float to diverge for any one month, these figures should converge over a period of several months.

Net Collected Balance. The net collected balance is the average amount of collected funds that the customer left with the bank after deducting clearing float from the average ledger balance; it is often referred to as the compensating balance.

Net Adjustment. The account analysis statement is prepared from different data streams within the bank. Occasionally, there are errors in the data that require some type of adjustment, usually in subsequent months. This section enables the bank to reflect those adjustments. The net adjustment amount is often ignored by both the bank and the customer, but it fulfills a valuable purpose. It is used whenever the bank's automatic system for calculating average balances requires an adjustment or when an adjustment to a prior period is required. For example, suppose an incoming $500,000 wire transfer was temporarily misplaced (e.g., posted to a wrong account). The bank received the payment on Wednesday, but did not correct the error until the following Monday, or five days later. The bank's computer will understate the rightful owner's average ledger and collected balances, and it will overstate the balances in the account that temporarily held the funds, by $83,333 ($500,000 divided by 30 days in the month, multiplied by the 5 days during which the error persisted). The analysis for the former account would receive a positive adjustment and the analysis for the latter account would receive a negative adjustment for the $83,333.

Earnings Credit Rate. The earnings credit rate is set by the bank to reflect the bank's theoretical investment alternative, such as T–bills. Hypothetically, the bank could invest the collected balances in T–bills to generate the amount of earnings credit reflected in the account analysis statement. A bank can charge any rate it chooses to create the allowance against which the customer's charges are absorbed. Obviously, the lower the rate, the more favorable it is to the bank—and the less competitive the bank may be.

The Fed's reserve requirement must enter into the calculation of the earnings credit because the reserves are a nonearning asset that must be maintained on deposit at the Fed or in vault cash. (Concurrent with examining the issue of paying interest on demand deposits, the Fed is also examining the issue of paying interest to banks on their reserve deposits with the Fed.) Some banks customarily reduce net collected balances by the amount of required reserves to arrive at an amount often called available balances, to which the earnings credit rate is applied to derive the amount of the earnings allowance. Other banks elect to provide for reserves by reducing the earnings credit rate by the reserve requirement percentage, which is currently 12 percent of collected balances. The NCCMA used this latter approach in its standardized account analysis, but the result of both methods is identical.

Earnings Allowance. The earnings allowance is the amount of credit that the bank allows for the month based on the amount of collected balances maintained in the account and the earnings credit rate. The formula for converting from balances to income uses the actual number of days in the month and, in the NCCMA standard, a 365-day year. Some banks use a 360-day year because this is used in calculating interest on money market investment instruments. This convention results in a larger figure, either income or fee. Some banks divide a year into 12 equal months, which obviously does not reflect reality but is simpler to calculate.

Referring to Figure 10-3, in the month of August 1986, the customer maintained average collected balances of $193,250, which generated an earnings allowance of $1,174 for the month. This was based on the earnings credit rate of 8.125 percent, less 12 percent for reserves, for a net earnings credit rate of 7.15 percent. Using these figures, the earnings allowance is calculated as follows:

Actual earnings credit rate	8.125%	
Less: 12% for reserves	0.975	
Net earnings credit rate	7.150%	

$$\text{Earnings allowance} = \frac{\$193,250 \times 0.0715 \times 31 \text{ days}}{365 \text{ days}} = \$1,174$$

An alternative method may be used to handle reserve requirements that yield the same result. This method reduces balances rather than the earning credit rate for the reserve requirements and is calculated as follows:

Average collected balances	$193,250
Less: 12% for reserves	23,190
Available balances	$170,060

$$\text{Earnings allowance} = \frac{\$170,060 \times 0.08125 \times 31 \text{ days}}{365 \text{ days}} = \$1,174$$

Collected Balance Required. Collected balance required is the amount of average collected balances required by the bank each month to compensate the bank for credit and operating services.

Excess (Deficit) Collected Balance. Excess (deficit) collected balance is the difference between the average net collected balance and the collected balance required. It is the amount by which the customer has over- or under-compensated the bank for the month.

Total Service Charge. The total service charge is the sum of the charges for each type of activity in the account during the month. In the NCCMA's standardized account analysis, this detail is found in the section "Service Description and Cost Information," which is shown in Figure 10-4. Most banks list a brief (often cryptic) description of the services, the volume of activity for each, the unit prices, and the charges for the month for each service category. Some banks show a corresponding amount of collected balances in lieu of the fee that would be required for each category of service.

FIG. 10-4

Service Description and Cost Information

Section V. Service Description and Cost Information
Current Month—Account Detail

Reference #	Service Descriptions	Unit Price	Volume	Service Charge	Collected Balance Required
010	General Account Services			0.00	0.00
020	Depository Services			0.00	0.00
030 004	Retail Lockbox Monthly Maintenance	1.0000	175	175.00	28,817.96
030 020	Lockbox Items Processed	0.0500	2165	108.25	17,825.96
030 040	Lockbox Custom Processing	0.0700	4120	288.40	47,491.99
030	Lockbox Services			571.65	94,135.91
040	Disbursement Services			0.00	0.00
050 140	Wire Transfer	15.0000	3	45.00	7,410.33
050	Funds Transfer			45.00	7,410.33
060	Reconciliation Services			0.00	0.00
070 000	Balance Reporting	50.0000	1	50.00	8,233.70
070	Information Services			50.00	8,233.70
080	International Services			0.00	0.00
090	Securities Services			0.00	0.00
100	Trust Services			0.00	0.00
110	Credit Services			0.00	0.00
999	Miscellaneous Services			0.00	0.00
			Total	666.65	109,779.95

Source: © National Corporate Cash Management Association. Reprinted with permission.

In the example shown in Figure 10-3, the total service charge for the month of August is $667. The detail of that service charge is shown in Figure 10-4.

One of the principal reasons for a standardized account analysis is to dispel the confusion that arises because different banks use different terminology for the same services. The NCCMA's standard format establishes generic product families (e.g., "Depository Services," and "Information Services") and encourages banks to provide a detailed listing of these services within each product family. Moreover, by publishing a glossary of terms, the NCCMA laid the framework for banks to adopt common meanings for the terminology.

Excess (Deficit) Allowance. In Figure 10-3, service charges for account activity totaled $667 for August, resulting in an "excess allowance," which some banks would erroneously label as a profit, of $507 for the month. It is erroneous to label this a profit because the bank customarily includes a profit factor in its service charges. For example, if the bank's products are priced to yield a 25 percent gross profit, then the $667 of service charges already contains $167 of profit. If the earnings allowance exactly equals the total service charge, resulting in neither an excess nor deficit allowance, the bank would have received its intended profit on the services it rendered. Therefore, an excess allowance is actually overcompensation paid to the bank.

The total service charge can be converted to the equivalent collected balances required using the same formula as the one previously used to convert from balances to an earnings allowance:

Annualize the monthly service charge by:

$$\frac{\$666.67 \times 365 \text{ days}}{31 \text{ days}} = \$7,849.50$$

Derive the amount of funds needed to earn $7,849.50:

$$\frac{\$7,849.50}{0.0715} = \$109,780$$

The actual collected balances required in August 1986 to offset the activity charges was $109,780 (rounded). The actual collected balance maintained during the month was $193,250 for an excess collected balance of $83,470. This is equivalent to an excess earnings allowance of $507 for the month at the earnings credit rate of 7.15 percent. Under Regulation Q, as previously described, the $507 may not legally be paid to the customer. However, its equivalent of $83,470 of excess collected balances may legally be carried back to prior periods or forward to subsequent periods to offset balance deficits incurred during those periods.

CASH MANAGEMENT SUGGESTION:

> The cash manager should attempt to negotiate as long a settlement period as possible. Many banks seek to charge their customers monthly for any deficit earnings allowance. If some months generate an excess allowance, for which the bank is not permitted to pay the customer, the customer should attempt to defer settlement to quarterly periods, or even annually, in order to take advantage of any situation in which an excess allowance develops.

Managing Average Balances

CASH MANAGEMENT SUGGESTION:

> The cash manager should consider adopting a cash management strategy of generating a deficit earnings allowance each month and paying the bank a fee equal to this amount. This will ensure that all balances maintained at the bank will always be working toward maximizing profits, with no excess balances lost because of Regulation Q.

When this suggestion is carried to an extreme, the cash manager may actually add to the profitability of the firm, unless the bank alters the slope of the playing field with penalty pricing for payment of fees in lieu of compensating balances. This practice has surfaced in the 1980s as cash managers increasingly opt to compensate their banks through fees rather than balances.

The CFO of an $800 million (sales) high-tech company criticized the cash manager for maintaining as much as $2.5 million in average collected balances to compensate the bank for monthly activity charges. At the same time, the bank was pressing the cash manager for additional balances, since the $2.5 million did not generate a sufficiently large earnings allowance to offset activity charges, thereby generating monthly account analysis losses.

A new assistant treasurer arrived on the scene and resolved the problem to the satisfaction of all. The solution was to manage the company's cash position aggressively, resulting in average collected balances of only $200,000, while investing the difference of $2.3 million in money market investments. A typical interest rate scenario can illustrate why everyone was happy with this arrangement:

FIG. 10-5

Generating Net Profit by Reducing Balances

	Before	After	Change
Collected balances	$2,500,000	$200,000	$2,300,000
Reserves @ 12 percent	300,000	24,000	-0-
Available balance	$2,200,000	$176,000	$2,300,000
Earnings credit rate	6.1%	6.1%	6.5%
Monthly earnings credit amount	$11,183	$ 895	$12,458

- Earnings credit rate (three-month T–bills)   6.1 percent
- Money market yields (composite)   6.5 percent
- Bank reserve requirement   12.0 percent

As Figure 10-5 shows, by investing the $2.3 million in money market instruments, the cash manager was able to generate additional monthly income of $12,458 ($2,300,000 × 0.065 ÷ 12). Because the bank balances were reduced by $2.3 million, the deficit earnings allowance now payable to the bank as a fee in lieu of balances increased by $10,289 ($2,300,000 × 0.88 [1 − 12] percent reserves] × 0.061 ÷ 12). This resulted in net revenues to the company of $2,169 ($12,458 − $10,289) for the month, or more than $26,000 per year more than before to support bank activity charges, and no more hassles from the boss and the bank.

There are two reasons for this positive differential in the company's favor:

1. The company can invest the full amount of the balance reduction, where the bank could invest only 88 percent of the balances because the bank is required to hold 12 percent in uninvested reserves; and

2. The company can invest in money market instruments yielding a higher return than the earnings credit rate.

In this example, the bank's operations department was quite pleased to be fully reimbursed for any deficit earnings allowance, which assured it of earning its target profit on the account activity. In addition, the bank's lending department required average collected balances of $300,000 to compensate for a line of credit. This was paid for with an additional fee in lieu of balances.

There is usually a margin in favor of the customer paying a fee instead of maintaining balances because of the reserve requirement and the difference in yields available in the money markets compared to the earnings credit rate allowed by the bank. However, some banks seek to encourage compensation through balances rather than fees by requiring a surcharge on any fee paid in lieu of balances. This surcharge is usually negotiable, however. Bankers prefer balances in the long run because balances provide the funding for loans. This has a multiplier effect as new balances fund new loans, which generate additional new compensating balances. However, in the short run fees have an immediate and very measurable effect on the bank's income statement, which is attractive to banks more concerned about current earnings than future growth.

When comparing the cost of paying fees to compensating through balances at various banks, it is essential to adjust the listed prices for the earnings credit. The following is an example of a price comparison between two banks:

	Bank A	Bank B
Price for one unit of specified activity	$1	$1.05
Earnings credit rate	6.0%	6.3%
Required reserves	12%	12%
Collected balances required to compensate for one unit of activity	$227.27	$227.27

While Bank A charges $1 compared to Bank B's price of $1.05 for the same service, Bank B allows a higher earnings credit for balances. If the company were to compensate its bank using balances, the price of these two banks would be virtually identical. If, however, the company were to compensate its bank by paying a fee, Bank A would clearly be the choice. The equation becomes tilted, however, if Bank A places a surcharge of more than 5 percent for payment of fees in lieu of balances. That surcharge would more than offset Bank A's lower stated price.

PART V

Liquidity

CHAPTER **11**

Managing Liquidity

IN GENERAL

Liquidity management in any firm is the primary responsibility of the treasury department, and the main job of the cash manager in particular. The tasks involved with managing liquidity include ensuring that funds and funding are available when needed and that funds remain invested or unborrowed in the meantime.

Managing liquidity involves more than merely managing credit sources and investment portfolios. Over the long run, liquidity is affected by the overall scheme of working capital management. Ineffective controls and operating methods consume too much working capital, thereby affecting the liquidity of the firm. Too much inventory, ineffective selling terms and collection practices, or inadequate controls to prevent early payment of trade accounts all sap the firm of working capital. While the current ratio and calculated amount of working capital in an accounting sense may look good on an analyst's spreadsheet, the firm may actually have too much working capital requiring too much permanent capital or resulting in too little liquidity.

Liquidity is derived from an appropriate balance among the assets, liabilities, and funds flows of the firm. This balance is made appropriate by the amount of permanent or long-term capital that is invested in the firm. An insufficient amount of capital almost always is reflected in liquidity problems.

LIQUIDITY AND THE CASH FLOW CYCLE

Liquidity may be reflected in the form of available funds, unused borrowing capacity, or a combination of both. The volatility of the funds flows of the particular enterprise determines the size of the liquidity cushion required, and short-term funds flow forecasting is essential to monitor the volatility and anticipate liquidity needs.[1] Therefore, it is necessary to maintain a liquidity cushion to absorb the shortfall when it occurs.

All firms occasionally experience negative cash flows for short periods. This may occur when accounts receivable are not collected until after the costs are paid, or it may be caused by the purchase of fixed assets, a large amount of inventory, the repayment of debt, or the payment of dividends. The manufacturer of seasonal merchandise, for example, pays virtually all costs well in advance of receiving the sale proceeds. Therefore, at the conclusion of the season, the manufacturer hopes to be flush with funds and unused bank credit in preparation for the next season. A nonseasonal manufacturer that acquires additional plant and equipment must take care to fund the acquisition without impinging on the firm's liquidity. To use short-term borrowed funds may not be sufficient to reach its operating potential because its liquidity has been depleted by the acquisition of fixed assets.

Liquidity

Perfect liquidity exists only in the form of funds on deposit in a healthy bank and in short-term U.S. government debt obligations. The term "funds" refers to unencumbered bank deposits. In the context of most businesses, liquidity refers not only to the firm's ability to convert a portfolio of investments to funds but to the on-going stream of funds flowing from the sale of products, services, and conversion of accounts receivable to funds. Cash in the form of coin and currency is not perfect liquidity for most businesses because of the logistical difficulties of processing, securing, and transporting it. Unused bank lines of credit provide liquidity but not perfect liquidity since the availability of the credit is subject to the decision of another person to make the loan.

Solvency

Liquidity should not be confused with solvency. Solvency describes a situation in which a firm's asset values exceed the amount of its liabilities. This is largely an accounting concept and states nothing about liquidity. For example, a company operating under the bankruptcy laws as a "debtor-in-possession" may be insolvent because its liabilities exceed its assets. But because bankruptcy liabilities are frozen, the company has the opportunity to reorganize and build liquidity even though it is insolvent. On the other

---

[1] See Chapter 12 for a detailed discussion of short-term funds flow forecasting.

hand, a real estate company may be quite solvent in the sense that the value of its assets exceeds the amount of its liabilities. However, if there is a shortage of funds or unused credit with which to make the monthly mortgage payments, the firm is suffering a lack of liquidity since its real estate assets cannot be converted to funds quickly.

Mining Liquidity From Working Capital

It is easy to buy liquidity. The commercial banking and investment banking industries exist for the purpose of providing liquidity to businesses. Debt has an interest cost, equity has a "cost of capital," and both have placement costs. All told, the cost of obtaining permanent or long-term capital is high, especially if this capital is to be invested in working capital rather than fixed or productive assets. Most businesses have untapped sources of liquidity buried in their capital structure. These sources include excessive inventory, unbilled or uncollected accounts receivable, and accounts payable that are paid sooner than necessary. Most businesses play according to the rules governing use of trade credit, although they often do not take full advantage of the exceptions and waivers available to them. For example, the sales volume of a business, and its turnover of receivables, are directly affected by the firm's credit policy, payment terms offered, and collection tactics. Too frequently, management points to competitive pressures as the reason for not being able to collect receivables sooner. However, a sharp pencil can sometimes show that profitability—and liquidity—can be enhanced through a more conservative policy. In a high interest rate environment, for example, it is expensive to carry receivables. A company selling its product or service on a thin profit margin may increase profits and liquidity by curtailing sales to slow payers. Moreover, delays in rendering invoices result in delays in collecting open accounts.

Careful working capital management can enhance cash flow. For example, improved systems and techniques for managing funds flows often can generate usable funds from the funds flow pipeline by accelerating receipts and delaying disbursements.

Cash. Managing the cash asset can generate more working funds for the company by:

- Managing a negative general ledger balance that is consistent with the volume, volatility, and predictability of the firm's receipts;
- Anticipating receipts and accelerating their concentration to the central point of use;

- Using float management techniques to accelerate collections and delay disbursements; and

- Paying fees for bank services instead of maintaining compensating balances.

Accounts Receivable. Use of aggressive sales terms and collection techniques to encourage timely collection and discourage late payment will add to liquidity.

Inventory. Reducing order lead times through electronic purchasing can reduce safety stocks of inventory dramatically. Also, careful analysis of turnover by product may indicate the unprofitability of continuing to stock certain product lines. Elimination of these will convert working capital from slow moving inventory to cash.

Accounts Payable. Providing controls to pay bills on a timely basis can add to working capital. "Timely" means two things in accounts payable management: (1) not paying any bills earlier than needed; and (2) paying bills as late as possible without adversely affecting the company's credit standing with its vendors and service providers. The company should always be careful about not losing early payment discounts, however. For example, terms of "2/10 net 30" are equivalent to interest at approximately 37.4 percent per annum. To lose this discount by delaying payment is expensive.

Taxes. Using legitimate means to reduce income tax liability and to defer payment of that liability adds directly to the liquidity of the firm. Not only is good tax advice essential, but devices such as Employee Stock Ownership Plans (ESOPs) may be used to generate new capital funds for the company at a low cost, while also providing important tax benefits to the company.

This discussion shows that liquidity reserves can be relatively inexpensive if they are mined from existing capital. The firm's liquidity can be increased to the extent that cash, receivables, and inventory are converted to spendable funds and payables are increased, all without negative effects. Working capital management is a frontline on-going effort. When it has reached its effective limit, liquidity reserves must then be purchased in the form of external debt or additional equity.

Most businesses are both solvent and liquid; if they are not liquid in the form of available or investable funds, they usually have liquidity reserves in the form of unused credit. This credit may be from a bank or other lender whose reliability and capability to lend is not subject to question. Otherwise, the unused credit may not be available when the firm has a borrowing requirement.

When the firm develops a stream of transactions so that it generates a positive flow of funds over time, then the business has reached a viable and self-sustaining level of operation. Even so, external events can impinge on the firm's equilibrium and the liquidity reserve would then be called into action.

All firms may experience imbalances between receipts and disbursements during any short-term interval. On any given day, week, month, or quarter, disbursements may exceed receipts. However, negative funds flow is not at all unusual for a short time. Management's responsibility is to anticipate funds shortfalls, understand their causes, and take steps to prevent and rectify this condition. Short-term funds flow forecasting and appropriate financial reporting and controls are essential tools for executing this responsibility.[2]

Cost of Liquidity Reserve

The cost of maintaining a liquidity reserve varies with its source and size, but it is indeed a necessary business expense. If the liquidity reserve is in the form of proceeds from the sale of permanent capital debt or long-term securities, then its cost is relatively high. If the liquidity reserve is in the form of unused bank credit, then the cost may be relatively low.

Funds Pool. A liquidity reserve in the form of a funds pool can be derived from either internally generated funds from operations or from external sources such as capital markets. Internally generated funds have no direct capital cost other than the opportunity cost of not paying the funds out to stockholders as a dividend. Externally derived funds, on the other hand, must be purchased at a price, the "cost of capital." To the extent that these funds are invested in short-term income-producing instruments, the cost of capital is mitigated somewhat but not completely, since the cost of long-term capital always exceeds the yield from short-term investments.

Credit Lines. Lenders extend credit under either committed or uncommitted lines. While both lines may be advised to the borrower in writing, the uncommitted line expresses only a willingness to lend at the time the letter is written, and the letter is not legally binding. A cost of a reserve of unused uncommitted credit, albeit not a financial one, is the possibility that the

---

[2] See Chapter 8 for a detailed discussion of information reporting and control systems for cash management; see Chapter 9 for a detailed discussion of treasury workstations.

FIG. 11-1
Funds Flow Time Line

Seller

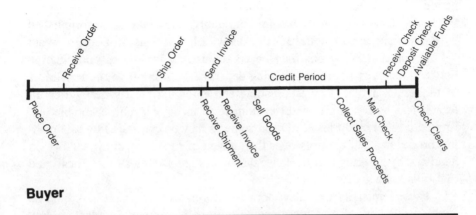

Buyer

credit reserve may not exist when the firm most needs it. It is perhaps unfair to predict that a lender will not be around when a borrower needs it the most. However, the cash manager must be aware of the possibility that a lender may decline to lend at any time that it is not legally compelled to do so.

A committed line, on the other hand, legally obligates the lender to make loans to the borrower as long as the borrower meets certain clearly defined criteria and convenants. Committed lines usually entail payment of a commitment fee and sometimes compensating balance by the borrower.

MANAGING THE FUNDS FLOW TIME LINE

The funds flow cycle, or "funds flow time line," depicted in Figure 11-1 illustrates the working capital process. In a typical manufacturing firm, for example, raw materials are purchased on open account, value is added by the manufacturing process, the resulting inventory is sold on credit terms, the account receivable is collected and converted to funds, and the funds are used to pay the accounts payable, payrolls, and other expenses.

Funds imbalances occur because in most firms the liabilities for accounts payable, payroll, and other operating expenses must be paid well before the funds are collected from the customer. Therein lies the need for capital to bridge the time gaps that inevitably exist in the funds flow cycle.

To maintain a firm's liquidity reserve at an optimally low cost, the size of the liquidity pool and the amount of its use should be minimized. In order to minimize the size of the liquidity pool, management should take those actions deemed necessary by the funds flow forecast to manage the firm's working capital and boost "natural" liquidity. This may be accomplished by trying to accelerate collections or delay disbursements, or both, to avoid a funds pinch. Collections may be accelerated by improving coordination between the billing and the shipping departments to improve the timeliness of rendering invoices, by establishing and enforcing clearly defined credit terms, and by screening credit customers to incur only an acceptable and limited level of credit losses. Disbursements may be controlled by establishing procedures and controls over the amount of materials and inventory on hand and by ensuring that purchase discounts are taken on a timely basis and that bills are not paid prematurely.

These formal activities, supported by formal sources of data, should be supplemented by information gathered informally. Network contacts in key parts of the organization are always helpful in managing and forecasting a firm's working capital.

Forecasting Short-Term Funds Flows

Short-term funds flow forecasting is an important tool for a company to use in managing its working capital actively. Most often, forecasting is undertaken by firms that tend to be net borrowers rather than investors. Suprisingly, some managers believe that short-term forecasting is less important when the firm is a net investor. Actually, the only difference in motivation of net borrowers and net investors should be the differential in interest rates between the cost of borrowing and the yield from investing. A borrower of liquidity funds, for example, may have a borrowing cost of 10 percent. Alternatively, if the firm had excess funds to invest short-term and the yield was 9 percent, then management's interest in aggressively managing working capital would be only 100 basis points less important. Nevertheless, some managers erroneously believe that when they cross the line from being a borrower to being an investor they no longer need to be so attentive to working capital. It pays to monitor and maintain tight controls over working capital regardless of whether the firm is a borrower or an investor.

Funds Forecasting and Budgeting

In order to minimize the cost of maintaining a liquidity reserve, and to assure its availability when needed, management usually prepares forecasts of funds flows over several time horizons. An annual budget describes in accounting terms the anticipated operations of the firm for a full year. This annual budget is then broken down into monthly or quarterly intervals, again for the purpose of monitoring the results of actual operations against the annual plan.

In addition to the annual budget with monthly or quarterly intervals, the cash manager often prepares a funds flow forecast with a very short time horizon, ranging perhaps from a daily forecast to a weekly forecast for several weeks. Unlike the format of the annual plan, the short-term funds flow forecast is not accounting-oriented but shows actual receipts and disbursements as they clear the firm's bank accounts. Therefore, the format of this short-term forecast may reflect the structure of the firm's bank accounts and cash management system rather than being net income oriented.[3]

This forecast of receipts and disbursements becomes the acid test of a firm's liquidity and its need for a liquidity reserve because it disregards allocation of nonfunds expenses over time, such as depreciation and amortization of major expenditures. It views an expenditure of funds as occurring only once: at the time the check clears the bank account. The short-term funds flow forecast, moreover, is concerned with the collection of accounts receivable rather than sales. A sale may occur in one period and be booked according to generally accepted accounting principles; but the collection of funds from a customer is a real event, rather than an accounting entry, that directly affects a firm's liquidity.

A daily schedule of forecasted receipts, disbursements, and bank balances can be constructed and operated rather neatly on a single spreadsheet and projected for one or two weeks. Weekly forecasts in the same format may extend for four to six weeks or more.

Aside from exercising good management skills, these forecasts are particularly useful when managing the investment of liquidity reserve funds. Forecasting of short-term funds flows gives the investment manager the ability to improve investment yields by anticipating funding needs and planning investment maturities carefully. Liquidity reserve funds are most often invested in money market instruments, each of which has a stated maturity and fixed interest rate.[4] When the money markets behave according to a

---

[3] Id. See Chapter 12.

[4] See Chapter 14 for a detailed discussion of short-term investing.

normal yield curve, the investor reaps a higher yield by investing in longer maturities. Without an available forecast, the investment manager has no way of knowing the capacity of the firm to invest for an extra period and to hold the instrument until maturity.

An investment manager should be concerned about holding the instrument until maturity, even when it is of high credit quality and there is an active market in which to sell if it must be converted to funds. If interest rates rose while the instrument sat in the portfolio, then selling it prior to maturity will result at worst in a loss or at best in a lower return than originally anticipated. Therefore, there is an advantage in buying an instrument with the intent and probable ability to hold it to maturity. In periods where interest rates decline, there is often an advantage to selling the instrument at a premium prior to maturity and investing the proceeds at a higher yield and a longer maturity.

The Players

Every company is unique in its organizational structure, and the organizational differences between a large and a middle market firm are often more than just size. In a large company, the organization often is rationalized to the point where departments become fiefdoms headed by feudal lords who oversee a particular aspect of production, sales, or administration. Middle market companies (those with sales of less than $200 million), on the other hand, often require managers to cross these turf lines and to become more involved in multiple functions.

When it comes to managing a firm's working capital, the task is a shared responsibility among all managers in the firm. Unfortunately, the very fact of sharing usually means that no one person has the responsibility—or the authority—to manage actively the firm's overall working capital position. Most firms, however, have a treasurer, who is responsible for managing the loose collection of financial tasks generically termed "treasury." A treasurer seldom feels comfortable being assertive in acting to reduce inventories or accounts receivable, however, because these tasks normally fall to the other financial manager, the controller. Responsibility for balancing the firm's liquidity through borrowing and investing operations clearly lies within the bounds of the treasury. In a typical $300 million (annual gross sales) company, for example, the treasurer's staff might consist solely of a cash manager who handles both borrowing and investing. In a large company, with annual sales of perhaps $1 billion or more, there might be additional staff support for short-term forecasting of funds flows, and the functions of borrowing and investing might be split between two people. This reflects how subtle differences in performance in the management of large amounts of loans and investments can affect a firm's profits. Therefore, while the principles of management do not change with size, these subtle performance differences require greater management expertise.

In smaller companies, such as those with less than $50 million in annual sales, the chief financial officer may tend to all the financial responsibilities. This is much more an economic reality than a reflection of super-human capabilities necessary for the job. The functional titles of "investment manager," "banking manager," and "cash manager" refer generically to the individual who has responsibility for making relevant decisions and executing related transactions. The actual corporate title and other functions performed by the person are of no immediate significance.

CAPITAL FUNDING ALTERNATIVE STRATEGIES

All businesses require permanent capital to survive, and firms use different forms of capital, each of which may have varying degrees of permanence. Moreover, the capital structure of a business continually changes as operating cash flow is retained, as new capital funds are obtained, and as debt is repaid. However, despite the shifting sands of capital structures, three distinct capital funding strategies can be identified: prefunding, postfunding, and balanced funding. Each has a major impact on a firm's short-term borrowing or investing program.

Prefunding

Firms that prefund obtain their permanent or long-term capital before the need for the funds arises. Such firms are regarded as "well capitalized." Available funds are usually placed in an investing program until they are needed in the business.

Postfunding

Firms that postfund generally finance their growth out of a combination of internally generated cash flow and short-term debt. When a sufficient amount of short-term debt has been incurred and the capital markets are favorable, permanent or long-term capital is raised and the proceeds are used to repay the short-term debt. Such firms often are considered "under-capitalized," and they seldom have a pool of funds to invest, except perhaps in overnight maturities. Their liquidity is managed through the use of credit rather than a liquid pool of funds.

Balanced Funding

Most firms prefer to maintain a balance between their internally generated cash flow and their use of funds, acting alternatively as a short-term borrower and as a short-term investor. Major capital expenditures are often funded with new permanent or long-term capital.

INVESTING LIQUIDITY FUNDS

Once the infrastructure of systems, procedures, controls, and staff are implemented to allow active management of the firm's working capital, the size of the required liquidity reserve may be estimated. The relative size of the pool will depend on the volatility of working capital in a particular firm. The volatility of a firm's working capital depends on two factors:

1. The size of a typical sale or purchase transaction relative to total sales or purchases; and
2. The velocity of funds flowing through the firm, as measured by the relationship between sales and permanent capital.

If the firm is a net borrower, then its liquidity pool will be in the form of unused credit lines from banks or other lenders. If the firm has prefunded its capital requirements, its liquidity pool will be in the form of funds available for investment in short-term instruments.

Investing Terminology

In the game of investing, short-term refers to securities that mature from one day to one year after the date of reference, which usually would be "today." For example, a U.S. government bond that was issued $19\frac{1}{2}$ years ago with a 20-year maturity is now an instrument that will mature in six months. Therefore, that bond would fall within the domain of short-term investment instruments.

Most short-term investments for liquidity portfolios are made in taxable money market instruments, including certificates of deposit (CDs), bankers acceptances (BAs), commercial paper, and Treasury bills (T-bills). Other taxable investments include Eurodollar time deposits and CDs, and project notes. Short-term portfolios of taxpaying investors may also include tax-advantaged money market instruments such as preferred stock, whose dividend is determined at periodic intervals by Dutch auction, tax anticipation notes, revenue anticipation notes, and variable rate demand notes issued by municipalities, which are popularly known as low floaters.

Intermediate-term refers to securities that mature between one and five years from the date of reference. These securities are often referred to as notes. Long-term refers to securities that mature more than five years from the date of reference, and they are usually referred to as bonds.

Credit risk is the potential inability of the debt security issuer to pay interest and principal when they fall due. Credit risk is measured by careful analysis of a firm's financial statements, its management capabilities, its industry trends, and other indicators. To most investors, credit risk is measured in terms of a credit rating supplied by a rating agency such as Standard & Poor's Corporation; Moody's Investors Service; Fitch; Duff & Phelps; or Keefe BankWatch.

Market risk is the element in the marketplace that causes the market value (or price) of a fixed-income security to vary inversely with changes in interest rates. When interest rates rise, for example, the value of a bond decreases.

Developing a Strategy

Given a pool of funds available for short-term investment, management should determine the strategy for handling this liquidity resource. The annual budget, and perhaps even a longer range plan, may indicate whether the pool of funds will become depleted within the time horizon of available forecasts. To the extent that the pool of funds, or at least part of it, will remain intact, the portion of the pool that must be retained in short-term instruments may be kept rather small since there is usually a yield advantage to investing in longer maturities. Because the short-term forecast of funds flows may indicate an occasional dip into the liquidity reserve, part of the pool should be kept in short-term, highly liquid instruments. Otherwise, the firm would be exposed to unnecessary market risk when it needs to liquidate securities prior to maturity.

The principal investment vehicles that businesses use for their excess funds are short-term and intermediate-term fixed-income instruments. Fixed-income securities come in various levels of risk, liquidity, and yield.[5]

---

[5] Id.

Assessing Investor's Aversion to Risk. While a company's degree of risk aversion is often a function of the "corporate culture" in which it operates, even risk-tolerant managers often prefer to maintain safety of principal and high liquidity in their short-term investment portfolios at the expense of yield.

Short-term investment portfolios often serve a particular purpose. Sometimes the purpose is not very clearly defined, but it nevertheless dictates the degree of liquidity required in the portfolio. For example, the firm may be on an aggressive acquisition hunt. Since management knows that acquisitions generally close with two or three months advance notice, liquidity may be sacrificed to gain a little extra yield. In this situation, the investment manager can use portfolio management techniques to increase yield without incurring greater credit risk and perhaps even without any greater market or interest rate risk. This compares with the situation in which the portfolio is a buffer against the sudden need for funds in the firm's daily cash management operations.

The purpose for which the investment funds are held usually dictates the degree of risk that the investment manager is willing to accept. The nature of the investor's business may not give a clue as to the investor's level of risk aversion in short-term investing. Stockholders of publicly owned enterprises can understand losses from normal business operations, but they seldom understand securities losses. In 1970, when the Penn Central Railroad surprised the business community by suddenly filing for bankruptcy, its $82 million in outstanding commercial paper carried the rating agencies' highest credit ratings. A major oil company held Penn Central commercial paper in its short-term investment portfolio. Although the oil company's management was embarrassed by the loss it took on this episode and fired its investment manager, it was not in the least embarrassed when it later announced the routine plugging of dry holes on which it had lost considerably more capital while exploring for oil. In short, investors and those looking over their shoulders do not expect losses on short-term investment portfolios.

Among known conservative investors are some of the larger Hollywood entertainment companies, which almost routinely risk $15 million or more on the production of a motion picture that may have a long gestation period and absolutely no assurance of any financial return. At least oil well drillers have some geological and engineering data to guide them, but no such data or market research has turned up a formula for making successful movies. When it comes to investing temporarily excess funds, these risk-taking moguls often retreat to rather conservative roles.

Investors with appetites for high risk—and the rewards that are expected to accompany it—usually are not fettered by public stockholders; maybe they do not have to protect a nonprofit status, or perhaps they have no public regulatory authorities or other constituents to please. Having only to represent themselves, they may exercise their entrepreneurial instincts to the fullest. Their interest in high yield securities is legitimate.

Investing Policy and Guidelines

The owner or chief executive officer of a company seldom conducts the actual investing operations. In publicly owned companies, the board of directors has ultimate authority and responsibility for investing. Unlike deployment of any other assets, investing funds in securities involves using discretion and judgment without the luxury of time to consult others and to obtain approval. Therefore, the investment manager must have clearly defined written parameters and guidelines in selecting particular investment instruments. This document becomes the contract between the board of directors and the investment manager for the conduct of the investing program. It should clearly state the firm's investing objectives, and it should define the priorities of the objectives. The paramount statement of policy usually names liquidity, safety of principal, and yield as the firm's objectives in its investing operations. Moreover, conservative investors will make sure that yield takes a back seat to liquidity and safety of principal.

In addition to a policy statement about the objectives and their order of priority, a written set of investing guidelines is necessary. The guidelines should:

- Describe the types of instruments and maturities that are acceptable;
- Delegate authority and responsibility for conducting the investing program;
- Discuss requirements for safekeeping of securities;
- Set criteria for acceptable levels of credit quality; and
- Prescribe requirements to assure that only reputable dealers and advisors will be used.

A well-crafted set of investing guidelines will simultaneously provide for investing limits and flexibility as markets and instruments change and the firm grows.

Money Markets

The money markets consist of several hundred professional securities dealers and thousands of investors, including corporations, individuals, pension funds, foundations, and financial institutions, investing for their own accounts. The money markets are dealer-based; that is, securities firms act as principals in the transactions rather than as brokers who bring the buyer and seller together. The money markets function "over-the-counter"; there is no central exchange for transacting business. Securities offerings are disseminated by telephone and various forms of wire and electronic transmission services; bids are submitted by buyers and accepted by sellers via telephone. Written confirmations of transactions follow by mail, and funds settlement is made as agreed to verbally.

The money markets largely developed in the 1960s. Until then, the only instruments that traded widely were U.S. Treasury securities and a modest volume of BAs. One investment alternative was commercial paper, but there was no active secondary market to provide liquidity. In 1961, Citibank (then known as the First National City Bank of New York) invented the negotiable time CD, which marked the beginning of a viable market in short-term fixed-income non-government securities. Until then, treasurers usually allowed their liquidity pools to lie fallow in checking accounts. But as interest rates began to rise in the late 1950s and early 1960s, treasurers realized that they could earn a modest return by placing these funds into fixed time deposits at the bank. The disadvantage of the fixed time deposit, however, was that it was not liquid. Citibank's contribution to the evolution of this money market instrument was specifically to allow the deposit to be negotiable. By accepting the time deposit and issuing a receipt payable to "bearer," the treasurer could sell the negotiable time deposit if funds were needed before maturity. As banks and investment dealers began to buy and sell these negotiable CDs, an active secondary market developed, providing liquidity to the investment portfolio.

In the 1980s, the money markets expanded with the proliferation of new types of securities arising from creative financing of borrowers, creative funding of traditional lenders, and peculiarities of tax laws. Moreover, faced with regulatory pressure to increase the ratio of capital to loans, banks found it immensely easier to reduce loans than to raise capital. Reduction in lending activities is anathema to most lenders, however. Therefore, the creative packaging and selling of loans to investors has been a convenient solution. Banks, captive finance companies, mortgage lenders, and others have "securitized" significant portions of their loan portfolios by issuing and selling participation certificates representing undivided interests in a portfolio of loans receivable. This effectively removes the receivables from the lender's books, thereby increasing its ratio of capital to loans. The maturities of most of these participation certificates are usually about three years or longer, yet investment bankers are inexorably finding ways to shorten the maturities in order to tap into new groups of investors.

Perhaps more illustrative of the proliferation of short-term investment/ borrowing instruments are certain securities that are best described as variations on commercial paper. Commercial paper has traditionally been defined as an unsecured promissory note of a manufacturing or financial services corporation. In the 1970s, the definition was widely adjusted to delete reference to the word unsecured, as many companies induced banks to guarantee payment of the commercial paper through the issuance of a letter of credit (LOC) that is attached to the commercial paper instrument. The LOC effectively upgrades the quality of the commercial paper to the credit rating of the guarantor bank, which is higher than the credit rating of the company that issued the commercial paper.

Increasing Rate Note. Another innovation in commercial paper in the late 1980s was an instrument called an increasing rate note. This promissory note issued by a corporation can help finance a large corporate acquisition, often a hostile one. In such transactions, the acquirer usually did not have enough time to arrange permanent or long-term capital funding before the transaction was completed. Therefore, short-term notes maturing in six to nine months were issued. The notes, which carried an interest rate that initially reflected the credit risk of the issuer and the current market interest rate level, also carried a provision that the interest rate would rise automatically by predetermined increments on certain dates during the term of the instrument. Of course, the instruments were redeemable at any time by the issuer. This gave the issuer an incentive to obtain its permanent or long-term funding quickly, lest it end up paying penalty interest rates for the privilege of owning the acquired company.

Loan Participation Certificates. Loan participation certificates are another creative development in the late 1980s. Commercial banks, prohibited from underwriting commercial paper by the Banking Act of 1933 (popularly known as the Glass-Steagall Act), found themselves unable to compete with investment banks in providing short-term funding for large companies. As a result, commercial banks watched their loan commitments and profitability erode sharply in the 1980s as their large corporate customers tapped the commercial paper markets and repaid their bank loans. In response, several major banks[6] created a new twist on an old banking device called the loan

---

[6] The banks leading the way in development of the loan participation market appeared to be as of the first quarter of 1988 Security Pacific Bank, Los Angeles, Cal.

participation. For many years, banks would share loan risk by selling participations in large loans to their good correspondent banks. The buyer of a loan participation bears full responsibility for making a diligent review of the borrower's credit and the loan documentation. In 1987, this concept was expanded to selling loan participation to corporate and institutional investors. To do so, the originating banks wrote standardized loan agreements and used standardized loan documents, and their borrowers agreed to have the loans sold to investors, with the originating bank servicing the loan.

Thus, loan participations and other instruments, such as increasing rate notes, illustrate the creativity that has attracted buyers/investors and provided liquidity to the marketplace. The lesson in all of this is that in the 1980s, instruments that had been traditionally considered debt became two-faced; they became debt instruments to the borrower and investment securities to the investor. This was not a new concept since bonds have been considered both debt and investment instruments for years. However, the innovation was to bring this concept into the short-term money markets.

The following are three other innovations in money markets that were developed in the late 1980s to take advantage of the tax laws.

Money Market Preferred Stock. The term "Money Market Preferred Stock" was copyrighted by Shearson, Lehman, Hutton, but it describes a generic group of similar instruments that use the Dutch auction method for setting the yield. Money market preferred stock looks like a stock, accounts like a stock, and is called a stock. Accordingly, under certain circumstances, a corporation that owns this kind of security may exclude from taxable income a substantial portion of the dividend it receives. Yet the security has other attributes that give it many characteristics of a money market instrument. Liquidity exists through remarketing agreements, "Dutch Auctions," and other devices to provide liquidity to the holder.

Adjustable Rate Preferred Stock. This stock provides liquidity by being listed and traded on securities exchanges. When adjustable rate preferred stock (ARPs) is first issued, it carries a provision that its dividend rate will be adjusted periodically, usually quarterly or semiannually, in accordance with changes in some preselected long-term interest rate. This feature is designed to insulate the investor from market risk so that the security will normally trade close to par value. Usually, however, there is an upper limit, or cap, to

---

and Bankers Trust, Chemical Bank, Morgan Guaranty, Citibank, and Chase Manhattan Bank, all of New York.

the dividend rate, and when interest rates meet or exceed that level, ARPs may decline in market price. ARPs are also subject to credit risk.

Variable Rate Demand Notes. These notes were invented to provide liquidity for investors seeking tax-exempt interest income. Municipalities have traditionally raised capital by issuing long-term bonds. But with interest rate volatility and limited liquidity in municipal bond markets, short-term investors were limited to buying short-term tax or revenue anticipation notes. In the mid-1980s, some creative investment bankers devised methods for adjusting the interest rate on long-term municipal bonds and for providing put options to assure investors liquidity. This attracted short-term investors to a new variation on an old theme.

CHANGING MARKETS

The proliferation of short-term investment securities has created a "good news/ bad news" situation. The good news is that the borrower has a broad array of alternative sources of liquidity funds, ranging from unsecured bank credit lines to asset-based loans to securitized packages of accounts receivable. The investor, too, has a much broader array of vehicles for short-term funds than ever before. With increasing varieties of investment vehicles, the size of the market has grown and the increased number of players has broadened the investor's and borrower's alternatives, and deepened the market's liquidity.

However, the increased variety of securities and players and the larger size of the market have introduced a new class of risk that requires greater sophistication among borrowers and investors alike. While investors need to ensure the safety of principal, borrowers need to ensure the reliability and availability of sources of liquidity funding.

Perhaps this new class of risk might be termed "game-playing risk," for it arises not from changes in market interest rates or from changes in the credit quality of a particular issuer. Rather, game-playing risk is introduced by the number of new and unsuspecting players who may fail to grasp some subtle feature or anomaly of an unusual instrument or transaction. The failures of several government securities dealers, for example, costing thousands of investors millions of dollars of losses, has caused market participants to reevaluate the precise nature of the repurchase agreement. For borrowers, the spate of bank failures in the 1980s, as well as the failures of several securities dealers, introduced a degree of uncertainty into the process of liquidity management. Accordingly, both borrower and investor must investigate and fully comprehend the nature of instruments and business relationships.

CHAPTER **12**

Short-Term Funds Flow Forecasting

OVERVIEW

The budgeting and profit planning process is usually discussed with a time frame of one year or more in mind, divided into quarterly or monthly intervals. Management's budget, in effect, sets financial goals and suggests a road map for operating units to reach those goals. Management also establishes some milestones—balance sheet values, income, or expense levels to be attained—by which progress toward those goals can be measured.

Many financial managers of publicly owned companies necessarily consider the most important forecast to be the annual plan. Others, particularly owner-managers who have no compulsion to pay taxes on reported taxable earnings, often consider the most important budget to be the funds flow forecast. Funds flow is affected by every receipt, disbursement, and change in each asset and liability on the balance sheet. Obviously, the generation of positive funds flow over time is essential to the viability of the enterprise, and the funds flow forecast is the road map required to get there.

Reasons to Forecast Short-Term Funds Flows

In the short run (daily through quarterly), many companies experience occasional periods of negative funds flow, sometimes of varying intensity and duration. Short-term funds forecasts can help prepare for these events both financially and emotionally. Without this tool, a manager may be taken by surprise and overract, or may react in a detrimental manner, possibly turning a short-term problem into a long-term one.

Many successful companies do not prepare short-term funds forecasts other than to refine the next month's interval in the annual budget. There are many reasons for the absence of a daily or weekly funds forecast, but three appear to predominate:

1. The firm may be a continual net borrower, and the net borrowed position can be adjusted daily without advance notice to the lender. However, borrowers themselves may be missing out on some profit-making opportunities. This is particularly true if the company is on a growth track or is in a business where funds flow is volatile, or both. Without adequate short-term funds flow forecasts, excessive borrowings may occur and excessively large credit lines—with attendant fees—must be maintained.

2. The firm may be a continual net investor whose investment position is adjusted daily in the overnight investment market. Unfortunately, this firm may carry more than it needs in overnight or very short maturities, thereby under-utilizing its investment abilities and sacrificing yield to the normal yield curve.

3. The firm may be either a borrower or an investor, and management simply carries more funds balances as a liquidity reserve than is really needed to cover unforeseen funds shortfalls. In this case, management probably is foregoing profits in order to maintain unnecessarily excessive liquidity.

In a firm with multiple business units that function with some operational autonomy, the short-term funds forecast, and the subsequent monitoring of results and variances, can be used by management to monitor the health of each unit and of the consolidated enterprise itself. By measuring the cumulative results of receipts and disbursements over any time period, management can reach conclusions about its overall corporate and individual business units' net funds flows without having to wait for monthly financial reports. The receipts/disbursements schedule provides a much more immediate and blunt report of what is happening within the firm than is provided even by conventional accounting reports. Moreover, the conventional accounting reports and the related budget may show that net positive funds flows are expected during the interval, but will not disclose any interim timing imbalances. Such timing imbalances may, for example, cause the firm to borrow for two weeks in the middle of the month to take its purchase discounts while awaiting receipt of the large collection whose payor insists that, "The check is in the mail." Preparing the daily cash schedule for the next one or two weeks, and weekly for the remainder of the interval, will allow the cash manager to anticipate collection of the large item and to adjust daily for its delay.

Firms that are required to keep a targeted level of compensating balances at the bank should also prepare short-term funds forecasts to assure attainment of those balance targets.

Predictability of Near-Term Funds Flows

Among the more predictable businesses from a receipts and disbursements scheduling viewpoint is the large, established retail business with numerous outlets that are widely dispersed geographically. (A typical retail funds flow pattern is shown in Figure 12-1.) Each retail location has its own historic sales patterns based on season, month, day of the week, and holidays. The aggregate cash receipts of a chain of such stores is highly predictable because the forecasting errors for each location tend to average out over all the stores. Nevertheless, this kind of business should not be managed without a daily forecast of receipts because, typically, today's receipts are used to cover today's check clearings. Any slight imbalance between daily receipts and disbursements will generate surplus funds, which need to be invested if only overnight, or will necessitate a loan to cover the funds shortfall. No monthly funds forecast can predict the occurrence, let alone the magnitude or duration, of such temporary imbalances.

Another type of funds flow cycle belongs to the packager or processor of agricultural products (refer to the tomato packer also represented in Figure 12-1). The growing season ends with the harvest and processing, which must occur within a few weeks in order to avoid spoilage. This is virtually the only "manufacturing" done, and it produces the entire inventory that will be sold throughout the year. Accordingly, a tremendous funds outflow is needed for this short period in order to pay pickers, packers, processors, and package makers. The tomato packer's cash manager needs to forecast the amount and duration of the shortfall in order to negotiate appropriate credit lines with lenders. For the remaining 11 months of the year, the funds inflow is steady as the inventory is sold and receivables are collected.

FIG. 12-1

Monthly Funds Flow Patterns of Selected Industries

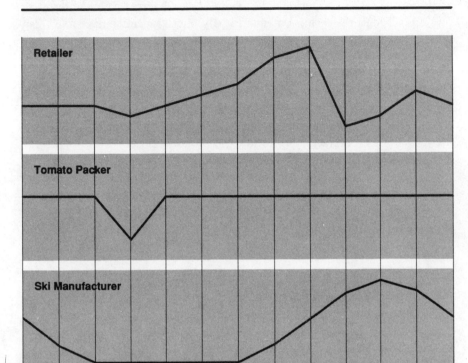

An industry with the opposite type of funds flow cycle might be a manufacturer of snow skis (also depicted in Figure 12-1). The selling season for skis is quite short—only two or three months—for which the successful manufacturer must produce throughout the year in order to have an appropriate amount of inventory when the selling season arrives. In this case, the cash manager must incorporate into the short-term funds forecast any unusual collections (e.g. special payment terms such as seasonal dating extended to large customers), as well as the collection of slow accounts. In addition, the cash manager must be aware of any deferred payment terms in order to schedule the cash payments. Finally, the ski manufacturer must also be able to project its net funds flows rather accurately in order to negotiate appropriate credit lines from lenders.

Perhaps a more customary, but somewhat more difficult, situation to predict is that of the construction contractor (also reflected in Figure 12-1). A construction project may call for certain completion milestones that, when attained, trigger large payments. The contractor's cash manager may know the terms of the contract, may follow the progress closely with the project manager, and may know precisely the amount of a particular payment. The exact timing of the receipt of payment may be unpredictable, however. Because the payment amount is so large, the effect of any delay can be devastating. In such a case, a funds flow schedule is crucial in planning alternative sources of funding until the payment is received.

Short-Term Funds Forecasting and Profits

When interest rates are high, funds imbalances will significantly affect the interest income or interest expense on the income statement. To the extent that the cash manager's schedule of receipts and disbursements is prepared early enough and predicts a funds shortfall, management can usually employ tactics to reduce or avoid borrowing before it becomes inevitable. Such tactics may involve delaying the release of certain disbursements, mounting a special collection effort with respect to past due accounts, contacting selected customers to accelerate the payment of open invoices, or a combination of these efforts. Of course, many firms practice these tactics continuously, which leaves them with little latitude when faced with a predicted cash squeeze.

In periods of high interest rates, businesses may find that interest earned on their invested cash may even exceed the rate of return derived from normal operations on invested capital. No one suggests liquidating the business in order to become a money market mutual fund. However, tactics to delay disbursements and accelerate receipts may prove profitable in order to minimize borrowings or maximize invested funds, even if there is no funds flow imbalance anticipated. Indeed, many businesses complain about slow collections during high interest rate periods because their customers are slowing their payments intentionally. The short-term funds forecast can help a business play this game more effectively, from both sides.

DEFINITION OF A SHORT-TERM FUNDS FLOW FORECAST

The focus of short-term funds flow forecasting is to predict the flow of funds and resulting balances on a daily basis. Unlike a budget, with its time horizons of a year or more, the short-term funds flow forecast has a total time horizon of from one day to not more than a few weeks. The long-range intervals in the short-term funds flow forecast are measured in weeks, and in the foreground the intervals are days.

The annual budget of a year or more usually uses the adjusted net income approach and is prepared after all other budget plans are prepared. In the adjusted net income approach, the budget manager begins with net income after taxes, adds back all noncash charges, and further adjusts for changes in balance sheet accounts to arrive at a forecast of funds flow for the interval involved. This approach is useful to the budget manager in long range growth planning but is not very useful to the cash manager because it fails to account for temporary timing imbalances between receipts and disbursements. Therefore, it may easily fail to predict borrowing requirements or investing opportunities during that period.

Thus, the short-term funds forecast is actually a schedule of receipts and disbursements by time intervals of days or weeks and the resulting funds balances. This schedule becomes a framework for monitoring completion of virtually all of the financial transactions in the firm. Routine transactions such as accounts receivable collections, accounts payable disbursements, payrolls, dividends, debt service, and rents become a predictable set of funds streams. A few larger transactions, such as major sales and capital expenditures, can be predicted and monitored individually for their timing and impact on the schedule of receipts and disbursements.

STRUCTURING THE SHORT-TERM FUNDS FLOW FORECAST

Who Prepares the Forecast

Unlike the annual budget, which usually is prepared by the budget manager or the financial planning executive for a diverse audience of users, the short-term funds forecast is used virtually exclusively by the cash manager. Moreover, this forecast may diverge significantly from the annual budget because of timing differences: the timing of particular receipts and disbursements is calculated more precisely in the funds flow forecast. Accordingly, the short-term funds forecast is usually prepared in the treasury department, often by the cash manager or by an analyst working closely with the cash manager.

The person who prepares the forecast must understand the company's organization and operations and must establish and maintain good communication with all levels of authority throughout the organization. The successful forecaster is able to ferret out information, to distinguish significant data, and to interact with managers of production, sales, and administration as well as senior management. The forecaster must also be able to organize results clearly before using the data or issuing it to others. For purposes of this chapter, it is assumed that the cash manager prepares the short-term cash forecast.

Designing a Format

The cash manager adjusts the flows of receipts and disbursements to minimize borrowings or maximize funds invested and to meet compensating balance requirements. The single most important element of the forecast, which represents the goal of the process, is the ending balance for the period being forecasted. This figure indicates the likely course of action for the cash manager, whether it be borrowing, investment, or repayment of loans. If the ending balance is negative or tends to be below the target level, the cash manager must adjust the forecast to include borrowing or otherwise to generate an amount sufficient to keep it at the desired positive level.

It can be noted that, apart from the forecasting process, a decision must be made (and periodically re-evaluated) about what the appropriate average or absolute level should be for the ending balance. Typically, management will determine that the objective is to maintain collected bank balances at:

- The lowest possible level without becoming overdrawn;

- An average level sufficient to meet compensating balance requirements for loans;

- An average level sufficient to meet compensating balance requirements for loans plus an amount sufficient to cover all account activity charges;

- An absolute level sufficient to meet most major disbursement contingencies;

- An absolute level sufficient to maintain the organization's general ledger balance greater than zero; or

- Some combination of these options.

A simple and logical layout is most appropriate for the short-term funds forecast. The format in Figure 12-2 highlights the ending balance and its three principal components: starting balance, total receipts, and total disbursements. Regardless of whether the format follows a horizontal or verti-

FIG. 12-2

Format for Vertical Axis of Short-Term Funds Flow Forecast

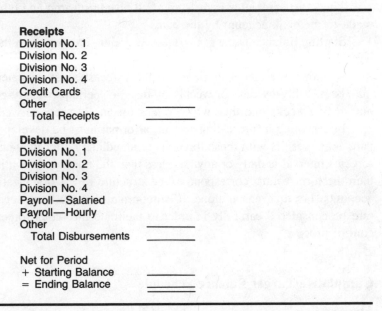

Receipts
Division No. 1
Division No. 2
Division No. 3
Division No. 4
Credit Cards
Other   _____
   Total Receipts   _____

Disbursements
Division No. 1
Division No. 2
Division No. 3
Division No. 4
Payroll—Salaried
Payroll—Hourly
Other   _____
   Total Disbursements   _____

Net for Period
+ Starting Balance   _____
= Ending Balance   _____

cal orientation, it will usually show a balance at the beginning of the period; for each interval it will show total receipts, total disbursements, and the ending balance. Receipts and disbursements are broken down into the smallest significant components that correspond to the bank account structure. For example, if each division has its own zero balance depository account and zero balance disbursing account, credit card receipts flow through a separate account, and two payroll accounts handle all payroll activity, the forecast format might look as it does in Figure 12-2.

Total Receipts is the sum of all funds in-flows during the period as reflected by credits to the bank account on the bank's books. This amount may differ from debits to the company's cash account in the general ledger due to delays between the time a bank deposit is made and the credit is posted in the general ledger. In short-term funds flow forecasting, the goal is to maintain a bank balance that will meet management's objectives. This can be attained only by managing the bank balances directly, not by managing them indirectly through control of the general ledger balances. General ledger balances are reduced too quickly, as checks are issued rather than as they clear the banks, and deposits often are not posted to the general ledger on the same day as they reach the bank. Therefore, bank balances are better managed directly, rather than after being filtered through the accrual-oriented accounting system.

Total Disbursements is the sum of all checks cleared and other charges made to the bank account by the bank.

Starting Balance is the same figure as ending balance from the previous period.

An appropriate time horizon for the forecast must be determined. It may be monthly-by-days or weekly-by-days, or perhaps weekly-by-days for one or two weeks and then whole weeks for another several weeks.

In designing a forecasting system, a format must be developed to compare actual results with those forecasted immediately after they occur. If the forecast interval is daily or anything less than the normal accounting period, then the format must correspond to the structure of the organization's bank accounts. For this reason alone, it is important that the bank account structure be considered carefully in order to facilitate the funds forecasting and control process.

Cumulative Target Balance Schedule

With the bank account structure in place, the cash manager can prepare the short-term funds flow forecast. To assist the cash manager in this process, a cumulative target balance schedule is prepared, usually for a monthly interval and possibly for quarterly and annual cumulative intervals as well. The frequency of the interval depends on the company's need to compensate the bank through cumulative average balances and on the settlement period negotiated with the bank.

Even companies that pay fees in lieu of maintaining compensating balances must m., itor balances using a cumulative target balance schedule. While no minimum balance may be required, a positive average collected balance level should be maintained. Furthermore, when reviewing the bank's monthly account analysis statement, it is helpful to have the company's own estimate of average collected balances as a point of comparison.

Where compensating balances are required for a credit line, the following is an example of a typical compensating balance arrangement: 5 percent of the amount of the credit line plus 5 percent of the average amount borrowed, plus collected balances sufficient to cover activity charges.

The cash manager can forecast the average collected balance requirement by compiling the following information:

Information	Forecasted Value	Source
Amount of credit line	$1,000,000	Loan agreement
Average loan	$ 700,000	Short-term cash forecast
Activity charges (monthly)	$ 110	Prior A/C analysis statements
Earnings credit rate	6 percent	Bank officer
Reserve requirement	12 percent	Bank officer
Collected balance required for activity	$ 25,000	Computation*

* Collected balances required to compensate for activity charges are calculated by annualizing the monthly charge ($110 X 12), dividing the result by the reciprocal of the reserve requirement (1 − 0.12 = 0.88) and dividing that result by the earnings credit rate (0.06).

The monthly target balance can then be compiled. Collected balances to compenstate for the availability and use of the credit line and account activity are:

Line of credit (5 percent of $1,000,000)	$ 50,000
Credit usage (5 percent of $700,000)	35,000
Account activity	25,000
Total monthly target average balance	$110,000

This amount is the target average collected balance for the month unless, by prior agreement with the bank, any excess or deficiency from the prior month may be carried forward. In that case, the $110,000 would be adjusted by the amount of excess or deficiency carried forward from prior periods.

The cash manager manipulates daily balances throughout the month to achieve the target balance. Progress toward that objective is monitored by using the daily bank balance report concerning ending balances, check clearing float, and collected balances.

A typical target balance schedule appears in Figure 12-3. Each day's collected balance in the concentration account—or the aggregate balances in all general and imprest accounts—is accumulated in a month-to-date total and then divided by the number of calendar days elapsed, which gives the month-to-date average collected balance. This figure is compared to the target balance, and an interim adjusted target balance is calculated for the remainder of the month in order to reach the overall monthly target. For

FIG. 12-3

Target Balance Schedule

Windy Widget Company
(dollars in thousands)

Month: April 19xx

Target balance: $110
Target dollar days (30 X 110): $3,300

Date	Day	Ledger Balance	Less: Float =	Collected Balance	Cumulative Dollar-Days	Average Collected Balance
1	Monday	$174	$ 67	$107	$ 107	$107
2	Tuesday	163	42	121	228	114
3	Wednesday	138	36	102	330	110
4	Thursday	112	25	87	417	104
5	Friday	96	10	86	503	101
6	Saturday	96	2	94	597	100
7	Sunday	96	0	96	693	99
8	Monday	170	86	84	777	97
9	Tuesday	187	62	125	902	100
10	Wednesday	240	74	166	1,068	107
11	Thursday	320	120	200	1,268	115
12	Friday	160	14	146	1,414	118
13	Saturday	160	5	155	1,569	121
14	Sunday	160	0	160	1,729	124
15	Monday	180	64	116	1,845	123
16	Tuesday	172	37	135	1,980	124
17	Wednesday	155	45	110	2,090	123
18	Thursday	136	29	107	2,197	122
19	Friday	110	20	90	2,287	120
20	Saturday	110	7	103	2,390	120
21	Sunday	110	0	110	2,500	119
22	Monday	105	44	61	2,561	116
23	Tuesday	99	19	80	2,641	115
24	Wednesday	89	32	57	2,698	112
25	Thursday	98	26	72	2,770	111
26	Friday	115	9	106	2,876	111
27	Saturday	115	2	113	2,989	111
28	Sunday	115	0	115	3,104	111
29	Monday	125	37	88	3,192	110
30	Tuesday	130	22	108	3,300	110

---

example, if the target for the month is $110,000, and there are 30 days in the month (nonworking days count), then exactly 3,300,000 cumulative "dollar-days" are required to meet the target. By using a working target that the cash manager adjusts throughout the month, the actual balances over the remaining days of the month can be manipulated to reach the overall target.

Calculation of the working target entails subtracting the actual dollar-days accumulated month-to-date from the goal and dividing the difference by the number of days remaining in the month. For example, in Figure 12-3, as of the eighth of the month the company accumulated 777,000 dollar-days for an average daily balance of $97,000 (against the target of $110,000). The revised working target is derived by subtracting the 777,000 accumulated dollar-days from the goal of 3,300,000, leaving 2,523,000 dollar-days to be accumulated over the remaining 22 days of the month, or $115,000 per day. Accordingly, on the morning of the ninth, the cash manager adjusts the working target balance from the original target of $110,000 to a new working target of $115,000 and begins to boost actual balances accordingly.

After pushing balances upward for more than a week, the cash manager finds that the month-to-date average has risen above the working target to $124,000 as of the close of business on the sixteenth, with 1,980,000 dollar-days accumulated toward the overall goal of 3,300,000. This leaves 1,320,000 dollar-days to be accumulated over the remaining 14 days, for a new working target of $94,000.

Offsetting any significant difference between the monthly goal and the cumulative actual position becomes increasingly difficult as the number of days remaining in the month dwindles. Therefore, the cash manager usually tries to stay close to the overall goal by using this methodology daily throughout the month.

BANK ACCOUNT STRUCTURE

It is important to have a bank account system that is structured appropriately, not only to facilitate funds flow forecasting but to facilitate the funds management function itself. The configuration and operation of the bank accounts should allow for the routine flow of receipts and disbursements.

Separation of the flow of receipts from the flow of disbursements is important both from the standpoint of forecasting and for purposes of audit and control. Staff concerned with making or accounting for deposits deal only with depository accounts, and staff preparing and accounting for disbursements work only with disbursing accounts. Since both sets of accounts have zero balances, information concerning the amount of the company's balances can be kept confidential.

Figure 12-4 depicts a classic bank account structure for forecasting and tracking cash. The banking structure involves a single concentration account to which zero balance accounts (ZBAs) for deposits and disbursements are appended. Deposits flow through the respective ZBA depositories into the

FIG. 12-4

Effective Bank Account Structure for Forecasting and Tracking Funds Flows

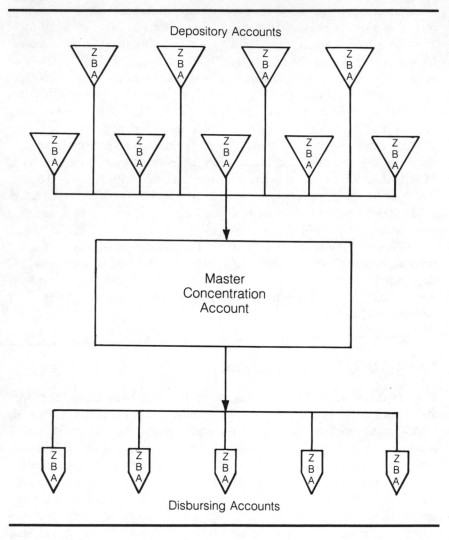

concentration account, and exact amounts of funds flow from the concentration account into the disbursing ZBAs as checks are presented to the bank for payment. In this system, each business unit has one or more depository ZBAs and one or more disbursing ZBAs. Each ZBA handles a significant

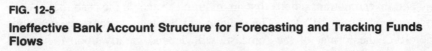

FIG. 12-5

Ineffective Bank Account Structure for Forecasting and Tracking Funds Flows

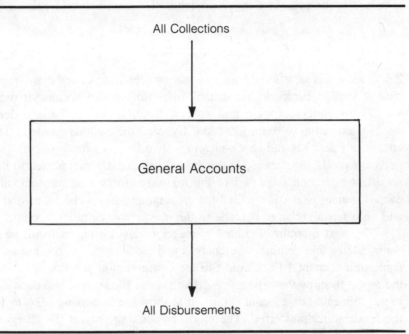

All Collections

General Accounts

All Disbursements

stream of funds that corresponds to a line in the short-term funds flow forecast format.

Because each ZBA reflects a significant stream of funds, the cash manager can forecast each stream and then monitor it, thereby forecasting the balance in the concentration account.

Figure 12-5 depicts a relatively ineffective bank account structure for forecasting net funds flows. This illustration employs general accounts, which tend to mask the visibility and predictability of the separate streams of receipts and disbursements. This system shows net changes in balances but fails to explain how those changes occur. Furthermore, the balances are spread among the accounts of the various units, making it necessary to total them and to take overt actions to concentrate the funds to avoid borrowing or to make investments.

Given a bank account structure that uses ZBAs and a master concentration account, the short-term funds flow forecast seeks to predict the bank's ledger balance in the concentration account. It also seeks to predict borrowing and investing transactions that are required to enable the cash manager to maintain the target balance. The structure of the bank account system and, therefore, the format of the forecast, will depend greatly upon the actual structure of the organization whose funds flows are being forecasted.

ZBAs and Funds Concentration Systems

ZBAs are a service offered by major money center banks and many regional banks. Smaller banks do not usually offer this service because it requires special computer software and special handling in the bank's demand deposit accounting system. Conceptually, after the bank has posted all of its customer's deposits and check clearings, two flows of funds occur: 1) each depository ZBA is charged for the total amount of deposits posted to it, and an offsetting credit is passed to the master concentration account; and 2) each disbursing ZBA is credited for the total amount of checks posted to it, and an offsetting charge is made to the master concentration account.

The next morning, the cash manager receives a report from the bank summarizing and detailing the charges and credits made to the master concentration account.[1] Each credit to the concentration account is labeled in the report to show the depository ZBA that was the source, and each charge to the concentration account is labeled to show the disbursing ZBA to which the funds were transferred. Therefore, by looking only at the charges and credits made to the concentration account, the cash manager can identify virtually all receipts and disbursements in the system for the day.

In offering the concentration/ZBA service to business customers, most banks do not limit the number of ZBAs that may be hooked up to a master concentration account. The only limits are the imagination of the cash manager about how best to organize the bank account structure and the cash manager's willingness to pay a premium maintenance fee for each ZBA. The premium fee covers the cost of transferring funds between the concentration account and the ZBA. When establishing the bank account structure, the cash manager needs to balance the cost of additional ZBAs against the benefit that they may be expected to bring.

Some banks offer a form of ZBA in which both deposits and disbursements are posted to the same account. After the close of each business day, the bank restores the balance to zero with either a debit or a credit for the net amount required as an offset. While this type of account may be useful for

---

[1] For a detailed description of Balance Reporting Service see Chapter 8; for a brief description, see p. 12-20 and Figure 12-8.

certain purposes, it is counterproductive for short-term funds flow forecasting because it masks the separate flows of receipts and disbursements.

Forecasting Check Clearings

From the standpoint of forecasting and tracking check clearings, there are three categories of check clearings:

1. Payroll checks

2. Large accounts payable checks

3. All other checks

Payroll check clearings are relatively easy to forecast because payroll disbursement cycles occur frequently, the amounts and check release dates are well defined, and clearing patterns are usually quite consistent. Dividend payments might also be included in the same category because they have predictable clearing patterns. The Distribution Approach is used most appropriately in forecasting these types of check clearings. In a payroll situation, for example, the net amount of payroll checks for a particular cycle is spread over the several business days following release of the checks. When multiple payrolls exist, each with a different cycle, each cycle can be isolated and forecasted separately. In this connection, it is preferable to use a separate disbursing ZBA for each type of payroll.

Some cash managers find it useful to separate large checks from the mainstream, tracking and forecasting their clearing individually by drawing them against a separate ZBA. By removing the large checks from the mainstream, the flow of checks that remains will have considerably less volatility and, therefore, greater predictability.

Whether or not a check can be considered ''large'' depends upon the size of the company and the typical payments that it makes. It may be convenient to select a cut-off level that will result in tracking approximately 40 to 60 checks per month in a large company and perhaps only 10 checks in a small company. The key here is the 80-20 rule: In this case, 80 percent of the volatility of check clearings is caused by probably fewer than 20 percent of the checks issued.

The Payments Pattern Approach may be used initially in disbursement forecasts to estimate the total dollar amount of checks to be cleared during a particular period. The length of time between the release of a check and when it clears the bank is called ''disbursement float,'' which is the sum of the following components:

1. Mail (or other delivery) time that it takes for the item to travel from issuer to payee;

2. Processing time by the payee upon receipt of the check; and

3. Clearing time by the banking system, from the time the payee deposits the check to the time the check is charged to the issuer's bank account.

In predicting the disbursement float of any particular check, the best guide is experience with checks sent to the same payee in the past. There is no useful formula that combines the three elements of disbursement float, since mail times and check clearing times vary among different pairs of cities, and different companies process their incoming checks with varying degrees of expediency. For example, a check that is mailed to a lockbox will enter the clearings sooner than a check that is deposited over the counter at a bank branch office; a check deposited through a lockbox may clear a full day sooner. Moreover, if the check is physically received at the payee's office, it may not be deposited the same day that it is received, causing further delay in its clearing.

A database of past clearing times of checks sent to each payee is necessary to predict the clearance of large items. The development and maintenance of the database need not be a burdensome task because the large checks paid by a firm are probably issued to a limited number of payees. An electronic spreadsheet or a simple card file may be very helpful here to keep track of historical clearing times by payees.

This historical database forms the basis for determining the probable clearing time of the next check issued. For any given payee, the database will show the historic minimum and maximum clearing times and an entire array of intermediate clearing times. From this data, the forecaster can either estimate intuitively the clearing time of the next check or use statistical techniques to estimate the probability of the check clearing on a certain date. This process is repeated for each large check outstanding, and a matrix is prepared that might look like either Figure 12-6 or Figure 12-7, depending on whether the intuitive approach or statistical probability approach is used.

Note that in the intuitive approach, as depicted in Figure 12-6, whole check amounts are recorded in the matrix, whereas in the statistical probability approach, each check is split and spread across several days to reflect the less than 100 percent probability of payment on any one day. For instance, a check may have no probability of clearing on January 25, a 75 percent probability of clearing on January 26, and a 25 percent probability

FIG. 12-6

Intuitive Approach to Funds Flow Forecasting

Forecasted Clearings of Large Checks
Today = Friday, January 23
(dollars in thousands)

Check	Amount	Date Mailed	1/23 Fri.	1/26 Mon.	1/27 Tue.	1/28 Wed.	1/29 Thur.	1/30 Fri.	2/2 Mon.
2069	$25	1/15	$25						
2070	cleared								
2071	60	1/19			$60				
2072	40	1/20			40				
2073	42	1/20				$42			
2074	37	1/21					$37		
2075	24	1/21					24		
2076	20	1/22					20		
2077	30	1/23							$30
Totals	$278		$25	$0	$100	$42	$81	$0	$30

FIG. 12-7

Statistical Probability Approach to Funds Flow Forecasting

Forecasted Clearings of Large Checks
Today = Friday, January 23
(dollars in thousands)

Check	Amount	Date Mailed	1/23 Fri.	1/26 Mon.	1/27 Tue.	1/28 Wed.	1/29 Thur.	1/30 Fri.	2/2 Mon.
2069	$25	1/15	$25						
2070	cleared								
2071	60	1/19			$45	$15			
2072	40	1/20			30	10			
2073	42	1/20			10	32			
2074	37	1/21				9	$28		
2075	24	1/21				6	18		
2076	20	1/22					15	$ 5	
2077	30	1/23						10	$20
Totals	$278		$25	$0	$85	$72	$61	$15	$20

for January 27. This is illustrated in Figure 12-6 by check #2072 for $40,000. If this check fails to clear on January 27, then the probability that it will clear the next day increases. In the case of check #2069, the probable clearing date has already passed. Therefore, there is virtually a 100 percent probability that the check will clear "today" (January 23). In both Figures 12-6 and 12-7, after spreading the checks according to their probable clearing dates, the columns for each day are summed to determine the forecast of large checks clearing each day.

Bank Balance Reporting Service

In order for the cash manager to monitor the actual flows of funds through the bank accounts and measure these flows and the resulting balances against the forecast, a bank balance report must be received daily from the bank (similar to the one shown in Figure 12-8). In order to be useful, the bank balance report must:

1. Be available to the cash manager upon (or before) opening for business;

2. Reflect all transactions and balances occurring in the concentration bank account the preceding day; and

3. Balance; that is, the report must reconcile the bank's ending ledger balance from the prior day with the current day's ending ledger balance, and the reason for all charges and credits must be readily apparent.

When these conditions are satisfied, the cash manager then may be assured that the data is valid.

Banks that offer the ZBA/concentration account service also offer an electronic balance reporting service. Many banks that do not offer the ZBA/concentration account service do, however, offer some form of balance reporting, either electronic or verbal. The electronic daily report of transactions and balances is more reliable, accurate, and timely than a verbal report received over the telephone. Electronic reports are received in formats designed by each bank; the reports are obtainable via touch-tone telephone, interactive terminal, personal computer, and mainframe computer.

For the sophisticated cash manager, pure data files rather than formatted reports may be downloaded from the bank or its third party time-share vendor to the user's computer. The user's computer then manipulates the data into a format designed by the cash manager, such as the format shown in Figure 12-9. One advantage of receiving data files instead of reports is that the cash manager may view the data from several banks in a common format.

FIG. 12-8

Bank Balance Report—Sample

Windy Widget Company
Summary Report
4/12/8x
as of 4/11/8x
Master Concentration Account #001-4379218

Ledger Balance	$319,954.88
1 Day Float	90,437.92
2 Day Float	29,677.22
Collected Balance	199,839.74
Total Credits	165,797.82
Total Debits	85,506.10

Detail Credits/Debits Report
4/12/8x
As of 4/11/8x
Master Concentration Account #001-4379218

Credits	$43,219.72	ZBA 4377811
	84,857.20	ZBA 4376731
	25,899.56	ZBA 4376523
	11,821.34	ZBA 4376383
Credits Total	165,797.82	
Debits	$31,209.50	ZBA 4375249
	27,642.00	ZBA 4374494
	15,387.06	ZBA 4374376
	11,267.54	ZBA 4373956
Debits Total	85,506.10	

Electronic Data Interchange in Funds Flow Forecasting[2]

Use of electronic data interchange (EDI), greatly improves the accuracy of funds flow forecasting. (EDI uses standardized data formats developed by the Accredited Standards Committee X12 of the American National Standards Institute for use by all industries in communicating computerized routine business data.) The X12 formats encourage electronic communication of virtually all elements of the materials purchase/sale transaction and the payment transaction, including:

- Request for quotation
- Price quotations
- Shipping notices
- Invoices

---

[2] See Chapter 7 for a more detailed discussion of electronic data interchange; see also Ben Milbrandt, Electronic Data Interchange: Making Business More Efficient (New Jersey: EDI in Business, 1988).

- Purchase orders
- Materials releases
- Payment order and remittance advice

Both the buyer and seller can use EDI to track shipping dates, which by prior negotiation may automatically determine payment due dates. This is important to the cash managers of both the buyer and seller, because the value date (date of settlement) for the transfer of funds becomes set—and known to both sides—well in advance of its occurrence. Then, the payment can be effected electronically via ACH with the value date known with certainty.

EDI has been adopted as a data communications standard by dozens of industries. Its appeal is expected to grow at a geometric pace through the early 1990s as its existence and usefulness become more well known and as EDI management software proliferates in large and small companies.

Reconciling the Short-Term Funds Flow Forecast

More than a few cash managers and accountants have wrestled with the task of reconciling the short-term funds flow forecast to the longer-term budget. Most are usually unsuccessful at the task because they are dealing with two very different kinds of statements that have no common base. Unless the budget is prepared in the same manner as the short-term funds flow forecast, as a schedule of receipts and disbursements, it is very difficult to reconcile the two, principally because of accruals. If, for example, the longer-term budget is prepared using either the "adjusted net income method" or the "working capital differential method,"[3] two very different kinds of data are being reconciled.

On the other hand, reconciling the forecast-to-actual for each type of forecast or budget is not only possible but could be a regular part of the forecasting process. Since the forecast elements and the actual data are similar but perhaps different only in amount and timing, they are easily reconcilable.

PREPARING AND USING THE SHORT-TERM FUNDS FLOW FORECAST

Collecting Data

Each figure or line item in the forecast is generated from available information. The accuracy of any particular forecasted number depends on the amount, quality, and reliability of information obtained. For example, in

---

[3] James D. Willson, Budgeting and Profit Planning Manual Ch. 23, Warren, Gorham & Lamont, Inc. (Boston: 2d ed. 1989).

forecasting the amount of daily collections for Company A, its collection history should be a readily available, fairly reliable source of information. For instance, it is known that:

1. Company A sells on terms of "2 percent 10th proximo," which means that customers may take a 2 percent discount if they pay by the tenth of the month following the date of the invoice;

2. About 70 to 75 percent of Company A's customers take the discount and pay by the tenth (allowing some slippage to the eleventh and twelfth); and

3. Sales during the previous month were very good (at $2.5 million), compared to lower sales in earlier months and for the same month last year.

These are key elements of information to use in forecasting collections for Company A. The quickly prepared forecast would show about 70 percent of last month's sales, or $1.8 million, being collected between the tenth and twelfth of the month, with the remainder (plus prior months' past due accounts) spread over the remaining days of the month. If the forecast is built solely on this data, it should be validated. For instance, the credit department might indicate that some past due accounts that were expected to be collected this month now need to be written off, or that several historically slow accounts will be paid sooner than expected. The sales department may confirm the "80-20" rule, that 80 percent of the business comes from 20 percent of the customers; or that the monthly sales hit a record level because of a blockbuster shipment to one customer totaling $450,000 or 18 percent of the $2.5 million total sales for the month. Now the question arises whether the cash manager can count on receiving payment from that client by the tenth of the month. If the payment is not received by then, the cash manager may have to borrow from the bank until payment is received. However, the line of credit may not be large enough to accommodate a bank loan of this size.

A solution to this dilemma is for the cash manager to pencil in the blockbuster collection on the tenth, assuming that it will be received on a timely basis. Then the cash manager and the sales manager should discreetly attempt to verify the customer's intention regarding payment.

Validating Data

Putting numbers on paper and labeling the page "Forecast" is not useful until the numbers are tested. Statisticians test the accuracy of numbers by evaluating historic patterns and by using various sophisticated statistical techniques. However, most cash managers lack the time, and occasionally the training, to use these sophisticated techniques. Instead, the cash manager often uses the "reasonableness" test. If the numbers on the page look reasonable based on the cash manager's experience, then they are probably sufficiently reliable.

This is not really a haphazard procedure; forecasting errors often average themselves out, if not by coincidence then by design. The cash manager should make offsetting changes throughout the forecasting process as more information is gained that can affect the forecast.

In the example on Company A, the cash manager learned that the customer plans to mail the huge payment on the twentieth of the month, assuming 10 days' grace because the sales and credit departments agreed to this at the customer's demand in order to make the sale. This information is very valuable to the cash manager, who must now adjust the forecast. But two questions immediately arise from this new information:

1. How reliable is the customer's word that "the check will be in the mail on the twentieth"?; and

2. How long will it take to receive the check through the mail?

The cash manager may talk to the sales manager again to convince him to extract one concession from the customer—to allow the salesman to pick up the check personally. This concession will immensely improve the forecast because the cash manager can adjust it for the proper check deposit date.

Where Company A's historic collection patterns showed that the $1.8 million of collections would normally be received between the tenth and twelfth of the month, collections of about $1.4 million can be more reliably predicted in that short period, and a $450,000 slug can be added on the twentieth.

Since Company A pays most of its own bills on the tenth of the month to take advantage of prompt payment discounts, the account will be short of funds until the blockbuster collection is received on the twentieth. Company A's checks that are due to go out on the tenth haven't been mailed yet, so the cash manager can still discuss the situation with the accounts payable and purchasing managers. They may agree to release certain checks late or to call a major vendor to request special dispensation because of the unusual circumstance. Clearly, the adjustment to the "receipts" side of the forecast necessitates an offsetting adjustment to the "disbursements" side. This is the reason that funds flow forecasting is so important to financial managers in the short run. Funds flow forecasting is not just the act of assembling some numbers into a forecast; it is the act of preparing for any impending situations that affect the company's business.

There is always an element of uncertainty in any cash forecasting situation. Good news is easily accepted, and bad news can be managed, but uncertainty has a way of being neither acceptable nor manageable. Therefore, whether the news is good or bad, the task of preparing accurate forecasts is to eliminate uncertainty wherever possible.

It is also extremely important that the cash manager avoid being lulled by averages and "gross numbers;" the cash manager must examine underlying transaction details for anomalies that may cause current events to differ from historic patterns. In small firms, the president many know every open invoice and expected collection date from memory, but as an organization grows and becomes more complex, it becomes necessary to implement a forecasting system tailored to the nature and scope of the organization it serves.

Identifying Historic Patterns

A forecast is a simulation, or model, of a firm's expected behavior; it is generally assumed that historic patterns will be repeated in the future. Four statistical methods that take historical patterns into account are used frequently to predict future financial events. These include simple moving average, exponential smoothing, regression, and sophisticated "time series" models such as the model developed by G.E.P. Box and G.M. Jenkins.[4]

In the simple moving average method, past values are expected to be repeated into the future. All values comprising the average are assigned equal weight so that trends will move slowly. The formula for the simple moving average is:

$$V_{t+1} = \frac{(V_t + V_{t-1} + V_{t-2})}{3}$$

where V_{t+1} is the value in the next time period and is based on the arithmetic average of the same values in the immediate past three time periods. Each of the values from the past three time periods carry equal weight in determining the moving average.

For example, assume Company A had net funds flow in each of the past six months as follows:

---

[4] G.E.P. Box and G.M. Jenkins, Time Series Analysis: Forecasting and Control. (San Francisco: Holden-Day, 1970).

June	$37	Three-month moving average = $34
May	35	
April	30	
March	32	
February	28	
January	25	
Six-month Average	$31.2	

Based on the three-month moving average, the predicted net funds for July would be $34.

The next level of sophistication recognizes that among the past values comprising a moving average, the most relevant values are likely to be those that have occurred most recently. For example, where the values reflect a rising trend, the most recent value is probably closer to the next value than the oldest one. Therefore, the most current values are assigned greater weight in the average than those occurring earlier in the series. This method of weighting the values is called exponential smoothing. The formula for the next value in this time series using exponential smoothing is:

$$V_{t+1} = V_t + S(X_t - V_t)$$

where V_t is the value that had been predicted for the current period, S is the statistical adjustment amount (or smoothing constant), and X_t is the actual value for the current period. Applying exponential smoothing to this time series for company A's net funds flow, the predicted value for the next period is equal to the value of the current period plus the amount of the adjustment to correct for the most recent forecast error. Accordingly, the forecast is based on the current period's forecast, with a statistical adjustment to correct for trends in recent values in the time series. Such corrections may adjust for seasonal variations or other external influences and often incorporate the forecasting error encountered in the most recent period.

The cash manager frequently uses the simple moving average together with some degree of exponential smoothing. At the simplest level, the cash manager can intuitively smooth the average and derive the predicted value by looking at a series of values.

Other statistical techniques require the use of a computer and specialized software. Regression analysis, for example, attempts to define a linear relationship between the input variables and the predicted funds flow element. Box-Jenkins models are complicated methods for identifying, estimating, and testing various time series. Although the Box-Jenkins techniques often prove to be accurate in forecasting funds flows, their use requires specialized training.

FIG. 12-9

Payments Pattern Approach to Funds Flow Forecasting

			Windy Widget Company (dollars in thousands)			
	March	**April**	**May**	**June**	**July**	**August**
Sales	$100	$120	$140	$110	$ 90	$ 80
Collections:						
March		70	20	10		
April			84	24	12	
May				98	28	14
June					77	22
July						63
August						
Total collected	$ 0	$ 70	$104	$132	$117	$ 99

Statistical Approaches

Two distinct statistical approaches predominate in short-term funds flow forecasting. These methods have been characterized as the Payments Pattern Approach and the Distribution Approach; they may be used by the cash manager on an intuitive level or may be created on a computer. Both approaches may be employed in forecasting the same funds flow element, depending on its nature. The Payments Pattern Approach, based on a model developed by Professor Bernell K. Stone,[5] operates on the premise that if the pattern of the source event can be determined, then the pattern of the resulting funds flow element can be predicted. The time delay from the source event to the occurrence of the funds flow element is estimated, and the result is entered into the forecast. For example, Company A's collection experience shows that sales in a given month are typically turned into collections at a rate of 70 percent of sales in the first month following the sale, 20 percent in the second month, and 10 percent in the third. Figure 12-9 shows how collections would result if this pattern holds true.

The Payments Pattern Approach is particularly useful in forecasting certain funds flow elements, such as collections of accounts receivable, which have a definite cycle or an identifiable origin. In many companies, there is a strong correlation between the timing of collection of the receiva-

---

[5] B.K. Stone, *The Payments Pattern Model to Forecasting and Control of Accounts Receivable*, Fin. Mgmt. 65–82 (Autumn 1976).

ble and the date of the invoice and credit terms allowed, because most payers pay with an eye to the credit terms allowed. However, where there is not such a strong correlation, the Payments Pattern Approach tends to become ineffective. This may occur, for example, where customers pay at random times from month-end statements. If a prompt payment discount is not offered, remittances may be received without any reliable pattern other than that established by the paying habits of the customers. The correlation is further weakened by the collection of past due accounts because it often defies any predictable pattern. In such a case, the Distribution Approach may work to better advantage.

The Distribution Approach uses previous payment patterns to predict the distribution of a known quantity over a specific number of days. In Figure 12-10, where the month's collections are anticipated to be $132,000, the distribution approach may be used to predict each day's collections using payment patterns derived from previous months. The Distribution Approach may incorporate payment patterns based on the particular day of the week and the date of the month.[6] One may also use the week-of-the-month to advantage when weekly transaction cycles exist.

The days-of-the-week pattern is important because of the effect of weekends on funds flow elements. For instance, the U.S. Postal Service moves mail on weekends, but there is only limited processing of checks by banks on weekends. Consequently, banks process massive volumes of checks on Mondays, both from checks being received by payees and deposited to their bank accounts and checks being charged to the accounts of issuers. Monday, therefore, is an important day in the funds flow forecast.

The day-of-the-month effect is driven by a combination of invoice dates and payment terms. If invoices are rendered evenly throughout the month and payment terms are net 30 days, then collections should be relatively constant throughout the ensuing month after accounting for weekends. Alternatively, if payment terms call for payment by the tenth of the next month, then there will be a skewing of collections around that date, again taking weekends into account.

To forecast collections by considering both the day-of-the-week and the day-of-the-month effects, the cash manager might simply combine the two effects into a table and multiply one by the other, as shown in Figure 12-10. The expected monthly collections total $132,000, derived by using the payments pattern approach based on collections of 70 percent, 20 percent, and

---

[6] For a more complete description of the Distribution Approach, see B.K. Stone and R.A. Wood, *Daily Cash Forecasting: A Simple Method for Implementing the Distribution Approach*, Fin. Mgmt. 40–50 (Fall 1977).

FIG. 12-10

Distribution Approach to Funds Flow Forecasting

Windy Widget Company

Days-of-the-Week Distribution of Cash Collections

Monday	30%
Tuesday	18
Wednesday	22
Thursday	14
Friday	16

Expected Collections for the Month
Combining Days-of-Week and Days-of-Month
for Cash Collections
(dollars in thousands)

(1) Business Day	(2) Monthly Historic	(3) Raw Amount	(4) Day	(5) Week Total	(6) Day-of- Week Factor	(7) Forecast Collection Amount
1	2%	$ 2,640	Monday		30%	$ 4,752
2	2	2,640	Tuesday		18	2,851
3	2	2,640	Wednesday		22	3,485
4	3	3,960	Thursday		14	2,218
5	3	3,960	Friday	$ 15,840	16	2,534
6	4	5,280	Monday		30	12,276
7	4	5,280	Tuesday		18	7,366
8	6	7,920	Wednesday		22	9,002
9	8	10,560	Thursday		14	5,729
10	9	11,880	Friday	40,920	16	6,547
11	10	13,200	Monday		30	15,840
12	10	13,200	Tuesday		18	9,504
13	9	11,880	Wednesday		22	11,616
14	7	9,240	Thursday		14	7,392
15	4	5,280	Friday	52,800	16	8,448
16	4	5,280	Monday		30	5,940
17	3	3,960	Tuesday		18	3,564
18	3	3,960	Wednesday		22	4,356
19	3	3,960	Thursday		14	2,772
20	2	2,640	Friday	19,800	16	3,168
21	2	2,640	Monday	2,640	30	2,640
	100%	$132,000		$132,000		$132,000

---

10 percent. Using the percentages of the total monthly collections that have been realized historically on each business day (Column 2), the cash manager can derive the expected (raw) collection amount for each day (Column 3) by muliplying each day's percentage by $132,000. However, the resulting daily amounts must be adjusted to take weekends into account. There-

fore, each business date has been labeled to indicate the day of the week for this month (Column 4), and the amount of expected weekly total collections has been inserted into Column 5, which is the sum of the raw amounts for Monday through Friday. Next, the factor for collections on each day of the week is entered into Column 6. The adjusted forecasted collection amount is then calculated in Column 7 by multiplying the weekly total by the respective day-of-the-week factor.

The forgoing example illustrates how these methods may be used in tandem to forecast at least one of the funds flow elements. The Payments Pattern Approach is used initially to estimate the total for the month. The Distribution Approach is then employed to spread that total over each of the days of the month.

Forecasting Error

The experienced forecaster attempts to improve the accuracy of future forecasts by tracking the distribution of forecast error. Vander Wiede and Maier[7] discuss three types of error distribution: normal, dependent-independent variables, and stable patterns.

Normal distribution reflects those kinds of forecasting errors that occur in the familiar bell-shaped pattern, where approximately half the forecasted amounts were too large and half were too small. In addition to the direction of the errors, the magnitude of the errors will vary approximately on the order of one or two standard deviations in a normal distribution of error. The forecaster will continously determine which elements of the funds flow forecast are subject to a normal distribution of error by monitoring variances of the actual results from the forecast. When the distribution varies from the norm, the forecaster immediately suspects that trends may be changing.

Many variances do not occur in a normal (bell-shaped) pattern, however, because they are dependent on other variables. For example, in an accounts payable disbursing bank account, more dollars may clear on a particular day than had been expected. Since only a certain amount of checks are outstanding, the amount clearing the following day will probably be less than forecasted. In this case, this amount is a variable factor dependent on the amount of checks paid the preceding day.

---

[7] James H. Vander Weide and Steven F. Maier, Managing Corporate Liquidity: An Introduction to Working Capital Management (New York: John Wiley & Sons, 1985).

Organizing Data: The Electronic Spreadsheet

The sheer amount of data and complex statistical approaches used in forecasting make the electronic spreadsheet an invaluable tool for the cash manager. An electronic spreadsheet, which may be accessed on a mainframe computer from a remote terminal or in a desktop computer, consists of rows and columns similar to the columnar pad. It can be programmed easily to do many functions automatically, including simple arithmetic and complex algebraic equations involving various cells and sets of cells on the spreadsheet.

The cash manager can develop a template to replicate the forecast format for each day, week, month, quarter, or other interval by using an electronic spreadsheet. Then the cash manager enters the forecasted values for each category of receipt and disbursement and for each interval in the forecast horizon. In Figure 12-11, the line items for each day's receipts and disbursements are entered into the appropriate cells on the spreadsheet. The computer then calculates the forecasted funds position for each day and the cumulative weekly funds flows and balance.

As the week progresses, the actual values for each day are entered in the "Actual" column, and the funds flows for the day and cumulatively for the week are automatically calculated. At this point, the cash manager begins to formulate possible decisions and test them for reasonableness. First, as the actual transactions occur and balances become known, they are compared to the forecasted values and the variances are analyzed. The variance analysis may involve nothing more than a mental comparison of the forecasted values to the actual, or it may be computer-assisted and more thorough.

After reviewing the variance between the actual and forecasted figures, the cash manager then adjusts the forecast for the current day and the next few days. For example, if collections have been exceeding the forecast, then an assumption might be made that future collections may be below the forecast because a significant amount was collected sooner than anticipated. Accordingly, the forecasted collections would need to be reduced by the estimated amount of the excess.

This updating process, which often occurs daily, uncovers any new imbalances between receipts and disbursements. At this point, further adjustments may be required to achieve the target balance. In these cases, the cash manager may need to revisit the managers of sales, purchasing, credit, and accounts payable to discuss delaying payments, accelerating collections, renegotiating purchase terms, or a combination of these tactics.

FIG. 12-11

Format for Weekly Funds Flow Forecast by Days

	Week Ending												
	Monday		Tuesday		Wednesday		Thursday		Friday		Total Week	
	Forecast	Actual	Forecast	Actual	Forecast	Actual	Forecast	Actual	Forecast	Actual	Forecast	Actual
Receipts												
Division no. 1 ZBA												
Division no. 2 ZBA												
Division no. 3 ZBA												
Division no. 4 ZBA												
Credit cards ZBA												
Other												
Total receipts												
Disbursements												
Division no. 1 ZBA												
Division no. 2 ZBA												
Division no. 3 ZBA												
Division no. 4 ZBA												
Payroll—salaried ZBA												
Payroll—hourly ZBA												
Other												
Total Disbursements												
Net for day												
+ BANK BALANCE @ BEGINNING												
= BANK BALANCE @ END												

Monitoring Patterns and Trends

For most commerce and industry, a month is usually the relevant billing and payment cycle. Trends develop over the course of several cycles, the lifetime of which will differ from company to company and from industry to industry. In the wholesale food and grocery business, for example, deliveries and payments usually occur weekly. In construction, the relevant cycle usually is the project life, with the contract dictating the completion milestones and payments. Whatever the relevant cycle may be, once the cash manager has identified a pattern for any funds flow element, that pattern must be monitored.

In short-term funds flow forecasting, daily funds flow elements are accumulated into weekly totals, and weekly totals are accumulated into monthly or quarterly totals. The weekly totals seem to be most valuable for monitoring trends because of their short and consistent length. In Figure 12-12, the cash manager builds a valuable database from which forecasts may be extrapolated by preserving the weekly actual totals. This may be accomplished by transferring the final column from the "weekly funds flow forecast by days" spreadsheet to a separate "actual weekly totals" spreadsheet.

Before locking away an "actual weekly totals" column, the cash manager should identify any unusual or nonrecurring transactions in the data and move these amounts to an "other" line in the format. This will adjust the total for the regular line items to an amount that is not distorted by any irregular or unusual transactions. In using this data base to extrapolate a new forecast, the cash manager will appreciate the purity of the regular line item. Furthermore, the frequency of the unusual transactions appearing in the "other" line will warn the cash manager about whether such irregular or unexpected transactions should be forecasted regularly as a separate category.

Keeping Management Informed

Senior management usually is more concerned with the firm's progress toward meeting quarterly and annual goals than with the daily funds flow forecast. It is the cash manager's responsibility, therefore, to determine whether any activity is significant enough to bring to senior management's attention.

The monthly or quarterly budget, which is prepared along with the annual plan, usually forms the basis for senior management's view of the firm's current position. Generally, as long as the short-term cash forecast corresponds closely to the annual plan, most senior managers tend to ignore

FIG. 12-12

Summary of Actual Weekly Funds Flows Forecast by Days

Windy Widget Company
Concentration Bank: First National Bank
(dollars in thousands)

Weeks ended

	1/7	1/14	1/21	1/28	2/4	2/11	2/18	2/25	3/4	3/11	3/18	3/25	4/1
Receipts													
Division no. 1	$12	$18	$14	$13	$8	$12	$14	$10	$8	$15	$17	$11	$13
Division no. 2	10	17	12	10	9	12	21	15	6	13	14	12	10
Division no. 3	8	12	10	10	7	4	7	6	12	6	7	10	8
Division no. 4	5	9	7	6	7	8	13	12	10	6	9	9	7
Special items		20	12		7	19	8	3	10	22	7	3	10
Credit cards	2	3	3	2	3	2	3	2	2	5	2	2	3
Other	1	2	1	4	2	4	1	2	2	3	2	3	6
Total Receipts	38	81	59	45	43	61	67	50	50	70	58	50	57
Disbursements													
Division no. 1	7	16	8	3	5	12	18	9	11	16	11	6	9
Division no. 2	6	13	8	2	2	11	9	5	8	7	9	4	10
Division no. 3	5	11	5	7	3	8	12	5	7	9	6	9	9
Division no. 4	3	9	3	4	6	7	7	4	3	8	6	7	8
Payroll—salaried	13	20		20	12		22		22		19		20
Payroll—hourly			15				14		16		16		15
Construction disbursements			10				13				15		
Other								14				16	
Total disbursements	34	69	49	36	28	38	95	37	67	40	82	42	71
Net for day	4	12	10	9	15	23	-28	13	-17	30	-24	8	-14
+ BANK BALANCE @ BEGINNING	21	25	37	47	56	71	94	66	79	62	92	68	76
= BANK BALANCE @ END	$25	$37	$47	$56	$71	$94	$66	$79	$62	$92	$68	$76	$62

daily cash trends. However, if the short-term funds forecast uncovers an unanticipated borrowing need, or the need to borrow an amount that is materially larger than originally anticipated, the cash manager is obliged to communicate that unpleasant news to management. By alerting the appropriate financial officer early, unexpected adverse occurrences may be examined and alternatives considered in a timely manner.

A routine weekly report of actual receipts and disbursements may be routed upward to management through the treasurer. This report, perhaps in the form of Figure 12-12, is actually a copy of the cash manager's current database, so it requires no additional production effort. The cash manager should attach a brief explanation highlighting the noteworthy transactions that occurred and the expected ones that failed to occur during the week.

In addition, the cash manager might prepare an extension of the "days-of-the-week" forecast to include several weeks beyond the current one. These extra weeks do not have to be broken down into days at this point since there is a good chance that any significant variations from the annual plan will readily be apparent.

Taken together, the weekly report of actual transactions over the past several weeks and the weekly forecast of transactions for the next several weeks will help apprise the financial officer of the firm's current and future financial status.

Unexpected Transactions

If unexpected transactions of a significant size occur with some frequency and on very short notice, then the forecast might be constructed to contain a margin for contingencies. This is particularly important if the unexpected transactions are usually disbursements. Businesses that tend to experience these events usually are "deal oriented" enterprises such as real estate or entertainment companies where deals are negotiated quietly and quickly, at least as far as the cash manager is concerned, and large payments must be made on very short notice. When such a situation prevails, it is imperative that the company have a liquidity reserve that can be tapped on short notice. This preserves the integrity of the forecast and the sanity of the cash manager. Since the cash manager's objective is to maintain liquidity with as low a funds balance as possible, the liquidity reserve may be either a line of credit for borrowing or a pool of short-term invested funds.

INTERMEDIATE-TERM FUNDS FLOW FORECASTING

Forecasting funds flows in the very short term using the receipts and disbursements scheduling technique previously described can be quite accurate on a daily basis for several weeks. But, as the forecast horizon is pushed out to the third or fourth week and beyond, the degree of accuracy deteriorates markedly. This deterioration happens when daily variances accumulate. The accumulation of such variances over 10 or 15 business days makes the forecast intervals beyond that time frame of dubious value. Cash managers who prepare weekly forecasts going beyond three weeks or so usually accept this deterioration in quality with equanimity because they do not use more than the first two weeks of their forecast in managing the company's funds position. Forecasts of the intervals beyond two or three weeks are prepared for two reasons: 1) senior management may want to review the funds forecast on a "best guess" basis; and 2) the exercise of identifying future expected large receipts and disbursements can be monitored.

One successful method for improving the quality of weekly funds forecasts beyond the very near term horizon is the "Accrual Addback Technique," developed by Alan M. Cunningham.[8] Using the best features of both the receipts and disbursements schedule and the adjusted net income approach, the accrual addback technique avoids the problem of cumulative errors and forms an effective bridge to the longer term forecast based on the adjusted net income approach.

The accrual addback technique starts with the forecasted pretax profit for a month or a quarter and adds back noncash charges such as depreciation and amortization and deducts large capital expenditures. The resulting "funds flow" is spread over the weeks of the forecast period, either equally or according to an algorithm based on the Distribution Approach described earlier. The weekly funds flow figures are then adjusted for: 1) the lag between sales and collections, based on days' sales outstanding (DSO) or other appropriate measures; 2) expected large collections and disbursements; and 3) intraperiod accruals such as payroll, taxes, insurance, and other similar expenses, which may best be based on quarterly or annual expense levels and then converted to average weekly amounts.

The elegance of this approach is that its accuracy depends on actual versus forecasted profits, which presumably is the focus of management's continual attention. Errors in profit projections are normally small in relation to sales volume, and the funds flow forecast inherits only this slight inaccuracy. The accrual addback technique, therefore, can be an effective tool in forecasting the intermediate time period between two or three weeks and two or three months from the reference point.

---

[8] Alan M. Cunningham, *The Accrual Addback Technique for Medium-Term Cash Forecasting,* Journal of Cash Mgmt. 46 (Sept./Oct. 1988).

SUMMARY

Preparation of a short-term funds flow forecast that has some degree of accuracy and relevance requires painstaking attention to detail and the organization of data into a rational format. No forecast can be prepared merely by shoveling massive amounts of data into the front of a computer and watching a forecast print out of the back.

The short-term funds flow forecast depends on organizing the bank account structure into discrete flows of receipts and disbursements and then forecasting those discrete flows. Then, as forecast intervals occur, the actual results are added to the database so that trends may be identified. Separation of the flows of receipts from the flows of disbursements is crucial to accurately forecasting net funds flows and balances.

Forecasters depend on historic data to project funds transactions and balances into the future. Gathering the data on completed transactions uses computerized bank reporting systems, electronic spreadsheets, and data base management systems. In time, uncertainty over the timing of many transactions will be reduced as buyers and sellers negotiate value dates for the settlement of payments, and this will be facilitated by computer-to-computer communications that will slowly replace paper flows.

Computers may be useful in keeping track of the numbers—and adjustments—that make up a short-term funds flow forecast. Computers may also be helpful in identifying trends through the use of various statistical techniques. However, the glue that holds the model together is the ability of the cash manager to maintain a network of contacts throughout the firm in order to stay abreast of transactions even before they occur.

SUGGESTED READINGS

Cunningham, Alan M. "The Accrual Addback Technique for Medium-Term Cash Forecasting." *Journal of Cash Mgmt.* (Sept./Oct. 1988).

Stone, Bernell K. "The Payments Pattern Approach to the Forecasting and Control of Accounts Receivable." *Fin. Mgmt.* (Autumn, 1976), pp. 65–82.

Stone, Bernell K. and Robert A. Wood. "Daily Cash Forecasting: A Simple Method for Implementing the Distribution Approach." *Fin. Mgmt.* (Fall 1977), pp. 40–50.

Vander Weide, James and Steven F. Maier. *Managing Corporate Liquidity: An Introduction to Working Capital Management.* New York: John Wiley & Sons, 1986.

Willson, James D. *The Budgeting and Profit Planning Manual,* 2d ed. Boston and New York: Warren, Gorham & Lamont Inc., 1989.

Wismer, David A. "Approaches to Cash Flow Forecasting: Part I." *Journal of Cash Mgmt.* (Jan.–Feb. 1985), pp. 12–16.

———. "Approaches to Cash Flow Forecasting: Part II." *Journal of Cash Mgmt. (July-Aug. 1985), pp. 50–57.*

———. "Approaches to Cash Flow Forecasting: Part III." *Journal of Cash Mgmt. (Nov.-Dec. 1985), pp. 85–90.*

CHAPTER 13

Short-Term Borrowing

Paul Peterik

PLANNING THE COMPANY'S BORROWING REQUIREMENTS

Short-term borrowing should be viewed in the context of overall strategic planning. In general, there are two ways to plan and manage the debt and capital structure of a company: the "At Any Cost Theory" and the "Strategic Planning Theory."

The "At Any Cost Theory" and its variations advocate that any treasurer, chief financial officer, or other appropriate financial manager can raise the capital necessary for a business if enough pressure is applied to do so. This theory usually follows traditional "supply and demand" thinking. Since capital is like any commodity—the greater the need, the higher the cost—this approach suggests that the best time to borrow money is when it is not really needed. For example, in some instances, "blind" acquisition financings are less restrictive and less expensive than financing when the acquisition target has been identified and the bankers know the money is needed quickly. However, if the acquisition is not completed, a company will be obligated for fees and costs, which can be an expensive proposition.

The preferable capital and debt management approach is to include acquisitions and their financing within the company's overall strategic planning. Planning the company's capital and debt structure should be as important as making sales projections and evaluating expansion and acquisition plans. Knowing the company's long range objectives enables management to match the variety of available options with the company's goals. Without such strategic planning, the liability side of a company's balance sheet could become a hodge-podge of debt, perhaps with conflicting covenants and restrictions.

Overall Strategic Financial Plan

The financial manager must be involved in the process of planning the capital and debt structure of the company. In this way, the financial manager will be in "synch" with the overall strategic plan, and other members of management will be exposed to the financing requirements of their business plan.

In developing the financing portion of the strategic plan, the most important concept is to let the plan dictate the financing requirements, not the reverse. Few companies would have achieved profitability if they had used only immediately available resources. Of course, financial strategic plans are inevitably imperfect due to unforeseen changes in business conditions, customer preferences, and similar uncertainties. However, the best plans are flexible and answer as many conditional or continuing issues as possible.

A strategic plan should take into account the company's existing assets, its available internal sources of funds, and management's growth plan for the company. Factors to be considered are:

- The company's mission statement or charter and its philosophical approach to debt financing;

- The company's financial and operational goals and how they may affect the company's approach to the use of leverage;

- Market and competitive analyses to see how competitors have leveraged their balance sheets;

- The company's competitive advantages and disadvantages and how the additional debt may affect these; and

- The company's strategies for achieving goals and objectives to see if additional debt conforms with the overall business plan of the company.

Clarifying the Company's Strategic Objectives

Examples of questions relating to the company's mission and charter that must be considered when analyzing a company's strategic choices include:

- Who are the owners of the business? Private or controlling stockholders often have a more entrepreneurial approach than public shareholders.
- What are their plans? Will additional debt help realize those plans?
- Does the company want new owners?
- Does the company want to be private or public?
- What amount of risk is appropriate?
- How much interest cost is desirable and/or affordable?
- Does the company want to give future returns such as stock or a percentage of profits?
- Does the company want to provide collateral security such as stock or assets?
- Are the principals of the business willing to sign a personal guarantee?
- How many covenants or restrictions will a company tolerate?
- How much control does the company want to retain?
- What happens in a worst case scenario?
- What limitations from other agreements does the company have in pledging assets?
- How important are ''committed'' versus ''uncommitted'' facilities?

Similarly, examples of questions relating to evaluating a company's competitive market position would include:

- The size of the total market?
- Who is the customer?
- What is the company's current market share?

- How can the company increase its market share?
- Who is the competition?
- What are the strengths and weaknesses of the competition?
- What are the company's competitive strengths and weaknesses?
- What are the market trends?
- What are the company's product and price point position?

Similar questions need to be asked about all phases of the strategic planning process.

The answers to these questions should fit together to form a clear picture of the current status of the company, as well as its actual and intended directions. The evaluation process, the result of realistically answering these questions, will help to narrow the choices of alternative financing and to keep short-term strategy consistent with long-term capital management objectives. For example, if a business is publicly owned, the interests of the shareholders (who seek quarterly earnings and annual dividends on their stock or appreciation in share values) must be addressed first. This will result in an emphasis on consistent growth, no matter how small. If the company is privately held, strategic objectives can often be much more flexible because the primary shareholders may not necessarily require regular quarterly profits if they feel that the company's investments will pay off in the long term.

Similarly, a major consideration when trying to determine a company's strategic objectives is how committed the company is to meeting the competition. If a company is small and aggressive, its long-term strategy may be to find a market niche for itself. If a company is large and more conservative, its strategies may include an emphasis on the service aspects of its product.

If a company does not evaluate itself—does not consider most (or all) of these types of questions—it runs the risk of obtaining funding from an inappropriate source. The result may be that the financing will not allow successful completion of the company's strategic plan.

Short-Term Requirements

A part of any plan should focus on evaluating the need for short-term borrowing as a way to finance the business. Before such a plan can be developed, however, the financial manager must thoroughly understand the company's cash flow on a monthly, weekly, and daily basis, including:

- Seasonality of sales
- Timing of collections and disbursements
- Economic trends
- Need for back-up plans in the event that the primary operating plan does not work well

The seasonality of sales, as well as the timing of collections and disbursements, can affect a company's short-term borrowing requirements. A company's short-term needs can be misleading if one month is particularly profitable, or if another has a particularly large number of disbursements. For example, if Company A receives most of its orders and remittances during the summer, it may be tempted to reduce its short-term borrowing forecast. However, if the first and second quarters are also a time for incurring extremely large production or maintenance costs, Company A may want to maintain a static borrowing requirement for the entire year.

The timing of major capital expenditures will also affect a company's borrowing requirements. Such expenditures may be timed so that they occur when cash is plentiful; however, the importance of an expenditure for new machinery, for example, could affect later periods if it is not installed to meet an anticipated increase in orders requiring additional plant capacity.

Economic trends also need to be reviewed. For example, companies in the automotive industry key on new car sales and interest rates in making assumptions on short-term borrowing requirements. In particular, they focus on the state of the economy and the consumer, and try to anticipate sales trends.

Contingency plans also need to be considered. Although downturns in sales usually spell trouble, companies that have the ability to eliminate variable expenses such as fixed sales expenses may generate additional cash in a downturn.

As these examples illustrate, the financial manager must be attuned to all the sources of changes in business circumstances. The ability to understand the interaction of these many factors will create the basis for successful forecasting.

STEPS TO SUCCESSFUL BORROWING

Once the company's strategic objectives and borrowing requirements are known, the necessary funds can be raised by taking the following steps:

1. Understanding the basic concept of debt;

2. Understanding the lender and credit process;

3. Understanding the advantages and disadvantages of short-term borrowing alternatives;

4. Matching the best type of financing to the strategic objectives; and

5. Preparing and presenting a loan request package.

The Basic Concept of Debt

"Neither a borrower nor a lender be" may be a wise proverb, but debt is the way of life for most consumers and institutions. It is important to recognize that investing and borrowing are the flip side of the same coin. For example, what a company can expect to pay for a 10-year mortgage can be determined by finding out initially what an investor who purchases 10-year government securities would pay and adjusting this "yield" for factors such as liquidity and risk or reward.

Definition of Capital. In broad terms, "capital" comprises the resources that are required to achieve a financial objective. The two broad classifications of capital are debt and equity. Equity is the owner's money, while debt is another person's money. Borrowed funds, or debt, carry an obligation to repay the source providing the money. Owners of capital make it available only for one reason: the return. Thus, the only real difference between debt and equity appears to be who provides the capital and what type of return the provider is seeking.

Risk and Reward. While debt and equity are similar, the nature of the returns sought by each source usually varies greatly. An owner or entrepreneur is often willing to receive little for his efforts in exchange for an opportunity to see his business idea germinate. On the other hand, a lender financing a risky venture would expect to receive a large return for the higher risk taken.

Generally, the cost of debt is represented by an interest rate, while equity is represented by appreciation in the company's stock or the value of the underlying assets. In both cases, the applicable tax implications will be factored into the desired return.

The most important element in the pricing of debt or equity is the trade-off between risk and reward: the greater the risk, the greater the reward. The high yield (junk) bond market that developed in the 1980s is a good illustration. A long-term bond issued by a noninvestment grade company returns more than a similar bond of an investment grade issuer. A debt manager must look at the risk factors of the company and assess the potential impact of availability and cost on equity and debt investors.

Leverage. If risk and reward are the most important elements of determining the return an investor seeks, then leverage is the most common benchmark for both investor and investee. Leverage is simply the use of another person's resources. The more leverage (i.e., the greater the proportion of debt to equity), the greater the risk that the scale of leverage may tip to the source providing the capital.

Leverage levels and limits vary widely from company to company and industry to industry. However, financial statements of other companies that are similarly situated can help determine an appropriate leverage range. These items will help in focusing on the different alternatives available.

Reasons for Borrowing. The three reasons to borrow money are

1. To purchase an asset;
2. To pay an expense; or
3. To make an investment (to buy net worth).

Knowing the reasons why funds are needed will help in looking for those funds. For example, leasing companies can be a source of money in an asset purchase, but typically they have no interest in financing working capital. Likewise, a venture capital firm seeks the upside equity potential of a highly leveraged transaction but typically is not interested in solely loaning money.

The Lender and Credit Process

It is important to understand the elements that a lender looks for in the decision to provide capital. Like any decision, there are two facets that need to be examined. The first is the emotional side of the lender's decision, while the second is the logic or information that is necessary to support the decision.

It is important to understand that the decision to provide capital can be an emotional one based on the personalities involved. The consumer's decision to purchase a new car, for example, is quite often done emotionally on impulse and then justified logically by citing factors such as low repair bills, better engine performance, and good gas mileage. Lenders, like used-car salesmen, too often are stereotyped; they are viewed as being conservative, cautious, pessimistic, and always looking for what's wrong with a business. While such stereotypes are inadequate, lenders certainly are not all alike. They do, however, have some attitudes in common when it comes to evaluating a loan proposal, and the borrower must play to these attitudes to be successful in presenting the loan proposal.

The process of presenting a loan proposal is the same for a small or large company. Success depends on differentiating the "deal" from all the others being evaluated and helping justify logically what an investor believes emotionally. The investor has his own stereotype of people presenting an investment—unprepared, overly optimistic, and out of touch with reality. Differentiating a loan proposal from the others is simple, just as the whole process of raising money is simple. It is like learning how a magic trick is done. What seemed mystifying at first suddenly looks easy when it is explained by the magician. In presenting a loan proposal, the financial manager must demonstrate that he is prepared, knowledgeable, and has a good chance to repay. In just understanding the process and being prepared, the applicant has an advantage over the average borrower.

In order for a borrower to evaluate this level of "preparedness," he should be able to answer the banker's questions very quickly and openly. Answering these questions may not be easy, but knowing the answers and seeing how they apply to a particular situation is crucial to success in raising money.

Concerns of Lenders and Bankers. In evaluating a loan proposal, the lender typically asks five key questions:

1. Why do you want the money?

2. How much money do you need?

3. How long will it take you to pay it back?

4. How will you repay my principal and return?

5. What will you do if that does not work?

The answers to these questions dictate the terms and conditions of the capital source. The first question addresses the business need for the funds, either to purchase an asset, pay an expense, or make an investment. The answers to the questions how much is needed and when will it be repaid, are derived from the funds flow forecast that management must prepare as part of its homework and the business plan. The most important of these five questions are the source of repayment and the contingency plans. The contingency plan explains what the borrower will do if the investment cannot be repaid the way it was intended. Bankers, like all investors, are particularly concerned with this aspect. Prospective borrowers must be prepared to show the investor how he is going to get his money back.

Evaluating the Loan Application. The criteria on which any investment decision is based are the following seven items:

1. Character of management (which is probably worth 80 percent of the decision);
2. Capital;
3. Capacity to earn;
4. Cash flow (earnings and depreciation);
5. Conditions of the market;
6. Current credit rating; and
7. Collateral.

The two most critical criteria are the character of management and cash flow. Character is the intangible determination (or lack thereof) in management to repay the loan even if the business plan fails to work as anticipated. Without strong character, any minor interruption of the business plan could doom the loan to an early write-off. Cash flow is the actual primary source of repayment. Without cash flow there is no assured source of repayment, despite management's strong character. The absence of one or more of the other criteria may alter the source, approach, or interest rate, but will not prevent the company from raising money. The lack of character in management or lack of cash flow will preclude raising capital for any company.

How Lenders and Bankers Receive Returns. The four ways to repay lenders are:

1. To borrow more;
2. To find another lender;
3. To sell assets; or
4. To use earnings and cash flow.

Borrowing more or obtaining another lender are often legitimate ways to refinance or restructure a company's capital. However, in today's complex world of convertible debentures, interest rate swaps, securitized assets, and other financing vehicles, this approach may be very expensive or have hidden costs and, accordingly, must be approached cautiously. Likewise, selling assets can be acceptable, especially as a contingency plan. However, the best way to repay a loan is by generating cash flow and profits.

Reinvestment and Refinancing. The two reasons for reinvestment or refinancing, other than to achieve an overall debt restructuring, are:

1. The plan did not work; or

2. The company did something else with the money.

If the company does something else with the money, no one will be sympathetic. However, most lenders or bankers understand when a business plan does not work. In fact, most business plans work only after changes or modifications. Business planning is a dynamic process and adjustments are part of the game.

Short-Term Borrowing Alternatives

The differences among the various short-term borrowing alternatives stem from the use to which the funds will be placed and the requirements of the particular type of lender, which are based on the following concerns:

1. How much money is needed? The lender wants some assurance that the need for funds is fully, not just partially, satisfied. If a whole loaf is required, half a loaf can create problems in the future.

2. How long will the funds be required before payment? If the funds are required for a long term and the lender's sources of funds are short-term, problems arise when the lender seeks repayment before the borrower is ready.

3. What form and rate of return will the lender require? The lender may be willing to accept equity in one form or another, or just a simple interest rate yield. This must be determined at an early stage.

There are two basic forms of short-term borrowing, with many variations of each: unsecured loans and secured loans. The differences between these types of loans go beyond the mere presence or absence of pledged collateral as security for the repayment of the loan.

Unsecured Loans. Borrowing without the pledge of assets as collateral reflects the ultimate in creditworthiness of the borrower. Personal guarantees of the owners of privately held companies are "standard operating procedure;" for public companies, even those controlled by one stockholder, personal guarantees are not common. Unsecured loans are the most flexible type of financing for both the lender and the borrower because there is no collateral to be maintained. The maximum amount of an unsecured loan depends on the financial condition and cash flow of the borrower rather than on the value of the collateral. The lender's principal consideration in making an unsecured loan is the borrower's ability to generate repayment from multiple cash flow sources simultaneously.

Secured Loans. Loans can be secured by any form of asset: tangible (such as inventories or equipment); intangible (such as accounts receivable); financial (such as stocks and bonds); or even intellectual (such as the right to provide a valuable service such as lease rights or motion picture distribution rights in a certain territory).

While no lender will ever make a loan with the intent to foreclose on the collateral for repayment, the collateral does provide a very important contingent source of repayment in the event that the primary source fails. This implies that collateral is usually required by the lender where alternative sources are few or of unproven reliability. Because of this uncertainty, secured loans are usually limited by the value of the assets that are pledged, although borrowers with good borrowing records occasionally are permitted to borrow in excess of the loan value of the collateral. In this case, the collateral exists merely as a symbol of security for the lender.

Young companies experiencing rapid growth often secure their loans by pledging the company's accounts receivable, inventory, and "proceeds therefrom." The combination of these assets tends to grow as the company grows and to form a pool of viable collateral to which the lender could gain quick access and liquidate if necessary. The combination of the three assets (accounts receivable, inventory, and cash proceeds) is necessary because it usually is nearly impossible to draw a precise line between when the asset is inventory and when it becomes an account receivable. Likewise, when "the check is in the mail," the asset may be an account receivable or it may be cash. Therefore, lenders typically require the pledge of all three assets in order to avoid legal and definitional questions.

The pledge of fixed assets, such as equipment, often forms the basis for loans but the collateral value of this form of asset is much harder to determine. The more specialized the equipment, the more difficult it is for the lender to realize enough proceeds from its sale to repay the loan.

Matching Capital to Strategic Objectives

The financial manager's life is complicated by the fact that one borrowing alternative may raise the most funds, while another has the longest term, and a third has the lowest cost. As discussed in the following paragraphs, evaluating loan alternatives can also become complicated by less tangible factors.

One factor is the need for lender flexibility to structure the transaction to meet the company's needs. The loan must fit the borrower's needs, not just the lender's. The covenants and restrictions that are designed to protect the lender's position must nevertheless allow the borrower sufficient latitude to operate its business.

Another factor is the borrower's confidence in the lender's ability and willingness to complete the transaction in a timely manner and in a form that meets the borrower's needs. With all the credit investigation and analysis, loan agreement negotiating, and legal drafting necessary to complete most loan documentation, the borrower should feel comfortable in dealing with the lender and have confidence that the lender can complete the tasks and make the loan in time for the borrower to use the proceeds.

Legal documentation carries steep costs, in terms of both the legal fees incurred by the borrower and lender (borrower pays both) and in terms of the financial manager's ability to monitor compliance with the loan agreement. The more complex the documentation, the higher the legal fees and the more difficult the task of monitoring compliance.

The timing and amount of front-end fees, if any, required by the lender must also be considered. Legal fees are only a portion of the cost of obtaining credit. The lender may charge a one-time fee to compensate for the lender's time in putting the loan together and negotiating the loan agreement, and there may be other periodic fees in addition to interest, such as commitment fees. All of these affect the borrower's cash flow and reported earnings.

It is also important to consider the issue of the borrower's right to prepay the loan if funds become available either from internal sources or from lower-cost financing. The borrower and lender may be in conflict on this issue, with the borrower wanting the freedom to prepay the loan in whole or in part either from internally generated funds or from proceeds of more attractive financing. The lender, on the other hand, has made an investment in the deal and is counting on the loan and the revenue it produces as a part of an overall portfolio. Often, the lender does not want to permit loans, especially term loans, to be prepaid—at least without any prepayment penalty.

The lender's requirement for credit support or enhancement of the credit risk through guarantees of others must also be considered. The lender's unwillingness to lend without credit enhancement is clear. What is not clear, however, is when the lender offers to accept a lower interest rate if the borrower could enhance the credit. Credit enhancement often is available at a price, which adds to the borrower's cost while reducing the interest expense. The borrower, naturally, seeks the lower overall cost.

Matching the best type of capital to a company's strategic objectives can be difficult. When trying to do so, the financial manager should:

1. Rate or rank strategic objectives;

2. Reduce alternatives to a one-page written summary;

3. Consult with other people in the decision process; and

4. Make a considered decision.

The first two items, which involve ranking objectives and alternatives, help to focus on the critical issues. In a given situation, the relative priorities of different strategic objectives will vary. Reducing various proposals to a one-page summary requires identification of the principal attributes and evaluation of major advantages and disadvantages of each source of capital.

Postponing a final decision by a day or a week can provide the reflective time necessary to assure that strategic objectives are being met. The most important thing is to make a decision after all of the alternatives have been evaluated. Many treasurers are often guilty of trying to find the perfect "deal," only to find that interest rates are rising or that sources of financing are becoming disinterested because they perceive the company to be "shopping." Generating competition among financing sources is desirable, but the number of institutions and the amount of time should be limited to assure that the company's objectives are met.

PREPARING THE FINANCING PROPOSAL PACKAGE

Once the type of financing has been determined, the financial manager must assemble a financing proposal package. This package generally contains a term sheet, a brief overview of the business plan, and financial statements. These elements provide the lender with all the pertinent information with which to make the initial decision regarding the loan application.

Term Sheet

The term sheet, consisting of not more than two pages, contains the answers to the five basic questions: how much, how long, what for, how to repay, and the contingent source of repayment.

Overview of the Plan

Another key element of any financing proposal is a short overview. Most investment decisions are made quickly and review committees often rely on a subordinate's written summary to make a determination, sometimes spending less than three minutes looking at what took the company weeks, or even months, to prepare. So when the business plan is translated into a presentation package, this summary overview must be included.

The overview should contain information on the character of the business, the nature of the product, and the people involved. These facts should give the investor an emotional feeling for what the business is all about. Product brochures can be helpful, and some companies use video presentations. A set of financial statements is essential since it will constitute the basis for determining terms and conditions. If the balance sheet has some quirks (e.g., companies using the "Last In, First Out" (LIFO) method of inventory valuation), it is usually helpful to prepare pro forma or alternative balance sheets. In a period of rising prices, LIFO valuations cause the balance sheet to be understated; thus, an alternative presentation would be helpful.

The Business Plan

The business plan needs to cover such basics as marketing, production, and accounting. The plan should be credible since optimistic or aggressive sales figures will make most investors skeptical. An investor's trust can more easily be gained with conservative calculations. It it always better to provide investors or lenders with better than expected results than to have results be below or even equal to the original projections. Showing sales increases of 150 to 200 percent per annum is not wise unless such increases are well documented and can be expected realistically.

The business plan must be highly professional and geared to the lender. Attention to detail is essential, as even a small error, such as an erroneous mathematical calculation, can threaten a plan's integrity. This is a particular caution with the prevalent use of electronic spreadsheets where a last minute change might be most embarrassing.

Finally, the business plan must exude confidence of a company's management. Even in difficult times, the companies that are successful in obtaining financing can change their fortunes and believe in their futures. Every company has a good story; the financing presentation is the time to capitalize on it.

Presenting the Business Plan

The financial manager must meet cordially with potential lenders, investors, or groups of investors and effectively communicate the plan. In this process, he must distinguish the company from the alternatives in which these sources of capital might otherwise invest. The professional treasurer who sells an investor on his company's loan proposal performs as a professional salesperson. He "warms-up" his investor, probes with questions, makes a pointed presentation, handles questions and objections smoothly, and, most importantly, knows how to end the presentation and "close the sale."

Importance of Questions. The presenter can obtain valuable information and keep control of the presentation by consistently asking questions of the potential lender. The presenter should avoid being put under scrutiny before receiving all the necessary information; by probing the investor with questions, the financial officer can test assumptions, confirm suspicions, and get a sense of the lender's concerns before making an outright request for funds.

A question period need not be clinical, technical, or legal in nature. Questions can be used to keep the conversation going and to relax everyone in the room. Even simple questions such as the following are useful: "Do you have similar investments in your portfolio?" A "yes" answer leads to another question: "Then you do know all about our particular industry, don't you?" If the investor says no, then you might ask: "Isn't it good to diversify your risk?" Other questions that might be asked include the following:

- Do you see any problem with my plan?
- Are you going to recommend this proposal to your loan committee?
- What is your loan approval process and funding procedure?
- How long does it take to get funded?
- Who makes the decision?

• If we provide the back-up data, are we in the "ball park?"

• Are you looking for business?

While these questions may appear procedural in nature, they elicit responses so that the presenter can push "hot buttons" and learn of possible objections that can be overcome later in discussions with a potential financing source.

The financial manager should not be embarrassed to ask about the credit approval and funding process, and to request copies of standard forms and the credit analysis of the company. These questions help to gain valuable information. Additionally, they mark the company as a sharper-than-average lending opportunity.

Answering major objections can also be done through questions. For example, if collateral is an issue, the financial manager might ask of the investor, "Isn't it true that in a bankruptcy, collateral generally goes down in value and that liabilities increase because of legal expenses?" The financial manager then asks, "Isn't it also true that the real value is cash flow and earnings power and that if you make a bad investment, it often doesn't matter how much collateral there is?" This approach can be taken with practically any objection if it is thought through to find the other side of the question. It is important to understand the motivation of the investor to provide insight into the appropriate response.

Improving the Presentation. There are many "common sense" suggestions that may assist a financial manager in enhancing a financing presentation. Although none of these suggestions individually will enhance the chances of a successful presentation, their cumulative effect may again differentiate one financing opportunity from another. For example, preliminary meetings with investors prior to a formal presentation are quite common and very important. The financial manager should get the investors to visit the company. Person-to-person contact is far more effective than using the telephone. Introductions to key managers, tours of facilities, and samples of products all aid in getting an investor emotionally involved with the company. These meetings should be free from distractions, and they should be planned or loosely structured to obtain the maximum benefit. They can be an excellent opportunity to learn what elements need to be highlighted in a formal presentation.

Using other people in the financial manager's presentation should be considered. Obvious possibilities would include the company's chairman, chief executive officer, and sales manager. Not so obvious possibilities could come from a number of sources. For example, a McDonald's franchise seeking a loan might consider someone from the corporate office to provide relative performance comparisons to other locations. Of course, the incremental value of such a co-presenter must be evaluated.

Another suggestion is to create a competitive situation among potential lenders. For instance, informing Bank A that Bank B is also considering a loan is a much better position than informing Bank A that Bank B has turned down a loan request. Again, "shopping" a deal should be avoided and could have adverse effects. This is especially true in the mortgage area where many transactions are made through brokers who all contact the same sources. Using multiple brokers is possible provided that the financial manager controls to whom the transaction is disclosed.

Often in the process of raising money, nerves become frayed. It is important that the financial manager never lose his or her temper unless on purpose. Controlled temper tantrums or "outrage" can be effective, but it can backfire. To avoid unnecessary confrontations, it would be beneficial to consider the lender as a business associate or even a friend. It is much easier for either party to accept a condition in an agreement when the parties know the business reasons behind it without seeing it as a personal battle. Another suggestion is to try to get terms and conditions in writing. Memoranda describing meetings become more reliable than memory as time goes on and sometimes as principals change.

One often overlooked suggestion that can pay dividends is simply saying "thank you," whether it is the mere words or a lunch after the proceeds are received. Good manners are as appropriate in raising financing as they are in a social environment.

Attitude. Notwithstanding the above suggestions, 90 percent of a speaker's effectiveness is determined before the presentation begins. The financial manager must be thoroughly prepared and must show competence and enthusiasm. People are more convinced by the depth of the manager's feelings than by the logic of his words. Even investors make decisions based on conviction and feeling. So, in addition to understanding the logic of the investing process and writing an acceptable business plan, the financial manager must be convinced of the company's ability to meet its plans and objectives. Such preparation, commitment, and conviction are the primary ingredients to getting the financing that is needed.

Salvaging a Rejection

The most important questions occur when a proposal is turned down. It is here that the financial manager discovers his mistakes or miscalculation of the objectives of the lender by asking pointed questions. This is a lesson that the manager will use to improve the next presentation. Questions that might salvage the rejection or provide another opportunity are:

- Why are you turning this proposal down?
- What would you do if you were in my situation?
- Where would you go? Why?
- Whom should I see there?
- If I go there and say that I just got turned down by you, what are you going to tell him when he calls you?

Again, these questions provide the financial manager with control, information, and feedback with which to adjust the next presentation. Many financial managers have been known to role-play this sequence, substituting various reasons for rejection, to see how effective these questions can be.

Demeanor and style are important in making an effective presentation. Rather than making demands, it is more productive to ask additional questions. This method pulls the lender into helping the company immediately following the rejection.

SHORT-TERM SOURCES OF FUNDS

Internal Sources

Before a financial manager decides to borrow for the short term, internal sources of funds should be evaluated and explored since these sources are usually less costly than outside alternatives. Some of the internal sources could include the following:

1. Increasing sales;
2. Accelerating accounts receivable collections;
3. Reducing inventory levels;
4. Improving accounts payable management;
5. Reducing expenses; and
6. Selling nonproductive assets.

Most of these items revolve around working capital management. The financial manager must ascertain whether any incremental cash can be obtained from these sources.

Increasing Sales. By increasing sales, a company can improve its financing capability, unless the cash flow time line generated from the conversion of cash, to inventory, to sales, to receivables, to cash is too long a cycle and requires yet additional borrowing. For a growing company, increased sales can cause additional borrowing requirements. Nonetheless, the financial manager needs to explore whether prices can be raised or if cash sales can be increased through special promotions or discounts.

Improving Accounts Receivable Collections. The financial manager needs to be aware of financing working capital borrowing needs through improved receivable collections. Understaffed and unsophisticated collection departments improperly supervised may not get consistent coverage of the receivable base. Another source of cash might be to settle past-due accounts, which can often create cash that otherwise would not be received.

Reducing Inventory Levels. A financial or treasury manager can often create financing through better inventory management. The interdepartmental interaction over management of inventories is often difficult, but the results can be substantial. For example, U.S. automotive manufacturers have been trying to catch foreign competitors with "just-in-time" inventory concepts, which reduce inventory to minimal levels. That is, inventories of component parts are being received just prior to assembly, reducing inventory carrying costs.

Other potential opportunities abound for large and small companies alike in this area, such as:

- Improved sourcing (e.g., lower prices, better terms);
- Coordination of production and sales mix;
- Sale of slow-moving inventories or scrap;
- Reduction in order lead times; and
- Engineering lower cost products.

Improving Accounts Payable Management. An often overlooked major source of short-term funds is management of accounts payable. In a crisis situation, the management of accounts payable is often crucial to a company's survival. Establishing appropriate procedures and conditioning vendors is important long before any crisis occurs. Traditionally, a number of payment methods have been used in financing trade. They are:

- Cash in advance or on delivery
- Open accounts
- Payment on a documentary collection basis, and
- Documentary letters of credit

By insisting on cash in advance or on delivery, the seller obviously has complete assurance of obtaining payment. This method often is used in cases where the buyer is unknown, for example, at the time of the first sale to a customer when the seller is not familiar with the buyer's credit standing. Cash in advance also may be appropriate when the political, economic, or credit conditions in the buyer's company make payment uncertain. This method, unless pricing concessions are obtained, is not a desirable tool. In the United States, it is common to sell on open account with payment due in a specified number of days after the invoice date. The seller, in effect, finances the transaction for the buyer and relies upon the buyer's ability and willingness to pay on the due date. The financial manager should review whether these terms are consistent with the market and prevailing economic conditions. A "stretch" of one to two weeks could provide a one time increase in cash, usually without hurting vendor relations.

While this method is appropriate in domestic markets where close contact is maintained with customers, open account sales are offered less frequently in the international market. This is due, in part, to the risks involved in dealing with countries where political and economic conditions are uncertain or where dollar exchange may be limited. Either situation may preclude a willing and otherwise able buyer from making payment.

Payment on a documentary collection basis is very widely used in the purchase and sale of goods and services in international markets. Under this arrangement, the seller forwards shipping documents, invoices, insurance certificates, and other appropriate documents through its bank to the buyer's bank overseas. The seller includes with the documents a draft drawn against the buyer for collection. A draft is a negotiable instrument that contains a demand for payment.

The party demanding payment is the drawer (also known as the maker or originator) of the draft. The party responsible for honoring or paying the draft is the drawee. To be negotiable, the draft must:

- Be signed by the drawer
- Contain an unconditional demand to pay a certain sum of money
- Be payable on demand or at a definite time
- Be payable to order or to bearer

The payment of a draft on a collection basis may be due "at sight" (payable at the time of presentment to the drawee), or the draft may be a time draft due a certain number of days after sight, or presentment.

The payment arrangements under a letter of credit are somewhat similar to those used in a documentary collection. In both cases the seller obtains payment for the merchandise by presenting shipping and other documents along with a draft for the amount of the sale. However, whereas the documentary collection represents the liability of the buyer alone, the letter of credit is a legal instrument that obligates the issuing bank to pay the seller (or any legitimate presenter or holder of the documents) upon presentation of the documents required under the terms of the letter of credit. In effect, the issuing bank substitutes its creditworthiness for that of the buyer, which is easier for the seller to determine. The letter of credit is therefore attractive to the seller who can release the merchandise for shipment with the knowledge that payment is assured if the seller presents the proper documentation to the issuing bank. The buyer also benefits by use of a letter of credit because the documents assure that the seller ships the specified merchandise according to the terms of the documents. The payment is expedited if the buyer instructs the issuing bank to have clear reimbursement instructions included in the text of the letter of credit.

While letters of credit and payment on collection bases date back to ancient Babylonian civilization and are some of the oldest instruments used in international trade, their use can be confusing to the financial manager for various reasons. Major banks welcome this type of financing and can assist in clarifying terms such as revocable, irrevocable, confirmed, and advised, and often they can recommend the appropriate vehicle to finance such trade transactions.[1]

Reducing Expenses. Although constant monitoring of expenses is a must for all companies, it is also the most politically sensitive method of generating funds internally. The elimination of expense needs to be done objectively and is usually a question of priorities. A program to cut expenses and generate cash should include the following steps:

---

[1] See Chapter 16 for a detailed discussion of letters of credit.

1. Identify major expense categories, such as payroll, production overhead, and travel.

2. Question whether each expense is required.

3. If the answer is "no," eliminate the expense.

4. If the answer is "yes," ask:
   - What will happen if the expense is not made? and
   - Is there a better or cheaper alternative?

5. Review expenditure approval limits and controls.

Many chief executives or financial officers of small- to middle-market companies sign and review every disbursement, thereby routinely and informally implementing these steps. It is also well to remember that small amounts add up to big dollars.

Selling Nonproductive Assets. The sale of items such as obsolete machinery or idle land is often a source of converting nonproductive assets into productive assets. Also, donating obsolete but still usable inventories to charity can produce tax savings. Likewise, assets not recorded on the balance sheet (e.g., logo, trademarks, or licenses) should be reviewed to explore ways to raise cash. For example, the company could borrow against the cash surrender value of an officer's life insurance policy.

Once all such internal sources are considered, it is then time for the financial manager to explore external sources of financing.

Unsecured Bank Credit Lines

Unsecured bank credit lines are a very common form of short-term borrowing. Banks making these loans rely on the general credit and reputation of the company to repay. These lines can be either committed or uncommitted. A committed line is the bank's legal obligation to fund a loan, while an uncommitted line is not legally binding.

Committed Lines. Committed lines require a fee to ensure availability and covenants to ensure that certain basic conditions are met. In addition to requiring a company to be solvent, such conditions and covenants may require the maintenance of a certain minimal financial profile. This might include certain financial ratio tests such as the company's ratio of debt to net worth, minimum earnings, working capital, and other limitations. When these conditions are not met, the bank may "waive" these requirements in consideration for past fees paid and the bank's judgment that noncompliance will not hurt its chances for repayment; or the bank may declare the loan to be in default and demand immediate repayment. While there may be no immediate need to borrow from the bank, the company may desire to put the committed line in place in anticipation of the need to borrow in the future. This approach to borrowing obviously requires the company to evaluate the commitment fee, legal requirements, severity of covenants, and interest rate before entering into an arrangement.

Uncommitted Lines. The availability of funds under an uncommitted line of credit depends upon the company's previous drawing experience and the health of a company's business. The key to maintaining uncommitted lines is to stir the bank's interest in future business by using the lines occasionally and minimizing any surprises in the financial results. Another way to keep the bank interested in future business is to use the bank for cash management functions such as lockboxes and payroll and accounts payable disbursing accounts.

Since uncommitted loans are predicated on the borrower's general creditworthiness, the underlying documentation for an uncommitted loan is a short-term promissory note. Any other legal documentation is extremely simple but very much one-sided in favor of the lender because the loan is usually unsecured and based solely on the borrower's promise to repay. One risk of using uncommitted lines is that the availability of loans is related not only to a company's health, but is also a function of the internal funding position of the bank and external political events; thus, the internal performance of the bank will affect both availability and pricing. Uncommitted lines of credit make the most sense for companies with occasional borrowing requirements, that borrow for very short periods, that usually have a liquid cash position, or that have other committed sources of funding.

Loan Sale Programs. In loan sale programs, also referred to as loan participation programs, the bank originates the loan and then sells a portion of it to other banks or investors. The buyers often include foreign or regional banks, which derive much of their income from loan interest, and corporate and institutional investors seeking yields higher than commercial paper. The bank, on the other hand, generally seeks a trading commission, or retention of a portion of the interest income without retaining a loan receivable. This is achieved by selling the loan at a spread from the normal interest rate to an investor. Loan sale programs such as this started among banks with highly rated public companies many years ago, but now the banks are marketing loans made to noninvestment grade public companies to both bank and corporate investors.

When competition among banks forces the interest spreads between investment and noninvestment grade companies to narrow, such that the spreads do not appear to reflect an appropriate credit risk differential, loan sale programs can be very attractive to a borrower. While competition rages among money center banks for loan sale deals, the regional banks try to protect their "turf" by being competitive on other uncommitted lines as previously discussed.

While loan sale programs are an attractive borrowing alternative, they should be viewed with caution. The risks to the borrower are the same as with other uncommitted lines of credit. Further, market sensitivity is a factor in borrowing under loan sale programs. For example, many money center banks refuse to lend money under uncommitted lines unless the bank has the right to sell participations to investors as its quarter or year-end financial reporting dates approach. Additionally, the borrower should be concerned as to which lenders may be "at the table" in the event that its loans need to be renegotiated. It is conceivable that a company could have a competitor holding a senior debt position by virtue of having bought participations from the bank as an investor.

Secured Bank Credit Lines

Collateral security gives the lender a second source of repayment if the debt is not repaid in the manner originally intended. Interestingly, this type of loan usually costs more than an unsecured loan. Some of the factors that affect the price of such loans include the liquidity and safekeeping of the collateral, the bank's ability to service the loan, industry risk, and the form and perishability of the collateral. Loans to borrowers in a highly leveraged transaction, particularly where the collateral is intangible or perishable, can range several hundred basis points above the rate charged to a bank's best customer.

Accounts Receivable Financing. The most common form of short-term secured financing is a loan that is secured by the assignment of accounts receivable. Typically, such lenders are finance companies or the subsidiaries of banks that specialize in making asset-backed loans. For a lender to consider this type of financing, it needs to know the following information about the potential borrower:

- Type of customers, trade terms offered, payment patterns, and payment history
- Delinquency and loss experience
- Accounts receivable aging schedule

From this information, the lender develops a loan advance rate, which is the maximum percentage of the receivables that will be advanced by the lender. The loan advance rate provides a cushion for the lender against unexpected uncollectable accounts. The interest rate on the loan is usually stated in terms of a spread above prime rate that reflects the lender's assessment of both the level of risk of the loan and the amount of effort required to police the collateral.

The mechanics of the accounts receivable loan transaction may vary, but the concept is very simple from the borrower's viewpoint. The basic steps in this transaction include the following:

1. The company bills a customer;

2. A percentage of the billing is then borrowed from the lender;

3. The customer pays the invoice; and

4. The lender is repaid (and the company retains the amount not applied to the loan).

Unfortunately, a company's billing and disbursement schedules frequently do not coincide. This is especially true for companies that have a long production schedule or have seasonal sales without matching variable costs and expenses. Accounts receivable financing, therefore, requires the lender's close attention to the borrower's cash flows. Often, the lender may receive a lien on the borrower's inventory and fixed assets as additional collateral to induce the lender to increase the advance rate. There are as many variations of this financing, each with as many different features, as there are participants.

Inventory Financing. Like accounts receivable financing, financing secured by the pledge of inventories has many variations. Loans secured by finished inventory of heavy equipment or automobiles usually list the collateral by specific serial number, whereas loans secured by raw materials, work in progress, and commodity-type items are secured by a general pledge. Further, inventory may be in warehouses or it may be released to customers against trust receipts that are pledged as collateral. The amount of money that can be raised, however, is limited as lenders are usually concerned about the liquidity of inventory and the costs involved in converting raw materials into finished goods. Although a dental laboratory's inventory of gold is worth more as loan collateral than the dentures that comprise "work in process," advance rates generally are higher for finished goods than work-in-process. Banks will also audit the inventory to touch and feel it, and they will focus on traditional inventory measures such as inventory turnover, gross margins, and days' sales in inventory.

Bulk Asset Sale. This is not a true form of borrowing, but companies looking for an acceleration of cash flow or balance sheet improvement sometimes consider the bulk sale of their receivables on a discounted basis. In many cases, this sale can occur, and the company continues to service or collect the receivables. The key is to construct this transaction as a "true" sale in order to have it qualify as a sale and a resulting account receivable, which makes for more liquid collateral than does inventory.

Asset-Backed Securities. The financial manager must run fast to keep up with all the different ways to borrow, but the basics seldom change. Companies today are exploring new ways to borrow by substituting securities or security-type instruments that are sold in the public markets in place of bank loans. The motivation for the shift clearly is that securities market borrowings are cheaper than bank loans. Additionally, banks are looking to retain historical relationships and increase their profits by selling participations in their loans to other banks and investors. Today, money center banks behave more like investment banks, and competition is creating additional sources for borrowing. Similarly, European markets offer additional sources of funding for the larger companies.

LOAN AGREEMENTS

Loan agreements and documentation for any of the above short-term borrowing sources can range in length from one page to five volumes. The negotiation of many agreements falls under the "Full Employment Act for Attorneys," which often makes this process overly complex. The key to successful negotiation of a loan is to understand why certain language or covenants are in the document, and to separate business issues from legal issues. For example, the financial manager needs to know why the banker wants to limit the company's future capital expenditures and reacts accordingly. Bankers usually attempt to limit many areas of activity as a matter of habit, but they are only really concerned about a few key issues. The devices used to limit or restrict the company's activities are referred to as covenants, which can be affirmative covenants ("the company will. . .") or negative ("the company will not. . ."). Some of the more common covenants include:

1. Maximum debt to equity ratio, which measures a company's leverage, and helps ensure the lender his position as a creditor.

2. Minimum interest coverage ratio, which measures the company's ability to pay the interest due on a loan from the operating cash flow of the company. This ratio usually affords a safety margin for the lending institution. Thus, a fixed charge covenant of 1.5 means that for any given period, earnings usually before interest and taxes must be at least 150 percent of the interest amount. This ratio on occasion can be expanded through definition of terminology to include items such as dividend payments and income taxes.

3. Minimum current ratio or working capital requirements, which protect the bank by requiring that sufficient current assets exist to meet current liabilities. The minimum amount of working capital to be maintained usually depends on the nature of the borrower's business and its historic working capital ratios.

4. Minimum net worth, which provides an equity floor in addition to the debt-to-equity ratio. Often this covenant is expressed as "tangible" net worth, which discounts or eliminates any value for goodwill and other such "intangibles."

The only covenant absolutely required is the payment of principal and interest when due; however, it is difficult to negotiate any substantial document without at least a debt-to-equity and fixed charge covenant. In addition, reports covering the company's financial condition and operations and certification of compliance with the covenants are almost always required. Figure 13-1 lists some additional affirmative and negative covenants that may be included in the loan agreement.

While being subject to these covenants may appear onerous, there is some logic to these requirements, expecially in a highly leveraged or risky transaction. The financial manager needs to ensure that the covenants match the business plan and that they provide enough margin for error to avoid random violation of the agreement. An uncured violation of the loan agreement becomes an event of default after a short period.

Negotiating what will happen upon default often is more crucial than negotiating the covenants themselves. Defaults can either be technical or real. A technical default usually occurs from the parties' inability to foresee all possibilities, and a subsequent transaction triggers a violation that requires amendment or waiver to the agreement. Although it is recommended that these be

FIG. 13-1

Additional Loan Agreement Covenants

Payment of taxes and liens;

Preservation of corporate existence;

Maintenance of properties;

Maintenance of insurance;

Compliance with laws;

Inspection rights;

Keeping of records and books of account;

Pension plans;

Guarantees from new subsidiaries;

Incurrence of liens;

Sales of assets;

Acquisitions and mergers; (generally permitted provided that the principal line of business is unchanged, the borrower is the survivor, and no loan covenants are violated)

Capital expenditures;

Dividends and/or stock repurchases; (usually limited to 40–60 percent of cumulative net income plus a fixed amount)

Changes on fiscal periods;

Investments; (Lenders do not want company funds used for anything other than the principal business except for short-term investment of temporarily excess funds.)

Lease obligations; (Leases are another form of debt and are of concern to the lender. Thus, leases are usually limited to an aggregate maximum dollar amount.)

Other indebtedness; (Lenders always want to limit additional debt; control can be outright prohibition, a formula, or other form of limitation.)

Contingent obligations;

Management continuity; (The lender is comfortable with existing management and wants to receive the right to call the loan if management should change. This provision is also used by the borrower as a "poison pill" in the event of a hostile takeover attempt.)

---

avoided by careful legal drafting and review, technical defaults do occur and they require adjustment.

Substantive events of default are more serious, especially if the company fails to make payment to the bank when due or a major covenant is violated. The financial manager needs to protect the company, even in the event of default, by including cure and notice provisions in the loan agreement. Lenders are usually reasonable in this area as they do not want to manage the company, and many of the covenants are designed to have the parties discuss the situation long before a financial disaster occurs.

Provisions of a loan agreement are either operational (mechanical) or substantive in nature. Substantive items, such as the amount and terms of credit, are clearly the most important provisions. Commitment fees, participation fees, the interest rate spread, and amortization period all compute into the bank's "yield," and they vary according to risk and market conditions. The interest rate "credit spread" reductions often can be negotiated after achieving specified financial tests, or the spread may be determined by a "bidding" or auction process if several banks are involved.

Additionally, optional borrowing rates and currency options should be investigated. Few corporations borrow under the "prime rate" option only; they usually have the flexibility of other borrowing options such as pegging their interest rate to spreads above the lender's CD rates or the London Interbank Offered Rate (LIBOR) for time deposits.

TROUBLED LOANS

While most business plans require continual adjustment and fine tuning, there are some situations where a borrowing can become a problem or "workout" loan. A "workout loan" is one in which the borrower has defaulted and needs time to reorganize the business. Cash flow problems and the inability to make scheduled principal and interest payments are the obvious reasons for a bank to classify a loan as a problem; but banks try to recognize trouble long before it occurs. Bankers watch for clues that are easily identifiable, including deterioration of financial ratios, variances between budgets and actual performance, inventory build-up, slow collection of accounts receivable, reduced profit margins, stretched accounts payable, adverse economic conditions, and unfavorable variances from historical seasonal borrowings. Less obvious signs of distress include late submission of financial reports, questionable accounting treatment, profits tied to new markets or dependent on a few major customers, poor internal controls, high employee turnover (especially of key executives), and evasive management responses. While many of these signals are often prevalent in a troubled loan, the key factor is usually a continuing stream of unfavorable surprises.

The keys to maintaining a working relationship with the lender when business conditions deteriorate are the same ones that enabled the financial manager to obtain the loan in the first place: communication and planning. The financial manager's challenge in troubled times is to demonstrate clearly, in a professional fashion, how the bank will be repaid. Demonstrating evasive management techniques or offering incomplete or unsatisfactory answers only serve to aggravate the situation.

Again, the use of questions can provide guidance in a troubled situation:

- What does the bank perceive as the problem?
- Is the bank concerned with the company's ability to manage the problem?
- Does the bank have clients facing similar problems?
- Would the bank consider deferral of interest or other relief if the business plan was fundamentally sound?
- How does the bank handle other "problem loans?"

A financial manager whose company's loan is deemed to be a problem loan is faced with a seemingly overwhelming amount of uncertainty. This uncertainty may extend to the very viability of the borrower's business and the continued employment of the financial manager. One way to ease the uncertainty is to attempt to clarify the bank's process of working out the loan and returning the company to viability.

Historically, banks sought to attach the assets; however, because of certain legal liability issues, banks often decide to weather turnaround situations that can take six months to three years. These legal issues are usually described as "lender liability" issues and stem from lawsuits in which borrowers succeeded in proving damages to their businesses when banks refused to lend or otherwise declined to make promised credit available. These are very complex legal issues; suffice it to say that these issues have not helped the borrower/lender relationship in the 1980s and have served to fatten loan documentation (and legal) fees.

A bank's workout department is generally staffed by a team of seasoned lending officers, and often an attorney, who take over the account from the original lending officer. The workout mentality of these bankers often appears to be pessimistic; however, the bank tries to make objective decisions about its money and help the borrower avoid bankruptcy. Often the bank may even recommend that the company hire a consultant who specializes in distressed situations. It is very important to remain logical and to avoid becoming emotional in troubled situations. The bank cannot come in and run the company or have an outside consultant engaged unless the company agrees.

In most cases, the bank will not "call" a loan; rather, it prefers to provide operational suggestions and actions. The financial manager's role is to help the senior management of the company recognize operating deficiencies and to implement often unpopular steps to repay the loan that was originally borrowed in good faith.

SUGGESTED READINGS

Childs, John F. *The Encyclopedia of Long-Term Financing and Capital Management.* Englewood Cliffs, N.J.: P.H. Inc. (1976).

Hayes, Rick Stephan. *Business Loans: A Guide to Money Sources and How to Approach Them Successfully.* Boston: Cahners Books International (1977).

Nevitt, Peter K. *Project Financing.* London: Euromoney Publications Ltd. (1983).

Ramey, Emmett and Alex Wong. *The Loan Package.* California: Oasis Press (1981).

CHAPTER **14**

Investing Excess Funds*

---

* This chapter is based on Alan G. Seidner's *Corporate Investments Manual: Short- and Intermediate-Term Fixed-Income Securities* (Warren, Gorham & Lamont, Inc., 1989). Mr. Seidner's contribution is gratefully acknowledged.

INTRODUCTION

The focus of this chapter is on managing a firm's liquidity funds, which are usually considered to be available only temporarily. Liquidity funds provide a cushion for a company's operations in the event of a shortfall in cash flow and serve as a reservoir for capital expenditures or for acquisitions. Most business managers are very conservative when managing a program for investing liquidity funds, since the funds are critical to a company's financial success.

This chapter addresses primarily the short- and intermediate-term segment of marketable securities that are appropriate for a liquidity portfolio. High yield securities, long-term bonds, common stocks, convertibles, and related vehicles are seldom used for this purpose. Although most corporate investing programs are usually limited to short-term money market instruments, if additional return is desired and some volatility in the market value of the principal can be tolerated, high quality intermediate-term fixed-income securities are often added to the portfolio. Also, if the investor is tax conscious, tax-exempt instruments and dividend-paying preferred stock issues may be included. Some of these instruments are also discussed.

INVESTMENT DECISION MAKING

To invest funds successfully requires stated objectives and guidelines. Investing without clear goals is risky, particularly if the funds are managed in a fiduciary capacity, where one person manages assets owned by another. The fiduciary has a responsibility to the owner to be prudent. Fiduciary relationships exist in corporate settings when an employee manages company retirement, health insurance, or other employee benefit funds. However, whatever the type of funds managed, whether fiduciary or corporate excess cash, it is essential to both the owner of the funds and the employee managing them that a clear set of objectives and guidelines be mutually understood and agreed upon as a prerequisite to any investing program.

The first step in establishing an investing program is to determine the owner's aversion to risk of loss and appetite for return on investments. The balance between risk and potential profit must be evaluated and clearly understood by both the owner and the investment manager. In a business environment, the owner's preferences generally are manifested by the actions of the board of directors, which is the source of all authority and responsibility in a corporation. The investment manager is well-served by establishing a written set of investing objectives and guidelines that is approved by the board of directors so that the document becomes, in effect, a contract binding the board and the investment manager to a common understanding of the basis for the investing program.

The process of establishing and operating an investing program involves a series of discrete decisions. These decisions include:

- Specifying the owner's preferences and constraints with regard to specific types of securities and issuers;

- Determining the portfolio management policies, strategies, and tactics that may be employed;

- Developing a viewpoint regarding interest rates and the economic, social, and political factors that affect both interest rates and credit risk; and

- Assimilating the firm's funds flow forecasts across all time horizons.

When these elements have been determined, they form the foundation for the investing program. The decision-making process then continues as changes in economic conditions, the funds flow forecast, credit quality of issuers, new developments in securities markets, and portfolio management techniques are monitored and the necessary adjustments made. Meanwhile, the investment manager proceeds to assemble a portfolio that will meet the organization's objectives and that will be within the announced preferences, constraints, and risk parameters. Finally, the investment manager should develop a methodology for measuring compliance with the organization's requirements.

ESTABLISHING A COMPREHENSIVE INVESTMENT POLICY

Even though each corporation's investment requirements may vary, most investment programs should include the following:

1. *The investment committee.* It is extremely important for senior management to discuss and review the corporation's philosophy toward its investable funds and for management's attitude in this area to be communicated to corporate staff so that misunderstandings can be avoided.

2. *The investment policy.* The first action of the investment committee should be preparation of a summary statement of investment policy that addresses the degree of risk and yield that

are suitable for present and future funds, and the importance of yield in relation to safety of principal and liquidity of the portfolio.

3. *Investment responsibility*. Once an investment policy statement is formulated, the investment committee must designate those who will implement the policy, execute the investments, supervise operations, audit the investment activities, and provide backup support for all of those functions.

4. *Reporting requirements*. Reporting and auditing requirements must be established. These include the kind of reports that are best suited to management's needs, the frequency with which they are generated, who will issue and receive them, the elements to be presented, and provision for the analysis and audit of all information that they contain.

5. *Definition of permitted or prohibited investments*. The types of instruments in which the corporation is willing to invest should be carefully defined. For example, is the corporation unwilling to invest its funds in instruments issued by specific governments, such as those that suppress human rights? Is it interested in investing only in low-risk, low-yield issues, or is it willing to invest funds in securities with higher degrees of risk and potentially higher yields?

6. *Diversification of investments*. Diversification in the investment portfolio can greatly reduce its exposure to credit risk. Maximum allowable positions should be established for different types of issuers, industries, and country of issuers' origin in order to minimize the exposure to credit risk of the investment portfolio.

7. *Limitations on maturity*. Purchasing securities that mature many years later can create a market risk exposure to rising interest rates. Also, the maturity of an investment affects its liquidity. If an investment is not easily marketable or liquid, it may be unwise to purchase it if there is a possibility that the funds invested will be required on short notice.

8. *Safekeeping of securities*. A securities safekeeping or custodial arrangement should be established with the company's concentration bank to safeguard and facilitate the audit of securities held in the investment portfolio and to credit principal and interest payments immediately to the appropriate bank account.

Investment guidelines should be reviewed regularly and modified when necessary. There are several reasons why this is important. First, new investment instruments are often introduced that may be added to the portfolio's universe of acceptable instruments. Secondly, instruments that are presently acceptable may become unacceptable. An example of this situation would be debt of the Federal Farm Credit Banks, once considered a high credit quality and liquid government agency security. However, in 1986–1987, this entity encountered severe financial problems owing to adverse conditions in agricultural markets. As a result, Federal Farm Credit Bank obligations were temporarily eliminated from portfolios or were limited to short-term maturities until Congress provided financial support.

Finally, changes in the corporate outlook may require an adjustment in the investment policy itself. Perhaps the corporation has decided to make an acquisition, making the liquidity of the investment portfolio of critical importance. Therefore, maturity restrictions and other factors may have to be changed.

A simple yet effective way to mandate a regular review of the investment policy and guidelines is to include a "sunset" provision; that is, to state a specific expiration date for them. Most practically, this should occur annually, or more frequently as needed, and should not coincide with critical activity periods such as end of the fiscal quarter or year.

DETERMINING INVESTMENT REQUIREMENTS

Any investment decision should be judged against several different investment criteria. Two issues that first must be resolved are:

1. What needs are the investments to fill?

2. What particular functions must the company's investment program serve?

If the portfolio's function is to provide a liquidity cushion against sharp variations in receipts or disbursements, then it must be invested in very safe and highly liquid securities. On the other hand, if the portfolio is designed to generate long-term income to the firm, then the portfolio can be slightly more risk-oriented and have somewhat less liquidity.

Figure 14-1 is a checklist of items a corporate investment officer must resolve before implementing the investment program.

FIG. 14-1

Investment Checklist

☐ Risk to principal—Can the investment officer risk losing any of the funds for which he is responsible? If so, how much?

☐ Liquidity—Will the company need any of these invested funds on short notice? If so, how much and how quickly?

☐ Balance sheet—Must the company show a particular type of investment on its balance sheet to satisfy stockholders, lenders, and other creditors?

☐ Cash flow management—To what extent does the company rely on the income from investments for its operations and/or its dividend?

☐ Future funding needs—Does the company have a special project or situation that requires the funds to be available at some future date?

☐ Staffing—Is sufficient staff in place to operate the investment program successfully, including analysis of the corporate portfolio, making sound investment decisions, and following up with the paperwork?

☐ Income taxes—What is the company's marginal tax rate or tax-paying status? Will investments that generate totally or partially tax-exempt income maximize after-tax returns?

☐ Income (cash flow) requirements—Will the stream of net investment funds fluctuate, or will the investment officer be provided with a consistent and stable amount of investment funds?

☐ Other investment requirements:

• Does the company have an obligation to do business with local banking institutions as part of a community support program?

• Does the company have specific arrangements with banks regarding services in exchange for compensating balances?

• Are those institutions sound from a credit standpoint?

Risk to Principal

The investment officer must determine the degree of credit risk and market risk that can be accepted for the company's funds before establishing an investment program. This determination warrants input from senior management. Although the investment officer has the mandate to obtain the highest return possible, the safety of the investment dollar should be the primary consideration. There are two types of risk: credit risk and market risk.

Credit Risk. This type of risk, also known as default risk, refers to the possibility that invested funds (principal and interest) will not be returned if the issuer of the instrument fails. For example, a financially weak

FIG. 14-2

Money Market Securities Ranked by Default Risk

Risk Free	U.S. Treasury (bills, notes, bonds)
	U.S. Government Agencies
	Banker's Acceptances
	Bank certificates of deposit
	Commercial paper
	Eurodollar time deposits
More Risk	Repurchase agreements

manufacturing corporation experiencing depressed sales activity, unusually high debt, a poor credit rating, and a slim prospect for future improvement may need to raise funds through the sale of debt securities to the public. A company in this condition is often willing to pay high rates to attract investors to buy their debt obligations. Some investors are willing to assume the risk of loss because of the potentially high rate of return. Figure 14-2 provides a ranking of default risk among various short-term instruments.

Market Risk. Market (or price) risk refers to the inverse relationship between the price of the security and the movement of interest rates; that is, when interest rates go up, the market price of fixed-income securities goes down. Moreover, the longer the maturity of the instrument, the greater the potential for volatility in market price. From the perspective of profit potential rather than risk, when interest rates decline, the market price of fixed-income securities goes up. Again, the longer the maturity, the greater the expectation for price increase. Figure 14-3 shows the effect of a 100 basis point increase in interest rates on the market value of $1 million par value of bonds for various maturities along a yield curve. For example, $1 million of a 10-year bond whose yield increases from 9.25 percent to 10.25 percent will decline in value by $61,700.

Treasury securities have the highest credit rating, and therefore the lowest yield, of any available interest bearing securities since they are direct U.S. government obligations. Although U.S. government obligations are considered extremely safe from the standpoint of credit or default risk, they are still subject to market risk.

EXAMPLE: An investment officer purchased a Treasury security maturing in two years since the company's strategic plan did not require the

FIG. 14-3

Price Volatility of Bonds

Maturity	Yield Curve		Effect of 100 basis points yield change on market value of $1,000,000 par value of bonds
	Before	After	
1 month(s)	7.35%	8.35%	$ 833
3	8.66	9.66	2,500
6	8.66	9.66	5,000
1 year(s)	8.70	9.70	9,340
2	9.50	10.50	17,600
5	9.40	10.40	38,240
10	9.25	10.25	61,700
20	9.20	10.20	84,600
30	9.00	10.00	94,600

use of the funds for approximately that time period. However, because of unforeseen capital expenditures requiring the need for those invested funds at the end of only one year, the Treasury instruments had to be sold before maturity. During the one-year period in which these Treasury instruments were held, interest rates rose one percentage point (100 basis points). Consequently, the company suffered a loss of approximately $9,340 per $1 million par value of the instruments being sold.

Portfolio Liquidity

Portfolio liquidity is the ability to turn investments into readily usable cash without suffering loss of principal. Portfolio liquidity is an important consideration when a corporation depends on its investment portfolio to cushion short-term funds shortfalls. Liquidity of a portfolio invested in long-term fixed-income securities is limited and further reduced in a market in which interest rates have risen. Marketability of long-term fixed-income investments declines sharply as market values decline. Substantial loss of market value may be incurred if the funds are needed before maturity and have to be sold. Also, liquidity is a consideration when the funds of the corporation are invested in unmarketable instruments such as low credit quality commercial paper, certain junk bonds, and certificates of deposit (CDs) and fixed-time deposits in small financial institutions.

When the investment portfolio must have a high degree of liquidity, it should consist of instruments with the highest available credit quality and relatively short maturities. When liquidity is not the predominant factor in managing an investment portfolio, the investment officer may wish to consider matching the investment maturity to a particular date for some predetermined purpose such as tax payments, pension fund contributions, or dividends.

Funds Management

Good cash management enables the orchestration of funds inflows and outflows from all sources and to all destinations in order to achieve the most effective use of the company's assets. The investment officer must be aware of the intended use of funds being invested, which may be earmarked for the following:

- An acquisition, in which case they may be needed immediately;

- A bank debt payment;

- Bond sinking fund requirements;

- Tax payments;

- Contributions to employee pension or profit-sharing plans; or

- Other needs.

Specific fund disbursement dates can be anticipated and investments made with maturities to coincide with the forecasted disbursement requirements.

While charged with the responsibility to invest wisely to protect principal and optimize the profitability of the company's investments, the investment officer must be aware that the investment portfolio usually is a buffer against an immediate unforeseen funds shortfall. Depending upon the company's projected funds requirements, the investment officer must ensure the safety of principal and liquidity of the portfolio rather than attempt to achieve the highest rate of return. Of course there are instances in which a less conservative approach is justified, yielding higher returns at a greater risk.

Funds Flow Forecast

To plan a successful investment program, the investment officer must know whether current net cash flow will be consumed by current operations or if it will become part of the pool of funds used to meet the corporation's long-term strategic goals such as capital expansion or acquisitions. The short- and intermediate-term funds flow forecasts are very helpful here. If the funds are not needed immediately, the investment officer may invest in instruments with longer maturities that offer higher returns. In either case, the investment officer must know how and when the funds will be used to determine the appropriate funding requirements for the portfolio.

Other Investment Requirements

Other considerations often must be addressed when planning an investment program. For example, investing funds as compensating balances in a bank as part of an agreement either for credit or operating services is certainly a valid use of funds. Also, investing in deposits with small, local, or minority banks may be an integral part of a company's community support activities. However, this activity also carries with it the credit risk of the depository institution involved. Checking the credit rating of small banks is as important as researching and checking the credit rating of the issuer of a more traditional investment vehicle in which investment funds are placed.

MONEY MARKET INSTRUMENTS

There are many fixed-income instruments available in the money market. Some of these securities are taxable while others are tax exempt. Figure 14-4 provides a general overview of the available instruments.

U.S. Treasury Securities

U.S. Treasury securities are direct obligations of the United States government and carry its full faith and credit. These securities, which comprise the bulk of the national debt, are continually issued to raise funds to redeem maturing issues and to fund the operations of the government during periods of budget deficit. Banks, insurance companies, pension funds, and corporations, both foreign and domestic, are all major investors in Treasury securities. The market for government securities is huge and, particularly with short-term securities, multimillion dollar transactions are common. In fact, Treasury securities are routinely traded in blocks of $5 million and increments of $1 million above that.

The mechanism for issuing and selling Treasury securities is a competitive bid public auction. The competitive bid auction results in yields that

FIG. 14-4

Instruments at a Glance

Instrument	Guarantee	Liquidity Rating*	Interest Paid	Typical Maturity	State, Local Income Tax**
U.S. Treasury-Bills	U.S. Gov't	10	At maturity	3–6–12 months	Exempt
U.S. Treasury Notes	U.S. Gov't	9	Semiannual	2–7 years	Exempt
U.S. Treasury Bonds	U.S. Gov't	8+	Semiannual	7–30 years	Exempt
Federal Home Loan Bank Discount Notes	Issuing Agency	9	At maturity	30–360 days	Exempt
Federal Home Loan Bank Debentures	Issuing Agency	8	Semiannual	1–20 years	Exempt
Federal National Mortgage Ass'n. Discount Notes	Issuing Agency	9	At maturity	30–360 days	Not Exempt
Federal National Mortgage Ass'n Debentures	Issuing Agency	7	Semiannual	1 year to several years	Not Exempt
Federal Home Loan Mortgage Corp. Discount Notes	Issuing Agency	9	At maturity	5–360 days	Not Exempt
Federal Home Loan Mortgage Corp. Debentures	Issuing Agency	8	Semiannual	1–30 years	Not Exempt
Farm Credit Bank Discount Notes	Issuing Agency	9	At maturity	5–360 days	Exempt
Farm Credit Bank Debentures	Issuing Agency	6	Semiannual	6 months to several years	Exempt
Student Loan Marketing Ass'n Discount Notes	Issuing Agency	9	At maturity	5–360 days	Exempt
Student Loan Marketing Ass'n Debentures	Issuing Agency	7	Semiannual	1–30 years	Exempt
Int'l Bank for Reconstruction and Development Discount Notes	Issuing Agency	8	At maturity	30–360 days	Not Exempt
Government Nat'l Mortgage Ass'n Mortgage Pools	U.S. Gov't	7	Monthly	12–25 years	Not Exempt
Municipal Bonds	Varies by issue	7	Semiannual	5–30 years	Varies
Municipal Notes	Varies by issue	7	Semiannual	1–48 months	Varies
Municipal (Tax-Exempt) Commercial Paper	Varies by issue	7	At maturity	5–270 days	Varies
Municipal Floating Rate Notes	Varies by issue	9+	Monthly	1–30 days	Varies
Banker's Acceptances	Issuing Bank	8	At maturity	7–270 days	Not Exempt
Certificate of Deposit: (1) U.S. Bank (2) Foreign Bank	Issuing Institution	8,7,5	At maturity or Semiannual	7 days to several years	Not Exempt
(3) Savings & Loan					
Certificate of Deposit—Eurodollar: (1) U.S. Bank	Issuing Bank	7,5	At maturity or Semiannual	14 days to several years	Not Exempt
(2) Foreign Bank					
Certificate of Deposit—with Floating Rate	Issuing Bank	5	Varies	Varies	Not Exempt
Eurodollar Time Deposit—U.S. Bank or Foreign Bank	Issuing Bank	0	At maturity	360 days	Not Exempt
Commercial Paper	Issuing Corp.	8	At maturity	1–270 days	Not Exempt
Corporate Notes	Issuing Corp.	6	Semiannual	3–7 years	Not Exempt
Preferred Stock	Issuing Corp.	5	Quarterly	No maturity	Not Exempt
Repurchase Agreements	Firm Accepting Money	0	At maturity	1–360 days	Not Exempt

* Liquidity Rating: These ratings, from 1 through 10 (with 10 being the highest) represent an estimation of the ability to sell this instrument into the market under even the most adverse market environment. Although this rating does not, in every case, indicate the credit quality of the instrument, it does indicate how market participants would view the liquidity of this investment.

** Many states apply a "Franchise Tax" to corporate income and thus no exemptions are granted. Check with your tax counsel for specifics.

Reprinted with the permission of The Alan G. Seidner Company.

fully reflect market conditions and sentiment. Those investors who seek Treasury securities at original issue but are not confident or able to submit a competitive bid may submit a noncompetitive bid and buy them at a price that is the average of the high and the low price. The Treasury reserves a portion of every issue for satisfying noncompetitive bid demand at the average price of the competitive bids.

Individual and institutional investors may bid for U.S. government securities by placing a bid through a bank or a dealer or by going directly to a Federal Reserve district bank. There is no fee for this service, although a deposit is required with the bid and full payment is required on settlement date. An investor may also purchase securities in the secondary market. That is, Treasury (and other) securities may be purchased from a dealer or a bank investment department that initially purchased them through a Treasury auction or from some other source.

The auctions, which are announced well in advance, involve bidding specified prices in yield format for certain quantities of a specific security. After the auction deadline, the Treasury reviews all of the bids, establishes a high, low, and average price, and awards the instruments to those competitive bidders starting with the highest price. The Treasury also awards instruments at the average bid price to those who submitted noncompetitive bids.

Investors in Treasury notes or bonds may only receive those securities into an account at the Federal Reserve (the Fed). This is known as "book entry" delivery. This applies to all Treasury securities and most government agency securities.

U.S. Treasury securities are traded very actively in the secondary, or resale, market. They are not only purchased in volumes by dealers and other investors at the time of initial sale, but are bought and sold many times during their life since many investors do not hold instruments until they mature.

It is important to note that Treasury and most government agency securities have excellent call protection; that is, they are not subject to early call (or paid off early). In fact, most long-term U.S. government and agency securities are not callable until the last few years of their maturity. This makes them particularly attractive to investors when interest rates have declined sharply since the likelihood of the issue being called is minimal.

Treasury Bills. Treasury bills (T-bills) are the most liquid securities in the money market because of their impeccable credit quality, their relatively short maturities, and the substantial volume of trading activity. T-bills do not have coupons or any other form of fixed-interest payments. An investor's return on T-bills occurs because the bills are issued at a discount from face value and are redeemed for full face value, or par, at maturity. In other words, they are purchased at a discount from par and the difference between the purchase price and the maturity value is the interest for the period the security is held. T-bills are issued each week with maturities of 13 weeks (3 months), 26 weeks (6 months) and 52 weeks (12 months). Occasionally, the Treasury sells what is known as cash management bills, with maturities ranging from a few days to up to six months (usually for 45 to 60 days) to provide an interim source of funds before a tax receipt date by the Treasury. These bills are announced in advance of their sale. Interest on T-bills is calculated based on the actual number of elapsed days and a 360-day year, and T-bill prices are quoted in discount-yield terms in basis points (one one-hundreth of a percent).

The market for T-bills is the most active and carefully watched sector of the money market because of the high volume of transactions and the large amount of outstanding Treasury debt. At the heart of this market are some 44 primary dealers who make markets in substantially all government securities issues by standing ready to buy and sell large volumes of these instruments. These primary dealers trade actively, not only directly with investors or through brokers, but with each other, and they are subject to oversight (although not supervision or regulation) by the Fed. Other dealers, institutions, and investors are not subject to such oversight.

The dealer market is highly competitive. For example, prices quoted by major dealers on T-bills are usually separated by only a few basis points (0.01 percent). A basis point equals $25 per $1 million par value of a 90-day bill. Dealers frequently check prices with one another, and corporate and institutional investors check several dealers to take advantage of slight differences in prices.

Treasury Notes. The Treasury issues interest-bearing notes that are sold at or near par value and redeemed at par value. The original maturity of a Treasury note when initially sold is from more than one year up to 10 years. The Treasury issues two and four year notes regularly. Notes of other maturities are issued periodically, depending on the Treasury's funding requirements. Interest on Treasury notes is paid semiannually and calculated based on the actual number of elapsed days and a 365-day year. Treasury note prices are quoted in terms of a percentage of par to the nearest 1/32.

Treasury Bonds. The Treasury issues interest-bearing negotiable bonds that have a maturity of more than 10 years from the date of issue. The only difference between Treasury notes and Treasury bonds is length of maturity from original issue. Interest on Treasury bonds (like Treasury notes) is calculated based on the actual number of elapsed days and a 365-day year. Treasury bond prices are quoted in terms of a percentage of par to the nearest 1/32.

Bank and Corporate-Issued Money Market Instruments

Banker's Acceptances. A banker's acceptance (BA) is a short-term bank obligation resulting from a commercial trade transaction, often involving the international shipment of a product that frequently is pledged as collateral for the obligation.[1] The instrument arises when a loan is made by a bank in the form of a short-term negotiable discount time draft drawn on and "accepted" by the bank. The bank then sells the instrument to investors in the secondary market at the discount. The following is a discussion of the various types of BAs.

Working Capital BAs. Also known as "finance bills," Working Capital BAs do not involve underlying collateral or a product. The credit quality of the bank becomes particularly important when considering investing in a Working Capital BA since there are no "goods" to serve as collateral.

Edge Act BAs. International BAs or Edge Act BAs, are created by a subsidiary of a bank or a bank holding company outside of the bank's state of domicile. Edge Act corporations are permitted under federal law to engage in international financial transactions; Edge Act BAs may carry the full faith and credit of the parent bank through the issuance of a guarantee. Edge Act BAs sold without this guarantee normally trade at higher yields than BAs of the parent bank because of the difference in credit quality.

Eligible vs. Ineligible BAs. An Eligible BA may be discounted at the Fed by a depository institution. If a BA is issued by a nonapproved bank or is not collateralized by goods, or its maturity exceeds 270 days at the time of issue, it is not normally eligible to be discounted or used as collateral for loans at the Fed's discount window.

CDs and Time Deposits. Negotiable CDs are normally issued in units of $1 million and are sold at face value on an interest-bearing basis. CDs can have maturities of 14 days to five years and pay interest semiannually or at maturity, whichever occurs first. Most CDs, however, have an original

---

[1] See Chapter 16 for a detailed discussion of international trade transactions and the creation of banker's acceptances.

maturity of less than 12 months. CDs are either sold directly by banks to investors or issued through dealers who buy large blocks of CDs from the issuers and then sell them in the resale market. When sold before maturity by their original issuers, they are said to be traded in the secondary market.

Yields on CDs normally exceed those on U.S. Treasury and government agency instruments of similar maturities for two reasons: (1) there is a higher credit risk with the bank CD; and (2) a CD is less liquid than government obligations.

Floating (Variable) Rate CDs. In the mid-1980s, banks introduced a negotiable CD with a variable interest rate. Two types are the 6-month CD with a 30-day roll, in which interest is paid at the end of each 30-day period and a new interest rate is set, and CDs with 1-year or longer maturities with a 3-month roll. Banks may issue a variable rate CD with a "put" option, which allows the investor to put, or redeem, the instrument at the next roll date.

The interest rate established on a variable rate CD at issue and on roll dates is set at some increment above a base rate. This base rate may be anything from the current 90 day T-bill yield to a composite rate that banks are paying on new CDs with an original maturity equal to the length of the roll period. Still other base rates may be used depending on the roll dates. The increment above the base rate generally ranges from 10 to 30 basis points, depending on the credit quality of the issuer, the length of maturity, and the base rate used.

Variable rate CDs provide the investor with protection against an increase in interest rates, which would otherwise cause a fixed-rate security to decline in value. Variable rate CDs are less liquid than other CDs because subsequent investors must examine the instruments carefully to determine their unique features. Consequently, many investors do not purchase them. However, during their last roll period, variable rate CDs trade like regular CDs of similar maturity, which opens up the market during this short period.

Eurodollar Time Deposits. With all of the protection (except the $100,000 Federal Deposit Insurance Corporation insurance) that domestic bank deposits normally carry, Eurodollar time deposits are essentially non-negotiable full liability U.S. dollar-denominated deposits in an offshore branch of a U.S. or foreign bank. Eurodollar time deposits are not marketable or liquid, although in some situations a bank may agree to an "early out" from the deposit with little or no interest penalty. Therefore, Eurodollar time deposits are best suited to short-term maturities of 1 to 90 days for those investors who need liquidity. Since this is a fixed-time deposit and not a CD, no instrument is created. In addition, offshore time deposits are subject to sovereign or country risk. Sovereign risk exists to the extent that the host country may decide at any time not to permit the transfer of funds out of its banks. Investors would then find their deposits frozen until the restriction is lifted. This risk can be reduced by carefully selecting countries in which to place Eurodollar time deposits. Generally, most professional investors believe that the Cayman Islands, Nassau, and London are relatively safe places for investment dollars.

Eurodollar CDs. Banks in London and Nassau that accepted Eurodollar time deposits began to issue negotiable Eurodollar CDs to deal with the liquidity problem that a Eurodollar time deposit presented to investors. A Eurodollar CD resembles a domestic CD except that the liability for the deposit is on the books of the bank's offshore branch. Eurodollar CDs may be issued by any foreign bank or by a domestic bank with an offshore branch.

For the corporate investment officer, a key advantage of purchasing Eurodollar CDs is that they offer a higher return than the domestic CD. At the same time, Eurodollar CDs are slightly less liquid and expose the investor to sovereign risk. However, as long as they are U.S. dollar denominated, there is no exposure to changes in foreign exchange rates.

Yankee CDs. Foreign banks issue dollar-denominated CDs not only in the Eurodollar market but also in the U.S. market through branches usually located in New York. These are referred to as Yankee CDs, a name borrowed from Yankee bonds, which are bonds issued in the domestic market by foreign borrowers.

It should be noted that Yankee CDs offer somewhat less liquidity than domestic bank CDs because of less familiarity with the issuers. Consequently, Yankee CDs trade at yields close to those of Eurodollar CDs. The major purchasers of Yankee CDs are investors that are more yield-oriented.

However, the yield spread between domestic CDs and Yankee CDs has been small since 1980 as foreign banks became better known as strong, creditworthy entities. Also, in 1980, the Fed began requiring reserve deposits, thereby diminishing the ability of foreign banks to pay higher rates than domestic banks.

Master Notes. A master note is a variable rate debt instrument issued by a corporation to a trustee (usually a bank) with a maturity of several years. To an investor, a master note is essentially a money market or short-term investment because the investor may stipulate the following specific requirements:

- The amount of money invested may be increased or decreased on short notice;

- The investor's maturity date is not fixed, allowing the investor to liquidate the instrument on short notice; and

- The investor may stipulate the frequency of interest payments (monthly, quarterly, or semiannually).

Each master note has a particular set of terms. The yield on most master notes is set in relationship to a particular well-established base rate. For example, the daily Fed Funds rate minus 0.05 percent (five basis points) may be the floating daily yield on a particular master note. The yield on master notes may be at, or slightly less than, other money market instruments because they provide the investor with a great deal of liquidity and flexibility. Master notes are issued by the same types of corporate issuers that issue commercial paper and medium term notes. Master note investments are usually for larger increments of funds on the order of $5 million and up.

Repurchase Agreements

A repurchase agreement (repo) is a transaction between a dealer and an investor in which the dealer sells a security to the investor with an agreement to repurchase the security on a certain date in the future at a price that will result in a predetermined yield to the investor. Repos are exceptionally important to fixed-income securities dealers because they maintain large inventories of U.S. Treasury, government agency, and other money market securities pending sale to investors. Dealers must finance this inventory through a combination of bank loans and repos. The inventory of securities is put up as collateral for these agreements (discussed in the following paragraph) enabling the dealer to finance the carrying of those securities at the repo interest rate, which is generally lower than alternative sources of funds such as bank borrowings. Therefore, repos are a very important source of funds for dealers.

A repo is considered to be a collateralized transaction and is structured so that an investor simultaneously enters into two agreements with a counterparty such as a securities dealer or bank. In the first agreement, the investor agrees to buy particular securities for which an agreed upon payment will be made. In the second agreement, the investor agrees to sell the securities back to the counterparty at a specified future date (usually from 1 to 360 days) and at a higher price. The difference in these amounts is the investor's interest income on the transaction. Figure 14-5 depicts the flows of funds and securities in a repo transaction.

FIG. 14-5

Flow of Funds and Securities in a Repo Transaction

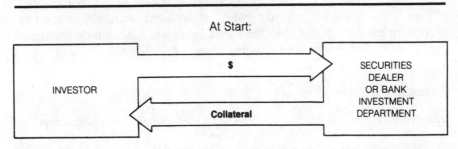

At Start:

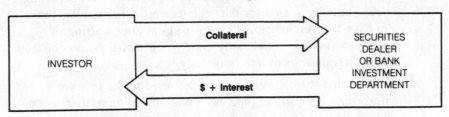

At Maturity:

Reprinted with permission of The Alan G. Seidner Company

Investors in repos historically had assumed that they owned the under-lying securities during the period that the transaction was in effect. How-ever, this concept was challenged in 1982 when a major securities firm, Lombard Wall, failed. In that case, the Bankruptcy Court refused to allow any of the repo investors to liquidate the underlying securities they were holding in order to obtain the return of their funds. Consequently, repos became a clouded investment, with many believing that the court had turned the repo transaction into an unsecured loan. As a result, many investors withdrew from the repo market. In 1984, federal bankruptcy laws were changed to help prevent repo collateral from being tied up in a bankruptcy situation. Although this change resolved some of the collateral questions, other questions still remain. Therefore, repos should still be executed with great caution and care.

It is important to note that under both prior and current law, the rules dealing with the safety of collateral only apply to securities dealers and not to banks and thrift institutions. Therefore, the status of a repo investor is not known if a bank or thrift institution failed. Thus, repo investors with banks are well-advised to require a written agreement with the bank—or any counterparty—that clearly sets forth the rights, duties, and responsibilities of each party in the event of the failure of the other. A model of such an agreement has been prepared by the Public Securities Association, and many banks readily offer it to their repo investors.

Executing a Repo

Investors are advised to take the following steps when executing a repo:

1. Verify that the counterparty is a creditworthy institution. The counterparty should have a high credit rating (by Keefe BankWatch, Moody's, or Standard & Poor's), have "net excess capital" of at least $35 million, or be a primary dealer reporting to the Fed. The reason for this requirement is that smaller firms can have their entire capital base wiped out after a string of trading losses; this could easily erase a substantial portion of their capital and push them into insolvency.

2. Confirm that the collateral will be delivered to the investor's safekeeping agent if the repo has a maturity of more than seven days. This will ensure that the collateral actually has been set aside and is under the control of a custodian independent of the counterparty.

3. Monitor the collateral to be sure that it has a continuing market value in excess of the amount invested in the repo. This can be done by obtaining a description of the collateral securities and checking their market value.

4. When entering into the transaction, ascertain whether the collateral is of acceptable quality in accordance with the investor's investment guidelines.

5. Ask the counterparty for a written agreement setting forth all terms and conditions, duties, rights, and responsibilities of both parties governing the transaction prior to executing the repo.

Alternatives to Repos

An investment manager has viable alternatives to repos when making short-term investments for anywhere from 1 to 30 days that provide an equal degree of credit quality and flexibility. Government agency discount notes, CDs, commercial paper, Eurodollar time deposits, tax-exempt put bonds, and money market funds are all viable alternatives. These instruments are available at competitive rates and enable the investment officer to spread the company's investment exposure.

Government Agency Discount Notes. These notes are available with very short maturities and are issued by such government agencies as the Student Loan Marketing Association (Sallie Mae), Federal Farm Credit Banks (FFCBs), and the Federal Home Loan Mortgage Corporation (Freddie Mac). Although there are other discount note issuers (Federal Home Loan Bank and Federal National Mortgage Association), the first three listed generally issue notes with very short maturities, ranging from 5 days (often shorter) to 360 days. These instruments are available as new issues and in the secondary market through many securities dealers and banks, and they can be purchased in quantities of $25,000 at original issue and in additional increments of $5,000 thereafter. In addition to their high credit quality and flexible purchase amounts, these instruments are generally very liquid.

Commercial Paper. Commercial paper is an unsecured promissory note issued for a specific amount and maturity on a specific day. Commercial paper is usually negotiable, although not as marketable or liquid as CDs, and commercial paper sold to investors typically is held to maturity. Commercial paper is issued not only by domestic and foreign industrial and manufacturing firms but also by finance companies. Finance companies normally sell their paper directly to investors or through banks, while industrial firms typically issue their paper through dealers.

Commerical paper may be issued in two different formats: interest bearing or discounted. In the interest-bearing format, the investor pays $1 million for a $1 million face value investment and interest is paid at maturity, similar to the way other interest-bearing securities, such as CDs, are issued. However, interest-bearing commercial paper is not very common except for very short maturities. Furthermore, the secondary market for interest-bearing commercial paper tends to be thin because most of it is held until maturity.

The most common form of commercial paper is discounted. The investor buys the instrument at a discount from the face or maturity value of the instrument. At maturity, the commercial paper issuer pays the face amount of the instrument, and the difference between the purchase price and maturity value is the investor's interest income for the period. This is identical to the way T-bills, BAs, and government agency discount notes are traded.

The maximum maturity for which commercial paper may be sold is 270 days, since instruments with a longer maturity must be registered with the

Securities and Exchange Commission (SEC), a costly procedure. In practice, however, very little 270-day paper is sold. Most commercial paper has maturities of up to 180 days. Since commercial paper typically has such short maturities, the issuer rarely has sufficient funds coming in before the paper matures to pay off the borrowing. Instead, the issuer normally expects to sell new paper to obtain funds to repay the maturing paper.

The rate offered on commercial paper depends on the credit rating of the issuer, the maturity date of the paper, how much the issuer wants to borrow, and the general level of money market interest rates. Most commercial paper issuers are rated by one or more of the rating services, such as Moody's, Standard and Poor's, and Duff and Phelps. Despite these highly competent rating agencies and their sophisticated analytical tools, there is still a risk that an issuer may default in payment of its debts. Therefore, yields on commercial paper are higher than those on Treasury obligations of similar maturities. The following is a discussion of the various types of commercial paper.

Bank holding company commercial paper. This commercial paper is issued by parent companies of major commercial banks to borrow money to fund holding company or bank operations.

Finance company commercial paper. This is usually issued by captive finance subsidiaries of major industrial concerns, which use the funds to make loans to buyers of their products. For example, General Motors sells commercial paper through its General Motors Acceptance Corporation subsidiary to generate funds to lend to purchasers of their new cars and trucks.

Industrial commercial paper. This commercial paper is issued by various major industrial concerns to provide short-term working capital for their operations.

Dealer commercial paper. Dealer commercial paper usually refers to commercial paper that is issued through securities dealers instead of banks, or sold directly to investors. Issuers are corporations borrowing for various uses. Dealer commercial paper is normally underwritten; that is, the dealer will buy the commercial paper from the issuer in bulk and "retail" it to investors from its own inventory. Until recently, this method of distribution was not available to banks that were prohibited from underwriting corporate securities by the Glass-Steagall Act. Banks could merely act as agents for the issuer, taking orders from investors but not investing any of the bank's funds in the commercial paper.

Foreign commercial paper. This is commercial paper issued by foreign industrial and financial concerns (including major foreign banks) in the U.S. market. This paper is denominated in U.S. dollars and is issued by U.S. subsidiaries of the foreign entities to raise funds, usually for working capital purposes. Foreign commercial paper usually carries the guarantee of the foreign parent corporation.

Collateralized commercial paper. Collateralized commercial paper is normally issued by savings and loans through major securities dealers where collateral in the form of U.S. government or agency securities has been pledged. This type of commercial paper is perceived as one of the more secure short-term investments, and proceeds from this type of borrowing are used for the thrift's lending activities.

Letter of credit commercial paper. Letter of credit (LOC) commercial paper contains a guaranty-type LOC to support its credit quality. This backing is usually issued by a major bank (either foreign or domestic) or an insurance company for a fee to a smaller or lesser known company seeking to enhance its credit rating. With a stronger credit standing, a smaller company can issue commercial paper in the national markets at a reasonable interest cost. However, the ultimate credit guarantee rests with the institution providing the LOC. There are various types of LOCs. The investor should be clear as to the features of each type prior to investing. These types of LOC backing include the following:

1. *Full and direct pay*—Under this arrangement, if the issuer of the commercial paper is unable to pay at the time of maturity, the LOC issuer will then pay the full amount directly to the commercial paper investor.
2. *Standby*—This is a general category of LOCs referring to various forms of guaranty that are not as direct or strong as the "full and direct pay" LOC. The standby LOC has many variations, including coverage of partial payments, and various types of delayed payments that, although acceptable, are not preferred by investors.
3. *Irrevocable*—A LOC that may be revoked or cancelled under certain conditions is not considered attractive.

Loan Participations. Some banks sell participations in loans made to their customers. Loan participations are similar to commercial paper from the standpoint of the investor, although loan participations are not liquid.

Money Market Mutual Funds. Money market mutual funds are professionally managed pools of funds that are invested in short-term fixed-income instruments. Money market mutual funds are occasionally used by institutional investors because they require relatively little time to manage.

To meet investment objectives, the investment officer must consider the redemption flexibility of shares (e.g., how funds are returned to the investor). In addition, investors can write checks against their balance in the fund or can redeem the invested funds via a telephone call. However, the shares are not negotiable. Many of these funds are specialized in that they are invested in short-term municipal instruments, thus providing tax-exempt returns. Since the average maturity of most money market mutual funds is 59 days or less, the market risk is quite limited. The market prices of short-term instruments are not very volatile as interest rates move up or down because of their short maturity. This translates into stability for the funds as well. For the investment officer considering an investment in money market mutual funds, most major newspapers carry a large listing of available funds showing their current yields and average maturity. Yield comparison of money market funds is relatively easy since most of these funds report their yields with a standard formula. Unlike investing in money market instruments, investing in a money market mutual fund does not permit safekeeping of the instrument.

Bond Mutual Funds. In recent years, bond mutual funds of all types have become popular with investors and heavily marketed by funds managers. To the corporate or institutional investor, however, these bond funds may not be an attractive short-term investment. There are several reasons for this. First, the yield advertised by these funds may be misleading. Usually bond funds are advertised showing a current yield, which is simply the weighted average interest rate of the securities in the fund. However, the current yield differs from the "total return," which includes the effect of changes in bond prices in the fund. When interest rates rise, bond prices decline, thereby reducing the net asset value of the fund. Thus, many investors are investing to obtain a "yield" that does not actually exist.

Second, since bond funds appear more attractive because of their high current yields, fund managers generally hold the longest maturity bonds to obtain the highest yields. However, long-term bonds suffer the greatest decline in price when interest rates increase; also, they may be the most difficult to sell in unsettled markets. Therefore, when interest rates increase, the market value of these funds decline relatively quickly.

Third, investors often are drawn to the so-called "no-load funds," (mutual funds with no front-end sales charge) believing that this allows them to buy fund shares at a lower transaction cost. Investors should be aware, however, that a no-load fund can charge a redemption fee or other fees under the "12b-1 fee" provision allowed by the SEC. The SEC provision allows funds managers to dip into the fund's assets to cover certain marketing costs. The investor may, therefore, have some of his principal used to cover advertising expenses to market the fund, which increases the fund and increases the management fee income to the company managing the fund. New federal laws require complete and standardized reporting of funds' yields and fees to eliminate misunderstanding in bond fund advertisements.

Finally, the liquidity of a large bond fund can be a problem when investors head en masse for the exits. When there are a lot of redemptions, and the bond funds begin to liquidate to their portfolios, there may not be a sufficient number of buyers available, causing prices to plummet. If the bonds are primarily U.S. Treasury securities, however, liquidation is usually orderly because the U.S. Treasury bond market is quite deep, active, and liquid. However, for bond funds specializing in municipal bonds, GNMA securities, and certain types of low-rated corporate bonds, the market is not nearly as liquid or stable. The supply offered in the market from the bond fund sales can further accelerate the decline in bond market prices and add to the instability of the market.

Floating Rate Instruments. A floating rate note (FRN) is a debt instrument that carries an interest rate that is periodically adjusted to reflect current interest rates. Typically, the yield is set at a fixed spread over or under a specific index rate. When the index rate goes up, the yield paid by the FRN goes up. Therefore, the market value of an FRN instrument should remain relatively close to par, assuming there is no change in the credit quality of the issuer. FRNs may have a maturity as long as 10 years, and many have put option features that allow them to be redeemed by the investor prior to maturity. Although the yield on an FRN floats in step with the current marketplace, some FRNs have limits on their yields. These limits, called collars, consist of a "cap" or maximum rate, and the "floor" or minimum rate. These features are identified in the issuer's prospectus or offering memorandum, and the investment officer must identify the precise interest rate risk and protection afforded by the collar before completing the purchase. As the yield approaches its cap or floor, the instrument may begin to act less like a floating-rate security and more like a fixed-rate security that has a coupon equal to the limit. This will affect the FRN's ability to trade close to par, thereby introducing some volatility to the market value of the principal.

Floating Rate Indexes

The various indexes that are used are usually based on one of the following:

Treasury Bills. The interest rates on "bill-based floaters" are periodically reset at some increment above the yield on 90-day T-bills. This index is not used frequently because T-bill yields can drop substantially during periods of financial uncertainty when investors flee to quality. This excessive demand for T-bills causes T-bill yields to become overly depressed. When T-bill yields are unusually low, the yield on FRNs indexed to T-bill yields will also be unusually low.

London Interbank Offered Rate. This rate is generally used to establish a basis for investment returns on numerous instruments and is used as a base rate for borrowing agreements, particularly for Eurodollar transactions. The London Interbank Offered Rate (LIBOR) is the rate at which funds are offered as deposits by one depository institution to another in London. The rate varies moment by moment and is an interbank, or wholesale, rate. This rate is quoted daily for various time periods, ranging from overnight to more than one year. On LIBOR floaters, a particular LIBOR maturity (such as the 90-day LIBOR rate) is selected as the index base and the yield on the floating rate instrument is reset at some increment (usually above) the LIBOR rate.

Composite CD Yields. Some floaters are based on the rates quoted by the Fed as composite yields on CDs for different maturities. Other variations include yield calculations based on commercial paper yields and Fed funds rates.

Although the interest rate on these instruments floats, providing some market price immunity from the effects of rising interest rates, the market value of the instruments is still subject to price swings, depending on such factors as the nature of the base index and changes in the credit quality of the issuing institution. In general, the investor should not buy these instruments thinking that their market price will not fluctuate. Moreover, the investor who owns an FRN or floating rate CD must verify:

- The accuracy of each new reset rate (based on the terms of the instrument);
- The correct dollar amount of each interest payment; and
- The timeliness of receipt of the interest payment.

Since most floating-rate CDs mature beyond one year from the date of issue, securities regulations require that they be registered with a transfer agent and that they not be issued in bearer form. These requirements do not exist for most other money market instruments that mature in less than a year and are usually in bearer form. A safekeeping agent should hold these securities in nominee name, which is a way to facilitate the transfer in the event of a sale. Investors should not have these instruments registered in their own names because of the considerable paperwork and legal documentation required to transfer ownership in the event they are sold. In addition, the corporate investment officer must also be aware that floating rate CDs require regularly updated portfolio records to reflect each new interest reset figure. There are many variations in yield reset dates and interest payment dates, and the administrative details involved may affect the attractiveness of these instruments.

Yield Curve Floaters. Yield curve floaters (also called Inverse Floaters) are a very unusual, although increasingly popular, method of setting yields on conventional floating rate investments. Normally, when market interest rates go up, the yield on floating rate instruments also goes up. However, yield curve floaters behave in the opposite manner. When market interest rates go down, the interest rate on yield curve floaters goes up. These instruments are structured so that a base interest rate is set and a spread is subtracted from the base rate to obtain the yield for the interest period.

> EXAMPLE: A base coupon rate of 17.40 percent is established for the life of the yield curve floater. Suppose the instrument's yield is based on the spread between the coupon and LIBOR for six month maturities. If LIBOR is 7.4 percent at the time of issuance, there is a net yield of 10 percent for the initial interest period. The six-month LIBOR is revised and subtracted from the base interest rate semiannually, resulting in a new yield to the investor for the ensuing six-month interest period. As the LIBOR goes down to perhaps 7 percent, reflecting market trends, the yield on the instrument increases. In this case, the reset yield would be 10.4 percent. Conversely, as market interest rates rise, including LIBOR, the yield on the yield curve floater declines.

These instruments are attractive to investors who believe that interest rates will decline but who are not willing to take the market risk by purchasing longer term securities to benefit in possible market price appreciation from falling interest rates.

"When-Issued" Trading in Government Securities

When a new security issue is announced, dealers may begin to make markets to buy and sell the new security before the instrument is issued. The period between announcement of the issue and its actual delivery to buyers is referred to as the "when issued" (WI) period. Transactions made during the WI period require little or no principal investment from the buyer until settlement date. Treasury and government agency obligations are often heavily traded during the WI period. It is possible to become an active speculator in WI securities with limited funds. Therefore, to avoid possible disaster, many investment advisors strongly suggest that investors (as differentiated from speculators) only commit to buy WI securities when they intend to pay for them and take delivery on settlement date.

Corporate Notes and Bonds

Corporate notes and bonds are issued by industrial corporations, utility companies, bank holding companies, and foreign firms issuing through their U.S. affiliates, often guaranteed by the foreign parent.

Medium Term Notes. Medium term notes are generally issued with maturities ranging from 9 months (picking up where commercial paper leaves off on the maturity spectrum) to approximately 10 years, and are subject to a continuing or "shelf" registration of the issue with the SEC. A group of dealers is selected to underwrite the securities, rates are set daily, and instruments are issued to investors in a continuing program. By offering medium term notes, the borrowing corporation can draw funds from 9 months to 10 years, depending on its funding needs, at rates it considers attractive.

Deposit Notes. Banks may issue deposit notes in much the same manner as corporate medium-term notes. Deposit notes are, in effect, longer-term CDs.

Credit Quality of Government Agency Securities

Although most investors consider government agency securities to be of extremely high credit quality (i.e., a very low possibility of default risk), certain factors need to be considered:

1. Not all actively traded government agency securities are guaranteed by the full faith and credit of the U.S. government. Therefore, many of them are "on their own" to maintain financial strength and stability.

2. Government agency securities generally are not provided with a credit rating by the major credit review services. Interestingly, the rating agencies usually provide an AAA rating to securities issued by others where some type of government agency backing is provided, such as a direct guarantee by the government agency or where securities issued by a government agency are provided as collateral. However, without credit ratings for government agencies themselves, it is difficult to find current information on their financial standing except in the press when a credit problem arises.

3. Government agencies can become involved in financial problems. Some of these problems can be so substantial that the agency needs to apply to the federal government for either direct or indirect assistance. Prime examples of this occurred in 1986–1987, when the Federal Farm Credit System developed severe financial problems.

YIELD CALCULATIONS

Many texts discuss at length how to calculate yields, prices, and equivalent yields. To the investor of short-term liquidity funds, however, a few simple rules on interest calculation should suffice.

1. Income is the difference between the total amount received and the total amount paid for an investment.

2. Yield is the amount of income received related to the total amount of funds invested and the amount of time it took to earn that income.

3. Money market instruments and other short-term fixed-income securities are traded on the basis of yield rather than price.

4. It is easier for the investor to check a dealer's yield and price calculations for accuracy than it is to do the calculations himself.

5. The conventional method for calculating yield is to use the actual number of elapsed days related to the total number of days in a year. The conventional year for instruments maturing in one year or less consists of 360 days; the conventional year for longer-term securities consists of 365 days (366 days in a leap year).

6. Conversion of a yield to an equivalent yield (e.g., bond equivalent, bank discount equivalent, or taxable equivalent) is meaningful only when considering or holding securities whose yields are calculated according to different conventions.

In comparing CDs to other instruments that accrue interest (interest bearing as opposed to discounted) it is important to note the formula differences. Specifically, CDs pay interest based on a 360-day year and governments pay based on the actual number of days in the year.

The following definitions apply to the formulas discussed in this section.

$$c = \text{coupon rate}$$
$$y = \text{yield at which the security is traded}$$
$$P = \text{price per \$1 of face value, accrued interest included}$$
$$t_{im} = \text{days from issue to maturity}$$
$$t_{is} = \text{days issue to settlement}$$
$$t_{sm} = \text{days from settlement to maturity}$$
$$a_i = \text{accrued interest}$$

What Is Price if Yield Is Known?

The following formula[2] for the yield on a CD can be used to obtain a formula for the price at which a CD will trade in the secondary market offered at a yield y. To do so, the following expression must be solved.

$$y = \left(\frac{1 + c \, \frac{t_{im}}{360}}{P} - 1 \right) \frac{360}{t_{sm}}$$

To find P, the following formula must be solved.

$$P = \left(\frac{1 + c \, \frac{t_{im}}{360}}{1 + y \, \frac{t_{sm}}{360}} \right)$$

EXAMPLE: If an investor buys a CD at a yield of 9.50 percent that carries a coupon of 10 percent with an original maturity of 90 days and a current maturity of 60 days, the price, P, which includes accrued interest that will be paid per \$1 of face value is

$$P = \left(\frac{1 + 0.100 \, \frac{90}{360}}{1 + 0.095 \, \frac{60}{360}} \right) = 1.009024$$

---

[2] For complete information on price and yield formulas, see Marcia Stigum and John Mann, Money Market Calculations, Yields, Breakevens, and Arbitrage (Dow Jones-Irwin, 1981).

Segregating Accrued Interest

Dividing the price P paid for a CD into principal and interest is calculated as follows:

$$a_i = \text{accrued interest}$$
$$t_{is} = \text{days from issue to settlement}$$

On a CD, accrued interest is given by the expression

$$a_t = c \, \frac{t_{is}}{360}$$

and

$$\text{Principal per \$1 of face value} = P - c \, \frac{t_{is}}{360}$$

Using these formulas for the previously mentioned example, it can be found that

$$a_i = 0.10 \, \frac{30}{360} = 0.008333$$

and

$$\text{Principal} = 1.009024 - 0.008333$$
$$= 1.000691$$

The CD in the example is selling at a premium above par. This is because it sold at a yield below its accrual or coupon rate.

Since the yield to the investor is the net amount of income earned related to the total cost of the investment over the number of days involved, the yield calculation is the same for both discounted instruments such as T-bills and BAs, and interest-bearing instruments such as CDs and repos.

Using a 360-day year, the money market yield provides five more days of income in a calendar year than does the bond yield. An investor in a one-year CD purchased on January 1 and maturing on December 31 would have accrued enough interest by December 26 to equal the amount of interest that it would take to accrue on a bond until December 31. The CD, therefore, produces an extra five days of interest even though the "coupon" is the same as on the bond.

The purpose of converting from a money market basis of 360 days to a bond equivalent basis of 365 days is simply to give the investment manager a point of comparison. If the investment manager is accustomed to working mostly with securities having maturities longer than a year, it would be desirable to convert money market instruments to a bond equivalent yield. If the investment manager is accustomed to working mostly with money market instruments, then it would be desirable to convert bond yields to their money market equivalent yields.

Likewise for tax-exempt securities, it is usually desirable to calculate the taxable equivalent yield. This is done simply by calculating the actual interest income from a tax-exempt security and dividing that amount by the reciprocal of the firm's marginal income tax rate, as follows:

$$\frac{\text{Tax exempt yield}}{1.00 - \text{Tax bracket}} = \text{Taxable equivalent yield}$$

Example:
$$5\% \div (1.00 - 0.41) = 8.47$$

This then represents the taxable equivalent income, which the investment manager may then compare to other taxable instruments.

PORTFOLIO MANAGEMENT TECHNIQUES

The financial manager is now ready to implement a well-managed portfolio of liquidity investments. The policy objectives and guidelines have been defined and committed to writing and the types of instruments for possible inclusion in the portfolio have been identified. What is often lacking, however, is the experience to manage a portfolio. Investing experience—or the lack thereof—is what differentiates an investment manager from a financial manager.

Yield curve analysis and yield spread analysis are two very important elements in the successful management of a short- to intermediate-term liquidity portfolio. An experienced investment manager should understand the historic yield spread among various instruments and how to use the sometimes tricky yield curve to advantage.

Yield Curve Analysis

Yield curve analysis enables an investment manager to compare yields at various maturities to gauge which securities offer the greatest yield reward with the least relative risk. In Figure 14-6, it can be observed that as maturities for a particular instrument extend from 30 through 360 days, yields become sharply higher until about 150 days at which time yields level off for longer maturities. In this case, the investment manager would probably decide to accept the attractive yields extending up to 150 days. However, beyond this point yields begin to increase much more slowly, and the reward for market risk in the form of higher yield is substantially less. Consequently, unless there is a compelling reason to purchase securities having maturities longer than 150 days, the investment manager would invest only up to that maturity point.

To create a yield curve for a particular security, one can simply plot the various time periods of a particular security on the horizontal (x) axis and the corresponding interest rate yields on the vertical (y) axis. If the investment manager also wanted to examine yield spreads (see below), he would obtain quotes for different maturities and plot the yield curves of each security using different colors. This generates a series of yield curves showing interest rate changes at various maturities as well as the yield relationships for the different securities being compared. This comparison, combined with the company's forecasted cash flow needs, helps the investment manager select an optimum maturity date for the next investment.

FIG. 14-6

Yield Curve

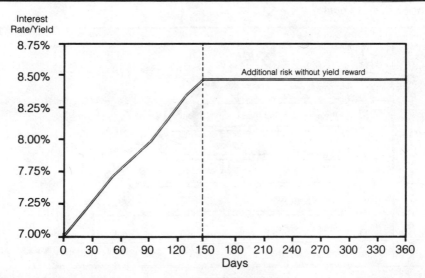

Reprinted with permission of The Alan G. Seidner Company

Yield Spread Analysis

Yield spread analysis examines the risk/reward relationships among various instruments. For example, instruments that are lower in liquidity or in credit quality should provide higher yields. The investment manager must learn how various instruments trade in relationship to one another to avoid the purchase of instruments at too low a yield. Also, as the relationship among instruments changes, the use of yield spread analysis allows the investment manager to sell one instrument and purchase another that is similar in maturity and risk for a yield improvement. Figure 14-7, which is not drawn to scale, describes the traditional approximate relationships between U.S. T-bills and other short-term instruments. When arrayed in this manner, it can quickly be seen how other securities trade in relation to each other in the market. For example, prime-rated commercial paper trades at yields higher than prime quality domestic bank CDs but at lower yields than foreign bank BAs.

FIG. 14-7

**Yield Spreads of Various Instruments Over U.S. T-bills
(not drawn to scale)**

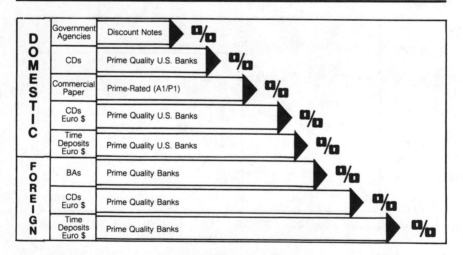

Reprinted with permission of The Alan G. Seidner Company

ROLE OF SECURITIES DEALERS

The role of the securities dealer is that of a middleman who purchases and sells instruments for its own account and generally maintains an inventory of securities. The dealer's profit is largely dependent upon successfully financing the inventory and the time involved in selling it. Thus, time can be the dealer's best friend or worst enemy. For example, a dealer purchases Instrument A in a special block trade at a discount from its retail market value. In order to obtain a profit, all the inventory of Instrument A must be sold quickly at the current market price. The longer the inventory sits, the smaller the profit will be as the interest cost on money borrowed to finance the inventory accrues. Instrument B, on the other hand, is purchased by the same dealer as a speculative opportunity. The dealer bought Instrument B anticipating that its price will improve in the near future, allowing it to be sold at a substantial profit. In both cases, the dealer must constantly weigh the carrying cost against the selling price and the amount of profit that can be obtained.

In addition to purchasing, selling, and maintaining an inventory of different instruments, dealers also may act as brokers. In this role, the dealer does not own a particular instrument. Instead, the dealer will go into the market and look for a particular instrument requested by a customer. Often the dealer finds the requested instrument at less than the retail price the customer has agreed to pay. The dealer then purchases the instrument, adds a markup, and resells it to the customer who placed the purchase order. In this type of transaction, the dealer has no market exposure or risk, a small profit is made, and the customer is satisfied.

Dealers also may act as sales agents, distributing securities issued by others. As a sales agent, the dealer arranges with several issuers (e.g., banks, savings and loan associations, and commercial paper issuers) to sell their instruments for a predetermined commission without actually purchasing them to resell from its own inventory. This type of transaction eliminates the dealer's risk of market exposure. Commissions for such transactions typically range from 0.02 percent to 0.125 percent, depending upon the type of instrument and its maturity.

Dealers often act as underwriters in the securities marketplace. Underwriters differ from dealers or brokers in that they purchase large quantities of an instrument, usually a new issue, and attempt to sell the complete quantity (or position) as quickly as possible at a higher price than its cost. If the underwriter is successful, a substantial profit can be made; however, if rates go up and prices go down before the complete position is sold, requiring an adjustment in the selling price, profitability is reduced and a major loss can occur.

Dealer Trading

Fixed-income securities, whether U.S. government securities or money market instruments, only trade in an over-the-counter market, not on a centralized exchange as do most major stocks. Therefore, there is no centralized location where all the transactions take place, and there are no reports issued at the end of the day indicating actual high, low, or last execution prices, or the volume of transactions. Trades of these instruments occur via telephone, telex, and through various other methods of decentralized electronic communication, which makes the collective reporting of execution details virtually impossible.

Rates on money market securities that are reported in newspapers are generally quotes rather than a set of specific execution prices. Therefore, they can be used only as general indicators of prices and yields. In preparing these quotes for public consumption, analysts typically use an actively traded current issue as a benchmark and then adjust the prices and yields of other less active issues to obtain an approximate indication of where instruments might have traded during the day. In addition, the rates reported for money market instruments, such as CDs and BAs, are based on a rather limited survey of the market and therefore should also serve only as an indication of the yield level. As a result of the fragmented data, there are usually wide variations in the execution prices of each fixed-income issue during a trading day. Therefore, it is important that the investment officer shop the markets for competitive prices once the type of instrument and the desired maturity date have been determined.

OPERATIONS

Proper operational procedures and controls are extremely important in the investment function. Failure to establish clear procedures and enforce their use in maintaining the investment portfolio can be extremely embarrassing and costly to the company and potentially dangerous to the continued employment of the investment officer. The investment officer should ensure that the operations program encompasses the following:

1. Verification of all dollar figures;
2. Verification of yields;
3. Maintenance of an accurate inventory of investments and a maturity "tickler"; and
4. Creation and retention of backup records for the accounting and auditing functions.

Despite the best intentions of all parties to a transaction, mistakes occur. Since the transactions are usually conducted on the telephone, the buyer and seller may have misunderstood or "misheard" each other, or the back office of the dealer may have made an error in processing the order. Therefore, it is incumbent upon the investor to check every detail of each transaction to verify that it has been completed in accordance with the investment officer's instructions.

Once the transaction is completed, the investor's records must be set up to reflect the portfolio inventory accurately. This includes ensuring that portfolio reports will be accurate and that maturing instruments will be highlighted for the investment officer's attention and action. Finally, an audit trail is essential to permit accountants and auditors to review all transactions.

SAFEKEEPING OF SECURITIES

The safekeeping agent is the custodian that physically receives, holds, and delivers each investment instrument in the portfolio. Most major money center banks, regional banks, and securities firms offer this service, typically through their investment departments. Similar custodial services are provided by their trust departments. However, most trust departments are not suited to meet the fast payment and delivery requirements that most short-term fixed-income securities transactions require. On the other hand, safekeeping services developed by the investment department were specifically created for client institutional investors who purchase short- and intermediate-term fixed-income instruments. In fact, many safekeeping departments that exist in banks were established to serve the bank's own investment department, which required the flexibility to move instruments in and out of an account frequently and effectively.

Most major banks hold in safekeeping all types of fixed-income securities for their customers even if the instrument was purchased through another firm. Investors that are not located in large urban areas will find that small regional banks usually have a correspondent relationship with a large money center bank to ensure that even small corporate investment portfolios will reside in a safe and convenient environment.

There are several important reasons why the corporate investment officer may want to place instruments with a bank for safekeeping. First, when instruments are held on neutral territory, such as in a bank's safekeeping department, it enables the investment officer to buy and sell freely using a number of different banks and securities dealers.

EXAMPLE: Corporation *X* has purchased instruments from *ABC* Securities, a dealer, and permits the dealer to retain the instruments in its own safekeeping department. After a few weeks, Corporation *X* wishes to sell the instruments purchased from *ABC* Securities. Corporation *X* goes to both dealer *ABC* and dealer *XYZ* for a bid. If the bid from *XYZ* is superior, the corporate investment officer is placed in the potentially embarrassing situation of asking *ABC* Securities to deliver out the instruments to *XYZ*. Not only could this situation weaken the customer/dealer relationship between Corporation *X* and *ABC*, depending upon the constraints that *ABC* has placed on moving instruments out of their safekeeping department, it may be more difficult to physically move the instruments to *XYZ* or to an alternate safekeeping facility in time to complete the sale. The investment officer would have been better served by using an independent third-party safekeeping agent, which would have enabled him to buy (receive) and sell (deliver) investment instruments from a number of firms efficiently.

Second, principal and interest payments on securities held by an independent bank safekeeping agent are credited directly to the customer's bank account for immediate use. Third, this arrangement facilitates the process for making claims for unpaid interest. The more time that passes, the more difficult it is to win a claim. Finally, audits to verify all instruments being held by the independent safekeeping agent are easy to initiate.

Delivery vs. Payment

When instruments are held in a carefully selected bank safekeeping department, each instrument usually goes through several audits before the purchase is final and the instrument is accepted or physically released. This is referred to as a delivery versus payment, or DVP, arrangement. If the type of security or the dollar amount involved in a transaction is not exactly what the investment officer ordered, the safekeeping agent will usually call the investment officer immediately for clarification of the order. Mistakes are usually caught and corrected before the securities are accepted for safekeeping. Conversely, any discrepancies with securities left for safekeeping with the dealer from which they were purchased may show up only at the end of the month on statements or confirmations. Because of the length of time between the transaction and the investor's statement date, it is very difficult to rectify an error at this point. Also, because the trade has already been settled, and payment and delivery have already been completed, the investment officer is not in an advantageous position to remedy the problem. The dealer has little incentive to solve the problem unless it would prevent him from conducting future transactions with a customer.

If an investor permitted each securities dealer to hold the instruments involved in a particular transaction, an audit would be extremely lengthy and cumbersome because each dealer would have to conduct its own audit and submit an individual report. The investment manager then would have to reconcile each audit to its portfolio. In a DVP arrangement, on the other hand, the physical securities are actually delivered to the independent central safekeeping agent of the investor. Moreover, DVP assures that the investor's payment is sent directly to the correct dealer.

Selecting a Safekeeping Agent

Before selecting a bank to use as a safekeeping agent, the investment officer should survey several banks. An important consideration when selecting a bank for a safekeeping agent is whether the bank provides direct safekeeping services or if safekeeping is offered through a correspondent bank. The investment officer must determine whether use of a correspondent bank is acceptable to the corporation. The investment officer should also be aware that the vast bulk of securities settlements occur at New York City banks, and it would be difficult and expensive to require delivery elsewhere. In addition, holding securities outside New York may impede delivery in the event a security is sold. Depending on the size of the corporate portfolio and the availability of larger banks, using a New York correspondent bank might be the best choice. Figure 14-8 is a checklist that will assist investment officers in determining the most efficient and economic investment portfolio safekeeping services.

CONCLUSION

The successful and effective program for investing liquidity funds begins with a careful description of investing policy objectives and investing guidelines. It includes designating personnel to carry out the program; it requires selecting securities, executing transactions, and carrying out reporting requirements; it requires establishing and maintaining appropriate controls. Once these elements are in place and functioning, the management of an investment portfolio will improve but should never be considered routine. Although this activity may consume relatively little managerial and staff resources, even for portfolios of $100 million and larger, it should be performed with great care and effort considering the possibility for substantial loss.

FIG. 14-8

Checklist for Safekeeping Services

- □ Investigate the type of safekeeping services used by other investment managers.

- □ Estimate the volume and types of transactions expected in the portfolio; obtain a complete fee schedule from several banks and compare prices on a total estimated cost basis for the various safekeeping services that may be required.

- □ Verify that the safekeeping service will handle all of the various instruments in which the company intends to deal.

- □ Confirm that the safekeeping agent is able to collect, receive, verify, record, and pay properly all types of interest payments, such as on floating rate securities, mortgage backed securities (paying back principal and interest), and odd coupon date payments.

- □ Determine if safekeeping services are directly provided through the bank or if they are provided through a correspondent bank; if the latter, investigate the capabilities of the correspondent bank.

- □ Verify that the safekeeping agent handles all transactions on a DVP basis and does not charge the investor's account on settlement date unless the instrument is received. Also, verify the bank's willingness to decline due bills (temporary receipts offered by the seller in lieu of the actual investment certificate).

- □ Verify that the safekeeping agent can provide prompt notification in the event that any discrepancy exists in connection with the delivery of an instrument. This is quite important because some safekeeping services will accept an instrument and automatically charge an account for a security without verifying that it has met all of the criteria required by the investment officer.

- □ Request information regarding the turnover of key personnel in the safekeeping department over the past few years. For example, if there have been five new department managers in the past two years, this could be a signal of problems in the department that could result in service deficiencies for the account.

- □ Verify that there always will be a responsible safekeeping contact person available during normal business hours.

- □ Have legal counsel review all contracts provided by the safekeeping department.

- □ Obtain a credit rating on the safekeeping bank to assure that it is a financially stable organization.

SUGGESTED READINGS

Bort, Richard and Alan G. Seidner. "Investing Surplus Funds: What to do With Your Everyday Cash." *Corp. Accounting* (Winter 1986).

Cook, Timothy Q., and Timothy D. Rowe, eds. *Instruments of the Money Market,* 6th ed. Virginia: Federal Reserve Bank of Richmond, Va., 1986.

Fabozzi, Frank J. and Leslie N. Masonson, eds. *Corporate Cash Management: Techniques and Analysis.* Homewood, Ill.: Dow Jones-Irwin, 1985.

———, and Irving M. Pollack. *The Handbook of Fixed Income Securities.* Homewood, Ill.: Dow Jones-Irwin, 1987.

———, and Sylvan G. Feldstein. "Tax Exempt Short-Term Investments," Chapter 11.

Seidner, Alan G. "Investment Policy and Guidelines." *Journal of Cash Mgmt.* (Nov./Dec. 1988).

———. *Corporate Investments Manual: Short- and Intermediate-Term Fixed-Income Securities.* Boston and New York: Warren, Gorham & Lamont, Inc., 1989.

Stigum, Marcia. "Taxable Money Market Instruments," Chapter 10.

———. "Using Futures and Options in Corporate Short-Term Portfolio Management," Chapter 13.

———. *The Money Market.* Homewood, Ill.: Dow Jones-Irwin, 1983.

———, and John Mann. *Money Market Calculations, Yields, Breakevens, and Arbitrage.* Homewood, Ill.: Dow Jones-Irwin, 1981.

PART VI

International Operations

CHAPTER 15

Managing Funds in Foreign Subsidiaries

ESTABLISHING A FOREIGN TREASURY OPERATION

Introduction

Managing the treasury operation of a foreign entity from its U.S. headquarters can be a continual challenge to the financial manager. The barriers are many: physical distance, language, volatility of the exchange markets, foreign and domestic tax rules, and the changing rules and regulations among all of the countries involved, including the United States. These are compounded by the differing payment systems, restrictions on cross-border data flows, and carloads of government regulations, most of which are imposed abroad. In addition, exchange rate fluctuations create unexpected gains and losses quite apart from the success or failure of the foreign business itself.

Against this somber background, the seemingly impossible task of managing international funds flows is necessary and actually quite possible. The international financial manager has many of the same concerns as the domestic financial manager—accelerating the collection of receivables; concentrating funds; controlling disbursements; developing useful data concerning transactions and balances; and maintaining liquidity at minimum costs and optimum returns.

Reality, however, requires that the financial manager recognize and accept social and cultural differences in the international arena because business customs and practices in other countries vary considerably from those in the United States and from one another. Therefore, the financial manager should not expect to impose the systems and procedures of a U.S. business on its foreign operations without allowing for many exceptions. Similarly, given a smoothly functioning financial operation in one foreign country, the financial manager must not assume that the same design or pattern will necessarily work as well, or at all, in another foreign country.

Location Requirements

It is important for a U.S.-based financial manager to realize that it is probably not possible to achieve the company's financial objectives from its U.S. base. Distance, coupled with all the different time zones, makes the task of dealing with the mundane details necessary to achieve these objectives very difficult. Therefore, the financial manager must seek the most efficient and effective location from which the treasury operation can be managed. In the search for that point, the manager often rejects the notion of installing regional cash managers. While regional cash managers may be a less expensive alternative than appointing a cash manager in each country and might mitigate the problems of time zone differences, all of the other external issues continue to exist, and each regional cash manager is still an outsider looking in except in the country in which he is located.

The issue is settled, therefore, by recognizing that the international treasury function is about the only exception to the rule that a centralized treasury management operation should be maintained. There are too many daily decisions regarding investment opportunities, borrowing requirements, and local banking practices to enable financial management from a distance. While the U.S. parent has certain global concerns that are best managed from home, the tasks of managing the treasury operations of each foreign entity are best placed in the hands of a strong financial manager located in each country. Only in that way will the foreign entity have the benefit of fully understanding the language, customs, laws, rules, regulations, and all of the subtle nuances of navigating the labyrinthian paths of each country's banking system and procedures, laws, and commercial and business practices.

Commercial and Financial Practices of the Host Country

The banking and financial operations of a foreign subsidiary must substantially comply with the normal practices of its host country. Attempting to operate abroad by using the same procedures and techniques used in the United States will likely create many problems, beginning with the negative image of a nonconforming foreigner.

Banking Practices. Banking practices are often very different outside the United States. With more than 15,000 U.S. commercial banks, competition for commercial and industrial business is keen. In many other countries, however, the number of banks capable of handling commercial and industrial business is limited to perhaps a half dozen or so major banks and a modest number of second-tier banks.

The banking customs of other countries vary not only from those in the United States, but from one another. In some countries, banks and their customers traditionally show great loyalty to one another, while in others, customers frequently shop around for banking services. Banks in some countries expect compensating balances even before credit or operating services have been rendered, whereas in other countries, overdrafts are as normal as positive balances. In some countries, checks are the predominant payment medium, while in other countries, commercial transactions may more often be settled through other means, such as electronic credit transfers through the banking or postal systems.

Commercial Practices. Common U.S. commercial practices frequently differ abroad. For example, while it is customary in the United States to sell on open account with payment of the net amount due (and usually paid) in 30 days, this practice is not common in countries such as Italy, France, Spain and Mexico. In Mexico, for instance, the customer must sign a document known as a "contrarecibo" to be legally bound to pay, and the credit period begins when the document is signed. In other countries, such as Germany and Japan, one's credibility and standing in the community may be jeopardized by failure to pay on time. In Australia, the practice of cash management involves stretching payments to the limit. Payment mechanisms differ, too, with many countries far ahead of the United States in using electronic methods for effecting corporate-to-corporate payments. And in some countries, like Japan, when a paper payment device is issued, it is more often a note or bill of exchange rather than a check.

Communications. Telecommunications systems in some countries are well developed and used by banks for transferring funds and data. This may not be the case in other countries, where even telephone service is spotty. In some countries, float occurs much like it does in the United States, whereas in others, value dating of deposits and payments occurs and must be negotiated quite separately and apart from the actual float involved. Companies in some countries try to locate their offices near the bank to facilitate even routine communications because mail and telephone service are undependable; in others, the banking system (like government) functions only upon financial incentives provided by the party wanting service. In contrast, the ethical standards and competence levels in some countries are high.

Generally, the very practice of cash management abroad often is unfamiliar to the indigenous banks, although it has become more common since U.S. banks became more aggressive and competitive abroad in the early 1980s. Many of the larger banks have developed sophisticated depository, disbursing, and information reporting products in many areas of cash management, and their capabilities in these previously ignored areas seem to be growing.

IMPLEMENTING FOREIGN CASH MANAGEMENT OPERATIONS

The establishment of a foreign operation frequently is a fait accompli as far as the U.S. financial manager is concerned. The operation either already exists by the time the financial manager arrives or the decision to establish an operation, including its location and form of organization, is made without consulting the financial manager. However, in the unusual event that the financial manager has an opportunity to provide some input on establishing or revising the foreign operation, some guidance into system structures and operational procedures would be helpful. The first step in designing a new cash management system or evaluating an existing one is to determine the unit's functional needs and to plan a strategy for meeting those needs. This strategy can be expressed in terms of a bank account configuration that would provide the required functionality. The banks that fit that structure can then be selected.

Bank Account Configuration

Bank accounts must be established within a country and configured to facilitate normal operations and provide controls. The system should be self-contained within the country in order to avoid exchanging currencies unnecessarily, yet it should allow for payments to suppliers in other countries and remittances to the United States. The system should also enable the U.S. parent to monitor and evaluate financial operations as well as to enforce guidelines and controls.

One banking system configuration that achieves this involves the use of dual bank accounts. As shown in Figure 15-1, a pair of bank accounts is opened, one for deposits and one for disbursements. The depository bank account is established under the control and sole signature authority of the U.S. parent, and the disbursing bank account is established under the operating control of local management but with U.S. signature authority as well.

Depository Account Operations

The depository account functions as a concentration account for all funds received in-country. Funds leave this account only under strict control by, and with authorization from, U.S. head office personnel; the number of such transactions is necessarily limited. Disbursements out of the depository account are made only to fund the disbursing account and for remittances to the United States. The depository bank should be furnished with standing written instructions that all deposits to the company must be made to the depository account and that no deposits are to be made to the disbursing account other than transfers from the depository account.

FIG. 15-1

Dual Bank Account Configuration for Host Country Banking

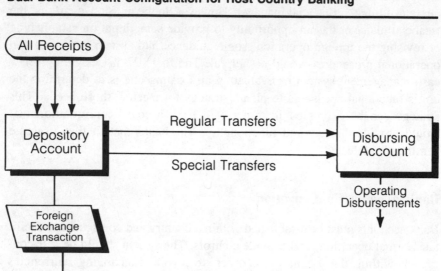

Disbursing Account Operations

The disbursing account is operated by local management to pay the bills and expenses of the foreign operation. Similar security features and controls should prevail for this account as for any company checking account, such as tightly controlled signature authority and written delegation of authority to initiate electronic funds transfers (EFTs) and conduct foreign exchange operations. These security and control features are generally available at all foreign banks, just as they are in the United States. The disbursing account is funded solely by transfers from the depository account with several transfer options available, none of which include discretionary action by local management.

Regular Periodic Transfer. The U.S. head office may give the depository bank standing instructions to make periodic (weekly, biweekly, or monthly) transfers from the depository to the disbursing account. The amount of the transfer is arbitrary but is usually based on the local company's budgeted overhead and operating expenses. This funding method is particularly appropriate where local expenses are relatively stable and predictable, such as in a sales operation.

Special Transfer. Upon the subsidiary's request for funds, a special transfer instruction must be given to the foreign bank by the company's U.S. head office before the disbursement can be made. Such a request might be to fund nonroutine or unusually large local disbursements such as taxes, a large procurement order, or capital expenditures. A special transfer would be initiated by a request for funds from the local manager to the U.S. parent. Approval of the transfer is based on the parent's knowledge and understanding of the underlying transaction that needs to be funded and is handled as an exception to normal operations.

Imprest Transfer. The U.S. head office may authorize a transfer to the disbursing account based on disbursements made, as reported by the local management. The disbursing account in this case would be an imprest account (a demand deposit bank account that is replenished periodically for the precise amount of disbursements made) funded initially with an amount estimated to be sufficient to carry the local company for a normal reimbursement period (weekly, biweekly, monthly). Such an imprest transfer system is appropriate for a manufacturing operation, where the amount of disbursements can vary considerably from one period to the next.

Remittances

A remittance of funds to the parent can occur whenever surplus funds are generated in the depository account, subject to local country rules and regulations and other legal and tax constraints. Local management's short-term funds flow forecast determines the existence of surplus funds, and local management initiates the remittance transaction by advising the U.S. parent as to the amount available for remittance.

The remittance transaction begins with the execution of a spot foreign exchange transaction conducted either by the U.S. parent or by local management. A spot transaction occurs when two parties agree to exchange currencies for settlement as soon as possible, normally in two days. Frequently, for hard currencies (currencies that are regularly traded in multiple markets outside the home country), the U.S. parent's treasury manager would conduct the exchange transactions in order to concentrate the company's worldwide foreign exchange trading transactions to the extent possible. This builds bargaining power. For a remittance to the United States from England, for example, pounds sterling can be sold for dollars in either London or the United States. The U.S. parent is likely to have access to at least as many foreign exchange traders in the United States as the London subsidiary, but the parent will have greater clout owing to the fact that it probably generates a greater number of foreign exchange transactions during the year. For soft currencies being exchanged into U.S. dollars or another hard currency, the exchange transaction may best be conducted locally. For example, for a remittance from Thailand, the transaction would best be conducted locally in Bangkok, since there is no reliable market outside Bangkok for Thai baht.

Authenticating Payments

Since all transfers from the depository account, except regular periodic transfers, are ordered from outside the foreign country (by the U.S. parent or a regional office), certain standing arrangements need to be made to ensure the integrity and authenticity of the payment order. If the payment order is issued by letter with a manual signature, the depository bank can verify the signature against the specimen signatures in its file. However, most international payments are ordered electronically via telex or other similar message carrier, which precludes verification of a signature. In this case, the standard means for verifying the authenticity of instructions is to use a "message authentication code" (MAC). A MAC is an algorithm that the bank and customer agree to use to verify the authenticity of a message. The key to the MAC is usually furnished by the bank to the customer, although some banks require that their codes be reserved for use only by correspondent banks. In this case, the customer may create its own MAC algorithm and request the bank to use it.[1]

Cash Operating Procedures

Local receipts are routinely deposited into the depository account; local expenses are paid from the disbursing account, which is funded through transfers from the depository account. If the local operation's expenses

---

[1] See Chapter 7 for a discussion of message authentication codes.

exceed its budget, the disbursements may exceed the funding, and the operation will run out of money. In this case, local management will be required to contact its parent to request a "special transfer" of funds from abroad, with the usual requirements for explanations.

Another approach to controlling expenditures in a foreign operation was implemented by a major American multinational manufacturer of high technology equipment.[2] The company's global strategy was to minimize idle funds, have each operating unit accountable on a timely basis, and control its expenditures without the need for a sophisticated staff. This company has its local controllers prepare detailed short-term funds forecasts, just like many companies do domestically. Each foreign controller determines its unit's beginning bank balance, adds the estimated customer receipts for the week, subtracts the estimated disbursements for the week's payroll and operating expenses, adjusts for the target balance position (usually an overdraft level), and determines the amount of excess funds. The excess is deemed to be available for remittance to the U.S. parent immediately.

It is interesting to note that, in this particular company, the remittance must be made at the start of the forecasted week, requiring the local unit to borrow from its local bank to obtain the funds. This places pressure on local management to make good on its forecasts, lest it end up with excessive bank borrowings or excessive funds in the bank account.

A third system, the "sweep account" system, is appropriate for companies having subsidiaries in several European countries. Such a company can establish accounts denominated in each currency involved with the Brussels or London branch of a major multinational bank, establishing disbursing accounts in each country with the local branches of that same bank. Frequently, as often as daily, the disbursing branches sweep all funds above a certain pegged level in each account out of the disbursing bank accounts into the Brussels or London concentration accounts. As balances fall below the peg in a disbursing account, the system draws funds back from the concentration account to the disbursing account.

This system, in various mutations and with numerous features, has been peddled for many years by several large multinational U.S. banks. The system is an excellent means for a bank to display its international cash management prowess but has several drawbacks from the customer's viewpoint.

---

[2] "How Digital Equipment's Weekly Cash Cycle Mobilizes Idle Funds," *Bus. Int'l Money Report*, 35 (Jan. 30, 1981).

Its principal advantages are:

1. It is a simple system requiring little involvement or effort on the part of the U.S.-based financial manager.

2. Account balances are more visible because the bank often can include the foreign currency balances in the daily balance report provided via terminal to the U.S. financial manager.

3. Payments in third-country currencies are facilitated.

Its principal disadvantages are:

1. The system is expensive to operate, requiring fee payments to maintain multicurrency sweep accounts at the concentration point and transaction charges to move the funds between the local operation and the concentration point.

2. The intercountry funds movements increase the likelihood of error and delay.

3. Information in the balance report may be misleading to the U.S. financial manager because it shows only the current bank balances and not the related checks and drafts outstanding or about to be issued against those balances by the units in each country.

4. The banking operations of a company involved in several different countries are locked into a single multinational bank, regardless of whether that bank is the best choice in each country.

5. The company remains a captive of the bank for foreign exchange transactions because of the ease of allowing that bank to handle everything. The "ease factor" can have a cost in terms of less than sharp exchange rate quotes when the bank knows it has no competition in the transaction.

Payment of Foreign Bills

Foreign operations frequently use suppliers in other countries, and provisions must be made for making routine payments in different currencies. If the company is using a sweep account system, where it maintains balances in various currencies under centralized control, the paying country may simply request that a payment be made by the regional controller out of the concentration account with the appropriate funds. This process may sound simple, but the intercompany bookkeeping may become somewhat cumbersome because the credit is in one currency while the debit is in another. The mutual exchange rates must be established by prior agreement and book-keeping accuracy must be tightly controlled.

Most companies rely on their local operations to pay their own bills, both domestic and foreign. Where the volume of foreign payments is small, local management can always buy a bank transfer or draft in a foreign currency to pay its foreign vendors. This retains the simplicity and low cost of keeping the transaction locally controlled without the unnecessary involvement of other parties, and it keeps local management fully accountable.

Information Reporting

Based on these considerations, the foreign units manage their own funds flows while the U.S.-based financial manager exercises its parental right to monitor the foreign operations. This is achieved by having each foreign unit report periodically (usually weekly) on its funds balances, investments (when authorized), borrowings, and intercompany transfers made and scheduled. Over time, a pattern should develop for each foreign unit. For example, a particular unit may historically function within a certain range of funds balances. A "spike," or sudden increase, in the actual level of balances may not cause alarm unless it persists for a prolonged period. When it does persist, the U.S. financial manager should question the foreign unit and receive an acceptable response. Of course, all reports and analyses should be made in local currency to isolate performance from currency exchange rate fluctuations.

Some major multinational banks offer terminal-based reporting of foreign bank balances as an optional module in the bank's domestic balance reporting system. Before buying this service, the U.S. financial manager should consider carefully the usefulness of this information. First, the reported balances are the bank balances rather than the foreign unit's book (general ledger) balances. Without knowing the amount of checks and drafts outstanding and about to be issued against the balance, the information is not very useful. Second, in order to report the balances, the foreign unit must maintain its accounts with the reporting bank. More important considerations than balance reporting usually lead to the decision to select local banks in foreign countries.

Bank Selection

The structure of foreign bank accounts often involves a depository account and a disbursing account and transfers between them to fund the disbursing account from the depository account (as depicted in Figure 15-1). However, this structure presents some problems for the financial manager in deciding upon a bank in the host country. For example, because of the need for frequent transfers, both accounts should be maintained at the same bank. The timeliness and accuracy of the transfers are improved, and the cost of making the transfers is minimized, if not eliminated. On the other hand, there is a float advantage to using an indigenous bank for deposits and a less-well-connected bank for disbursements. The indigenous bank can clear deposits and grant funds availability as soon as possible, while a foreign bank will probably take longer to have checks presented to it on the disbursement side. This combination allows the cash manager to use float to an advantage in some countries. Further, by using an indigenous bank, the company can more easily navigate local regulations and make important business and community contacts. And maintaining a relationship with a U.S.-based multinational bank is a plus because it is more likely to understand the U.S. business ethic and may have an even greater incentive to serve the company if its relationship is extended worldwide.

A blending of these objectives and strengths may therefore dictate using both banks within a country: placing the depository account with the indigenous bank and the disbursing account with the U.S. bank's foreign branch. This gives the company both the depository and disbursing float advantage, and it makes the resources of both banks available to the company. Generally, the only problem that might be encountered with this arrangement would be a language problem in U.S. headquarters dealing with the depository bank, particularly in situations involving Latin America, where English-speaking bankers are not always available. However, by using standardized telex messages (or other forms of electronic communication), misinterpretation can generally be avoided.

An example of what happens when the wrong indigenous bank is selected was when a well-known entertainment company with worldwide operations in more than 40 countries discovered a few years ago that it had selected the wrong banks in London. No one noticed this for years until the U.S.-based treasury manager visited the London office and learned something about the British banking system. British finance is centered in a one square mile section of London known as "The City of London." The five top-tier British banks (Lloyds, Barclays, Midland, National Westminster, and Standard Chartered) have standing arrangements for exchanging and clearing checks among each other. Other banks—British and foreign—must go through one of these clearing banks, which introduces a certain amount of inefficiency. Many years before, the entertainment company had inadvertently placed its depository account with the London branch of a U.S.-based lead bank and placed the disbursing account with one of the five clearing banks. Not only was this a disadvantage for float purposes, but it led to substantial messenger fees for sending deposits to the depository bank with a single branch located a considerable distance from the company's office. Of course, the disbursing bank had a branch directly across the street from the company but was not permitted by the company to take its deposits.

Another major consideration in selecting the bank or banks for the foreign operation is the same as at home: the attitude of the banker. The foreign financial manager and his domestic counterpart will experience severe frustration if they have selected a bank that specializes in some area of business that is not germane to the company's operations. For example, in some countries there are banks that specialize in certain industries; some banks prefer to make loans funded from sources other than customer deposits; and some banks use customer deposits to make investments other than loans to customers. In selecting an appropriate bank, the financial manager must explore whether these differences exist; and, if so, to find a bank that offers the company certain advantages. For example, if the company expects to borrow locally, and if the company is in a manufacturing business, it may not want to consider "land banks" specializing in agricultural lending and merchant banks investing deposits rather than lending them.

Managing Liquidity

The foreign financial manager performs the same functions in managing liquidity as his U.S.-based counterpart: forecasting and monitoring daily receipts and disbursements, maintaining communications (i.e., networking) with marketing, production, and financial managers to improve the quality of the funds forecast; arranging borrowings and investments when permitted; and informing management of any unusual aberrations in trends. As with its U.S. counterpart, the foreign unit should have a line of credit from a financial institution or a portfolio of short-term investments to ensure a balance of receipts and disbursements.

The parent company normally establishes policy guidelines regarding liquidity management. These guidelines might include:

1. A determination of the frequency of remittances from the foreign subsidiary to the parent:
   - Irregularly, whenever funds are in excess of local requirements; or
   - Regularly, perhaps quarterly, in the form of dividends from current earnings; or

- Regularly, usually monthly, in the form of royalties under license agreements or management fees; or
- Some combination of each of these.

2. An objective of maintaining the lowest possible average level of positive balances;

3. Preference for a liquidity cushion in the form of a bank credit line over idle funds in the bank; and

4. An instruction that the company's banks are to be compensated fairly, whether through fees or balances.

The U.S.-based financial manager must learn to accept and then deal with the "outpost mentality" governing much of the liquidity management process. An outpost mentality is commonly noticed among those who work a long distance away from the headquarters; it includes a number of features relating to communications breakdowns, elements of mutual respect and confidence, and the task of image management. In finance, an outpost mentality manifests itself in the reluctance of foreign managers to request funds from headquarters. In this respect, foreign managers follow the dictum, "It is better to give than to receive," even if there are good reasons for receiving. It is human nature to try to maintain comfort and avoid exposure to risk. Combining a natural inclination to avoid exposure to risk with outpost mentality leads to the hoarding of funds by the foreign manager. Remitting too much or too soon is often a cardinal error. Therefore, the task of the U.S. financial manager is to provide the cushions and escape valves to encourage the foreign manager to make remittances without jeopardizing the liquidity of the foreign operation. Two tools help achieve this: a local bank line of credit, and a demonstrated willingness and ability of the parent company to advance funds when needed.

As an example, the financial manager of the German sales subsidiary of an American company felt "broke" when his funds balances declined to about one month's net cash flow, the equivalent of about $300,000 in U.S. currency. To the U.S. parent, then borrowing from banks at short-term rates of about 10 percent, this hoarding of funds was expensive. The U.S. treasury manager broached the idea that a bank overdraft line of credit, rather than positive deposit balances, could be used as a liquidity cushion. This elicited fears among the German managers that the interest expense would adversely impact their bonuses, a visceral problem that could affect their willingness to cooperate. Investigation showed that the interest expense would not affect their bonuses, and this revelation dispelled any resistance to the plan. A credit line was arranged for the equivalent of $500,000 U.S.

dollars at the German bank's prime rate, guaranteed by the U.S. parent company. The size of the credit line allayed any fears by the German subsidiaries' managers that the cushion was insufficient, and no commitment or other fees were associated with this short-term credit facility. During the ensuing 12 months, the German subsidiary operated on average deposit balances equal to approximately $50,000, allowing the parent to repatriate $250,000 virtually permanently. Moreover, the subsidiary went into an overdraft condition only three times for a total of only 12 days, incurring an aggregate interest expense of only $300—a nominal amount compared to the interest expense of $25,000 saved by the parent company.

Tax Policy

Occasionally, the collective wisdom of the tax managers offsets the urge of other U.S.-based financial managers to repatriate funds from abroad. Tax managers are paid to minimize tax expense through any legal means possible. Taxes, of course, are a necessary cost of doing business. Occasionally, however, tax considerations carry more weight than they should, overwhelming sound business judgments.

The U.S.-based financial manager needs to be aware of tax treaties between the United States and the foreign countries in which the company operates. A tax treaty is an agreement between the two countries in which, among other things, the countries agree to give preferred tax treatment to residents and companies doing business in each other's country. Such preferred treatment usually takes the form of reduced withholding taxes on remittance of royalties, license fees, and dividends from the host country to the base country.

Another important matter for the U.S.-based financial manager is the set of requirements and restrictions governing the remittance of funds. This matter is totally foreign to people who never venture beyond the United States, where there are no restrictions on funds transfers or foreign exchange transactions. Many countries do, however, limit remittances. Some do it by controlling the amount of hard currencies available; some do it by law and regulation; and others do it through their domestic tax policy by placing a very high tax on remittances. The U.S.-based financial manager must understand the restrictions and limitations in each foreign country in which the company does business in order to avoid violating any of the host country's laws or regulations. This is also essential in finding the optimal route for repatriating funds quickly and with minimum taxes withheld.

For example, a particular Latin American country has rampant inflation and a confiscatory tax on dividends paid out in excess of a 12-percent return on capital. Working with the tax manager, the U.S. cash manager initiated a revision of the license agreement between the parent and the Latin American subsidiary to increase the license fee, the remittance of which was taxed very heavily, but at a lower tax rate than dividends. The cash manager then made the recommendation to pay dividends to the fullest extent possible and to pay the confiscatory tax because the tax rate was lower than the rate of devaluation of the currency.

Another case in point involved a medium-sized multinational company with exports to many countries. Exports were made to the company's foreign sales subsidiaries in each country under license agreements. The license agreements were flexible to allow variable license fees country-by-country and product-by-product. This enabled the company to follow a strategy of managing the profits of each foreign unit to generate a small but steady taxable income, with the bulk of the funds repatriated as license fees. (The strategy of allowing a small but positive taxable income in each country was used in order to gain the cooperation of local tax authorities in other tax matters.) After paying local expenses, the foreign sales units had little use for excess funds since they maintained little inventory, no production plants, and operated out of rented quarters. Accordingly, each subsidiary declared and paid a dividend annually to its U.S.-based parent. (It should be noted that the license agreements were occasionally routed circuitously through one or more intermediate subsidiaries to take advantage of more favorable tax treaties that reduced the amount of withholding taxes on remittances.)

For many years, the tax department was able to maximize cash flow because foreign income tax payments were used as a credit against the parent company's U.S. income taxes. However, a few years ago this public company was acquired by a wealthy individual in a leveraged buyout. Now that the company had no public stockholders, it had no incentive to report taxable income; it just needed cash flow to service its heavy debt burden and to maintain the owner in the style to which he had become accustomed. Finding enough expenses to offset income was not a problem. The tax department did a fine job in structuring the acquisition transaction in such a way that write-offs would continue for many years to shelter the cash flow that the company generated domestically. Unfortunately, the tax department forgot that the new owner enjoyed the fruits of his labors in the United States, not in several dozen countries abroad. With taxable income from U.S. operations now only nominal, so that there was no way to offset the taxes on foreign source income, the tax department ordered a halt to any further dividends from foreign subsidiaries, so informing the assistant treasurer responsible for effecting remittances.

The assistant treasurer met with the tax manager to discuss an accommodation. While the amount of funds withheld from any one country may have been immaterial in the overall scheme, the aggregate amount of these funds was significant and would be sorely missed. Moreover, the funds were not needed abroad but were desperately needed in the United States to service the parent company's debt.

The foreign tax credit would be lost, however, if the funds were repatriated because there was virtually no domestic source income against which to apply the foreign tax credits. The tax manager opined that this situation could continue virtually forever because the owner had a strong preference for avoiding taxes. It would not cost the company if foreign dividends were paid, but the company would forego a future tax benefit if the parent company were someday to report taxable earnings. This conflict was illustrated best when the assistant treasurer, pleading abject corporate poverty, informed the tax manager (who was of Pakistani descent) that henceforth the tax manager's salary would have to be payable in Pakistani rupees in Lahore, since the parent company did not have sufficient dollars both to service the debt and cover the payroll. The tax manager learned that a good tax recommendation can be a bad business decision.

SUMMARY

Managing a treasury operation in a foreign subsidiary is unlike managing a domestic treasury operation. The laws, rules, regulations, banking systems, and commercial practices are all different. Moreover, the physical distance, coupled with language differences and time zone disparities, makes the task nearly impossible to manage from the corporate headquarters.

One way for the foreign unit to have the operating flexibility it requires, and yet to maintain adequate financial controls over its operations, is to structure the bank accounts carefully. All incoming funds should be trapped into a bank account controlled by headquarters, and measured doses of funds should be sent to the local operation on some logical basis. That basis might be a forecast of net funds flow, an overhead budget, or some other basis mutually agreed to by the operating unit's management and the headquarters management to which it reports. In this way, local management has the ability to run its own operation and yet must seek additional funds from the parent if it deviates from the plan.

CHAPTER 16

Executing International Trade Transactions

FOREIGN EXCHANGE TRANSACTIONS

The payment of funds from one country to another, as in a dividend, royalty, or vendor payment, involves the exchange of one currency for another. This exchange transaction can only occur through a party such as a bank that is willing to hold balances in both currencies. With some notable exceptions, one may hold balances in a country only in the currency of that country. In the United States, until recently a depositor could hold only U.S. dollars in its U.S. bank account. That depositor may open a sterling deposit account in London with a British bank as well, to service its U.K. business. When the depositor wishes to repatriate some of its U.K. profits to the United States, the depositor gives up the desired amount of pounds sterling to a financial intermediary, usually a bank, in exchange for the delivery of an equivalent value of dollars paid simultaneously into the depositor's U.S. bank account. This is a foreign exchange transaction, the execution of which requires an intermediary willing to exchange the two particular currencies. The bank that is willing to exchange U.S. dollars for sterling may not be willing routinely to accept certain other currencies such as Brazilian cruzados or Egyptian pounds unless it has a particular need or the proper facilities to handle them.

There are five steps in a foreign exchange transaction, as illustrated by the following remittance transaction:

1. The company determines the amount of foreign currency that is available for remittance;

2. The company determines the value date on which the foreign currency will be available in the payor's bank account;

3. The company identifies a bank that is willing to execute the exchange transaction;

4. The parties negotiate the exchange rate and settlement date and execute the transaction;

5. The recipient monitors the depository bank account on the settlement date to ensure that a) funds are received in the correct amount and on a timely basis; and b) the offsetting remittance is properly paid to the counterparty institution.

Factors Affecting Exchange Rates

Money is defined by three fundamental attributes: it is a medium of exchange, a store of value, and a unit of measure. Any external factor affecting any of these characteristics of a particular currency likewise affects its value against other currencies. There are literally thousands of influencing factors, all of which add up to the exchange rate of one currency against all the others in the world. Considering the complexity of these factors, exchange rates cannot be predicted with any accuracy for any period, even with sophisticated computers, because contributing factors such as "investor sentiment" cannot be readily quantified. Most currency rate forecasting attempts are limited to estimating the general direction of a currency against the U.S. dollar over a certain period. The principal external factors affecting foreign exchange rates, from the viewpoint of the U.S.-based financial manager, are supply and demand for the particular currency. Therefore, an important consideration in conducting the exchange transaction is the country in which the transaction is to be conducted.

Country of Transaction. Selection of the country in which the exchange transaction is conducted may make a significant difference in the exchange rate. For "hard currencies," which are freely traded in various markets around the world, competition among currency traders helps to maintain small spreads between the bid and offered prices. However, the "soft currencies" are traded only in their home countries in exchange for "hard currencies,'' and they have very limited markets. Occasionally they are traded in certain other countries having an historical affinity. For example, currencies from certain former French colonies sometimes are traded in Paris. But Thai baht are best traded in Bangkok and Korean won in Seoul.

Supply and Demand. The price of a currency, like any commodity, is directly affected by supply and demand factors that are the result of other economic influences, most of which are related to each other in an economy. These factors include:

1. Interest rates, which reflect the rate of inflation;
2. Inflation, which reflects the relative balance of supply and demand in an economy for goods and services;
3. The international trade balance, which affects the amount of a country's currency owned by foreigners and, therefore, the potential demand for conversion;
4. Budget deficits, which affect interest rates through the government's demand for borrowed funds; and
5. Expectations regarding the direction of these factors, which tend to be self-fulfilling.

Because so many exceptions to these economic ''rules'' exist, very few corporations undertake any meaningful forecasting of foreign exchange rates. Dozens of banks, independent economic research organizations, the Federal Reserve (Fed), and other institutions support legions of economists armed with computer models attempting to predict the movement of foreign exchange rates. Perhaps their collective failure to achieve any reliability or consistent degree of accuracy in the long run (often measured in terms of one month) is due to the unusually large number of political, psychological, and perceptual factors that affect interest rates, in addition to the quantifiable statistical trends.

Despite these exceptions, however, some generalizations can be noted. High inflation rates cause high interest rates because no one wants to hold or invest money without demanding high interest to compensate for lost purchasing power. High interest rates, in turn, cause traders to incur high costs to carry their currency positions, which encourages continual pressure to sell the currency. On the other hand, high interest rates in countries with strong currencies attract worldwide investors because of the investment yields that can be obtained. In order to make investments in a country, the investor must first buy its currency. Traders in strong currencies can control their position more carefully and minimize interest expense in carrying their positions because the markets for hard currencies are deeper and more liquid.

Trade deficits increase the amount of a country's currency in the hands of foreigners. What those foreigners choose to do with the currency affects the value of the currency. For example, if the country is stable, and particularly if interest rates are attractive relative to other stable countries, foreigners may elect to hold the currency in the form of liquid investments, or invest it in hard assets in that country. On the other hand, if the country is unstable or if interest rates are not particularly attractive relative to other stable countries, foreigners may elect to sell the currency in favor of another more attractive currency.

A country whose national budget deficit must be funded through borrowing will tend to force its domestic interest rates upward in order to satisfy its appetite for borrowed funds. Rising interest rates in a stable economy tend to attract foreign investment, to a point. Beyond that undefinable point, foreign investors begin to perceive the possibility of less stability, which mitigates to some degree the attractiveness of the currency.

All of these factors affect and reflect the levels of supply and demand for a given currency. The greater the supply, the lower the price; the greater the demand, the higher the price. The price level exists where the supply and demand curves intersect.

Spot and Forward Exchange Transactions

A spot transaction occurs when two parties agree to exchange currencies at the current rate. Spot transactions normally settle on the second business day after entering into the agreement, except Canadian dollar transactions, which settle one day after entering into the agreement. A company that needs to buy (or sell) a foreign currency for settlement on next day rather than the normal two days can usually arrange this with a foreign exchange bank. The bank would execute a currency "swap," which is the purchase of the currency for settlement on one date and the simultaneous sale of that currency for settlement on another date. Swaps are priced by combining the current, or spot, price and the forward price of that currency.

A forward transaction occurs when two parties agree to exchange currencies with settlement on a specified date further in the future than the spot settlement date. The forward contract enables a company to lock in an exchange rate for later settlement, which can largely eliminate the risk of unexpected fluctuations in currency exchange rates. Forward contracts can be written to settle on any particular date in the future except weekends and holidays, not just month-ends or increments of a month, and they can be written for any amount agreed upon by both parties.

An illustration of how a forward contract can be useful in eliminating foreign exchange risk is the situation encountered by a U.S. importer/wholesaler of a line of high quality French bicycles. The factory sent its invoice for the shipment at the time the container left the factory. The invoice was denominated and payable in French francs, due 90 days after the invoice date. The bicycles arrived in 30 to 35 days and were sold almost immediately to bicycle shops. The wholesaler received payments from the retailers at approximately the time that the factory invoice was due (give or take a week or two), and the wholesaler worked on a gross margin of about 15 percent. Riding the coattails of a long trend toward a stronger dollar, the importer would save money by waiting until the due date to pay the franc-denominated invoice; that condition prevailed for a long time. But then things changed quickly: political and economic changes in France and the United States caused the dollar to weaken against the franc. Suddenly, it cost the importer more to pay the factory invoice than expected, virtually wiping out the gross profit margin. And because of weakening demand in the United States, the importer could not readily raise prices without losing competitiveness with domestically produced bicycles. It was clear that the importer had a problem, not the least of which was its new silent partner—the foreign exchange market. It was equally clear that the importer needed to fix the cost of the bicycles as soon as the shipment occurred, if not earlier. In fact, there was no reason why it could not set the foreign exchange cost of all of its imported product a year or two in advance by entering into one or a series of forward contracts to lock in the foreign exchange rate for delivery and payment at some later date.

Currency Swaps

A currency swap is the simultaneous purchase and sale of a given quantity of currency with different settlement dates. A swap may be used by a financial manager to shift the final settlement of a transaction. For example, if a foreign currency remittance is available today but the spot exchange rate is temporarily depressed, the financial manager may either do nothing, awaiting a more favorable exchange rate, or swap the currency out to a later date, affording some protection against sharp market price changes. The financial manager would normally want to accept delivery of the remittance, but may not want to dispose of it at the current price. A swap enables the financial manager to dispose of the currency temporarily, selling it at the spot rate for delivery in two days, while simultaneously agreeing to buy an equivalent amount of the currency for delivery in three days or more. If the financial manager believes that the spot rate will rise next week, then the forward component of the swap could be set to mature next week. At maturity, the financial manager could either sell the currency at the new spot rate or enter into another swap to push the maturity out again. If the forward rate is at a discount from the spot rate, a profit would be earned on each such swap, as the financial manager simultaneously contracts to buy forward at a lower price than the current spot rate at which the currency is sold.

Hedging Currency Exchange Rates

Earning a continuing profit for a business is not easy. But when this challenge is compounded by floating currency exchange rates, the atmosphere can become downright hazardous to a company's financial health. The financial manager can attempt to protect the profitability of the company's international transactions through hedging techniques that include forward contracts, futures contracts, options, foreign currency borrowings, and a technique called "leading and lagging" (defined later in this section).

A foreign currency exposure exists when a company has a net asset or a net liability position in a particular country other than its home country. For example, a U.S. company's British subsidiary has a net worth according to the subsidiary's balance sheet of £450,000; that is, total assets exceed liabilities by £450,000. If the exchange rate of the pound sterling is equal to $1.50, then the net worth of the subsidiary translates to $675,000. If the exchange rate of the pound were to decline to $1.45, then the value of the parent's investment would decline by $22,500 (£450,000 × $0.05).

This potential decline in value can be offset by entering into a forward foreign exchange contract to sell £450,000 for settlement at some date in the future. This firmly establishes the value of the foreign currency for as the current exchange rate declines, the economic value of the forward contract rises by an equal amount (plus or minus a forward premium or discount). That is, if the forward contract reflects the sale of £450,000 for settlement one year later at $1.49 and the actual exchange rate declines to $1.45 by then, the company will close out the forward contract at maturity and take a profit of $0.04 per pound to offset the translation loss of $0.05.

Forward Contracts. As discussed earlier in this section, a forward contract is an agreement between two parties, one of which is usually a bank, to exchange a certain quantity of two currencies on a certain date in the future. Each party designates the bank and account number to receive the respective currencies, and delivery is expected to occur in accordance with the contract, unless the contract is modified or terminated in advance of its maturity. Forward contracts may be made for any amount that suits the parties; however, the amount is usually the equivalent of at least $100,000.

Setting Foreign Exchange Rates. The rate of exchange for delivery of a foreign currency at a future date is a function of three key factors: current spot exchange rate, differential in interest rates between the two countries involved, and anticipated supply and demand for the two particular currencies at settlement date.

The forward rate is stated as a premium or discount from the spot exchange rate at the time of entering into the forward contract. Therefore, changes in the spot rate directly affect the forward rate. The premium or discount depends on the relative levels of interest rates in the two countries. For example, in pricing the forward exchange rate between the U.S. dollar and the British pound sterling for settlement in one year, the U.S. investor could look at one-year interest rates in the United States and the United Kingdom, as reflected by the yields on one-year Treasury bills (T-bills) in each country. Assuming the following interest rate yields—one year U.S. T-bills at 6.5 percent, and one year U.K. T-bills at 7.5 percent—the investor in U.K. T-bills will earn a higher yield. This could encourage the U.S. investor to convert from dollars to pounds sterling at the current spot rate, purchase the U.K. T-bills yielding 7.5 percent, and convert back to dollars at maturity. In doing so, however, the investor will want to arrange up front to sell the sterling for dollars for settlement at the maturity of U.K. T-bills, in order to avoid the risk of foreign exchange fluctuations. The investor, therefore, makes the following simple calculation of the forward rate, assuming a transaction size of $1 million for illustration purposes.

1. Start with $1 million on deposit at a U.S. bank.

2. Convert to pounds sterling at a current spot rate of $1.50, resulting in £666,667 on deposit at a U.K. bank.

3. Invest the £666,667 in one-year U.K. T-bills yielding 7.5 percent, or £716,667 at maturity.

4. The alternative investment of the $1 million in one-year U.S. T-bills at 6.5 percent would result in $1,065,000 at maturity.

5. The exchange rate at maturity that would convert £716,667 to $1,065,000 is $1.48605 (1,065,000 divided by 716,667).

Therefore, in the absence of any unusual events expected at the maturity date, the one-year forward rate would be quoted at approximately

$1.48605, perhaps minus a small amount to allow the bank a spread for its profit on the transaction.

Futures Contracts. As with forward contracts, a futures contract includes a fixed exchange rate and an agreed upon settlement date. However, that is where the similarities end. A futures contract involves a securities exchange, rather than a bank, as the counterparty. Where parties to a forward contract usually expect to settle by actually exchanging the currencies on the settlement date, the investor in a futures contract often only expects to pay or receive a net settlement amount at maturity of the contract. The amount of the settlement reflects the difference between the actual spot exchange rate on the maturity date and the rate specified in the futures contract. Another difference is that currency futures contracts are written for a certain amount of currency per contract set by the securities exchange (e.g., 25,000 pounds sterling, 125,000 German marks, 12,500,000 Japanese yen), whereas a forward contract can be written for any amount of a currency. In addition, a futures contract is executed through a broker who charges a commission. With the forward contract, the parties merely agree to exchange currencies at a certain rate, with no fees or commissions paid by either side. Futures contracts are frequently used by investors and speculators who want to bet on the direction of a currency over a certain period, as well as by businesses wishing to hedge modest-size foreign exchange translation or transaction exposures. Forward contracts, on the other hand, are mostly used by businesses to hedge larger currency exposures, generally the equivalent of about $1 million or more, owing to the flexibility afforded by the forward contract through negotiations with a counterparty to customize the amount and maturity of the transaction.

Options. A foreign currency option, like a commodity option, is the right to buy or sell a certain amount of a specified currency at a specific price, known as the strike price, on or before a certain date. The right to buy or sell is strictly at the option of the investor who pays an option fee, or premium, to the counterparty, which may be a bank or an options exchange. Options compete with forward and futures contracts, but are more expensive because of the lower volume of transactions, giving the counterparty less liquidity.

Foreign Currency Borrowings. Borrowing in a foreign currency is used as a hedge to offset a translation exposure or to cover an expected transaction. It can also be used in place of a forward contract, especially when the company is a domestic borrower as well. The funds are borrowed in a foreign currency, converted to dollars, and repatriated. If the purpose is to offset a translation exposure, the borrowing could be made by the parent. If the purpose is to cover an expected remittance by a foreign subsidiary, the borrowing would be made by the subsidiary and repaid from the subsidiary's cash flow.

Leading and Lagging. This foreign exposure management technique involves making payment earlier than its due date (leading) or later than its due date (lagging) in order to take advantage of current trends in the exchange rate between two currencies. For example, if the U.S. bicycle importer had anticipated the rise in value of the French franc, the importer could have paid the franc invoice earlier than the due date to avoid a greater dollar cost later. Obviously, financial managers do not want to set a policy of always leading or lagging payments in a particular currency, although this policy may remain in place for an extended period.

Executing the Foreign Exchange Transaction

The spot or forward foreign exchange transaction is typically conducted with a large money center bank as the counterparty. Although regional and smaller banks sometimes accommodate a customer's foreign exchange needs, they usually do so only by acting as agent for a large money center correspondent bank and by adding a markup to the customer. The financial manager with large transactions must decide whether to retain the smaller bank in the transaction or go directly to the larger bank. The principal criterion in evaluating this issue is the typical size of the transaction. The "round lot" size of a transaction will vary, depending on the particular currency involved. In interbank trading, a round lot is generally the equivalent of U.S. $5 million. In corporate dealing, banks readily trade in U.S. $1 million lots. If the transaction is a round lot size or if the company has a continual flow of foreign exchange transactions that may be somewhat smaller, the money center bank's foreign exchange trading department will usually be interested in dealing with the company. To set up a foreign exchange trading arrangement, the financial manager must contact the account officer or a customer liaison officer in the foreign exchange department of the bank.

Foreign exchange traders usually are not very customer-oriented and do not have a lot of time to spend answering customers' questions. Therefore, many banks use customer liaison officers who are thoroughly familiar with the trading operation and who work with customers to accommodate their transactions. In fact, these officers generally sit adjacent to the bank's trading floor and have direct access to the traders as well as to economic data and foreign exchange rate trends. They have been known to help many corporate treasury managers understand the intricacies and techniques in foreign exchange.

Foreign exchange traders are responsible for investing the bank's money in currencies assigned to them. This entails considerable focus and concentration on economic and political developments, and monitoring the flow of supply and demand for the particular currency in the marketplace. Foreign exchange traders are in constant contact with professional traders at other banks and some large corporations, but they do not have time both to manage their currency positions and to respond personally to each customer. The customer liaison officer will ask the corporate financial manager questions to determine the bank's interest in doing business with the company. If the bank is interested, the officer will solicit information to set up a foreign exchange line of credit. The customer liaison officer manages the customer contact and quickly obtains price quotes from the trader, informing the trader immediately of all completed trades.

Credit Line. The financial manager should contact the foreign exchange department at least several days prior to the first contemplated transaction, because the bank will need to evaluate the company's credit and establish a foreign exchange credit line before entering into the first transaction. The bank's credit exposure to the customer arises because there is a lag of at least two business days between the time the foreign exchange transaction is entered into and is settled. The bank needs assurance that the company has the financial capacity to complete its transactions, and it must verify that the company has a history of fulfilling its commitments and is authorized by its board to enter into foreign exchange contracts. A foreign exchange credit line enables the foreign exchange department to enter into transactions routinely knowing that the credit of the customer has been pre-approved.

Foreign exchange transactions generate two forms of potential customer risk for a bank: delivery risk and rate risk. Neither form of risk materializes, of course, as long as the customer fulfills its obligations under the contract to deliver the specified currency to the bank on the agreed date. However, problems occur when the customer fails to perform, or it becomes apparent that the customer will be unable to perform at the contract's maturity.

Delivery Risk. This form of risk materializes at maturity when the bank delivers its currency to the customer or to the party designated by the customer, but the customer fails to deliver its currency to the bank. If such a failure occurs, the bank stands to lose 100 percent of the value of the transaction. For this reason, the bank credit officer will want to specify not only the overall amount of a foreign exchange credit line, but also the maximum amount that may mature with the customer on any one day.

Rate Risk. This form of risk materializes prior to maturity when the bank discovers that the customer will not be able to deliver its currency at the maturity of the contract. The risk occurs because the bank probably has contracted with another party to offset the transaction with its customer, and it must now find another party to replace the customer's position. To the extent that the exchange rate has changed, the bank will realize a gain or loss upon replacing that position. For example, when LMN Company contracted with First National Bank to deliver 6 million French francs to the bank in 30 days against payment of $1 million by the bank to the company, the bank probably contracted immediately to re-sell the francs to another party for settlement on the same date. During the interim, however, LMN Company filed for bankruptcy and was unable to deliver the francs. This required the bank to go into the foreign exchange market to contract with a new source for the 6 million francs in order to settle its offsetting contract on the maturity date. If the price of the francs had increased since the transaction date, the bank would have had to pay more and therefore, would have incurred a loss on the transaction.

The bank's exposure to rate risk in any transaction is usually considered to be a fraction of the size of the transaction, and the amount of the exposure varies by the volatility of the particular currency involved and the length of time until settlement. For example, a line covering spot transactions in the relatively stable Canadian dollar has a very small exposure, perhaps only 0.5 percent to 1 percent of the amount of the transaction per day. Therefore, the risk to the bank on a transaction equivalent to U.S. $1 million may be only $5,000 to $10,000. This is because the Canadian dollar tends in the short run to fluctuate with the U.S. dollar rather than against it. In addition, Canadian dollar transactions settle in one day rather than two (it is the only currency that customarily settles in one day against the U.S. dollar). Therefore, the bank's exposure on a Canadian dollar spot transaction is limited to the amount by which the Canadian dollar is likely to vary against the U.S. dollar in one day. If the customer had failed to settle the transaction on a timely basis, the bank would have had to offset the transaction in the market and perhaps would have suffered a loss of one or two days' rate fluctuations. In fact, the bank may even make a profit if the currency floats in the right direction.

In a forward transaction, there is a longer elapsed time before settlement, with a potentially much greater fluctuation in value. The risk to the bank, therefore, is much greater. Because of this, the bank must know at the outset whether it should consider a foreign exchange line for spot transactions only, or for both spot and forward transactions.

Dealing

After making arrangements for a foreign exchange credit line, the company is free to execute transactions, or to deal, with the bank. Foreign exchange dealing is like commodity trading: transactions usually are executed based on price and availability rather than on a good relationship. The bank's foreign exchange trader (also known as a dealer) has his own profit goals and position exposures, and the fact that a modest-sized foreign exchange transaction involves a good deposit customer may have no influence on the trader. The foreign exchange trader is interested only in the frequency of foreign exchange transactions of round lot sizes or larger. This is another good reason for corporate financial managers to deal with the liaison officer rather than directly with the dealer.

A bank decides the currencies in which it will specialize, and it assigns those currencies to specific traders. However, banks are very circumspect about the number and selection of currencies in which they maintain positions for several reasons. First, a trader is expected to follow the economic and political trends and events in his assigned countries. This limits a trader in an active foreign exchange department to one or two currencies or a small, related group such as the Scandanavian currencies. Second, the overhead cost of making a market in a currency is high—comprised of compensation for an experienced trader that sometimes runs into six figures and the interest cost of maintaining a position in a currency.

While foreign exchange customer liaison officers claim (usually quite accurately) that they can serve the customer's needs for any currency in the world, it is useful to know the currencies in which the bank specializes; it is in those currencies that the bank maintains a book, or position, and acts as a wholesaler. At any given moment during the trading day the trader's book in a currency may be long or short. That is, the bank may own balances in that currency, which is a long position, or it may have a net negative (short) position in the currency, which it will soon need to cover by buying from other dealers. Banks usually establish internal position limits for each currency, and the trader often is required to "square up the position" (i.e., bring the position close to zero) by the end of each trading day. Knowledge of how the bank operates its book is important because if a dealer has a long position as the end of the day approaches, and the financial manager phones to sell that currency, the dealer may have little interest in buying it. The wise dealer will make a bid, but the price level will not be as high as that of another bank whose trader may have a short position in the currency and is anxious to cover it. Of course, a sharp dealer maintains contacts in the marketplace, and has an idea of which banks are short and which are long at any moment. The astute dealer who is long at the moment would probably bid slightly below market for the transaction and, if accepted, he would immediately sell the currency to the dealer with the short position at an advantageous price.

The financial manager who takes the time to understand the complexities and nuances of the foreign exchange marketplace will soon learn that no one bank always has the best price for a particular currency, and that no one bank is always better as a buyer or seller of foreign currency. It is possible that a bank's particular mix of customers could provide it with a steady stream of a particular currency, putting the bank into the position of usually offering an attractive price to sell that currency. But most large foreign exchange dealers are able to manage their positions without resorting to fire sale pricing, particularly through the use of a handful of private firms in New York that act as brokers for the wholesale traders.

CASH MANAGEMENT SUGGESTION:

Because no one bank will have the best price on all currencies all the time, the financial manager who has a decent volume of attractively sized transactions should establish foreign exchange dealing arrangements with at least two or three money center banks. When a transaction needs to be executed, the financial manager (perhaps with the assistance of one or two colleagues) should telephone several banks virtually simultaneously for quotes and take the best one at that moment. A foreign exchange quote is good only for a moment and may be subject to change even while the financial manager speaks with the bank's customer liaison officer. Alternatively, if the financial manager has confidence in one bank's foreign exchange department, a valid approach would be to place any sizeable transaction entirely in the hands of the bank to execute at the best price during some specified time period, perhaps in the course of an hour or two. This approach works particularly well when dealing with the softer currencies, where the trader may have to conduct some discreet shopping, or with very large hard currency transactions where the trader may want to control the size of the transaction in order not to move the market price. In any event, sometimes the advice given to the customer by the foreign exchange liaison officer can be worth much more than the few points the customer might save by shopping among different foreign exchange departments.

Just as no bank will have the best price all the time, neither should a bank consistently lose deals because of price. A bank should be expected to win a representative proportion of the deals it is offered; otherwise, the company should replace it with another foreign exchange bank.

For example, a major U.S. oil company had a sizeable pool of funds offshore that the company kept invested in money market instruments in various countries. The funds would have been subject to U.S. income taxes if repatriated, and since the parent had no use for them at home, other than to invest in U.S. money market instruments, the funds were kept offshore. The corporate treasury staff monitored investment rates and currency exchange rates in a dozen or so countries and moved funds among those countries as rates warranted. To do this, the staff established a list of 10 foreign exchange dealers with which it did business. As transactions came up, the staff called three dealers and executed the deal with the bank that offered the best price. They rotated the bidding among the 10 dealers to afford each one an equal opportunity for the company's business. After a few cycles, the oil company then ranked the 10 dealers by the number of transactions completed, with the ranking continually updated. The banks that consistently remained at the bottom of the list were not very price competitive and were soon replaced by other banks. Banks that were price competitive received their share of transactions and remained in the upper tier of the list.

MANAGING FOREIGN EXCHANGE EXPOSURES

Generally, translation exposures do not cause much excitement among U.S. financial managers who focus on current earnings per share. This is because the Financial Accounting Standards Board (FASB) Statement No. 52, which governs the accounting treatment of foreign exchange exposure, allows translation losses to flow directly to the equity portion of the parent's balance sheet without affecting the income statement. Transaction exposures, however, are another story because they have operating implications and have a more immediate effect on the flow of funds in the firm. In foreign exchange exposure management, however, even the direction of exchange rates, not to mention the approximate rate level, is so unpredictable that the only prudent course is to avoid exposure and to let rates fluctuate in their own way. For unknown reasons, some otherwise conservative financial managers do not believe that they are speculating when they retain an exposure to a foreign currency.

FIG. 16-1

Condensed Balance Sheet of Dutch Subsidiary (as of December 31, 19xx) (in Dfls)

Current Assets	1,000,000	Current Liabilities	600,000
Fixed Assets	400,000	Due to Parent	600,000
		Net Worth	200,000
Totals	1,400,000		1,400,000

Translation Exposure

A company has a foreign exchange translation exposure whenever it has net assets or net liabilities in a foreign currency. From an accounting perspective, FASB Statement No. 52 carefully prescribes the procedures for handling the translation of financial statements that are denominated in a foreign currency. Financial managers, however, must work to control exposures, not just to account for them, because a change in the exchange rate can have a large and immediate effect on the value of the parent company's investment in the subsidiary; the value of remittances can also change dramatically.

Translation exposure arises whenever a foreign subsidiary's assets and liabilities (to firms other than the parent) are not equal. A subsidiary with a positive net worth, or assets in excess of liabilities, usually has a net asset exposure. The subsidiary's books of accounts are kept in the foreign currency, and these accounts must be translated into U.S. dollars periodically for consolidation with the parent's financial statements. As the exchange rate between the U.S. dollar and the subsidiary's currency changes, the translated value of the subsidiary's net assets changes accordingly, thereby affecting the value of the parent's investment in the subsidiary.

Assume for a moment that the Dutch subsidiary of a U.S. parent has a condensed balance sheet in Dutch florins (also known as guilders) as shown in Figure 16-1. (Dfls is the customary international reference to currency of the Netherlands.)

If the guilder's value is $0.50 at December 31, then the value of the parent's investment (the sum of the amount due to the parent and the net worth of the subsidiary) is $400,000 (Dfls 800,000 × $0.50). Suppose that in the following quarter, the Dutch balance sheet remains substantially the same, but the value of the Dutch guilder declines $0.05 to $0.45. As a result, the value of the parent's advance and investment has dropped by

$40,000 to $360,000 (Dfls 800,000 × $0.45). This translation exposure results in an accounting gain or loss simply from translation of balance sheet accounts from the native currency to another currency from one date to another. The company can take steps to mitigate the effects of these currency exchange rate fluctuations in several ways.

To reduce its translation exposure, the company can reduce its investment in the subsidiary by transferring the subsidiary's amount due to parent to a lender in the country. This is done by the subsidiary borrowing from the bank and repaying the parent. Then the parent can repatriate the proceeds. This can be achieved by having the subsidiary in the previous example borrow Dfls 600,000 locally, convert the borrowed proceeds to dollars, and remit the dollars to the parent. If this had been done at year-end when the exchange rate was $0.05 per Dfl, the parent's investment would have been reduced to Dfls 200,000 and the drop in the value of the guilder by $0.05 during the next quarter would have resulted in a translation loss of only $10,000 instead of $40,000.

Transaction Exposure

Transaction exposure applies to the subsidiary's income statement rather than to its balance sheet, and it usually results from timing differences. If the foreign subsidiary could repatriate its funds flow instantaneously as the revenue is recorded, then there would be no transaction exposure. Since this is not often possible, transaction exposure exists.

Transaction exposure occurs when revenue and profit are booked in one period and translated into the parent's currency at one exchange rate and the remittance occurs later at another exchange rate. This delay is caused principally by two factors: the credit period between the moment of sale and the moment of collection of the receivable, and delays in making the remittance transaction following collection of the accounts. If the value of the foreign currency drops during this period, fewer dollars will be remitted than were booked by the parent at the last translation.

Two customary methods for covering foreign exchange transaction exposures are forward contracts and foreign currency borrowings. If the company is obligated to pay in a foreign currency at some future date, the forward contract locks in the price of the currency for delivery at that time. If the company is due to receive a foreign currency at a date in the future, a forward contract locks in the value of the proceeds on the settlement date. In both cases, the forward contract transfers the risk of exchange rate fluctuation to the counterparty in the transaction.

An extreme example of transaction exposure occurred when the Argentine economy suffered from an inflation rate of 50 percent per month. An American movie distributor doing business there learned firsthand about foreign exchange transaction exposure. The motion picture distribution business is based on film rentals paid by the theater operator to the distributor. The film rental is a negotiated percentage of the box office gross revenue, usually calculated after deducting a certain amount for "house" operating expenses. At an inflation rate of 50 percent per month, the Argentine peso was declining in value hourly. Moreover, the government, in an effort to maintain the availability of a basic form of entertainment for its populace, placed price controls on movie theaters, effectively restraining the ability of the theater owners and film distributors to stay even with inflation. The theater collected 10,000 pesos for a ticket, and at the end of the month remitted the film rental of 4,000 pesos to the distributor. The distributor paid local distribution and overhead expenses of 2,500 pesos and applied for permission to remit the remaining 1,500 pesos to the United States. This permission would usually be granted in three weeks, so the remittance was made about eight weeks after the box office revenue occurred. During that period, the exchange rate of the peso dropped by half, so that the American parent received only $0.075 per ticket instead of the $0.15 it had expected (and booked into the accounting records).

Another method of covering exposures is the foreign currency loan. In the case of the Dutch subsidiary described previously, the U.S. parent reduced its translation exposure by using a bank loan in the currency of the subsidiary. In the Argentine situation, if the local subsidiary had borrowed the amount to be remitted and had conducted the remittance transaction earlier (subject, of course, to the availability of loans and government approval), then it could have avoided at least part of the decline in the currency's value that it experienced by waiting. Unfortunately, however, in highly inflationary economies bank loans are often not available, or are available only at confiscatory interest rates. This places the financial manager in the uncomfortable position of having to choose between confiscatory interest rates or confiscatory exchange rates. This is like choosing one's form of execution—gas chamber or firing squad. In either case, one loses.

In more moderate situations, where bank loans are readily available, the financial manager usually has a clearer choice among loans, foreign exchange forward contracts, foreign exchange futures, and options, the prices and features of which should be compared carefully.

If the parent is not a borrower, then it may have little use for the proceeds of the foreign currency loan. In that case, a forward contract may be the preferred path. On the other hand, there are occasional situations in which certain foreign currencies can be borrowed at relatively low interest rates. When this situation arises, the company may have an interesting opportunity to earn a guaranteed profit through interest rate arbitrage. For example, if the company's German subsidiary has a net asset exposure of DM10,000,000 that the parent wishes to cover, the subsidiary (or the parent) could borrow DM10,000,000 for six months from a bank at an interest rate of 6 percent. The proceeds of the loan are converted to U.S. dollars, and deposited to the parent's bank account in the United States. Not needing the funds, the parent could invest the dollar proceeds in U.S. money market instruments maturing in six months, such as bank certificates of deposit yielding 7.25 percent. During the six-month period, the company will enjoy a profit of 125 basis points on the amount borrowed. At the end of the six months, any change in the exchange rate between the deutschemark and the dollar will result in a gain or loss in translation exposure; an offsetting loss or gain will occur in the exchange value of the investment.

If the loan device were used to cover a translation exposure, the cash flow generated by the subsidiary during the six months would be used to repay the loan.

Using hedging techniques such as foreign currency loans and forward contracts, the financial manager can plan more strategically for the future. Instead of hedging each transaction, or next month's remittance, the financial manager can hedge all transactions expected to occur over the next 6, 12, or 24 months through either borrowings or forward contracts, or a combination of both, depending on rates and the predictibility of funds flow.

For example, a French subsidiary of a U.S. company manufactures electronic components for consumer products sold in France. The company is profitable and growing, and remitting manufacturing license fees of approximately FF1,000,000 monthly plus dividends of FF400,000 quarterly. The U.S. financial manager wanted to assure the receipt of dollars over the next year regardless of what happened to exchange rates. He assumed that the French company would continue to operate in its current trend. The financial manager checked with two foreign exchange dealers to determine and verify the current spot and forward rates and contacted the French bank serving the subsidiary regarding loan rates. Using the rates shown in Figure 16-2, he calculated the total transaction exposure for the year at FF13,600,000 (FF1,000,000 per month plus four quarterly dividends of FF400,000).

These rates, representing the best available information at the time, indicated to the financial manager that the market expected the franc to decline in value against the dollar, and that the franc should therefore be hedged. Accordingly, the financial manager decided to hedge remittances over the first three months with a French franc loan of FF3,400,000 (3 months' remittances

FIG. 16-2

Forward Contract vs. Bank Loan

Term	Dollar Exchange Rate	Annual Discount Rate	Loan Interest Rate
Spot	$0.1750	——	——
1 month(s)	0.1735	10.3%	7.0%
3	0.1715	8.0	7.1
6	0.1690	6.9	7.2
12	0.1635	6.6	7.3

of license fees of FF1,000,000 each, and one dividend payment of FF400,000), and to cover the remaining 9 months' remittances of FF10,200,00 with a forward contract maturing in 12 months. The loan proceeds would be converted immediately to dollars at the spot rate, and would be repaid by diverting the monthly license fees and quarterly dividends to the lender to service the debt instead of being remitted to the U.S. parent. The parent will pay the interest of FF241,400 out of additional cash flow from the French subsidiary after the loan is repaid. Following repayment of the loan in the third month, the subsidiary will resume remitting the license fees and dividends to the United States as it had before. The francs will be converted to dollars at the then-current spot exchange rate.

As it turned out, according to Figure 16-3, the franc indeed declined in value against the dollar, and the hedge limited the loss to a relatively nominal amount. The company considered this net cost to be comparable to the premium on a property and casualty insurance policy.

Where did all of this get the company? The financial manager's goal was to protect the dollar value of the anticipated stream of funds from the French subsidiary. To do so, he was willing to incur a moderate cost. By covering the potential stream of funds with a hedge, the financial manager would be assured that if the value of the franc declined against the dollar, the U.S. parent would still receive the dollars at the current spot rate minus the cost of the hedge. The full cost of the hedge would not be known, however, until the transaction was completed or the hedge was unwound. If the value of the franc increased against the dollar, then the company would have foregone a large stream of funds plus the cost of the hedge, unless the financial manager recognized the trend and unwound the hedge; if the value of the franc had declined against the dollar, then

FIG. 16-3

Transaction Hedge Illustrated

Transactions in France in Francs (000's omitted)	Loan Balance	Exchange Rate	Amount of Remit.
I. Start: Loan made in French francs	3,400 ×	$0.1750 =	$595.0
II. Sell FF10,200 forward to end of twelfth month at:		0.1700	
III. Cash flow applied to repay loan:			

Month	License fees	Dividends	Total	Cumulative				
1	1,000		1,000	1,000	2,400			
2	1,000		1,000	2,000	1,400			
3	1,000	400	1,400	3,400	0			
	3,000	400	3,400					

IV. Remit Monthly at Actual Spot Rate								
4	1,000		1,000	4,400		×	0.1730 =	173.0
5	1,000		1,000	5,400		×	0.1720 =	172.0
6	1,000	400	1,400	6,800		×	0.1720 =	240.8
7	1,000		1,000	7,800		×	0.1700 =	170.0
8	1,000		1,000	8,800		×	0.1680 =	168.0
9	1,000	400	1,400	10,200		×	0.1660 =	232.4
10	1,000		1,000	11,200		×	0.1640 =	164.0
11	1,000		1,000	12,200		×	0.1620 =	162.0
12	1,000	400	1,400	13,600		×	0.1635 =	228.9

Total remitted	$2,306.1
Original value: FF13,600 × 0.1750	= $2,380.0
Loss on remittances	($73.9)

V. Unwind hedge:
Sold forward at start: FF10,200 at $0.1700 for
    settlement at end of month 12 $1,734
Bought FF10,200 at spot rate of $0.1635 $1,668

Gain on forward contract	$66.3
Gain or (loss) on overall transaction	($7.6)

the company would have preserved its funds flow intact, minus the cost of the hedge.

Once the hedge is on, the manager must monitor the direction of the foreign currency because movement in the wrong direction can become very costly to the company. Sophisticated computer models exist to monitor these price changes and, in particular, the spreads between two currencies against a third. Changes in the spreads often indicate an imminent change in direction, and the manager's timing in unwinding a hedge becomes critical.

INTERNATIONAL TRADE FINANCE

Facilitating trade transactions internationally is a specialized area of finance that often carries a mystique about it, similar to that of foreign exchange and investing. But it need not be so mysterious. Important techniques are available for the company that does business abroad, whether as an importer or exporter. The U.S. company that sells to, and collects from, its foreign customer quickly finds that doing business internationally is very different from doing business domestically on open account. Domestically, the financial manager may adjust lockbox arrangements to save a fraction of a day's collection float. Internationally, however, float can be measured in weeks unless appropriate steps are taken to protect the flow of funds to the seller.

The international trade transaction begins with the contract in which the buyer and seller agree to all the terms of the transaction. Those terms should include, among other things, the method of payment and the currency in which the transaction will be denominated. There are six methods by which the buyer can pay the seller:

1. Funds in advance

2. Open account

3. Consignment

4. Documentary collection

5. Letter of credit (LOC)

6. Barter

A sale with terms of funds in advance requires the buyer to advance funds to the seller prior to shipment of the goods. This clearly shifts the credit risk to the buyer, who now must depend on the seller to perform.

Open account terms are offered only when the seller has a great deal of confidence in the buyer's willingness and ability to pay. This confidence is developed in international transactions usually only after years of doing business.

Consignment terms place the seller at risk, dependent totally on the buyer's integrity to remit the sale proceeds, minus a commission, or to return the goods. In consignment, the buyer is actually an agent for the seller and technically never takes title to the goods.

Barter involves the exchange of unlike goods rather than the exchange of goods for money. Because the consideration is goods rather than money, the parties must negotiate the transaction very carefully and must have mutual confidence in each other's ability and willingness to deliver the quantity and quality of goods at the time and place promised. Also known as countertrade, barter is a method of payment dating back to ancient history; it was revived when the Dutch traded some seashells for Manhattan Island, and it has seen some fresh light in the 1980s. Barter is used principally where the currency of a country is not readily acceptable in the world markets and the country has limited access to hard currencies.

The LOC is by far the most important method for conducting transactions between unrelated parties. In international trade, evaluating the credit of a potential trading partner is nearly impossible in many countries. The LOC enables a seller to know that questions concerning a trading partner's ability and willingness to pay have been eliminated from the transaction by substituting the credit of a bank. All of the other methods except funds in advance introduce the element of credit risk to the transaction.

The documentary collection is also heavily used in international trade transactions. The documentary collection maintains some formality about the transaction in that it clearly places title to the goods, and it forces the buyer to acknowledge the obligation to pay simultaneously with the release of the goods.

The documentary collection may function in a similar manner to the LOC, except that no bank assures payment. Instead, the seller using the documentary collection method has developed a level of confidence in the buyer that eliminates the question of whether the buyer will pay. The documentary collection typically consists of a draft drawn by the seller against the buyer (rather than against the issuing bank), related documents such as an invoice and a bill of lading, and perhaps certain forms of certificates relating to insurance, inspection, or origin. This package is sent to the buyer through the seller's bank to the buyer's bank with a simple letter describing handling instructions. If the draft is a sight draft, the buyer's bank is instructed to release the documents to the buyer upon payment of the draft. If the draft is a time draft, due at some time in the future, the buyer's bank would normally be instructed to obtain the buyer's formal acceptance of the draft before releasing the documents. The buyer's bank would also be instructed whether to hold the accepted draft and collect it at maturity for the seller, or to return it to the seller's bank for holding.

LETTERS OF CREDIT

In international commerce, open account trade credit is very difficult to establish because of:

1. The lack of uniform credit reporting rules and methods;

2. The lack of standards and uniform laws governing trade terms, payments, and rules for recourse in the event of nonpayment;

3. The lack of a universally used payment mechanism; and

4. The distances between seller and buyer that make open account terms difficult to monitor and control.

Further, differences among nations affect commercial and accounting practices, payment practices for bills and expenses, and alternate payment mechanisms (e.g., checks, drafts, giros, and electronic funds transfers). The solution to these conflicts is the LOC once the buyer and seller have reached a meeting of the minds regarding the underlying transaction.

An LOC is a promise, usually made by a bank, to make payment to a party upon presentation of a draft provided that the party complies with certain documentary requirements stated in the LOC. The LOC is used in trade transactions to substitute the well-known good credit of a bank for the relatively unknown credit of the buyer.

Origin

LOCs were probably first issued by "factors." Although the origin of factoring is hazy, factors have played an important role in commerce and industry throughout the ages.

Factors were financial intermediaries who were financially responsible independent entrepreneurs. They went to the colonies initially as shipping agents to handle incoming shipments of goods. The seller relied on the factor to sell the goods and collect the proceeds of the sale from the buyer. Factors also assumed the risk of loss for failure to collect by paying the ship captain as he departed the port, so they had incentive to check carefully the buyer's credit and to arrange for collateral security. As factors prospered and their financial strength grew, they expanded their financial services to include lending to buyers secured by the pledge of the goods and often other assets. In addition, factors often issued a letter to the seller in the mother country undertaking to pay on behalf of the colonial buyer. These letters eventually became known as LOCs.

While factors still perform collection and trade financing functions today, LOCs have become the product of banks—principally the larger banks whose names are recognized around the world.

Relevant Parties

There are a number of parties to an LOC. They include the following:

1. *Account party*—The party that applies to the bank for the LOC, usually the buyer.
2. *Advising bank*—The bank in the beneficiary's country that acts as agent for the issuing bank to notify the beneficiary of the terms of the LOC.
3. *Beneficiary*—The party that is entitled to the payments under the LOC; usually the seller.
4. *Confirming bank*—A bank known to the beneficiary that adds its own irrevocable undertaking to pay the beneficiary on top of the issuing bank. The confirming bank may also be the advising bank as well as the negotiating bank.
5. *Issuing bank*—The bank that issues (or opens) the LOC and undertakes the obligation to pay when all documentation requirements described in the LOC are met.
6. *Negotiating bank*—The bank that accepts documents on behalf of the issuing bank from the beneficiary; this bank may advance funds to the beneficiary until funds are collected from the issuing bank. The negotiating bank may be the same as the advising bank.
7. *Paying bank*—The bank in the beneficiary's country that is appointed in the LOC to make payment to the beneficiary. This is usually the confirming bank or an office of the issuing bank.

Advantages

The LOC is a classic "win-win" device because it affords both the buyer and seller significant benefits. The buyer's benefits include:

1. Assurance that the seller complies with the terms of the LOC before payment is made; those terms are usually based on the underlying contract between the buyer and seller;
2. Deferred payment terms (often 30 to 180 days after presentation of the required documents) from the seller at a lower cost than interest on borrowed funds; and
3. The ability to finance the purchase of goods using the banker's acceptance (BA), a debt instrument made possible by the LOC.

FIG. 16-4

Specimen Import Letter of Credit

ISSUING BANK
437 Wall Street, New York, N.Y. 10015
Cable Address: "Issubank"

DATE: June 16, 19xx   Reference Credit No. 0032497

Irrevocable Negotiation Credit

MAIL TO:
Jacques Clermont-Ferrand Companie   All drafts drawn must be
2 Rue de Val   marked: Issuing Bank Ref.
Marseille, France   No. 673240

Dear Sirs:

At the request of: ABC Corporation
                   Moraga, Utah, U.S.A.

and for the account of ABC Corporation, we hereby open in your favor our Irrevocable Credit, numbered as indicated above, for a sum or sums not exceeding a total of U.S. $42,500 available by your drafts at SIGHT on us subject to the following:

Expiration Date: October 16, 19xx
Transshipment allowed.   Partial shipment not allowed.
Ship to: ABC Corporation
Latest shipment date: October 1, 19xx
accompanied by the following documents:

1. Original on board ocean bills of lading made out to order of Issuing Bank, Notify buyer.
2. Full set Marine and War Risk insurance policy or certificate in negotiable form.
3. Commercial invoice in triplicate stating that it covers: "Porcelain Tableware," C.I.F. Moraga, Utah, U.S.A.

This letter is to accompany all draft(s) and documents. When presenting your draft(s) and documents or when communicating with us, please refer to our reference number, which appears at the top of this document.

We hereby engage with the drawer, endorsers, and bona fide holders that each draft drawn under, and in compliance with, the terms of the said credit, and accompanied by the above-specified documents, will be duly honored if negotiated on or before the expiration date.

The credit is subject to the Uniform Customs and Practice for Documentary Credits, International Chamber of Commerce.

Very truly yours,

The seller's benefits include:

1. Extension of credit to a bank rather than to a merchant. This usually implies greater creditworthiness;

2. Less risk and apprehension about payment delays caused by external problems such as political risk, foreign exchange rate fluctuations, and availability of foreign currency; and

3. The ability to obtain financing of its manufacturing operation even when granting deferred credit terms through the LOC.

Figure 16-4 is a sample LOC.

Types of LOCs

Irrevocable. LOCs are not revocable by either the issuing bank or the account party. If an LOC were revocable without approval of the beneficiary, it would hardly be able to serve its function. Therefore, while the term irrevocable implies that there exists the revocable LOC, in fact revocable LOCs are seldom seen and are virtually worthless instruments for assuring compliance and payment.

Confirmed. An LOC may be confirmed by a bank known to the beneficiary, or it may remain unconfirmed. The beneficiary may not be aware of the soundness and reputation of the issuing bank, and confirmation by a local bank known to the beneficiary solves that problem. Confirmation by a local bank brings the point of negotiation and payment much closer to the beneficiary and can facilitate communications and operation of the payment mechanism.

Transferable. An LOC may be transferable by the beneficiary to another party. However, the LOC must explicitly permit transfer. Transfer of the LOC in whole or in part may be important to the seller in lining up its suppliers or subcontractors.

Straight or Negotiation. An LOC is either a straight credit or a negotiation credit, both of which refer to the timing required for the presentation of documents. In a straight credit, the documents must be presented to the issuing bank on or before the date the LOC expires. In a negotiation credit, the documents must be negotiated (presented) to the intermediary negotiating bank on or before expiry. In the latter case, the documents may reach the issuing bank after the LOC has expired, but that bank remains obligated to pay as long as the negotiation of documents occurred in a timely manner.

Documentary or Clean. An LOC is either a documentary credit or a clean credit. A documentary LOC is the type used to finance shipments of goods, in which various documents must be presented at the time funds are drawn. A clean LOC, as its name implies, is unaccompanied by documents and is often referred to as a guaranty, bank guaranty, performance, or stand-by LOC. The clean LOC serves as an indemnity covering a specified contract between the parties. The beneficiary of a clean credit is usually authorized in the credit to draw by presenting a draft and a signed statement, the essence of which is prescribed in the LOC.

An LOC is not:

- As detailed as the sales contract;
- Contingent upon the seller's compliance with the terms of the sales contract (compliance is only with the terms of the LOC);
- A guaranty of payment to anyone. It applies only to the seller if its terms and conditions are met; and
- A guaranty that the goods shipped are the same as the goods ordered under the contract.

Both parties to the transaction must bear in mind that the quality and quantity of goods shipped ultimately depends on the integrity of the seller, and that in operating the transaction and the LOC mechanism, banks deal only in documents, not the goods themselves.

OTHER ELEMENTS OF THE TRANSACTION

The other necessary elements of a trade transaction, in addition to the buyer, seller, and the goods, are the contract of sale, a transportation carrier, and the documents.

Contract of Sale

The contract of sale between the buyer and seller is the key to the entire trade transaction. The contract is separate and distinct from the LOC; it may be oral or written, and at minimum it should stipulate the following items in detail:

- Description of the goods
- Quantity of the goods to be shipped
- Price of the goods
- Method of shipment, and the payor of freight charges

- Party responsible for insurance in transit
- Method of payment and payment terms
- Specification of the currency to be paid

Carrier

The transportation carrier has the following responsibilities in the transaction: (1) transportation of the goods without negligence; (2) issuance of a receipt for the goods to the shipper; and (3) release of the goods at the destination to the holder of the bill of lading.

Documents

Trade transactions, especially international ones, seemingly deal more in documents than in the goods themselves. It is said that globally the function of processing the documents adds on the order of 7 percent to the cost of the transaction. This excludes insurance and freight charges. The documents most often encountered in international trade transactions are:

- Bills of lading
- Commercial invoices
- Customs invoices
- Certificates of origin

- Inspection or packing certificates
- Drafts or bills of exchange
- Insurance certificates

BANKER'S ACCEPTANCES

A BA is a time draft drawn against the buyer/importer and which is then accepted by a bank. Often, the BA is created as the financing vehicle for the buyer in an LOC transaction. A specimen of the instrument is shown in Figure 16-5.

The BA affords the buyer in a trade transacton the opportunity to finance its trading activities at attractive short-term money market rates. There are other benefits to using a BA:

FIG. 16-5

Specimen Banker's Acceptance

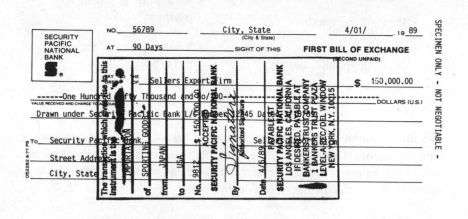

1. The buyer/importer can obtain deferred payment terms while the seller/exporter receives immediate payment for goods sold. This allows the buyer the time to receive the shipment, sell the goods, and collect the proceeds from its customers before having to pay for the goods;

2. Companies can use BA financing to differentiate and segregate their international trade financing from their continuing working capital financing;

3. BA financing usually is priced at attractive fixed short-term rates available to creditworthy companies that are not able to tap the commercial paper market for financing.

BAs are useful because a bank can provide financing to its customer without employing bank funds, by selling the instrument in the money markets at a discount. To achieve maximum marketability, a BA should comply with the Fed's requirements for eligibility of the instrument for sale to the Fed. Such Fed eligibility enhances the liquidity of the instrument in the money markets, which ultimately translates into a lower financing cost to the buyer/importer receiving the financing. To be eligible for a discount at the Fed, a BA must arise from at least one of the following:

- Importing or exporting goods;

- Shipping goods between foreign countries or within the United States;

- Storing readily marketable staples in the United States or abroad; or

- Furnishing dollar exchange in certain foreign countries to support U.S. dollar-denominated trade.

In addition to these eligibility criteria, negotiability is also enhanced if the instrument is created for a round lot amount of $5 million, which is most attractive to institutional and corporate investors. BAs of $1 million carry a small premium in interest rate, but are quite liquid in the money markets. Odd lots, meaning odd amounts such as $1,157,000 or amounts under $100,000, carry a much higher financing cost to the importer because their marketability tends to be impaired.

In order to create a BA, prior arrangements must be made between the buyer and its bank. At the time that financing is required, perhaps when a sight draft drawn under an import LOC is presented, the importer executes a time draft drawn against itself and discounts the draft with the bank. That is, the bank buys the draft from the importer at a discount, takes a commission for structuring the transaction, and deposits the net proceeds into the importer's account. The bank may, if desired, hold the draft until maturity, or it may accept liability for payment of the draft at maturity by writing "Accepted" across the face of the instrument, having it signed by a bank officer, and then re-discounting the instrument in the secondary money market. Similar results may occur if the draft drawn under the LOC is a time draft, in which case that draft may be accepted and discounted by the importer's bank.

Most BAs are created with maturities from 30 to 180 days, with a maximum legal tenor of 270 days. Beyond that period, the instrument becomes a security that must be registered with the Securities and Exchange Commission (SEC) before being sold. BAs are an important instrument in corporate and institutional short-term investment portfolios.[1]

SUMMARY

A business operating internationally, particularly with subsidiaries or other business units located abroad, inevitably must deal with remittances and

---

[1] See Chapter 14 for a discussion of short-term investing, including BAs.

payments in foreign currencies. Also, when foreign currency values make up part of the assets and liabilities of a firm's balance sheet, exposure to fluctuations in currency values create potential loss situations. Therefore, not only does a firm need to find convenient ways to handle its remittances and payment transactions in the foreign currencies, it must also learn to manage the transaction and translation exposures, and then to hedge the irreducible exposure that remains.

When extending credit to foreign customers, open account is somewhat rare. Instead, international sales are often consummated through the device of the LOC issued by a bank. The LOC is perhaps the most important international trade finance vehicle.

Index

INDEX

[References are to chapters followed by page number(s).]

B

[References are to chapters followed by page number(s).]

[References are to chapters followed by page number(s).]

[References are to chapters followed by page number(s).]

[References are to chapters followed by page number(s).]

[References are to chapters followed by page number(s).]

[References are to chapters followed by page number(s).]

[References are to chapters followed by page number(s).]

[References are to chapters followed by page number(s).]

[References are to chapters followed by page number(s).]

M

[References are to chapters followed by page number(s).]

[References are to chapters followed by page number(s).]

O

[References are to chapters followed by page number(s).]

[References are to chapters followed by page number(s).]

[References are to chapters followed by page number(s).]